OCCUPATIONAL FRAUD AND ABUSE

by Joseph T. Wells, CFE, CPA

Occupational Fraud and Abuse
published by the Obsidian Publishing Company, Inc.
© 1997

Printed by
Thomson-Shore Printing Company, Inc., Dexter, Michigan

Obsidian Publishing Company
800 West Avenue
Austin, Texas 78701
(800) 245-3321

Printed in the United States of America

10 11 12 13 14 15 16 17 18 19 20

ISBN 1-889277-08-8

This book is dedicated to Sgt. Jerry Gregor (1917-1996).
He wasn't my father, but he should have been.

FOREWORD

It is a pleasure to write the foreword for *Occupational Fraud and Abuse*, a book authored by my friend, Joseph T. Wells. I have known Joe for over ten years.

While most certified fraud examiners, fraud researchers, and others know Mr. Wells as the founder and chairman of the Association of Certified Fraud Examiners, I know Joe as a friend, as one who has influenced my thinking, knowledge, and research about fraud, and as a person who, although not positioned in the research confines of a university, is one of the most thorough and thoughtful fraud researchers I have ever met. And, as you will see from reading this book, Mr. Wells is an excellent writer and communicator who can make numerous fraud theories and schemes easy to understand.

It is my opinion that Joseph T. Wells, through his efforts with the Association of Certified Fraud Examiners (the Association), videos produced, books and articles written, and training courses taught, has made a greater contribution to the prevention, detection and investigation of fraud than any person in the world. Because of his work in fraud education and research and his vision in organizing the Association, there are at least 20,000 people who have a better understanding of fraud and who are working to reduce its cost and occurrence.

At Joe's gracious invitation, I read this book before it was published. I began reading the manuscript in the evening and, although I had only gotten two hours of sleep the previous night, could not put the manuscript down until I had read it all.

Occupational Fraud and Abuse provides an excellent description of, a summary of the seminal research related to, and an analysis of the various classes of fraud, each with its many and varied schemes. The concepts described in the book are sound and are based on the most extensive empirical research ever conducted on fraud. This book is must reading for anyone working in business, internal and external auditing, individuals involved in security or asset protection, law enforcement workers and litigators, and others interested in the subject of fraud.

Reading *Occupational Fraud and Abuse* will help you better understand the various ways occupational fraud and abuse occur, thus helping you identify exposures to loss and appropriate prevention, detection, and investigation approaches. And, as you will see, the book is written in a way that will capture and hold your attention. The numerous fraud stories and personal insights provided by the author will have you believing you are reading for enjoyment, while in fact, you will be learning from one of the true master educators.

I believe this book is destined to become one of the real classics and definitive works on the subject of occupational fraud and abuse.

W. Steve Albrecht, Ph.D., CFE, CPA, CIA
Director, School of Accounting and Information Systems, Brigham
    Young University
President, American Accounting Association

PREFACE

Few people begin their careers with the goal of becoming liars, cheats, and thieves. Yet that turns out to be the destiny of all too many. Occupational fraud and abuse cost organizations billions and billions annually. The losses in human terms are incalculable. And by some estimates, the problem is worsening.

This book is for those whose job it is to reduce these losses: fraud examiners, auditors, investigators, loss prevention specialists, managers and business owners, criminologists, human resources personnel, academicians, and law enforcement professionals, among others.

Occupational Fraud and Abuse has four broad objectives: First, to establish a classification system to explain the various schemes used by executives, owners, managers, and employees to commit these offenses. Second, to quantify the losses from these schemes. Third, to illustrate the human factors in fraud. And finally, to provide guidance in preventing and detecting occupational fraud and abuses.

How this book came about is a story in itself. As improbable as it seems looking back, I am approaching my fourth decade in the field of fraud detection and deterrence. Like many of you, my career path didn't start where it ended up. In the third grade, I distinctly remember pledging to be an astronomer. But by college, quantum physics had provided my undoing. Just a few credits shy of a math/physics degree, I switched to business school and majored in accounting.

After two years toiling in the ledgers of one of the large international auditing firms, I decided I couldn't stand it anymore; my life had to have more excitement. So I became a real-life, gun-toting

FBI Agent. Many times I have laughed to myself—and to others—that the FBI is the only organization I know that would attempt to make trained marksmen out of a bunch of CPAs. Thankfully, I didn't have to use my pistol too many times to track down heinous robbers. And I learned in a hurry that the expensive crimes weren't the bank robberies, anyhow—they were the bank embezzlements. For the next nine years, I specialized exclusively in investigating a wide range of white-collar crimes in which the federal government was a party at interest. The cases ran the gamut, from nickel-and-dime con artists to Watergate.

My second decade was with Wells & Associates, a group of consulting criminologists concentrating on white-collar crime prevention, detection, and education. That eventually led to the formation of a professional organization, the Association of Certified Fraud Examiners. For most of the third decade, I have been Chairman of the Board of Directors and CEO. In a few years, I hope to spend the fourth decade with what I have discovered to be my secret love: writing.

Occupational Fraud and Abuse is my fifth book. Its genesis was nearly six years ago. At the time, I was intrigued by the definition of *fraud* as classically set forth in Black's Law Dictionary:

> "All multifarious means which human ingenuity can devise, and which are resorted to by one individual to get an advantage over another by false suggestions or suppression of the truth. It includes all surprise, trick, cunning, or dissembling, and any unfair way which another is cheated."[1]

This definition implied to me that there was an almost unlimited number of ways people could think up to cheat one another. But my experience told me something else: after investigating and researching literally thousands of frauds, they seemed to fall into definite patterns. If we could somehow determine what those patterns were and in what frequency they occurred, it would aid greatly in understanding and ultimately preventing fraud. And since so much fraud occurs in the workplace, this particular area would be the starting point.

So in 1993, I began a research project with the aid of over 2,000 Certified Fraud Examiners. They typically work for organizations in which they are responsible for aspects of fraud detection and deterrence. Each CFE provided details on exactly how their organizations were being victimized from within. The amount of data analyzed was extensive: Actual fraud cases ranging from $22 to $2.5 billion, and totaling $15 billion, most of which occurred within the last ten years. That information was subsequently summarized in a document for public consumption, the 1995-96 Report to the Nation on Occupational Fraud and Abuse.

Although the Report provided a basic framework, this book is intended for a different audience—those of you who need to know all the details. You will discover that while fraud may outwardly seem complex, it rarely is. You don't need an accounting degree—just an understanding of fundamental business procedures and terminology. As the saying could go, fraud ain't rocket science.

Rather than an unlimited number of schemes, this book will suggest that occupational fraud and abuse can be divided into three main categories: Asset misappropriation, corruption, and fraudulent statements. From the three main categories, there were 44 separate schemes identified and classified, and they are covered in detail herein.

The book begins with an overview of the complex social factors that go into creating an occupational offender. People do things for a reason, and understanding why employees engage in this behavior is the key to creating ways to prevent it. You will therefore find these pages rich in personal detail.

Following the introduction, the book is divided into ten chapters devoted to the specific occupational fraud and abuse schemes. Each of the chapters is organized similarly. First, the scheme is illustrated and detailed. Then, a case study provides insights. Next, the scheme itself is flowcharted and the scheme variations are scheduled, along with statistics for each method. A second, longer case study follows. Finally, observations and conclusions on each chapter will help in devising prevention and detection strategies.

A project such as this is not a solo venture, even though I accept final responsibility for every word, right or wrong. I must first gratefully acknowledge the thousands of Certified Fraud Examiners who provided the case examples.

The core staff of the Association—better than thirty people— all helped to some degree. I am especially appreciative of the efforts of John Warren and Matt McCall, who did much of the detailed research. Kathie Green, Jim Ratley, Nancy Bradford, Jeanette LeVie, John Gill, and Julie Askanase merit special recognition.

Several writers assisted in preparing case studies: Michael C. Burton, Sean Guerrero, Brett Holloway-Reeves, Marty Kramer, Katherine McLane, Suzy Spencer, and Denise Worhach.

Technical support recognition goes to Mike Eisenberg, Richard C. Hollinger, Anthony Rezendes and Sandra Welch.

Special thanks goes to the Certified Fraud Examiners and other professionals who furnished details of their cases: Thomas D. Anderson, K. Patrick Batka, Danny R. Bauwens, William B. Bokel, Jr., Frederick Bornhofen, John R. Boyce, Bradley Brekke, Allen F. Brown, Stephen J. Burke, Anthony J. Carriuolo, Craig Christiansen, Dennis Coleman, John Combs, Thomas Cornelius, Harvey Creem, Jim Crowe, Harry D'Arcy, Tonya DiGiuseppe, Paul Dopp, Harold Dore, Marvin Doyal, Harold Dore, Jack Dunlap, Gerald Dunning, Tim Edwards, Peter Fogarty, Stephen Gaskell, Gerald L. Giles, Jr., Alan Graham, Paul Granetto, James Grosskopk, Michael Gruber, Ronald Hagenbaugh, Debra Hamilton, James Hansen, Paul Hayes, John D. Heeney, Charles Intriago, Terry Isbell, Allen R. Keown, Bobby R. King, Robert Klein, Douglas LeClaire, Tim Leech, Daniel Lentz, George Magula, Barry Masuda, Thomas McAuley, Debbie McCardle, David McGahan, Terrance McGrane, David McGuckin, Michael McLean, David Mensel, Michael Miller, Andrew Mintzer, Richard Nygaard, Richard Osborn, Frederick Pasteau, Vernon Pitsker, Dick, Polhemus, Allen Pruett, Trudy Riester, Calvin Robbins, Lee Roberts, Thomas Roberts, Peter Roman, Robert Rudloff, Allan Schuman, James Sell, David Sherick, Harry J. Smith III, Donald Stine, Alexis M. Stowe, Gayton Tis, Steve Vickers, H. Edward White, and Frances Zuniga.

Additional thanks goes to W. Steve Albrecht, C.N. Anin, G. Jack Bologna, Rob Bongenaar, Robert Basart, John Braithwaite, Claude K. Chappelear, Isabel Cumming, Iliana Colon-Carlo, Joe Dervaes, Bryan J. Farrell, Orrin F. Fuelling, Anne Graham, Tom Golden, Mason Haynesworth, John J. Hickey, Tom Hubbard, Franklyn J. Howatt, Joseph W. Koletar, W. Michael Kramer, Gary J. Kruchten, G. Michael Lawrence, Phil Levi, Robert J. Lindquist, Ed Madge, Judge Frank Maloney, Robert McEntee, Jeff Mirken, John J. O'Connor, Michael M. Ryman, Oliver "Buck" Revell, Jack Robertson, Donald K. Wall, and John Fisher Weber.

Finally, I must thank the one person without whom these pages would not have been written. My wife, Judy, has endured countless weekends and early mornings alone while I sat at this keyboard. She has become accustomed to me jumping up in the middle of dinner to write down a new thought on a scrap of paper. And she has done every bit of it by cheering me on, never complaining. She owes her positive attributes in no small part to the influence of her parents, Jerry and Jenny Bell Gregor. First to the memory of the late Jerry Gregor—then to those of you trying to make a better world by reducing fraud — this book is dedicated.

Joseph T. Wells
Austin, Texas
July, 1997

[1] Henry Campbell Black, *Black's Law Dictionary, Fifth Edition* (St. Paul: West Publishing Co., 1979), p. 468.

LIST OF CHAPTERS

TABLE OF CONTENTS

PART V – EPILOGUE

PART VI – APPENDIX

PART I - INTRODUCTION TO OCCUPATIONAL FRAUD AND ABUSE

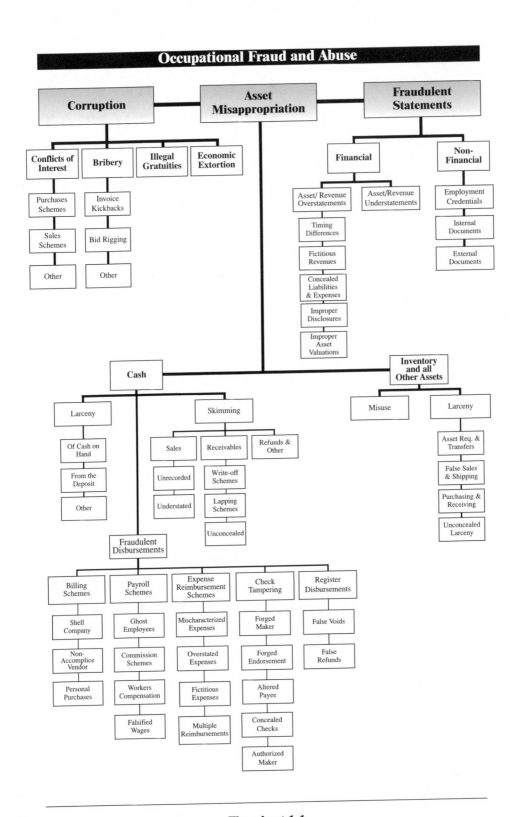

Flowchart 1-1

1. INTRODUCTION

In the world of commerce, organizations incur costs to produce and sell their products or services. These costs run the gamut: labor, taxes, advertising, occupancy, raw materials, research and development—and yes, fraud and abuse. The latter cost, however, is fundamentally different from the former — the true expense of fraud and abuse is hidden, even if it is reflected in the profit and loss figures.

For example, suppose the advertising expense of a company was $1.2 million. But unbeknownst to the company, its marketing manager is in collusion with an outside ad agency and has accepted $300,000 in kickbacks to steer business to them. That means the true advertising expense is overstated by at least the amount of the kickback — if not more. The result, of course, is that $300,000 comes directly off the bottom line, out of the pockets of the investors and the workforce.

Defining Occupational Fraud and Abuse

The above is a clear-cut example, but much about occupational fraud and abuse is not so well defined, as we will see. Indeed, there is widespread disagreement on what exactly constitutes these offenses.

For purposes of this book, *occupational fraud and abuse* is defined as:

> "The use of one's occupation for personal enrichment through the deliberate misuse or misapplication of the employing organization's resources or assets."[1]

By the breadth of the definition, it involves a wide variety of conduct by executives, employees, managers, and principals of organizations, ranging from sophisticated investment swindles to petty theft. Common violations include asset misappropriation, fraudulent statements, corruption, pilferage and petty theft, false overtime, using company property for personal benefit, and payroll and sick time abuses. As the Report states, "The key is that the activity (1) is clandestine, (2) violates the employee's fiduciary duties to the organization, (3) is committed for the purpose of direct or indirect financial benefit to the employee, and (4) costs the employing organization assets, revenues, or reserves" [2]

"Employee," in the context of this definition, is any person who receives regular and periodic compensation from an organization for his or her labor. The employee moniker is not restricted to the rank and file, but specifically includes corporate executives, company presidents, top and middle managers, and other workers.

Defining Fraud

In the broadest sense, fraud can encompass any crime for gain which uses deception as its principle modus operandi. There are but three ways to illegally relieve a victim of his money: Force, trickery, or larceny. All those offenses which employ trickery are frauds. Since deception is the linchpin of fraud, we will include Webster's synonyms: "'Deceive' implies imposing a false idea or belief that causes ignorance, bewilderment or helplessness; 'mislead' implies a leading astray that may or may not be intentional; 'delude' implies deceiving so thoroughly as to obscure the truth; 'beguile' stresses the use of charm and persuasion in deceiving."

All deceptions, though, aren't frauds. To meet the legal definition of a fraud, there must be damage, usually in terms of money, to the victim. Under the common law there are four general elements, all of which must be present for a fraud to exist: (1) a material false statement, (2) knowledge that the statement was false when it was uttered, (3) reliance on the false statement by the victim, and (4) damages as a result. The legal definition is the same whether the offense is criminal or civil; the difference is that criminal cases must meet a higher burden of proof.

Let's assume an employee didn't deceive anyone, but stole valuable computer chips while no one was looking and resold them to a competitor. Has he committed fraud? Has he committed theft?

The answer, of course, is that it depends. Employees have a recognized fiduciary relationship with their employers under the law.

The term *fiduciary*, according to *Black's Law Dictionary*, is of Roman origin and means "a person holding a character analogous to a trustee, in respect to the trust and confidence involved in it and the scrupulous good faith and candor which it requires. A person is said to act in a 'fiduciary capacity' when the business which he transacts, or the money or property which he handles, is not for his own benefit, but for another person, as to whom he stands in a relation implying and necessitating great confidence and trust on the one part and a high degree of good faith on the other part."

So, in our example, the employee has not only stolen the chips—in so doing, he has violated his fiduciary capacity. That makes him an embezzler. "To 'embezzle' means willfully to take, or convert to one's own use, another's money or property of which the wrongdoer acquired possession lawfully, by reason of some office or employment or position of trust. The elements of 'embezzlement' are that there must be a relationship such as that of employment or agency between the owner of the money and the defendant, the money alluded to have been embezzled must have come into the possession of defendant by virtue of that relationship and there must be an intentional and fraudulent appropriation or conversion of the money."[3] In other words, embezzlement is a special type of fraud.

Conversion, in the legal sense, is "an unauthorized assumption and exercise of the right of ownership over goods or personal chattels belonging to another, to the alteration of their condition or the exclusion of the owner's rights. An unauthorized act which deprives an owner of his property permanently or for an indefinite time. Unauthorized and wrongful exercise of dominion and control over another's personal property, to the exclusion of or inconsistent with the rights of owner." [4] So by stealing the chips, the employee also engages in conversion of the company's property.

The legal term for stealing is *larceny*, which is "felonious stealing, taking and carrying, leading, riding, or driving away with another's personal property, with the intent to convert it or to deprive the owner thereof. The unlawful taking and carrying away of property of another with the intent to appropriate it to a use inconsistent with the latter's rights. The essential elements of a 'larceny' are an actual or constructive taking away of the goods or property of another without the consent and against the will of the owner and with a felonious intent. Obtaining possession of property by fraud, trick or devise with preconceived design or intent to appropriate, convert, or steal is 'larceny.'"[5]

As a matter of law, the employee in question could be charged with a wide range of criminal and civil conduct: fraud, embezzlement, obtaining money under false pretenses, or larceny. As a practical matter, he will probably only be charged with one offense, commonly larceny.

Larceny by fraud or deception means that "a person has purposely obtained the property of another by deception. A person deceives if he purposely: (1) creates or reinforces a false impression, including false impressions as to law, value, intention or other state of mind; but deception as to a person's intention from the act alone that he did not subsequently perform the promise; or (2) prevents another from acquiring information which would affect his judgment of a transaction; or (3) fails to correct a false impression which the deceiver previously created or reinforced, or which the deceiver knows to be influencing another to whom he stands in a fiduciary or confidential relationship; or (4) fails to disclose a known lien, adverse claim, or other legal impediment to the enjoyment of property which he transfers or encumbers in consideration for the property obtained, whether such impediment is or is not valid, or is or is not a matter of official record." [6]

The fraudulent aspect of occupational frauds, then, deals with the employee's fiduciary duties to the organization. If those duties are violated, that action may be considered fraud in one of its many forms. Under the definition of occupational fraud and abuse in this book, the activity must be clandestine. Black's defines that as "secret, hidden, concealed; usually for some illegal or illicit purpose."

DEFINING ABUSE

A litany of abusive practices plagues organizations. Here are a few of the more common examples of how employees "cost" their employers. As any employer knows, it is hardly out of the ordinary for employees to:

- Use employee discounts to purchase goods for friends and relatives
- Take products belonging to the organization
- Get paid for more hours than worked
- Collect more money than due on expense reimbursements

- Take a long lunch or break without approval
- Come to work late or leave early
- Use sick leave when not sick
- Do slow or sloppy work
- Work under the influence of alcohol or drugs

Abuse has taken on a largely amphoteric meaning over the years; Webster's definition of abuse might surprise you. From the Latin word abusus—to consume—it means: "1. a deceitful act, deception; 2. a corrupt practice or custom; 3. improper use or treatment, misuse. . . ." To deceive is "to be false; to fail to fulfill; to cheat; to cause to accept as true or valid what is false or invalid."

Given the commonality of the language describing both fraud and abuse, what are the key differences? An example illustrates: Suppose a teller was employed by a bank and stole $100 from her cash drawer. We would define that broadly as fraud. But if she earns $500 a week and falsely calls in sick one day, we might call that abuse—even though each has the exact same economic impact to the company—in this case, $100.

And of course, each offense requires a dishonest intent on the part of the employee to victimize the company. Look at the way each is typically handled within an organization, though: in the case of the embezzlement, the employee gets fired; there is also the remotest of probabilities that she will be prosecuted. In the case in which the employee misuses her sick time, she perhaps—and this perhaps—gets reprimanded, or her pay is docked for the day.

But we can also change the "abuse" example slightly. Let's say the employee works for a governmental agency instead of in the private sector. Sick leave abuse—in its strictest interpretation—could be a fraud against the government. After all, the employee has made a false statement for financial gain (to keep from getting docked). Government agencies can and have prosecuted flagrant instances. Misuse of public money—in any form—can end up being a serious matter, and the prosecutive thresholds can be surprisingly low.

Here is one real example. Many years ago, in 1972, I was a rookie FBI agent assigned to El Paso, Texas. That division covered the Fort Bliss military reservation, a sprawling desert complex. There were rumors that civilian employees of the military commissary were stealing inventory and selling it out the back door. The rumors turned out to be true, albeit slightly overstated. But we didn't know that at the time.

So around Thanksgiving, the FBI spent a day surveying the commissary's back entrance. We had made provisions for all contingencies—lots of personnel, secret vans, long-range cameras—the works. But the day only produced one measly illegal sale out the back door: several frozen turkeys and a large bag of yams. The purchaser of the stolen goods tipped his buddy $10 for merchandise valued at about $60. The offense occurred late in the day. We were bored and irritated, and we pounced on the purchaser as he exited the base, following him out the gate in a caravan of unmarked cars with red lights. The poor bloke was shaking so badly that he wet his pants. I guess he knew better than we did what was at stake.

Because he was in the wrong place at the wrong time and did the wrong thing, our criminal paid dearly: he pled guilty to a charge of petty theft. So did his buddy at the commissary. The employee was fired. But the purchaser, it turned out, was a retired military colonel with a civilian job on the base—a person commonly known as a "double dipper." He was let go from a high-paying civilian job and now has a criminal record. But most expensively, I heard he lost several hundred thousand dollars in potential government retirement benefits. Would the same person be prosecuted for petty theft today? It depends entirely on the circumstances. But it could and does happen.

The point here is that abuse is often a way to describe a variety of petty crimes and other counterproductive behavior that have become common and even silently condoned in the workplace. The reasons employees engage in these abuses are varied and highly complex. Do abusive employees eventually turn into out-and-out thieves and criminals? In some instances, yes. We'll describe that later.

Research in Occupational Fraud and Abuse

EDWIN H. SUTHERLAND

Considering its enormous impact, relatively little research has been done on the subject of occupational fraud and abuse. Much of the current literature is based upon the early works of Edwin H. Sutherland (1883-1950), a criminologist at Indiana University. Sutherland was particularly interested in fraud committed by the elite upper world business executive, either against shareholders or the public. As Geis noted, Sutherland said, "General Motors does not have an inferiority complex, United States Steel does not suffer from an unresolved Oedipus problem, and the DuPonts do not desire to return to the womb. The assumption that an offender may have such pathological distortion of the intellect or the emotions seems to me absurd, and if it is absurd regarding the crimes of businessmen, it is equally absurd regarding the crimes of persons in the economic lower classes."

For the non-initiated, Sutherland is to the world of white-collar criminality what Freud is to psychology. Indeed, it was Sutherland who coined the term *white-collar crime* in 1939. He intended the definition to mean criminal acts of corporations and individuals acting in their corporate capacity. Since that time, however, the term has come to mean almost any financial or economic crime, from the mailroom to the boardroom.

Many criminologists, myself included, believe that Sutherland's most important contribution to criminal literature was elsewhere. Later in his career, he developed the "theory of differential association," which is now the most widely accepted theory of criminal behavior in the twentieth century. Until Sutherland's landmark work in the 1930s, most criminologists and sociologists held the view that crime was genetically based, that criminals beget criminal offspring.

While this argument may seem naive today, it was based largely on the observation of non-white-collar offenders — the murderers, rapists, sadists, and hooligans who plagued society. Numerous subsequent studies have indeed established a genetic base for "street" crime, which must be tempered by environmental considerations. (For a thorough explanation of the genetic base for criminality, see *Crime and Punishment* by Wilson and Herrnstein.) Sutherland was able to explain crime's environmental considerations through the theory of differential association. The theory's basic tenet is that crime is learned, much like we learn math, English, or guitar playing.[7]

Sutherland believed this learning of criminal behavior occurred with other persons in a process of communication. Therefore, he reasoned, criminality cannot occur without the assistance of other people. Sutherland further theorized that the learning of criminal activity usually occurred within intimate personal groups. This explains, in his view, how a dysfunctional parent is more likely to produce dysfunctional offspring. Sutherland believed that the learning process involved two specific areas: the techniques to commit the crime; and the attitudes, drives, rationalizations, and motives of the

criminal mind. You can see how Sutherland's differential association theory fits with occupational offenders. Organizations that have
dishonest employees will eventually infect a portion of honest ones.
It also goes the other way: honest employees will eventually have an
influence on some of those who are dishonest.

DONALD R. CRESSEY

One of Sutherland's brightest students at Indiana University
during the 1940s was Donald R. Cressey (1919-1987). While much
of Sutherland's research concentrated on upper world criminality,
Cressey took his own studies in a different direction. Working on his
Ph.D. in criminology, he decided his dissertation would concentrate
on embezzlers. Accordingly, Cressey arranged the necessary permission at prisons in the Midwest and eventually interviewed about
200 incarcerated inmates.

Cressey's Hypothesis

Cressey was intrigued by embezzlers, whom he called "trust
violators." He was especially interested in the circumstances that
led them to be overcome by temptation. For that reason, he excluded
from his research those employees who took their jobs for the purpose of stealing — a relatively minor number of offenders at that
time. Upon completion of his interviews, he developed what still
remains as the classic model for the occupational offender. His
research was published in *Other People's Money: A Study in the
Social Psychology of Embezzlement.*
Cressey's final hypothesis was:

"Trusted persons become trust violators when
they conceive of themselves as having a financial
problem which is nonsharable, are aware this problem can be secretly resolved by violation of the position of financial trust, and are able to apply to their
own conduct in that situation verbalizations which
enable them to adjust their conceptions of themselves
as trusted persons with their conceptions of themselves
as users of the entrusted funds or property." [8]

Over the years, the hypothesis has become more well known
as the "fraud triangle." One leg of the triangle represents a perceived

nonsharable financial need. The second leg is for perceived opportunity, and the final is for rationalization. The role of the nonsharable problem is important. Cressey said, "When the trust violators were asked to explain why they refrained from violation of other positions of trust they might have held at previous times, or why they had not violated the subject position at an earlier time, those who had an opinion expressed the equivalent of one or more of the following quotations: (a) 'There was no need for it like there was this time.' (b) 'The idea never entered my head.' (c) 'I thought it was dishonest then, but this time it did not seem dishonest at first.'"[9]

The Fraud Triangle

"In all cases of trust violation encountered, the violator considered that a financial problem which confronted him could not be shared with persons who, from a more objective point of view, probably could have aided in the solution of the problem." [10]

Nonsharable Problems

What, of course, is considered "nonsharable" is wholly in the eyes of the potential occupational offender, Cressey said. "Thus a man could lose considerable money at the race track daily but the loss, even if it construed a problem for the individual, might not constitute a nonsharable problem for him. Another man might define the problem as one which must be kept secret and private, that is, as one which is nonsharable. Similarly, a failing bank or business might be considered by one person as presenting problems which must be shared with business associates and members of the community, while another person might conceive these problems as nonsharable."[11]

Cressey divided these "'nonsharable" problems into six basic subtypes: violation of ascribed obligations, problems resulting from personal failure, business reversals, physical isolation, status gaining, and employer-employee relations. Violation of ascribed obligations—the specter of being unable to pay one's debts—has historically proved a strong motivator. "Financial problems incurred through non-financial violations of positions of trust often are considered as nonsharable by trusted persons since they represent a threat to the status which holding the position entails. Most individuals in positions of financial trust, and most employers of such individuals, consider that incumbency in such a position necessarily implies that, in addition to being honest, they should behave in certain ways and should refrain from participation in some other kinds of behavior."[12] In other words, the mere fact that a person has a trusted position brings with it the implication that he or she can and does properly manage money.

Violation of Ascribed Obligations

"When persons incur debts or in some other way become financially obligated as a result of violation of the obligations ascribed to the role of trusted person, they frequently consider that these debts must be kept secret, and that meeting them becomes a nonsharable financial problem. In many instances, the insurance of such debts is also considered incompatible with the duties and obligations of other roles which the person might be enacting, such as those of a husband or father, but the concern here is with such debts only as they represent conflict with the person's role as a trusted person."[13] Cressey describes a situation we can all appreciate — not being able to pay one's debts — and then having to admit it to one's employer, family, or friends.

Problems Resulting From Personal Failure

Problems resulting from personal failures, Cressey writes, can be of several different types. "While some pressing financial problems may be considered as having resulted from 'economic conditions'. . . . others are considered to have been created by the misguided or poorly planned activities of the individual trusted person. Because he fears a loss of status, the individual is afraid to admit to anyone who could alleviate the situation the fact that he has a problem which is a consequence of his 'own bad judgment' or 'own fault' or 'own stupidity.'"[14] In short, pride goeth before the fall. If the potential offender has a choice between covering his poor investment choices through a violation of trust and admitting that he is an unsophisticated investor, it is easy to see how some prideful people's judgment could be clouded.

Business Reversals

Business reversals were the third area Cressey detailed as a part of the nonsharable problem. He saw these differently from personal failures, since many business people consider their financial reverses as coming from conditions beyond their control: inflation, high interest rates, raising capital, and borrowing money. Cressey quoted the remarks of one businessman who borrowed money from a bank using fictitious collateral. "Case 36. 'There are very few people who are able to walk away from a failing business. When the bridge is falling, almost everyone will run for a piece of timber. In business there is this eternal optimism that things will get better tomorrow. We get to working on the business, keeping it going, and we almost get mesmerized by it . . . . Most of us don't know when to quit, when to say, "This one has me licked. Here's one for the opposition."'" [15]

Physical Isolation

The fourth category of nonsharable problems Cressey described is physical isolation, in which the person in financial straits is isolated from the people who can help him.

Status Gaining

The fifth are problems relating to status-gaining. Although these are easily passed off as living beyond one's means or spending money lavishly, Cressey was interested more in their behavioral implications. He noted, "The structuring of status ambitions as being non-sharable is not uncommon in our culture, and it again must be emphasized that the structuring of a situation as nonsharable is not alone the cause of trust violation. More specifically, in this type of case a problem appears when the individual realizes that he does not have the financial means necessary for continued association with persons on a desired status level, and this problem becomes nonsharable when he feels that he can neither renounce his aspirations for membership in the desired group nor obtain prestige symbols necessary to such membership."[16] He observed, then, that a lot of occupational offenders are afflicted with the "Keeping up with the Joneses" syndrome.

Employer-Employee Relations

Finally, Cressey described problems resulting from employer-employee relationships. The most common, he stated, was an employed person who resents his status within the organization in which he is trusted. The resentment can come from perceived economic inequities, such as pay, or from the feeling of being overworked or underappreciated. Cressey said this problem becomes non-sharable when the individual believes that making suggestions to alleviate his perceived maltreatment will possibly threaten his status in the organization. There is also a strong motivator for the perceived employee to want to "get even" when he feels ill treated.

A Personal Experience

One of my best-remembered examples involves a personal experience, and not a pleasant one. Most people — if they admit the truth — will have stolen on the job at some time in their careers. Some of the thefts are major, some minor. Some are uncovered; many never are. With this preamble (and the fact that the statute of limitations has long expired!) I will tell you the story of one employee thief — me.

The incident occurred during college. Like many of you, I didn't work my way through the university just for experience; it was a necessity. One of my part-time jobs was as a salesperson in a men's clothing store, a place I'll call Mr. Zac's. It seems that Mr. Zac had the imagination to name the store after himself, which may give you a clue as to the kind of person he was.

My first day on the job, it became clear by talking to the other employees that they had a strong dislike of Mr. Zac. It didn't take long to figure out why: he was cheap beyond all reason; he was sore-tempered, paranoid, and seemed to strongly resent having to pay the employees who were generating his sales. Mr. Zac was especially suspicious of the help stealing. He always eyed the employees warily when they left in the evening, I assume because he thought their clothing and bags were stuffed with his merchandise. So his employees figured out novel ways to steal for no other reason than to get back at Mr. Zac. I was above all that, or so I thought. But then Mr. Zac did something to me personally, and my attitude changed completely.

One day I was upstairs in the storeroom getting merchandise off the top shelf. Since the high reach had pulled my shirttail out, I was standing there tucking it in when Mr. Zac walked by. He didn't say a word. I went back downstairs to work and thought no more of it. But ten minutes later, Mr. Zac called me into his small, cubbyhole office, closed the door, and asked, "What were you tucking in your pants upstairs?" Just my shirt, I replied. "I don't believe you," Mr. Zac said. "Unless you unzip your pants right now and show me, you're fired." At first, of course, it didn't register that he was serious. When it finally did, I was faced with a dilemma—unzip my pants for the boss, or be late on the rent and face eviction. I chose the former, but as I stood there letting my pants fall down around my knees, my face burned with anger and embarrassment. Never before had I been placed in a position like this—having to undress to prove my innocence.

After seeing for himself that I didn't have any of his precious merchandise on my person, Mr. Zac sent me back to the sales floor. I was a different person, though. No longer was I interested in selling merchandise and being a good employee. I was interested in getting even and that's what I did. Over the next few months, I tried my best to steal him blind—clothing, underwear, outerwear, neckties—you name it. With the help of some of the other employees, we even stole a large display case. He never caught on, and eventually I quit the job. Was I justified in stealing from Mr. Zac? Absolutely not. At this age, given the same circumstances, would I do it again? No. But at that particular time, I was young, idealistic, very headstrong, and totally fearless. Criminologists have documented that the reason so many young people lack fear is because they do not yet realize actions can have serious consequences; it never occurred to me that I could have gone to jail for stealing from Mr. Zac.

The impact of job loyalty—or like Mr. Zac's employees, the lack of it—is an important consideration in the occupational fraud and abuse formula. With changes in the American workforce, we may or may not experience more fraud-related problems. Much has been written recently concerning the downsizing, outsourcing, and increased employee turnover in business. If the employee of the future is largely a contract worker, much of the incentive of loyalty toward organizations could be lost. Such a trend seems to be under-way, but its real fraud impact has not been determined. However, fraud is only one cost of doing business. If the outsourcing of corpo-rate America does indeed cause more occupational fraud and abuse, the benefits of restructuring may be seen as outweighing the cost of more crime, at least in the short term. In the long run, it is difficult to justify how employees stealing from organizations can be beneficial to anyone. That was Cressey's theory, too.

Sociological Factors

Since Cressey's study was done in the early 1950s, the workforce was obviously different from today's. But the employee faced with an immediate, nonsharable financial need hasn't changed much over the years. Cressey pointed out that for the trust violator, it was necessary that he believe his financial situation can be re-solved in secret. Cressey said, "In all cases [in the study] there was a distinct feeling that, because of activity prior to the defalcation, the approval of groups important to the trusted person had been lost, or a distinct feeling that present group approval would be lost if certain activity were revealed [the nonsharable financial problem], with the result that the trusted person was effectively isolated from persons who could assist him in solving problems arising from that activity.

"Although the clear conception of a financial problem as nonsharable does not invariably result in trust violation, it does es-tablish in trusted persons a desire for a specific kind of solution to their problems. The results desired in the cases encountered were uniform: the solution or partial solution of the problem by the use of funds which can be obtained in an independent, relatively secret, safe, and sure method in keeping with the 'rationalizations' avail-able to the person at the time."[17]   Cressey pointed out that many of his subjects in the study mentioned the importance of resolving the problem secretly.

Cressey also discovered, by talking to his trust violators, that they did not see their positions as a point of possible abuse until after they were confronted with the nonsharable financial problem. They used words such as "it occurred to me" or "it dawned on me" that the entrusted moneys could be used to cure their vexing situations. In Cressey's view, the trust violator must have two prerequisites: general information and technical skill. With respect to general information, the fiduciary capacity of an employee in and of itself implies that, since it is a position of trust (read: no one is checking) it can be violated.

Cressey said that in addition to general information, the trust violator must have the technical skills required to pull the fraud off in secret. He observed, "It is the next step which is significant to violation: the application of the general information to the specific situation, and conjointly, the perception of the fact that in addition to having general possibilities for violation, a specific position of trust can be used for the specific purpose of solving a nonsharable problem.... The statement that trusted persons must be cognizant of the fact that the entrusted funds can be used secretly to solve the nonsharable problem is based upon observations of such applications of general information to specific situations."[18] Cressey believed that based upon observations, it was difficult to distinguish which came first — the need for the funds, or the realization that they could be secretly used. In other words, did the person have a "legitimate" need for the funds before he figured out he could get his hands on them secretly? Or did he see secret access to funds and find a justification to use them?

Next, Cressey delved into the inner workings of the offender's minds—how were they able to convince themselves that stealing was okay? He found they were able to excuse their actions to themselves by viewing their crimes as: (1) non-criminal, (2) justified, or (3) part of a situation which the offender does not control. These methods he generalized as "rationalizations." In his studies, Cressey discovered "In cases of trust violation encountered, significant rationalizations were always present before the criminal act took place, or at least at the time it took place, and, in fact, after the act had taken place the rationalization often was abandoned."[19] That is, of course, because of the nature of us all: the first time we do something contrary to our morals, it bothers us. As we repeat the act, it becomes easier. One hallmark of occupational fraud and abuse offenders is that once the line is crossed, the illegal acts become more or less continuous.

One of the simplest ways to justify unacceptable conduct and avoid guilt feelings is to invent a good reason for embezzling — one sanctioned in the social group as a greater good. Thus, the trust violator's self-image, should he be discovered, must be explainable to himself and others around him.

Offender Types

For further analysis, Cressey divided the subjects into three groups: independent businessmen, long-term violators, and absconders. He discovered that each group had its own types of rationalizations.

INDEPENDENT BUSINESSMEN

Businessmen, for example, used one of two common excuses: (1) they were "borrowing" the money which they converted, or (2) the funds entrusted to them were really theirs—you can't steal from yourself. Cressey found the "borrowing" rationalization was the most frequently used. Many independent businessmen also expressed the belief that their practices were the rule of the day for other businesses. Nearly universally, the business owners felt their illegal actions were predicated by an "unusual situation," which Cressey perceived to be in reality an unsharable financial problem.

LONG-TERM VIOLATORS

The long-term violators Cressey studied also generally preferred the "borrowing" rationalization. Other rationalizations of long-term violators were described, too: (1) they were embezzling to keep their families from shame, disgrace, or poverty; (2) that theirs was a case of "necessity;" that their employers were cheating them financially; and (3) that their employers were dishonest towards others and deserved to be fleeced. Some even pointed out that it was more difficult to return the funds than to steal them in the first place, and claimed they did not pay back their "borrowings" out of detection fears. A few in the study actually kept track of their thefts, but most only did so at first. Later, as the embezzlements escalate, it is assumed that the offender would rather not know the extent of his "borrowings." All of the long-term violators in the study expressed a feeling that they would like to eventually "clean the slate" and repay their debt.

Cressey noted that many of the offenders finally realized they were "in too deep." This then forces the violator to think of the possible consequences of his actions. Cressey said the fear generated from being in over one's head is not caused by the thought of going to jail — after all, the offender doesn't generally consider his conduct illegal. As Cressey observed, "The trust violator cannot fear the treatment usually accorded criminals until he comes to look upon himself as a criminal."[20]

But at some point, Cressey noted, the offenders start becoming apprehensive about the possible social connotations, and later, the criminal possibilities. A number of offenders described themselves as extremely nervous and upset, tense, and unhappy. Cressey felt that without the rationalization that they are borrowing, long-term offenders in the study found it difficult to reconcile converting money, while at the same time seeing themselves as honest and trustworthy. If this is the situation, Cressey says that ". . . as a result, he either (a) readopts the attitudes of the groups with which he identified before he violated the trust, or (b) he adopts the attitudes of the new category of persons (offenders) with whom he now identifies."[21]

ABSCONDERS

The third group of offenders Cressey discussed was "absconders" — people who take the money and run. He was able to work this group into his theory of a nonsharable financial need by describing their behavior as "isolated." He observed, "While among persons who abscond with entrusted funds, as among other violators, almost any problem situation may be defined as nonsharable, the problems which are nonsharable for absconders are almost always of that nature, at least in part because the person is physically isolated from other persons with whom he can share his problems. Individuals who abscond with the funds or goods entrusted to them usually are unmarried or separated from their spouses, live in hotels or rooming houses, have few primary group associations of any sort, and own little property. Only one of the absconders interviewed had held a higher status position of trust, such as an accountant, business executive, or bookkeeper."[22]

Cressey says that although absconders recognize their behavior as criminal, they justify their actions by claiming their behavior is caused by outside influences beyond their control. Absconders also frequently express a "don't care" attitude. Moreover, they are more likely to claim their own personal "defects" led to their criminality.

In the 1950s, when this data was gathered by Cressey, embezzlers were considered "persons of higher socioeconomic status who took money over periods of time . . . while 'thieves' are persons of lower status who take whatever funds are at hand. Since most absconders identify with the lower status group, they look upon themselves as belonging to a special class of thieves rather than trust violators. Just as long-term violators and independent businessmen do not at first consider the possibility of absconding with the funds, absconders do not consider the possibility of taking relatively small amounts of money over a period of time."[23]

One of the most fundamental observations of the Cressey study was that it took all three elements — perceived motive, perceived opportunity, and the ability to rationalize — for the trust violation to occur.

Cressey concluded that ". . . [a] trust violation takes place when the position of trust is viewed by the trusted person according to culturally provided knowledge about and rationalizations for using the entrusted funds for solving a nonsharable problem, and that the absence of any of these events will preclude violation. The three events make up the conditions under which trust violation occurs and the term 'cause' may be applied to their conjecture since trust violation is dependent on that conjecture. Whenever the conjecture of events occurs, trust violation results, and if the conjecture does not take place there is no trust violation."[24]

Conclusion

Cressey's classic fraud triangle helps explain the nature of many—but not all—occupational offenders. For example, although academicians have tested his model, it has still not fully found its way into practice in terms of developing fraud prevention programs. Our sense tells us that one model—even Cressey's—will not fit all situations. Plus, the study is nearly half a century old. There has been considerable social change in the interim. And now, many antifraud professionals believe there is a new breed of occupational offender—one who simply lacks a conscience sufficient to overcome temptation.

Even Cressey saw the trend later in his life. After doing this landmark study in embezzlement, Cressey went on to a distinguished academic career, eventually authoring 13 books and nearly 300 articles on criminology matters. He rose to the position of Professor

Emeritus in Criminology at the University of California, Santa Barbara.

It was my honor to know Cressey personally. Indeed, he and I collaborated extensively before he died in 1987, and his influence on my own antifraud theories has been significant. Our families are acquainted; we stayed in each other's homes; we traveled together; he was my friend. In a way, we made the odd couple. He, the academic and me, the businessman. He, the theoretical and me, the practical.

I met him as the result of an assignment, in about 1983. A Fortune 500 company hired me on an investigative and consulting matter. They had a rather messy case of a high-level vice president who was put in charge of a large construction project for a new company plant. The $75 million budget for which he was responsible proved to be too much of a temptation. Construction companies wined and dined the vice president, eventually providing him with tempting and illegal bait: drugs and women.

He bit.

From there, the vice president succumbed to full kickbacks. By the time the dust settled, he had secretly pocketed about $3.5 million. After completing the internal investigation for the company, assembling the documentation and interviews, I worked with prosecutors at the company's request to put the guy in prison. Then the company came to me with a very simple question: "Why did he do it?" As a former FBI Agent with hundreds of fraud cases under my belt, I must admit I had not thought much about the motives of occupational offenders. To me, they committed these crimes because they were crooks. But the company—certainly progressive on the anti-fraud front at the time—wanted me to invest the resources to find out why and how employees go bad, so they could possibly do something to prevent it. This quest took me to the vast libraries of The University of Texas at Austin, which led me to Cressey's early research. After reading his book, I realized that Cressey had described the embezzlers I had encountered to a "T." I wanted to meet him.

Finding Cressey was easy enough. I made two phone calls and found that he was still alive, well, and teaching in Santa Barbara. He was in the telephone book and I called him. Immediately, he agreed to meet me the next time I came to California. That began what became a very close relationship between us which lasted until his untimely death in 1987. It was he who recognized the real value of combining the theorist with the practitioner. Cressey used to proclaim that he learned as much from me as I from him. But then, in addition to his brilliance, he was one of the most gracious people I have ever met. Although we were only together professionally for four years, we covered a lot of ground. Cressey was convinced there was a need for an organization devoted exclusively to fraud detection and deterrence. The Association of Certified Fraud Examiners, started about a year after his death, is in existence in large measure because of Cressey's vision. Moreover, although Cressey didn't know it at the time, he created the concept of what eventually became the Certified Fraud Examiner.

It happened like this. Don, his wife, Elaine, my wife, Judy, and I were returning from a fraud conference in Australia when we stopped over in Fiji for two days. As he and I were sitting on the beach talking, Cressey theorized that it was time for a new type of "corporate cop"—one trained in detecting and deterring the crime of the future: fraud. Cressey pointed out that the traditional policeman was ill-equipped to deal with sophisticated financial crimes, as were the traditional accountants. It was just one of many ideas he had discussed that day, but that one stuck.

Dr. W. Steve Albrecht

Not too long thereafter, I met another pioneer researcher in occupational fraud and abuse, Dr. Steve Albrecht of Brigham Young University. Unlike Cressey, Albrecht was educated as an accountant. We discussed, among other things, Cressey's vision. Albrecht agreed with Cressey—traditional accountants, he said, were ill-equipped to deal with complex financial crimes. Eventually, my colleagues and I decided that this new kind of "corporate cop" would have training in four disciplines: accounting, law, investigation, and criminology. And that new corporate cop is now the Certified Fraud Examiner.

The Albrecht Study

Steve was helpful in commencing the CFE program, and his research contributions in fraud have been enormous. He and two of his colleagues, Howe and Romney, conducted an analysis of 212 frauds in the early 1980s under a grant from the Institute of Internal Auditors Research Foundation, leading to their book entitled *Deter-*

ring Fraud: The Internal Auditor's Perspective. The study's methodology involved obtaining demographics and background information on the frauds through the extensive use of questionnaires. The participants in the survey were internal auditors of companies who had experienced frauds.

The study covered several areas, one of the most interesting of which concentrated on the motivations of the perpetrators of occupational frauds and abuses. They classified these motivators as one of nine different types:[25]

1. Living beyond their means
2. An overwhelming desire for personal gain
3. High personal debt
4. A close association with customers
5. Feeling pay was not commensurate with responsibility
6. A wheeler-dealer attitude
7. Strong challenge to beat the system
8. Excessive gambling habits
9. Undue family or peer pressure

As you can see from the list, these motivators are very similar to the nonsharable financial problems Cressey discussed. The study by Albrecht, et al., also disclosed several interesting relationships between the perpetrators and the frauds they committed. For example, perpetrators of large frauds used the proceeds to purchase new homes and expensive automobiles, recreation property, expensive vacations, support extramarital relationships, and make speculative investments. Those committing small frauds did not.

There were other observations: Perpetrators who were interested primarily in "beating the system" committed larger frauds. However, perpetrators who believed their pay was not adequate committed primarily small frauds. Lack of segregation of responsibilities, placing undeserved trust in key employees, imposing unrealistic goals, and operating on a crisis basis were all pressures or weaknesses associated with large frauds. College graduates were less likely to spend the proceeds of their loot to take extravagant vacations, purchase recreational property, support extramarital relationships, and buy expensive automobiles. Finally, those with lower salaries were more likely to have a prior criminal record.[26]

Like Cressey's study, the Albrecht study suggests there are three factors involved in occupational frauds: ". . . it appears that three elements must be present for a fraud to be committed: a situational pressure (nonsharable financial pressure), a perceived opportunity to commit and conceal the dishonest act (a way to secretly resolve the dishonest act or the lack of deterrence by management), and some way to rationalize (verbalize) the act as either being inconsistent with one's personal level of integrity or justifiable."

The Fraud Scale

To explain the concept, Albrecht developed the "Fraud Scale," which included the components of: situational pressures, perceived opportunities, and personal integrity.[27] When situational pressures and perceived opportunities are high and personal integrity is low, occupational fraud is much more likely to occur than when the opposite is true.[28]

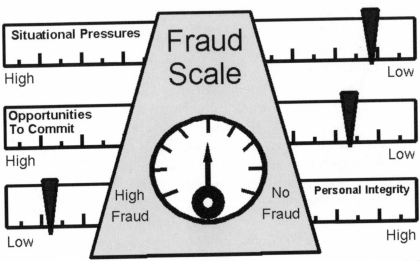

Albrecht, Howe, Romney, "Deterring Fraud: The Internal Auditor's Perspective," p6

The Fraud Scale

He describes situational pressures as ". . . the immediate problems individuals experience within their environments, the most overwhelming of which are probably high personal debts or financial losses."[29]   Opportunities to commit fraud, Albrecht says, may be created by deficient or missing internal controls—those of the employee or the company. Personal integrity ". . . refers to the personal code of ethical behavior each person adopts. While this factor appears to be a straightforward determination of whether the person is honest or dishonest, moral development research indicates that the issue is more complex."[30]

Albrecht and his colleagues believed that, taken as a group, occupational fraud perpetrators are hard to profile and that fraud is difficult to predict. His research examined comprehensive data sources to assemble a complete list of pressure, opportunity, and integrity variables, resulting in a list of 82 possible red flags or indicators of occupational fraud and abuse. The red flags ranged from unusually high personal debts, to belief that one's job is in jeopardy; from no separation of asset custodial procedures, to not adequately checking the potential employee's background.[31]

While such red flags may be present in many occupational fraud cases, one must re-emphasize Albrecht's caution that the perpetrators are hard to profile and fraud is difficult to predict. To underscore this point, Albrecht's research does not address—and no current research has been done to determine—if nonoffenders have many of the same characteristics. If so, then the list may not be discriminating enough to be useful. In short, while one should be mindful of potential red flags, they should not receive undue attention absent more compelling circumstances.

RICHARD C. HOLLINGER
The Hollinger - Clark Study

In 1983, Richard C. Hollinger of Purdue University and John P. Clark of the University of Minnesota published federally-funded research involving surveys of nearly 10,000 American workers. Their book, *Theft by Employees*, reached a different conclusion than Cressey. They concluded that employees steal primarily as a result of workplace conditions, and that the true costs of the problem are vastly understated: "In sum, when we take into consideration the incalculable social costs . . . the grand total paid for theft in the workplace is no doubt grossly underestimated by the available financial estimates."[32]

Hypotheses of Employee Theft

In reviewing the literature on employee theft, Hollinger and Clark concluded that experts had developed five separate but interrelated sets of hypotheses of employee theft. The first was external economic pressures, such as the "unsharable financial problem" that Cressey described. The second hypothesis was that contemporary employees, specifically young ones, are not as hardworking and honest as those in past generations. The third theory, advocated primarily by those with years of experience in the security and investigative industry, was that every employee can be tempted to steal from his employer. The theory basically assumes that people are greedy and dishonest by nature. The fourth theory was that job dissatisfaction is the primary cause of employee theft, and the fifth, that theft occurs because of the broadly shared formal and informal structure of organizations. That is, over time, the group norms — good or bad — become the standard of conduct. The sum of their research generally concluded that the fourth hypothesis was correct.

Employee Deviance

Employee theft is at one extreme of employee deviance, which can be defined as conduct detrimental to the organization and to the employee. At the other extreme is counterproductive employee behavior such as goldbricking, industrial sabotage, and even wildcat strikes. Hollinger and Clark define two basic categories of employee deviant behavior: (1) acts by employees against property, and (2) violations of the norms regulating acceptable levels of production. The latter relates to the impact employee deviance can have on sales.

During the three-year duration of the study, Hollinger and Clark developed a written questionnaire which was sent to employees in three different sectors: retail, hospital, and manufacturing. They eventually received 9,175 valid employee questionnaires, representing about 54% of those sampled. Below are the results of the questionnaires. The first table represents property deviance only.[33]

Combined Phase I and Phase II Property-Deviance Items and Percentage of Reported Involvement, by Sector

Items	Almost Daily	About Once a Week	Four to Twelve Times a Year	One to Three Times a Year	Total
Retail Sector (N= 3,567)					
Misuse the discount privilege	0.6	2.4	11	14.9	28.9
Take store merchandise	0.2	0.5	1.3	4.6	6.6
Get paid for more hours than were worked	0.2	0.4	1.2	4	5.8
Purposely underring a purchase	0.1	0.3	1.1	1.7	3.2
Borrow or take money from employer without approval	0.1	0.1	0.5	2	2.7
Be reimbursed for more money than spent on business expenses	0.1	0.2	0.5	1.3	2.1
Damage merchandise to buy it on discount	0	0.1	0.2	1	1.3
Total involved in property deviance					35.1
Hospital Sector (N=4,111)					
Take hospital supplies (e.g. linens, bandages)	0.2	0.8	8.4	17.9	27.3
Take or use medication intended for patients	0.1	0.3	1.9	5.5	7.8
Get paid for more hours than were worked	0.2	0.5	1.6	3.8	6.1
Take hospital equipment or tools	0.1	0.1	0.4	4.1	4.7
Be reimbursed for more money than spent on business expenses	0.1	0	0.2	0.8	1.1
Total involved in property deviance					33.3
Manufacturing Sector (N=1,497)					
Take raw materials used in production	0.1	0.3	3.5	10.4	14.3
Get paid for more hours than were worked	0.2	0.5	2.9	5.6	9.2
Take company tools or equipment	0	0.1	1.1	7.5	8.7
Be reimbursed for more money than spent on business expenses	0.1	0.6	1.4	5.6	7.7
Take finished products	0	0	0.4	2.7	3.1
Take precious metals (e.g. platinum, gold)	0.1	0.1	0.5	1.1	1.8
Total involved in property deviance					28.4

Adapted from Richard C. Hollinger, John P. Clark, *Theft by Employees*, Lexington: Lexington Books, 1983. p42.

Following is a summary of the Hollinger and Clark research with respect to production deviance. Not surprisingly, the most common violations were taking too long for lunch or breaks, with more than half of the employees involved in this activity.[34]

Combined Phase I and Phase II Production-Deviance Items and Percentage of Reported Involvement, by Sector

Items	Almost Daily	About Once a Week	Four to Twelve Times a Year	One to Three Times a Year	Total
			Involvement		
Retail Sector (N= 3,567)					
Take a long lunch or break without approval	6.9	13.3	15.5	20.3	56
Come to work late or leave early	0.9	3.4	10.8	17.2	32.3
Use sick leave when not sick	0.1	0.1	3.5	13.4	17.1
Do slow or sloppy work	0.3	1.5	4.1	9.8	15.7
Work under the influence of alcohol or drugs	0.5	0.8	1.6	4.6	7.5
Total involved in production deviance					65.4
Hospital Sector (N=4,111)					
Take a long lunch or break without approval	8.5	13.5	17.4	17.8	57.2
Come to work late or leave early	1	3.5	9.6	14.9	29
Use sick leave when not sick	0	0.2	5.7	26.9	32.8
Do slow or sloppy work	0.2	0.8	4.1	5.9	11
Work under the influence of alcohol or drugs	0.1	0.3	0.6	2.2	3.2
Total involved in production deviance					69.2
Manufacturing Sector (N=1,497)					
Take a long lunch or break without approval	18	23.5	22	8.5	72
Come to work late or leave early	1.9	9	19.4	13.8	44.1
Use sick leave when not sick	0	0.2	9.6	28.6	38.4
Do slow or sloppy work	0.5	1.3	5.7	5	12.5
Work under the influence of alcohol or drugs	1.1	1.3	3.1	7.3	12.8
Total involved in production deviance					82.2

Adapted from Richard C. Hollinger, John P. Clark, *Theft by Employees*, Lexington: Lexington Books, 1983. p45.

In order to empirically test whether economics had an effect on the level of theft, the researchers also sorted the data by household income, under the theory that the lower the level of income, the greater the degree of thefts. However, they were unable to confirm such a statistical relationship. This would tend to indicate—at least in this study—that absolute income is not a predictor of employee theft. But they were able to confirm that there was a statistical relationship between a person's "concern" over his financial situation and the level of theft.

Hollinger and Clark presented the employees with a list of eight major concerns, from personal health to education issues to financial problems. "Being concerned about finances and being under financial pressure are not necessarily the same. However, if a respondent considered his or her finances as one of the most important issues, that concern could be partially due to 'unsharable (sic) economic problems,' or it could also be that current realities are not matching one's financial aspirations regardless of the income presently being realized".[38]

The study concluded that "in each industry, the results are significant, with higher theft individuals more likely to be concerned about their finances, particularly those who ranked finances as the first or second most important issue."[35] The researchers were unable to confirm, though, any connection between community pressures and the level of theft.

Age and Theft

Hollinger and Clark believe there is a direct correlation between age and the level of theft. "Few other variables . . . have exhibited such a strong relationship to theft as the age of the employee."[36] The reason, they concluded, was that younger employees had less tenure with the organization and therefore lower levels of commitment to it. "By definition," they say, "these employees are more likely to be younger workers."[37] In addition, there is a long history of connection between many levels of crime and youth. Sociologists have suggested that the central process of control is determined by a person's "commitment to conformity." Under this model — assuming employees are all subject to the same deviant motives and opportunities — the probability of deviant involvement depends on the stakes that one has in conformity.

The researchers suggest that the policy implications from the commitment to conformity theory is that—rather than subject employees to draconian security measures, ". . . companies should afford younger workers many of the same rights, fringes, and privileges of the tenured, older employees. In fact, by signaling to the younger employee that he or she is temporary or expendable, the organization inadvertently may be encouraging its own victimization by the very group of employees that is already least committed to the expressed goals and objectives of the owners and managers."[38]

Although this may indeed affect the level of employee dissatisfaction, its policy implications are wide-ranging and may not be practical for non-fraud-related reasons.

Hollinger and Clark were able to confirm a direct relationship between an employee's position and the level of the theft, with those levels of theft highest in jobs with almost unrestricted access to the things of value in the work organization. Although they see obvious connections between opportunity and theft (for example, retail cashiers with daily access to cash had the highest incidence), the researchers believe opportunity to be ". . . only a secondary factor that constrains the manner in which the deviance is manifested."[39]

Job Satisfaction and Deviance

The research of Hollinger and Clark strongly suggests that all age groups of employees who are dissatisfied with their jobs, but especially the younger workers, are the most likely to seek redress through counterproductive or illegal behavior in order to right the perceived "inequity." Other writers, notably anthropologist Gerald Mars and researcher David Altheide, have commented on this connection. You can probably remember your own instances of "getting back" at the organization for its perceived shortcomings, like I did with Mr. Zac.

As another example, I heard a legendary story when I was in the FBI about an agent we'll call Willis. Stories such as this one have a way of taking on a life of their own, and I therefore cannot vouch for its complete accuracy. At any rate, Willis was apparently attempting to arrest a fugitive when his suit was ripped to shreds. On his next expense voucher, Willis claimed $200 for the suit. But a clerk in charge of paying the voucher for the FBI called him. "Willis," the clerk said, "there is no way the government is going to pay you for ripping your suit—forget it." Willis reasoned this was extremely unfair. After all, he would now have to come out-of-pocket for a new suit. This would not have been necessary were it not for his job, Willis rationalized. The clerk, however, was unimpressed.

The following month, the clerk received the FBI Agent's next expense voucher and examined it with a fine-tooth comb to make sure Willis didn't try again. Convinced the voucher was satisfactory, the clerk called Willis. "I'm glad to see you didn't try to claim the cost of that suit again," the clerk said. Willis reputedly replied, "That's where you're wrong. The cost of that suit is in the voucher. All you have to do is find it."

This story illustrates the same concept that Mars observed consistently among hotel dining room employees and dock workers. The employees believed that pilferage was not theft, but was "seen as a morally justified addition to wages; indeed, as an entitlement due from exploiting employers."[40] Altheide also documented that theft is often perceived by employees as a "way of getting back at the boss or supervisor."[41] From my own experience with Mr. Zac, I can verify this sentiment.

Jason Ditton documented a pattern in U.S. industries called "wages in kind," in which employees "situated in structurally disadvantaged parts [of the organization] receive large segments of their wages invisibly."[42]

Organizational Controls and Deviance

Try as they might, the researchers were unable to document a strong relationship between control and deviance. They examined five different control mechanisms: company policy, selection of personnel, inventory control, security, and punishment.

Company policy can be an effective control. Hollinger and Clark pointed out that companies with a strong policy against absenteeism have less of a problem with it. As a result, they would expect policies governing employee theft to have the same impact. Similarly, they feel employee education as an organizational policy has a deterrent effect. Control through selection of personnel is exerted by hiring persons who will conform to organizational expectations. Inventory control is required not only for theft, but for procedures to detect errors, avoid waste, and insure a proper amount of inventory is maintained. Security controls involve proactive and reactive measures, surveillance, internal investigations, and others. Control through punishment is designed to deter the specific individual, plus those who might be tempted to act illegally.

Hollinger and Clark interviewed numerous employees in an attempt to determine their attitudes toward control. With respect to policy, they concluded ". . . the issue of theft by employees is a sensitive one in organizations and must be handled with some discretion. A concern for theft must be expressed without creating an atmosphere of distrust and paranoia. If an organization places too much stress on the topic, honest employees may feel unfairly suspected, resulting in lowered morale and higher turnover."[43]

Employees in the study also perceived, in general, that computerized inventory records added security and made theft more difficult. With respect to security control, the researchers discovered that the employees regarded the purpose of a security division as taking care of outside—rather than inside—security. Few of the employees were aware that security departments investigate employee theft, and most such departments had a poor image among the workers. With respect to punishment, the employees interviewed felt theft would result in job termination in a worst-case scenario. They perceived that minor thefts would be handled by reprimands only.

Hollinger and Clark conclude that formal organizational controls provide both good and bad news. "The good news is that employee theft does seem to be susceptible to control efforts . . . . Our data also indicate, however, that the impact of organizational controls is neither uniform nor very strong. In sum, formal organizational controls do negatively influence theft prevalence, but these effects must be understood in combination with the other factors influencing this phenomenon."[44]

Employee Perception of Control

The researchers examined the perception—not necessarily the reality—of employees believing they would be caught if they committed theft. "We find that perceived certainty of detection is inversely related to employee theft for respondents in all three industry sectors—that is, the stronger the perception that theft would be detected, the less the likelihood that the employee would engage in deviant behavior."[45]

Social control in the workplace, according to Hollinger and Clark, consists of both formal and informal social controls. The former control can be described as the internalization by the employee of the group norms of the organization; the latter, external pressures through both positive and negative sanctions. These researchers, along with a host of others, have concluded that—as a general proposition—informal social controls provide the best deterrent. "These data clearly indicate that the loss of respect among one's acquaintances was the single most effective variable in predicting future deviant involvement." Furthermore, ". . . in general, the probability of suffering informal sanction is far more important than fear of formal sanctions in deterring deviant activity."[46]

Conclusion

Hollinger and Clark reached several other conclusions based on their work. First, they believe that ". . . substantially increasing the internal security presence does not seem to be appropriate, given the prevalence of the problem. In fact, doing so may make things worse."[47] Second, they conclude that the same kinds of employees who engage in other workplace deviance are also principally the ones who engage in employee theft. They found persuasive evidence that slow or sloppy workmanship, sick-leave abuses, long coffee breaks, alcohol and drug use at work, coming in late and/or leaving early were more likely to be present in the employee-thief.

Third, the researchers hypothesize that if efforts are made to reduce employee theft without reducing its underlying causes (e.g., employee dissatisfaction, lack of ethics), the result could create a "hydraulic effect." That is, tightening controls over property deviance may create more detrimental acts affecting the productivity of the organization—if we push down employee theft, that action may push up goldbricking. Fourth, they agreed that increased management sensitivity to its employees will reduce all forms of workplace deviance. Fifth, they believe special attention should be afforded young employees, as these are the ones statistically the most likely to steal. However, it must be pointed out that although the incidence of theft is higher among younger employees, the losses are typically lower than those of more senior employees with financial authority.

Hollinger and Clark believe management must pay attention to four aspects of policy development: (1) a clear understanding regarding theft behavior, (2) continuous dissemination of positive information reflective of the company's policies, (3) enforcement of sanctions, and (4) publicizing the sanctions.

The researchers sum up their observations by saying, ". . . perhaps the most important overall policy implication that can be drawn . . . is that theft and work place deviance are in large part a reflection of how management at all levels of the organization is perceived by the employee. Specifically, if the employee is permitted to conclude that his or her contribution to the workplace is not appreciated or that the organization does not seem to care about the theft of its property, we expect to find greater involvement. In conclusion, a lowered prevalence of employee theft may be one valuable consequence of a management team that is responsive to the current perceptions and attitudes of its workforce."[48]

THE REPORT TO THE NATION ON OCCUPATIONAL FRAUD AND ABUSE

Dr. Gilbert Geis, the Association's president and Professor Emeritus in Criminology at the University of California-Irvine, has done a lot of original research in white-collar crime. Since Geis and Cressey were contemporaries, I don't take it as an insult when Geis describes me as a "frustrated researcher." For as long as I can remember, I have had this unquenchable quantitative curiosity. As stated, I conceived this project with one major goal: To classify occupational fraud and abuses by the methods used to commit them. There were other objectives, too. One was to get an idea of how the professionals—the CFEs—see the fraud problems in their own companies. After all, they deal with fraud and abuse on a daily basis.

Another goal was to gather demographics on the perpetrators themselves: How old are they? How well educated? What percentage of offenders are men? Were there any correlations that we could identify with respect to the offenders? What about the victim companies: how large were they? What industries did they cover?

For good measure, I also decided to ask the CFEs to take an educated guess — based upon their experience—of (1) how much fraud and abuse occurs within their own organizations, and (2) how much other U.S. organizations are losing to all forms of occupational fraud and abuse. In 1992, several professional colleagues and I designed a questionnaire that could be mailed to Certified Fraud Examiners. Dr. Sandra Welch of The University of Texas at San Antonio and Dr. Sarah A. Reed of Texas A & M University were instrumental in developing the survey form and in analyzing the first layer of data.

The final questionnaire was four pages in length and contained 20 multi-part questions organized into four sections: the victim, perpetrator, scheme, and detection method. Beginning in 1993, the form was mailed to about 10,000 Certified Fraud Examiners. By early 1995, 2,608 usable surveys had been returned for analysis. Although the survey design was not perfect, the sheer number of responses made it — to our knowledge — the largest such study on this subject to date, loaded to the brim with useful data. Of the cases analyzed, the total pilfered was about $15 billion, ranging from a low of $22 to a high of $2.5 billion. Most of the cases occurred during the last ten years, and represent 12 different major industry groups, including government.

The 1996 *Report to the Nation on Occupational Fraud and Abuse* was drawn directly from the 2,608 responses. And this book is drawn from the Report, but with several major differences. First, the *Report to the Nation* was intended for a general audience; this book is aimed at antifraud practitioners. Second, much of the data contained in this book had not been analyzed for the Report. Third, the Report presented only summary information on schemes used to defraud organizations.

Association President Gil Geis decided that *Report to the Nation on Occupational Fraud and Abuse* was a bit long, so he also titled it the "Wells Report." Other than making me feel a little like Mr. Zac, it is certainly an honor. The Report was organized into the following major areas: the cost of fraud and abuse, the perpetrators, the victims, and the schemes.

Costs

The Report disclosed that Certified Fraud Examiners believe organizations lose about 6% of their revenues to all forms of fraud and abuse. If multiplied by the U.S. Gross Domestic Product — which exceeds $7 trillion annually for the latter 1990s — then the total cost to organizations in the U.S. exceeds $400 billion annually. It is a staggering sum, twice what we pay to defend our country. It is more than we spend on education and roads, not to mention six times what we pay for the criminal justice system.

But what does the figure really mean? It is simply the collective opinions of those who work in the antifraud field. Unfortunately, finding the actual cost may not be possible by any method. One obvious approach would be to take a scientific poll of the workforce and ask them the tough questions: Have you stolen or committed fraud against your organization? If so, how? And how much was the value of the fraud or abuse you committed? But the unlikelihood of people answering such questions candidly throws the reliability of this information into doubt.

Another approach to finding the cost of fraud is to do a scientific poll of a representative sample of organizations. Assuming the respondents answered the poll correctly, there is an obvious flaw in the data: Organizations typically don't know when they are being victimized. And of course, there is the definitional issue which plagues all the methods: Where do we draw the line on what constitutes occupational fraud and abuse? So asking the experts—the approach used here—may be as reliable as anything else. But the reader must be cautioned that, by any method of estimation, the numbers on fraud and abuse are soft and subject to various interpretations.

Whatever the actual costs, organizations are unwittingly paying them already as a part of their total operating expenses. Such is the insidious nature of fraud, and what to do? How can we possibly detect something we don't about in the first place? It's as if a secret "fraud tax" has been levied on organizations. And interestingly, many organizations may silently condone fraud and abuse, which is committed from the top down. Indeed, some sociologists see abuse as an informal employment benefit, and have even suggested that chronic pilferage and certain other abuses might actually have a positive effect on morale and therefore increase productivity.[49]

The Perpetrators of Fraud

In all instances, the perpetrators of fraud were employed by the organization they defrauded. The Report gathered data on the perpetrator's position, age, sex, marital status, education, and the amount of loss.

Position in the Organization

Personal data gathered about the perpetrators indicated that, with respect to numbers of offenders in this study, about 58% were employees, 30% managers, and about 12% owners or equity executives.

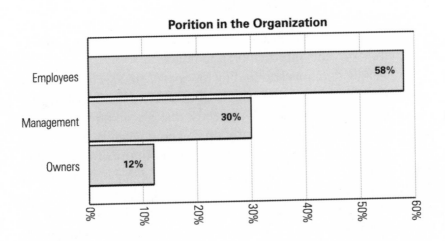

**Report to the Nation 1: Offenders' Position
Within the Victim Organization**

Although most perpetrators were employees, their median losses were the lowest at $60,000 per incident. Their managers' losses were about $250,000 per incident, and the owner/executives losses were about $1 million. In other words, the manager's losses were four times those of the employees, and the executive's losses were four times of those of their managers. We concluded the differences in the loss amounts were because of the degree of financial control exercised at each level; those with the highest positions also have the greatest access to company funds and assets.

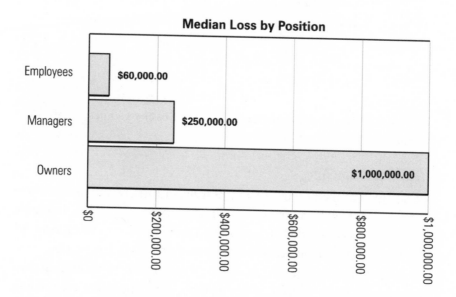

Report to the Nation 2: Median Loss by Position

Median Loss by Gender

The *Wells Report* concluded that male employees caused median losses four times those of female employees, with $185,000 representing the mean for men and $48,000 for women. The Report drew no official conclusions from this particular data, but one could easily speculate: Generally, in the U.S., men occupy higher paying positions than their female counterparts. And as we have seen, there is a direct correlation between median loss and position.

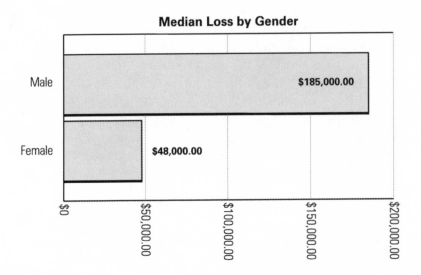

Report to the Nation 3: Median Loss by Gender

Median Loss by Age

One of the most meaningful trends of the survey is the direct and linear correlation between age and median loss. The reason for the trend, we concluded, was because those in an organization who are older generally tend to occupy higher-ranking positions with greater access to revenues, assets, and resources. It should also be noted that those in the oldest age group were responsible for median losses 28 times those of the youngest. The implications for auditors applying these data are obvious. If the auditor is able to capture data concerning the ages of the client's employees, it would be possible to design new and completely different audit tests to help assess risk on the basis of age and other personal demographic information. Perhaps this approach will be explored by auditors in the future, as it has a strong logical appeal: People commit fraud and abuse, not systems. But to some, keeping track of such personal data may smack of "Big Brother."

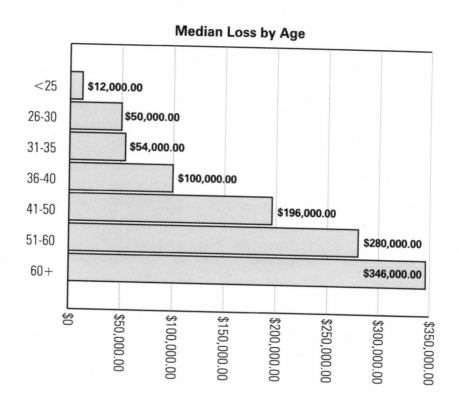

Report to the Nation 4: Median Loss by Age

Median Loss by Marital Status

Married employees commit frauds with a median of about $150,000—about three times those of single people at $54,000. The reasons for this are unclear from the data we analyzed. But as most of us who are already married know, it certainly seems to cast doubt on the saying, "two can live as cheaply as one."

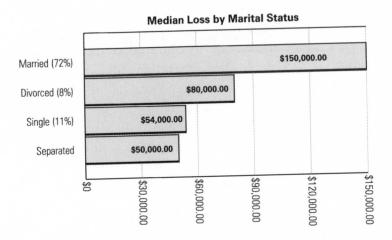

Report to the Nation 5: Median Loss by Marital Status

Median Loss by Education

Education was a consistent predictor of loss amounts. The fraudulent actions of employees with postgraduate degrees resulted in losses of over five times greater than the actions of those employees armed with a high school education. Again, the apparent reason is because employees with higher educations are more likely to occupy higher-ranking positions within the organization.

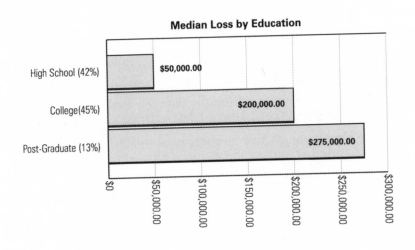

Report to the Nation 6: Median Loss by Education

The Victims

The organizational victims were divided into 12 different industry groups, classified by the median losses for each. The losses in the real estate financing industry are skewed because of the large savings and loan losses of the late 1980s. There was not enough information to determine exactly why some industries are more susceptible than others. For example, median losses in manufacturing were nearly nine times as high as those in education. But one can draw an inference, which will require further study to validate. It could well be that the median losses are in proportion to the profit margins of the respective industries—the higher the profit margin of the industry, the more employees feel entitled to "share" the margin. As an illustration, the median losses for education, utility, and government are quite low, as are the historic returns in these three industries; they operate primarily on a cost basis. At the other extreme, manufacturing has relatively large margins based on volume—the more there is available, the more employees can use these profits for their own personal benefit.

Median Loss per Number of Employees

The data for median loss per number of employees confirms what we always suspected, but did not know quantitatively. Accountants would logically conclude that small organizations, those with 100 employees or less, are particularly vulnerable to occupational fraud and abuse. What we didn't know was the depth of that vulnerability — about 100 times more than the largest organizations. We theorize that this phenomenon exists for two reasons. First, smaller businesses have fewer divisions of responsibility, meaning that fewer people must perform more functions. One of the most common frauds encountered in this study resulted from small business operations that have a one-person accounting department—that employee writes checks, reconciles the accounts, and posts the books. An entry level accounting student could spot the internal control deficiencies in that scenario, but apparently many small business owners cannot or do not.

Which brings up the second reason losses are so high in small organizations: There is a greater degree of trust inherent in a situation where everyone knows each other by name and face. Who of us would like to think our coworkers would or do commit these offenses? As a result, our defenses are naturally relaxed. There again is the dichotomy of fraud: It cannot occur without trust, but neither can commerce. Trust is an essential ingredient at all levels of business—we can and do make handshake deals every day. Transactions in capitalism simply cannot occur without trust. The key is seeking the right balance between too much and too little.

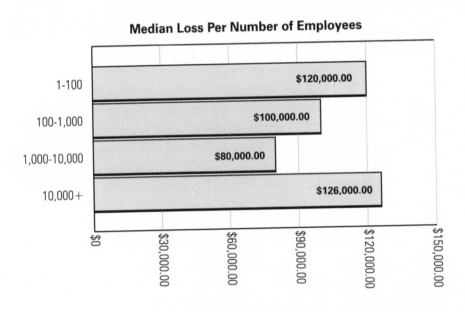

Report to the Nation 7: Median Loss per Number of Employees

The Methods

The Report classified occupational fraud and abuse schemes into three types: asset misappropriations, corruption, and fraudulent statements. In terms of volume of cases, asset misappropriations accounted for about 80%; corruption, 15%; fraudulent statements, 4%; and "other," 1%. Once we established the three broad categories, we then examined and classified separate schemes within the categories. For purposes of this book, the schemes were re-examined and further refinements were made to the classification method. This latter classification system is used herein, and much of this book reviews the details of those classifications.

Total Losses by Type

As chart 1-1 illustrates, the majority of "losses" resulting from occupational fraud resulted from fraudulent statements. This data may be somewhat misleading, however, since the data from fraudulent statements often represents the size of a *misstatement* rather than the size of actual cash losses. For instance, to defraud investors, an employee might overstate his company's net worth by $5,000,000. This does not mean the employee has stolen $5,000,000 from his employer. He has simply misstated his company's financial standing to the tune of $5,000,000.

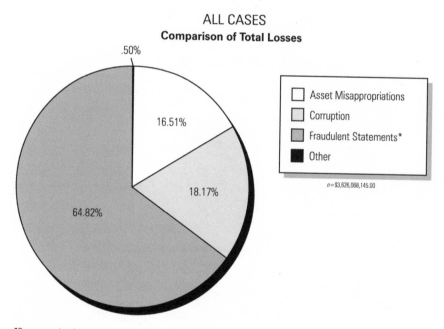

ALL CASES
Comparison of Total Losses

.50%

16.51%

18.17%

64.82%

Asset Misappropriations
Corruption
Fraudulent Statements*
Other

n = $3,626,068,145.00

*Represents size of misstatement rather than actual cash loss.

Chart 1-1: All Cases - Comparison of total Losses

Median Loss by Type

Chart 1-2 also shows a vast disparity between the losses associated with fraudulent statements and other types of fraud. Again, the data reflected in this chart actually refers to the median size of misstatements associated with fraudulent statement schemes. Disregarding these, we see that corruption schemes, on average, cause the greatest loss to a victim company: over $400,000.

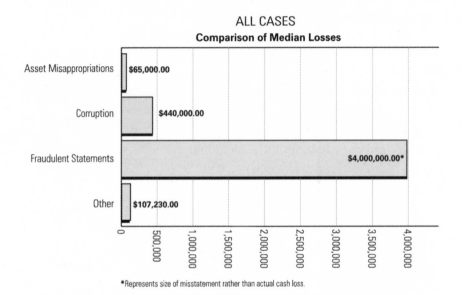

*Represents size of misstatement rather than actual cash loss.

Chart 1-2: All Cases - Comparison of Median Losses

Number of Cases per Type

    Asset misappropriations were the least harmful of the three fraud types in terms of median loss, but they were by far the most prevalent. Asset misappropriations accounted for over 80% of the cases in our study (see chart 1-3). This may make asset misappropriations the most dangerous of the three fraud types. While the median loss associated with these schemes is much less than that of the other two types, your company is much more likely to be victimized by an asset misappropriation scheme.

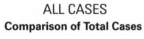

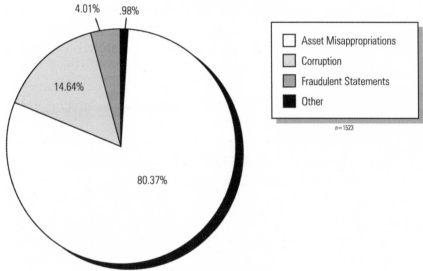

Chart 1-3: All Cases - Comparison of Total Cases

Scheme Statistics

After establishing the three broad categories for occupational fraud, we broke down each category into several distinct scheme types. They are listed below:

Asset Misappropriations
>   Skimming Schemes
>   Cash Larceny Schemes
>   Check Tampering Schemes
>   Register Disbursement Schemes
>   Billing Schemes
>   Expense Schemes
>   Payroll Schemes
>   Other Fraudulent Disbursements
>   Inventory and Other Assets Schemes

Corruption
>   Bribery Schemes
>   Conflict of Interest Schemes

Economic Extortion Schemes
Illegal Gratuities Schemes
Fraudulent Statements
Financial Statements Schemes
Non-Financial Statements Schemes

Loss and Case Statistics

ALL CASES
Comparison of Total Losses

Schemes	Total Losses
*Financial Statements	$2,112,756,500.00
Bribery	$587,834,495.00
*Non-Financial Statements	$237,764,400.00
Billing	$191,436,030.00
Skimming	$142,904,482.00
Inventory & Assets	$79,190,221.00
Other Fraudulent Disbursement	$75,566,120.00
Conflict of Interest	$59,375,000.00
Check Tampering	$48,908,776.00
Payroll	$39,650,462.00
Other	$17,801,730.00
Expense	$14,957,672.00
Economic Extortion	$10,532,000.00
Cash Larceny	$5,493,842.00
Illegal Gratuities	$1,272,215.00
Register	$624,200.00

*Represents size of misstatement rather than actual cash loss.

Chart 1-4: All Cases - Comparison of Total Losses (all schemes)

Charts 1-4, 1-5, and 1-6 provide comparative information for the various scheme types. For instance, we see that of all schemes, skimming was the most common, with 20.75% of the total cases in our study. Meanwhile, economic extortion and illegal gratuities schemes, two forms of corruption, were the least commonly encountered schemes. On the other hand, bribery (another form of corruption) generated the largest total and median cash losses of any scheme type. (Remember that the figures for financial statements and non-financial statements represent the size of the misstatement, not the size of the cash loss).

As our discussion of each scheme type broadens throughout this book, the data in these graphs will take on a more substantive meaning. Occasional reference back to these pages may help put our discussions of individual schemes into the context of occupational fraud as a whole.

ALL CASES
Comparison of Median Losses

Schemes	Total Losses
*Financial Statements	$5,000,000.00
*Non-Financial Statements	$3,050,000.00
Bribery	$500,000.00
Conflict of Interest	$500,000.00
Billing	$250,000.00
Economic Extortion	$167,000.00
Other Fraudulent Disbursement	$140,000.00
Other	$107,230.00
Inventory & Assets	$100,000.00
Check Tampering	$96,432.00
Skimming	$50,000.00
Payroll	$50,000.00
Register	$22,500.00
Cash Larceny	$22,000.00
Expense	$20,000.00
Illegal Gratuities	$8,107.00

*Represents size of misstatement rather than actual cash loss.

Chart 1-5: All Cases - Comparison of Median Losses (all schemes)

ALL CASES
Comparison of Total Cases

Schemes	% of Cases
Skimming	20.75%
Billing	16.02%
Bribery	11.82%
Check Tampering	11.75%
Inventory & Assets	8.60%
Payroll	7.94%
Expense	7.16%
Other Fraudulent Disbursement	3.87%
Financial Statements	3.09%
Cash Larceny	2.95%
Conflict of Interest	1.71%
Register	1.32%
Other	.98%
Non-Financial Statements	.92%
Economic Extortion	.66%
Illegal Gratuities	.46%

Chart 1-6: All Cases - Comparison of Total Cases (all schemes)

Time to Detection

Chart 1-7 measures the median duration of the various scheme types. This data provides a good measure of the relative sophistication of the schemes we have identified. For example, financial statements schemes went on for an average of 36 months before they were detected and false billings lasted an average of 24 months before they were detected. In general, these tend to be fairly sophisticated schemes. Register disbursements and thefts of inventory and other assets, on the other hand, are generally less sophisticated and are therefore easier to detect. This is reflected by the fact that these schemes had the shortest lifespans of any in our study.

ALL CASES
Median Lengths of Schemes

Schemes	Median*
Financial Statements	36.00
Billing	24.00
Bribery	24.00
Other Fraudulent Disbursement	24.00
Expense	18.00
Non-Financial Statements	18.00
Skimming	18.00
Payroll	16.00
Check Tampering	14.50
Cash Larceny	12.00
Conflicts of Interest	12.00
Illegal Gratuities	12.00
Extortion	11.00
Other	11.00
Inventory & Other Assets	10.00
Register Disbursements	6.50

*Median # of months to detection

Chart 1-7: All Cases - Median Lengths of Schemes

Commonness of Schemes

Each Certified Fraud Examiner who participated in our study was asked to rank the relative commonness of the scheme he or she had described. Based on their experience in dealing with occupational fraud, the CFEs ranked their schemes on a scale of one to seven (one being a rare scheme, seven being a common scheme). Chart 1-8 lists the average rating for each of the scheme types we have identified. From the data gathered we see that fraud prevention professionals rated conflicts of interest and illegal gratuities schemes as very uncommon, while skimming, expense reimbursement schemes and register disbursement schemes were rated as fairly common.

ALL CASES
**Fraud Examiners' Rating of the Level of
Commonness of Schemes**

Schemes	Common
Conflicts of Interest	3.35
Illegal Gratuities	3.43
OTHER	3.67
Payroll	3.87
Other Fraudulent Disbursement	3.95
Check Tampering	4.00
Financial Statements	4.06
Billing	4.10
Non-Financial Statements	4.11
Inventory & Other Assets	4.23
Cash Larceny	4.41
Bribery	4.42
Skimming	4.50
Expense	4.55
Register Disbursements	5.00
Economic Extortion	5.00

1 = Rare
7 = Common

**Chart 1-8: All Cases - Fraud Examiners' Rating
of the Level of Commonness of Schemes**

Difficulty to Detect

The CFEs who participated in our study were also asked to rank the difficulty they had in detecting the schemes they described. Chart 1-9 summarizes the results of this inquiry. We see that the top half of the chart (the schemes which are the most difficult to detect) is dominated by fraudulent statements schemes and corruption schemes, while the bottom half is mostly populated by asset misappropriation schemes.

ALL CASES
Fraud Examiners' Rating of the Difficulty in Detecting Schemes

Schemes	Difficult
Extortion	2.50
Illegal Gratuities	2.86
Non-Financial Statements	3.22
OTHER	3.53
Conflicts of Interest	3.54
Bribery	3.65
Inventory & Other Assets	3.73
Other Fraudulent Disbursement	3.95
Billing	4.01
Payroll	4.20
Skimming	4.24
Financial Statements	4.28
Expense	4.34
Register Disbursements	4.35
Check Tampering	4.40
Cash Larceny	5.04

1 = Difficult to Detect
7 = Easy to Detect

Chart 1-9: All Cases - Fraud Examiners' Rating of the Difficulty in Detecting Schemes

[1] The Association of Certified Fraud Examiners, *The Report to the Nation on Occupational Fraud and Abuse* (Austin: ACFE, 1996), p 4.

[2] ACFE, p. 9.

[3] Black, p. 468.

[4] Black, p. 300.

[5] Black, p. 792.

[6] Black, p. 793.

[7] Black, p. 225.

[8] *Webster's Dictionary* (Boston: Houghton Mifflin Company, 1996), p. 47.

[9] Gilbert Geis, *On White Collar Crime* (Lexington: Lexington Books, 1982).

[10] Larry J. Siegel, *Criminology, 3rd Edition* (New York: West Publishing Company, 1989) p. 193.

[11] Donald R. Cressey, *Other People's Money* (Montclair: Patterson Smith, 1973) p. 30.

[12] Cressey, p. 33.

[11] Cressey, p. 34.

[12] Cressey, p. 35.

[13] Cressey, p. 36.

[14] Cressey, p. 38.

[15] Cressey, p. 42.

[16] Cressey, p. 47.

[17] Cressey, p. 54.

[18] Cressey, p. 66-67.

[19] Cressey, p. 86.

[20] Cressey, p. 94.

[21] Cressey, p. 121.

[22] Cressey, p. 122.

[23] Cressey, p. 128.

[24] Cressey, p. 133.

[25] Cressey, p. 139.

[26] W. Steve Albrecht, Keith R. Howe, and Marshall B. Romney, Deterring Fraud: The Internal Auditor's Perspective (Altamonte Springs: The Institute of Internal Auditor's Research Foundation, 1984), p.xiv.

[27] Albrecht, et.al., p.xv.

[28] Albrecht, et.al., p. 5.

[29] Albrecht, et.al., p. 6.

[30] Albrecht, et.al., p. 5.

[31] Albrecht, et.al., p. 6.

[32] Albrecht, et.al., p. 12-13.

[33] Richard C. Hollinger and John P. Clark, *Theft by Employees* (Lexington: Lexington Books, 1983), p. 6.

[34] Hollinger and Clark, p. 42.

[35] Hollinger and Clark, p. 57.

[36] Hollinger and Clark, p. 57.

[36] Hollinger and Clark, p. 57.

[37] Hollinger and Clark, p. 63.

[38] Hollinger and Clark, p. 67.

[39] Hollinger and Clark, p. 68.

[40] Hollinger and Clark, p. 77.

[41] Hollinger and Clark, p. 86.

[42] Hollinger and Clark, p. 86.

[43] Hollinger and Clark, p. 86.

[44] Hollinger and Clark, p. 106.

[45] Hollinger and Clark, p. 117.

[46] Hollinger and Clark, p. 120.

[47] Hollinger and Clark, p. 121.

[48] Hollinger and Clark, p. 144.

[49] Hollinger and Clark, p. 146.

[50] Norman Jaspan, *Mind Your Own Business* (Englewood: Prentice-Hall, Inc., 1974).

PART II - ASSET MISAPPROPRIATIONS

Asset Misappropriation

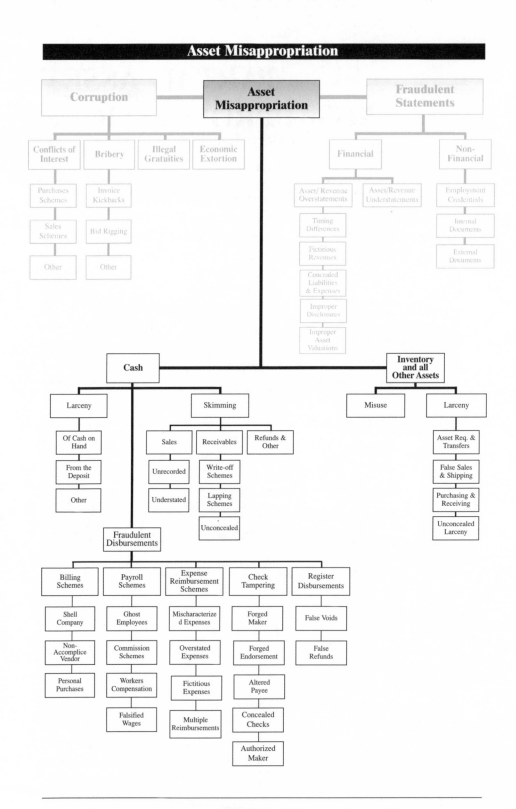

2. INTRODUCTION TO ASSET MISAPPROPRIATIONS

History of Asset Misappropriations

Employee theft by means of embezzlement has been entrenched in the workplace seemingly since the first business system was introduced. Many sociologists, such as Jerald Greenberg and Kimberly S. Scott, hypothesize that employee theft is more permissible in the capitalist society precisely because it is a "capitalistic" venture—the taking of goods for potential gain.

In fact, the taking of "company assets" was once a commonly accepted practice, openly conducted by workers throughout sixteenth and seventeenth century Europe. Until England passed the Acts of Enclosure, workers at the lord's manor were permitted to take, within reason, raw supplies such as wood, hay, or food from the manor for personal use. The Acts of Enclosure prohibited such pilfering, instigating a small rebellion of peasants against the English nobility and causing a mass exodus of rural laborers to the English cities for better-paying work.[1]

The first known case of embezzlement to be tried in a court of law is known as the Carrier's Case. The facts surrounding the case are quite simple: the defendant in that trial was hired to carry bales to Southampton, but the defendant was accused of instead taking the bales to another location, breaking them open, and taking the bales' contents. The defendant had been given the bales by the bales' owner, so the Court of the Star Chamber had a difficult time deciphering exactly how to rule on the case.

The Carrier's Case is notable for several reasons. Up to this point in English history, around 1473, thefts tried in the English court systems had all involved cattle and the law covered only direct acts of this type of theft. The bales at the center of the Carrier's Case, however, contained wool and textile products, goods which had recently become England's primary exports.[2]

The case presented entirely new questions to the Star Chamber. When the bales were given to the defendant, did he legally obtain possession of the bales to do as he pleased? Or was the defendant merely given possession of the bales to deliver, but never given possession of the bales' contents? England's Chief Justice Brian, as well as high court Judges Choke and Nedham, argued endlessly as to how to rule on the matter. They decided after much deliberation that the defendant was entrusted with the bales, but was never given direct possession of the wool and textile products contained in the bales. Therefore, the defendant was ruled guilty by a majority of the court and a precedent was set concerning what has come to be known as embezzlement.

Another infamous embezzlement case from England took place in the late 1970s. The Norton Warburg Group Ltd. was a reputable and firmly established investment management firm in London, servicing the financial investments of wealthy clients since the corporation had been established in 1973. The firm managed pensioners and employee accounts of prestigious companies such as British Airways, Unilever, the British Broadcasting Company, and even the Bank of England. But the company's most famous client and business partner was the musical group Pink Floyd; the group also happened to be Norton Warburg's largest client. The band's financial resources were intricately tied to Norton Warburg's various company arms, such as the venture capital arm, Norton Warburg Investments Ltd. The investment company could not have been more financially sound in 1978.

That year, however, Pink Floyd abruptly pulled its approximately £860,000 out of the firm, which would be expected to put a dent in the company's finances. But when Norton Warburg's financial report was released the next year, the company looked as financially sound as it had ever been.

The truth of the matter did not come to light until early 1981, when the company quickly unraveled and voluntarily liquidated its assets. Andrew Warburg, cofounder and managing partner, admitted that upon the withdrawal of the company's "Pink Floyd funds," a gaping hole appeared in the venture capital arm of Norton Warburg Investment Ltd. As well, the company deceived several of its clients about the returns on one investment opportunity, the company's subsidiary, TFA Electrasound. To cover the company's wounded financial tracks, Norton Warburg embezzled investor funds to plug the monetary gaps. The company admitted to snatching more than 4.5 million pounds and Andrew Warburg was sent to prison.

Few crimes can match the devious nature of the embezzlement scheme that former United Way of American president William Aramony undertook in the early 1990s. Aramony stooped so low as to snatch more than $1.2 million from the charity organization, a move which not only cost the organization the embezzled funds but millions more in contributions which were withheld after the public debacle.

Aramony, a 67-year-old man who had headed United Way for more than 22 years before stepping down in 1992, was an extravagant leader even before he was under any legal suspicions. Earning more than $463,000 a year in salary and benefits, Aramony had a reputation for enjoying a lavish lifestyle and was also known to be quite a womanizer.[3] However, the United Way organization knew that Aramony was an outstanding field general, and Aramony's attorney, William Moffitt, argued at trial that Aromony had to keep a high standard of living in order to convince other high-powered executives from large corporations to do business with United Way.

Aramony's bloated salary was apparently not enough to appease his luxurious appetite. The president used $1.2 million in United Way funds to maintain apartments in Coral Gables, Florida, and East Manhattan, New York, for himself and his 17-year-old girlfriend, Lori Villasor, a United Way employee. Company records also proved that the former executive used company funds to pay for extended vacations with Villasor to London, Paris, Egypt, and Las Vegas. When these indiscretions came to light, many company volunteers and employees became extremely irritated and United Way donations dropped precipitously. Aramony claims that other United Way executives knew very well of his actions, but did not disapprove of the lavish lifestyle until the details hit the morning papers.[4]

Aramony didn't conceal his embezzlements and was found guilty of 25 counts of mail and wire fraud, filing false income tax reports, and conspiracy. The United Way has to an extent recovered from the fraudulent episode, but the public relations disaster the organization faced is not something the nonprofit organization would like to face again.

One of the more flamboyant embezzlers in recent times is relatively famous not for his illicit escapades, but instead for his ability to toss a pizza pie. Andrew Bellucci gained prominence in the New

York area by promoting a local pizzeria, proclaiming himself a pizza historian to anyone who would listen. Bellucci was loud and jovial, recounting the evolution of the New York pizza to countless television and newspaper reporters. Various food critics acclaimed Bellucci's enthusiasm, but more importantly for the supposed owner of Lombardi's Pizzeria, they loved his pies. The large entrepreneur who claimed roots in Brooklyn seemed omnipresent, on television and radio interviews and advertisements, a virtual budding superstar of the pizzerias.[5]

There was only one hitch: Bellucci was not the true owner of Lombardi's; he was not, as he had claimed, from Brooklyn; but he was a tried and true embezzler. Bellucci had previously been employed as an administrator at the law firm of Newman Schlau Fitch & Lane, and the FBI had issued a warrant for his arrest. The feds had been searching for Bellucci for over five years, attempting to apprehend him for 54 counts of fraud. Bellucci had stolen hundreds of thousands from the law firm.

So the question begs to be answered: Why would a known embezzler turn to touting pizzas on television? After all, the FBI, whose notes on the case indicated that their suspect had fled to France, was tipped off to his whereabouts by one of the television commercials Bellucci was featured in. The fraudster's answer is naive and yet understandable: He didn't realize that anyone had discovered his thefts. In an interview with the *New York Times*, Bellucci discussed why he hopped on television after swindling his former employers and was quoted as saying, "To be honest, I didn't give the matter too much thought."[6] The former pizza king of New York was sentenced to 13 months in prison to reflect on the matter.

An embezzlement scandal reared its head within the Bank of Tokyo at the worst possible time: as the bank was in the process of merging with Mitsubishi Bank in April 1996, resulting in the world's largest bank. Company executives discovered that over 1.02 billion yen (approximately $9 million) had been pilfered from the bank's coffers. When the investigation led back to Hideki Nishiyama, an assistant manager at one Bank of Tokyo branch, he quickly admitted his wrongdoings.

Nishiyama attempted to cover his embezzlements by forging loan applications, making it appear that the funds were to be directed to a fictitious bank customer. The fraudster explained to authorities that he had a gambling addiction and had "borrowed" the ill-gotten moneys to bet at a local race track. Because he was so forthright in admitting his crime, Nishiyama was sentenced to only five years in prison, instead of the ten he would have normally faced.

In a recent court battle that can only be described as bizarre, a founder of a controversial revisionist group was accused of embezzling $6.4 million. Willis A. Carto was instrumental in the founding of the Institute for Historical Review, a powerful group whose main goal is to refute all accounts of the Holocaust.   The group forced Carto out in 1994, accusing him of embezzling over $7.5 million. To make matters just a touch more surreal, the money in question was a bequest from Jean Edison Farrel, the granddaughter of inventor Thomas Alva Edison. Apparently, Carto and cofounder Henry Fischer traveled to Switzerland to meet with Farrel and receive the bequest. However, the organization never saw any of the money.[7]

When the organization brought a civil suit against Carto (authorities declined to press criminal charges), the court ruled that Carto owed $6.4 million back to the organization and its parent company, the Legion for the Survival of Freedom. Carto countered by suing the organization for court costs, but when the court hearing came around, Carto did not appear and has not been heard from since. At that point, a warrant was issued for his arrest, but the controversial group has not received a cent of the money owed to them by Carto.

Overview

The purpose of this chapter is to provide you an overview of the favorite target of occupational fraud offenders: the organization's assets. Before detailing a definition of assets, let us first learn what constitutes *misappropriation*. According to *Black's Law Dictionary*, it is "the act of misappropriating or turning to a wrong purpose; wrong appropriation, a term that does not necessarily mean peculation, although it may mean that. The term may also embrace the taking and using of another's property for sole purpose of capitalizing unfairly on good will and reputation of property owner."[8] The definition in *Webster's* is a little more pointed: "to appropriate wrongly (as by theft or embezzlement)."[9] For our purposes, misappropriation includes more than theft or embezzlement. It involves the misuse of any company asset for personal gain. Therefore, an employee using a company computer after hours for his own side business has not stolen an asset. But he has misappropriated it for his own benefit.

DEFINITION OF ASSETS

In commerce, the purpose of assets is to produce income. If a business produces oil, the rigs, trucks, and even the land are all assets. Should the business sell clothing, their merchandise and display cases are assets. According to Marshall and McManus, "Assets are probable future economic benefits obtained or controlled by a particular entity as a result of past transactions or events. In brief, assets represent the amount of resources owned by the entity."[10]

Because of the breadth of this accounting definition, exactly what constitutes an asset can become very esoteric to the nonaccountant. For example, the logo of the Coca Cola Company is recognized worldwide. For many people, all they need to know about a soft drink is its logo before they buy. As a result, the trademarked logo of Coke is worth millions, perhaps billions. Just exactly how much it is worth can't be determined accurately unless Coke decides to sell the logo itself—an unlikely event. The logo alone is called an intangible asset, one of the two types of assets in commerce.

Intangible Assets

According to Marshall and McManus, *intangible assets* are ". . . long-lived assets that differ from property, plant, and equipment that has been purchased outright or acquired under a capital lease — either because the asset is represented by a contractual right, or because the asset results from a purchase transaction but is not physically identifiable. Examples of the first type of intangible assets are leaseholds, patents, and trademarks; the second type of asset is known as goodwill."[11]

You can readily see that intangible assets are difficult to misappropriate because they are not "physically identifiable." Anything that cannot be physically identified cannot be stolen. Therefore, for all practical purposes, asset misappropriations are restricted to *tangible assets*.

Tangible Assets

Webster's defines tangible as ". . . (1a) capable of being perceived, especially by the sense of touch: palatable; (b) substantially real: material; (2) capable of being precisely identified or realized by the mind; (3) capable of being appraised at an actual or approximate value, e.g assets . . . ."[12] If we can't see it, feel it, or smell it, chances are the asset isn't tangible. Tangible assets of a business or organization, for accounting purposes, are classified on the entity's books as one of five principal types: cash, accounts receivable, inventory, plant and equipment, or investments. And of course, it is invariably one or more of these types of assets that are misappropriated by employees.

But some of the assets subject to misappropriation within an organization are not necessarily classified as such in the books. For example, we have included in our particular definition of assets the two categories of supplies and information. Supplies are normally carried on an organization's books as expenses. This is because they tend to be consumed by the organization within a year of purchase. And information does not find its way directly to the entity's books. Instead, it is recognized when the information is sold at a later time. But any organization would tell you that information is one of its most valuable resources—employees who engage in industrial spying and sabotage for a competing organization are becoming increasingly common and expensive.

How Asset Misappropriations Affect Books of Account

You don't need to know much accounting at all to understand how asset misappropriations affect the organization's books. And this book assumes that you don't know anything about accounting. For the reader with an accounting background, you will find the following material elementary. You may even be amused at my efforts to explain basic accounting. But even if you are experienced in this area, the review of the following concepts in light of possible fraud will be a good refresher.

Let's assume you own a small business of restoring and selling rock 'n' roll guitars. And let's say your assets are $225,000, but you owe $75,000 on the business. Your equity in the business is then $150,000, the difference. One of your employees steals a rare 1954 Fender Telecaster, for which you paid $3,000, excluding $500 in parts, labor, and other costs to restore it. You were going to sell the restored guitar for $6,000.

So to the question: How does this theft affect your books? Did you lose $3,000; $3,500; or $6,000? Under what are called "generally accepted accounting principles" your loss is $3,500—what you paid for the guitar plus the repairs. But why isn't the loss what you would have gotten when you sold the guitar? Because the generally accepted accounting principle of conservatism requires us to keep our books to reflect the cost of the product, not the amount for which it sells. A more complete discussion of accounting concepts can be found in the Fraudulent Financial Statements chapter.

The accounting profession prefers companies to keep their books so that the value of all the assets is at least what is reflected on the financial statements. If the value is more, then so be it. We will recognize the value of that rare guitar when it is finally sold. In that particular transaction, we will effectively trade one asset (the restored Fender Telecaster) for another asset: $6,000 in cash. The difference is called our "gross profit."

So when the guitar is stolen by an employee, how do we record that loss on our books, and what effect does it have on you, the owner of the guitar shop? That accounting transaction is quite simple: the stolen asset comes directly out of your equity in the business. You had a beginning equity of $150,000. Now you must bear the entire $3,500 loss yourself. So your total assets are now $221,500, and your total equity is $146,500.

The fact that you might owe money on the guitar is irrelevant to the amount you lost — you still must pay your bills. There is, then, a dollar-for-dollar set-off to your equity when someone steals an asset. You can't claim the $6,000 for which the guitar would have sold; this $2,500 you would have made is called a "lost profit." The reason you cannot claim it is because you did not have the guitar to sell—it has been stolen; your potential profit is moot, even though it is a real loss to you.

The Accounting Equation

The above example is actually an illustration of the accounting equation, which is:

$$Assets = Liabilities + Owner's\ Equity$$

This equation is self-balancing. That is, increases or decreases on one side of the equation will always be reflected on the other side as increases or decreases. Liabilities are ". . . probable future sacrifices of economic benefits arising from present obligations of a particular entity to transfer assets or provide services to other entities in the future as a result of past transactions of events. In brief, liabilities are amounts owed to other entities."[13]

As stated, asset misappropriations have no effect whatsoever on the liabilities of the organization. And of course, no one misappropriates liabilities. But if you would like to steal some of my bills and pay them, help yourself. Although asset misappropriations have no effect on the liabilities, they do have the direct effect we described on the equity account. You can consider the equity account for what it is: simply the difference between the assets and liabilities. But how does that difference arise? In one of two basic ways. First, if you put your own money into the guitar shop, it goes directly to the equity account. So do the profits and losses your guitar shop makes. The profits will increase your equity, and the losses will decrease it.

In the guitar shop illustration, our equity before the misappropriation was $150,000. Suppose that you put $10,000 in the business when it was started. Then the remaining $140,000 consists of profits you have not taken out of the business. If for example, you had—over a period of several years—accumulated $200,000 in profits, but you had taken out $60,000 for yourself, your earned equity portion of the $150,000 is $140,000. The remainder is called "contributed capital."

The Balance Sheet and Income Statement

Financial records of commercial enterprises are kept in order to produce two key statements: the balance sheet and the income statement. The balance sheet uses the exact formula of the accounting equation, Assets = Liabilities + Owner's Equity. The purpose of the balance sheet is to allow the owner, investors, creditors, and others with an interest to know the approximate book worth of the business at a particular date in time. The book worth of the business and its actual value are not the same. The net worth for purposes of the books should always be lower. Its actual value can't be precisely determined until the business is sold. If the business has been historically profitable, a potential purchaser will determine the value of the business primarily by what it earns. But whatever the real value of the business, asset misappropriations affect the balance sheet dollar for dollar. They are difficult to detect at the balance sheet level itself, however, unless the misappropriation is quite large. The way asset misappropriations affect the balance sheet through the equity account is via the income statement, sometimes called the statement of profit and loss.

Where the formula for the balance sheet is Assets = Liabilities + Owner's Equity, the formula for the income statement is *Revenue - Expenses = Profit or (Loss)*. Revenue results from selling a product or service; expenses result from those costs incurred—both direct and indirect—to sell the product or service. And while the balance sheet takes a "picture" of the business at a particular date, the income statement is historical, covering a specified period of time, most commonly a year. The two statements tie together through the equity account. Remember, profits increase the equity account while losses decrease it.

In the guitar example, we said that the theft of the $3,500 guitar is a dollar-for-dollar set-off to the equity account. That set-off is accomplished by recognizing the theft of the $3,500 guitar as an expense called Cost of Goods Sold, listed on the income statement. The income statement is closed to profit and loss, which is then transferred to the equity account. So as we said much earlier, occupational fraud and abuse is an expense of doing business, in much the same way that we pay expenses for electricity, taxes, and wages.

The big difference, though, is that we always know what we are paying for electricity. We only know what we pay for fraud when it is discovered, like in the example of the stolen guitar. If the theft of the guitar went undetected because you failed to inventory your merchandise one year, you may never recognize that theft. But it still cost $3,500—you just don't know it yet. And you may never know it.

There are several concepts used in accounting for income and expense that have application in asset misappropriations; however, keep your eye on the ball—people steal assets, not income or expense.

Cash versus Accrual Accounting

Businesses have an option to keep their books on the cash basis or the accrual basis, whichever provides the more accurate and conservative picture of the business. On the cash basis, income is recognized when it is collected, and expenses are incurred when they are paid. But if you stop and think, that method usually doesn't properly reflect what you've made in a year—only what you've collected and paid out. When we try to match those income and expenses year by year, this is called the accrual basis. Most businesses keep their books on an accrual basis, even though their tax returns may be filed on a cash basis.

Accountants use the matching concept to tie the balance sheet and the income statement together in accrual basis accounting. The logical idea is that the expenses used to produce income—all of them—should be matched in a consistent manner against that income. Since, for example, you are in the guitar business and want to match all expenses in the years they produced income, then what do you do about having to purchase brand new woodworking equipment every three years? Since your statement of profit and loss is kept by the year, the matching concept would require you to write off one-third of the value of that equipment each year as an expense.

This write-off is called *depreciation*, and it has no application to asset misappropriations, except to help determine the amount of book value write-off to be taken if that equipment is misappropriated. And often, what the equipment is valued at on the books and what it will actually bring if sold are two different numbers. The third number is replacement cost. Let's take again the example of the woodworking equipment.

If you paid $9,000 for it and the equipment was stolen at the end of the first year, the amount valued on your books would be $6,000. But perhaps the equipment would have only brought $2,000 if sold in an emergency. And perhaps the $9,000 equipment would cost $11,000 to replace. Still, generally accepted accounting principles would necessitate the loss to be written off against profit, and equity would be $6,000.

Depreciation is especially applicable when companies try to overvalue their assets and net worth; the lower their depreciation expense, the higher the company's profits. That—and many other accounting concepts used to do the same thing—will be discussed in the False Statement section of this book.

Another accounting term that has no bearing on asset misappropriations is called *accruals*. Under the matching concept, we need to make sure that any expenses incurred but not paid by the end of the year are counted in our records of profit and loss. For example, if our guitar shop paid its insurance premiums every September but kept its books on a calendar year basis, then one-fourth of the premium should be shown as an expense for this year, and three-fourths for next year, no matter when it is actually paid. These are called accrued expenses, and accountants figure out how much this totals, so they can be included in the correct year. After making all the necessary adjustments to a company's books to match the income with the expenses, a final profit is determined for the company. Remember, the profit figure the company shows and the amount of cash it collected will not be the same under accrual basis accounting.

Organization of Financial Records

The way financial records are organized varies somewhat by entity. For example, some companies computerize their entire record-keeping process, while others use the pen-and-ink system that has been around for centuries. Regardless, the applications are largely the same. Books are organized by "accounts" which are individual captions in the financial statements. For each item of income, expense, asset, liability, and equity, a separate account is created to keep track of their changes.

The heart of the bookkeeping system is the checkbook. All enterprises—no matter what they do—collect revenue and pay out expenses. But the checkbook is inadequate for bookkeeping purposes. Again, the amount of profit a company makes and its receipts over disbursements (the balance in the checkbook at a particular date) will be different. To help keep track of the differences, companies keep journals.

Books of Account

There are two types of books of account: journals and ledgers. A *journal* "(derived from the French word jour, meaning day) is a day-by-day, or chronological, record of transactions."[14] Financial information is taken from source documents and recorded in the journals. Most businesses will typically have at least four journals: a cash receipts and disbursements journal; a sales or accounts receivable journal, in which all sales made on credit or cash are listed; a purchases (or accounts payable) journal, which records all acquisitions of merchandise or services purchased on credit; and a general journal, which reflects transactions not covered by other journals. It is also the journal used to adjust the books.

The journals are kept and summarized, usually monthly, in a ledger. This process is called *posting*. In a manual bookkeeping system, a ledger is usually a loose-leaf notebook, with entries made only once per month. At the end of the year, the net of these ledger accounts is carried directly to the financial statements. In other words, the financial statements are a summary of the account balances carried in the ledger.

For example, in order to prepare financial statements, the bookkeeper for your guitar shop would go through your checkbook regularly. For each item of deposit, he would record its source in a journal; in this case, the cash receipts and disbursements journal.

And for every check, he would also record what that disbursement paid. In a simple illustration, presume the bookkeeper noticed one deposit in the checkbook contained two items: sales of merchandise amounting to $500, and a bank loan of $7,500, for a total deposit of $8,000.

In order to accurately keep your books, he must separate the item of income, which determines your profit or loss, from the item of the loan, which is not income; it must be repaid. In the cash receipts and disbursements journal, your bookkeeper would "spread" or code these two transactions, recording one in the journal's income column and one in the liability column. And the checks you wrote during the month for labor, parts, electricity, repayment of bank loans, and other expenses would be recorded by the bookkeeper in the expense portion of the journal, with an account for each item of expense. In order for the bookkeeper to make sure he has accounts for all your transactions, he will prepare a chart of accounts. Most of the time, this is simply a piece of paper with numbers on it for each account. The bookkeeper would record in the checkbook the number of the account (instead of its name) to which he posted the transaction.

Once your bookkeeper has recorded all the transactions, he can adjust the books through a process called *journal entries*. They are for one and only one purpose: to try to agree the books of the company to the accounting equation. And journal entries are used mostly for transactions that do not go through the checkbook. For example, each month, the bank deducts a service charge from your bank account. That is an item for which a check has not been written. If over a period of a year, the bank charged you $100 in service charges, then your books must be adjusted downward by that amount, or the balance in your checking account will not agree with what's on your books by that $100. Your bookkeeper or accountant, then, will make a journal entry lowering your bank balance by $100, which he offsets against your profit as an expense in the same amount. Now, your books agree with what is in the bank. The bookkeeper keeps a written record of all the journal entries he makes during a year. Each journal entry should contain an explanation as to why it was made.

Double entry bookkeeping, invented in the 14th century, is an extension of the accounting equation, Assets = Liabilities + Equity. Since this equation is always in balance, both sides of any transaction are recorded. The asset side is known also as the debit side or the charge side, and it is reflected on the left. The right-hand side of the equation is also known as the credit side. Each transaction then, is both a debit and a credit. Here is how debits and credits affect the financial accounts:

> *Debits*:   Increase assets and expenses and/or decrease liabilities and/or equity.

> *Credits*:   Decrease assets and expenses, and/or increase liabilities and/or equity.

The normal balances of the accounts, then, are as follows:
Asset or Expenses   *Debits*
Income, Equity, or Liability   *Credits*

This produces the following formula for the balance sheet:
Debits (Assets) = Credits (Liabilities + Equity)

which in turn produces the following formula for the income statement:
Credits (Income) = Debits (Expenses + Profit [or loss])

The excess credits (or debits) on the income statement are then used to increase (or decrease) the equity account. Journal entries and transactions from the journals are used to adjust the ledgers to the proper amount through debits and credits.

Let us again return to the guitar example. Since the guitar valued at $3,500 was stolen, that transaction is not reflected in the books until we make an adjustment—by hand if you will—to show it. After all, the theft did not go through the checkbook, and it was not posted to a journal. Since we already have discussed the fact that the theft of the guitar is an expense—which offsets directly against our equity, the bookkeeper will make the following journal entry in the form of debits and credits:

Journal Entry #1
Debit (Dr.)
     Cost of Goods Sold (an expense account) $3,500
   Credit(Cr.)
     Inventory (an asset account) $3,500
To record the theft of 1954 Fender Telecaster Guitar by employee

As a result of the above transaction, our books are now in balance again. The debits equal the credits. By debiting an expense account, we will ultimately reduce our equity by the same amount when our books are closed and the loss is tallied. By crediting the inventory account, we are reducing our assets—inventory—to reflect the fact that the guitar is missing and now can't be sold. Again, we get to claim nothing on our books for the profit we would have made as a result of the ultimate sale of the guitar.

Concealing Asset Misappropriations

Asset misappropriations are generally concealed in the books of account as either false debits or omitted credits. However, many misappropriations are not concealed at all, and they will be reflected in the books as an out-of-balance condition.

Out-of-Balance Conditions

By removing a tangible asset from the business (a debit), the books will be out-of-balance by the exact amount of the tangible asset misappropriated. Therefore, if all tangible assets were counted after a theft, the debits and credits would not equal. Of course, tangible assets are rarely counted in their entirety. As a result, the out of balance condition may not be known.

Let's take an absurdly simple example. Wendall works at McDonald's as a cashier. One day, you go to Mickey D's and order a Big Mac, large order of fries, soft drink, and one of those hot apple pies that seem to come out of the oven at about 3,000 degrees. You give Wendall the exact change, in this case, $4.22. Rather than ringing the sale on the register, Wendall simply puts the money in his pocket. He has now appropriated an asset: $4.22 in currency. If we could stop the business right after the theft and close our books, we would find that the credits exceed the debits by $3.51, the cost to McDonald's for the Big Mac, large order of fries, soft drink, and hot apple pie. The 71-cent difference is the gross profit on the sale, which Wendall also stole. But McDonald's will not account for that loss until they determine their profits at the end of the year.

Out of balance conditions occur during larcenies, when there is no attempt by the thief to conceal the fact that the debits and credits do not match. Of course, the perpetrator is counting on the fact that McDonald's will not close immediately after his theft and count debits and credits, and therefore his scheme will not be detected.

That alone is the perpetrator's "concealment method"—his thefts are lost in the shuffle.

False Debits

Let's carry the example further, and presume that McDonald's would be dumb enough (they're not) to let Wendall not only be a cashier, but to keep the books, too. Now Wendall controls both the money and how it is counted. Since he knows the credits really exceed the debits by $3.51, he decides to do some "creative accounting" to take care of the difference. He creates a journal entry and debits "miscellaneous expense" on the books for $3.51; and he credits the food inventory account for $3.51. His books are now in balance. The debit to miscellaneous expense in this case is false, and designed to replace the cash Wendall stole. Wendall had his choice of false debits: to expenses or to assets.

Expenses

Smart perpetrators like Wendall who have chosen to cover their trails will invariably select an expense account over an asset account to create a false debit. The fictitious entry to an expense account accomplishes two different but interrelated objectives. First, many expense items are not represented by "hard" merchandise, which can be counted and inventoried. Second, on an annual basis, expense accounts are closed to a zero balance and the remainders are transferred to the profit and loss account. Once the expense account is closed, it becomes a historical item, and will probably never be reviewed again. If the false debit is not detected in the expense account by the time the books are closed, it is gone forever, as my colleague Steve Albrecht once observed.

Forced Balances

A variation to the out-of-balance condition is a forced balance. Those using this technique invariably have access to the books and records. In this method, an incorrect total is carried from the journal to the ledger, or from the ledger to the financial statements. Let us return for a moment to the example of Wendall as a bookkeeper for McDonald's. The only indication we have in our books that Wendall skimmed $4.22 is the fact that our inventory is short by its cost, $3.51. Let's assume that Wendall wanted to "cover" that loss in McDonald's books. He can do so by forcing his inventory balance. Rather than making a journal entry reducing the inventory account, Wendall can purposely add incorrectly when he is totaling up the inventory.

For example, if inventory of food at McDonald's was counted and totaled $4,680.44, then this amount should be reflected in the inventory or purchases journal. But Wendall adds $3.51 to that figure, and makes the total of the numbers $4,683.95. When the balance of the inventory is transferred from the journal to the ledger, the latter will be overstated by $3.51. When the ledgers are used to prepare the financial statements, inventory will be overstated by $3.51 and expenses by the same amount. But the only way to detect the forced balance is to go back and add the original column of figures in the inventory account, which will be off by the $3.51.

Assets

Wendall also could have created his fictitious journal entry to debit an asset. It matters not what the asset is, although he probably will not chose a fictitious debit to the cash account, because the asset of cash is watched closely and accounted for to the penny. Since McDonald's doesn't have charge accounts, Wendall probably wouldn't show his debit as accounts receivable. But he could add it to any fixed asset account—furniture and fixtures, investments, plant and equipment—or a host of others. The point is that the false debit to an asset account is much easier to detect. And the false asset debit stays on the books until some action is taken to remove it.

Omitted Credits

Omitted credits are used to conceal revenue skimmed from the organization. In Wendall's case, he failed to ring up a sale on the cash register. The credit he omitted was to sales, and he stole the debit portion—$4.22 in cash. The books are therefore technically in balance, but merchandise is missing. The principal way to detect omitted credits from books of account is through trend analysis—a form of indirect proof. That's because of the method Wendall chose to commit his theft. By not ringing the sale on the cash register, McDonald's never knew a sale occurred. But, as we have stated, if they stopped and added their debits and credits, the credits would exceed the debits by $3.51, the amount of the missing merchandise. All we know from that scenario, though, is that merchandise—the burger, fries, soft drink, and pie—is missing. We don't know where it is, who took it, or whether it was stolen at all. It could have been accidentally thrown away, spoiled, or even eaten by a hungry employee.

Let's take a separate illustration of omitted credits, one much more difficult to detect. Say Wendall worked for a dry cleaning establishment and did exactly the same thing: took $4.22 from a customer for laundry, pocketed the money, and failed to ring up the sale. Remember, our books are still in balance—Wendall omitted the credit (the sale) and stole the debit ($4.22 in currency). Since we are not missing merchandise, the indirect proof will be that our profits are lower by the cost of the service we provided. If our direct costs to launder the clothing amount to $3.51, then our profits suffer by the same amount. The remaining 71 cents is lost revenue, which will not be reflected in the books at all. Detecting thefts such as this requires sophisticated revenue and expense analysis on a line-by-line basis. And of course, if the thefts are at a level where they leave no obvious trends, the odds of detecting such a loss from the dry cleaner's books of account is small. If, for example, Wendall confined his thefts to that one transaction, it would hardly be noticeable in a dry cleaning operation that grossed several hundred thousand dollars a year.

But we know from examining thousands of occupational fraud cases that the single, individual theft is exceedingly rare. The basic trend seems to be for such frauds to start off small, but grow larger as time progresses. Of course, that makes sense—if Wendall isn't detected the first time, why should he stop? And by the time he has gotten away with the theft ten times, he gets a feeling of invincibility, and escalates the frequency and the amounts he steals. If he were smart, he would determine a threshold amount he could steal without arousing suspicion. There is no way of knowing how many such smart people there are, since we certainly aren't catching them. The cases in this book, as you will see, show a consistent trend of excess by the perpetrators. Some might assume such people secretly want to be caught. Although that is certainly possible, those cases are far outweighed by people who simply lose sight of the amount of money they are stealing—they either don't know or don't want to know.

In fraud classes I have taught over the years, a common question asked is, "What is the most effective technique to catch employees stealing?" Only partially in jest, I reply, "Time is the most effective detection technique. Left unchecked, many occupational frauds will finally surface when there is nothing left for the employee to steal and the company goes broke." Such a comment underscores a key element of occupational fraud and abuse — its repetitive nature feeds on itself. It's not just a "good idea" to control fraud and abuse; it is an economic necessity.

Statistics

Cash vs. Non-Cash Assets

Cash schemes dominated the asset misappropriations cases in our study. As the following charts illustrate, 89.3% of the total losses and 86.8% total cases in the asset misappropriation category came from the theft or misapplication of cash. Schemes involving inventory and other assets were not nearly as common, but when they occurred they tended to be costly. The median loss for a non-cash asset scheme in our study was $100,000, almost twice the median loss for cash schemes.

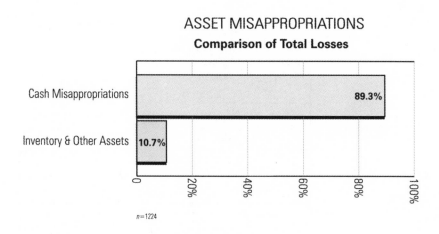

Chart 2-1: Asset Misappropriations - Comparison of Total Losses (Cash vs. Non-cash)

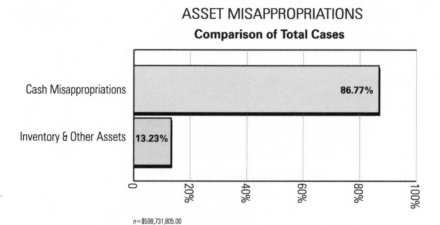

Chart 2-2: Asset Misappropriations - Comparison of Total Cases
(Cash vs. Non-cash)

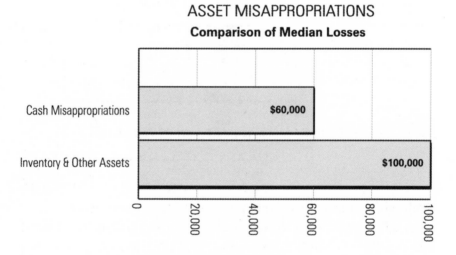

Chart 2-3: Asset Missappropriations - Comparison of Median Losses
(Cash vs. Non-cash)

CASH SCHEMES

Frauds involving the misappropriation of cash can be broken down into three groups; skimming schemes, cash larceny schemes, and fraudulent disbursements of cash. As the following data illustrates, fraudulent disbursements made up the majority of the cash schemes in our study. Fraudulent disbursements are schemes that involve false payments by the victim company. Examples include false billings, payroll fraud, and fraudulent expense reimbursements.

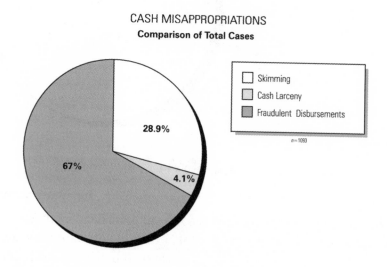

Chart 2-4: Cash Misappropriations - Comparison of Total Cases

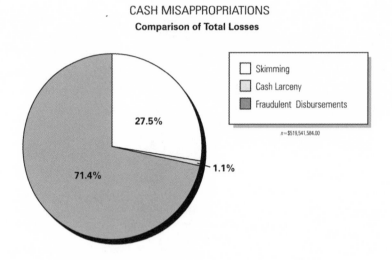

Chart 2-5: Cash Misappropriations - Comparison of Total Losses

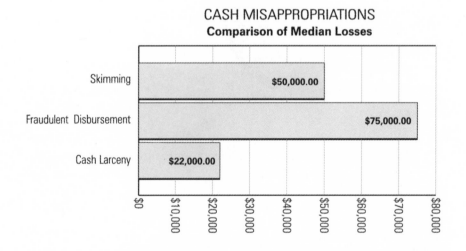

Chart 2-6: Cash Misappropriations - Comparison of Median Losses

FRAUDULENT DISBURSEMENTS

Fraudulent disbursements as a group made up over 48% of all the cases in our study. This group has been broken down into the following scheme types:

Check Tampering Schemes
Register Disbursements Schemes
Billing Schemes
Expense Schemes
Payroll Schemes
Other Fraudulent Disbursements

As the charts below illustrate, billing schemes are the most common and most costly of the fraudulent disbursement schemes. They comprise 33.3% of the cases and over 51.6 % of the losses attributable to fraudulent disbursement schemes. In addition, their median cost of $250,000 is by far the highest of any type of fraudulent disbursement. The median loss for fraudulent disbursement schemes in our study as a whole is $75,000.

FRAUDULENT DISBURSEMENTS
Comparison of Total Cases

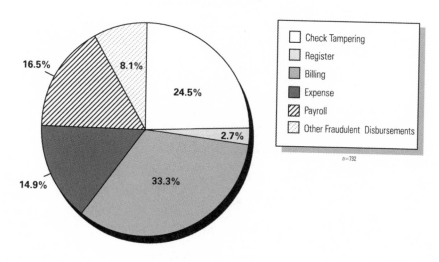

Charts 2-7: Fraudulent Disbursements - Comparison of Total Cases

FRAUDULENT DISBURSEMENTS
Comparison of Total Losses

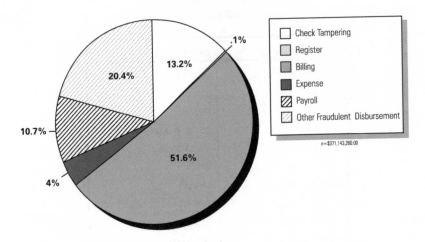

Chart 2-8: Fraudulent Disbursements - Comparison of Total Losses

FRAUDULENT DISBURSEMENTS
Comparison of Median Losses

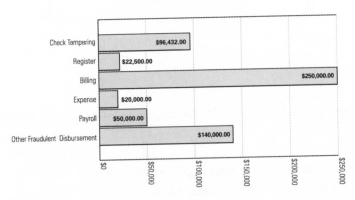

Chart 2-9: Fraudulent Disbursements - Comparison of Median Losses

ASSET MISAPPROPRIATIONS AS A WHOLE

The following charts provide comparative data for all nine scheme types that make up asset misappropriations.

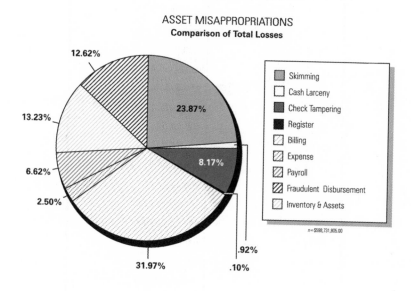

Chart 2-10: Asset Misappropriations - Comparison of Total Losses (All Schemes)

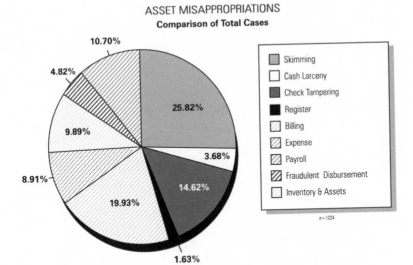

Chart 2-11: Asset Misappropriations - Comparison of Total Cases (All Schemes)

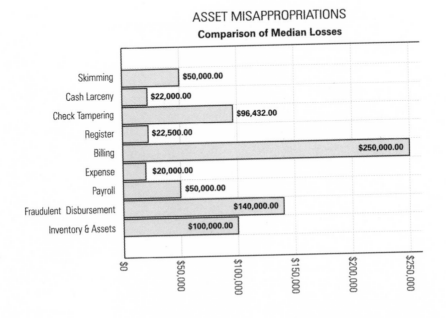

Chart 2.12: Asset Misappropriations - Comparison of Median Losses

[1] Jerome Hall, *Theft, Law and Society, 2nd Edition*, 1960

[2] Hall.

[3] Karen W. Arenson, "Former United Way Chief Guilty in Theft of More Than $600,00," *The New York Times*, April 4, 1995

[4] Arenson.

[5] Eric Asimov, "Too Hot Out of the Kitchen," *The New York Times*, May 22, 1996.

[6] Asimov.

[7] "Arrest Ordered in Alleged Embezzlement from Revisionist Group," *San Diego Daily*, November 22, 1996.

[8] *Webster's Dictionary*, p. 901.

[9] *Webster's*, p. 759.

[10] David H. Marshall and Wayne W. McManus, *Accounting: What the Numbers Mean*, Third Edition (Chicago: Irwin, 1981), p. 32.

[11] Marshall and McManus, p. 217.

[12] *Webster's*, p. 1205.

[13] Marshall and McManus, p. 32.

[14] Marshall and McManus, p. 107.

Skimming Schemes

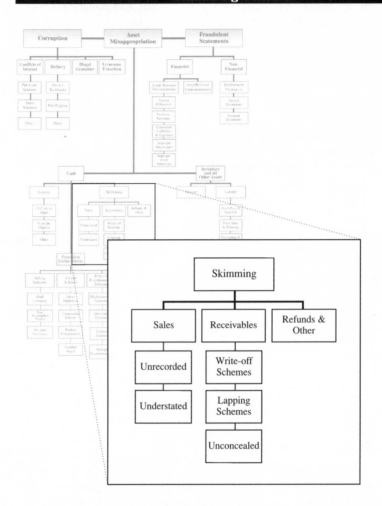

Flowchart 3-1

3. SKIMMING

*****

Case Study: Shy Doc Gave Good Face
*Several names have been changed to preserve anonymity

Brian Lee excelled as a top-notch plastic surgeon. His patients touted Lee's skill and artistry when privately confiding the secret of their improved appearance to their closest friends. Exuding a serious yet gentle manner, the 42-year-old bachelor took quiet pride in his beautification efforts — mainly nose jobs, face lifts, tummy tucks, and breast enhancements.

Lee practiced out of a large physician-owned clinic of assorted specialties, housed in several facilities scattered throughout a growing suburb in the Southwest. As its top producer, Lee billed more than $1 million annually and took home $300,000 to $800,000 a year in salary and bonus. But during one four-year stretch, Lee also kept his own secret stash of unaccounted revenue — possibly hundreds of thousands of dollars.

Once Lee's dishonesty came to light, the clinic's board of directors (made up of fellow physician-shareholders) demanded an exact accounting. Acting on behalf of the clinic, its big-city law firm hired Doug Leclaire to conduct a private investigation. Leclaire is a CFE based in Flower Mound, Texas, who had worked well with the lawyers earlier that year on an unrelated case.

"The doctors wanted an independent person to root around and document how much money was missing," recalled Leclaire. "They also wanted to see how deep this scam ran. As far as I could determine, no one else was involved." Lee's secretary and nurse knew that Lee was performing the surgeries, but they were unaware that the doctor was withholding patient payments from the clinic. Leclaire marveled at the simplicity of the fraud. He said Lee's ill-gotten gains came easily, given the discreet nature of his business.

Leclaire first familiarized himself with both clinic and office policies. (Doctors ran their offices as autonomous units.) During a confidential, free consultation, Lee would examine the patient and explain various options, the expected results, and his total fee. The doctor or his secretary would then discuss payment requirements.

According to Leclaire, "If the patient planned on filing an insurance claim for covered procedures — such as nonemergency, reconstructive surgery for a car crash victim whose nose smashed into a windshield — the patient must pay the deductible beforehand." For pure cosmetic surgery like liposuction, which is not covered by insurance, patients had to pay the entire amount by cash or check prior to the procedure. Like many plastic surgeons, Lee accepted no credit cards, presumably to guard against economic reprisals from "buyer's remorse." The one-time payment included all post-op visits as well.

Once a patient decided to go under the knife, Lee or his secretary would schedule another appointment or review the doctor's master surgery log to schedule a mutually agreeable date and time. Lee performed the surgeries at the clinic or an affiliated hospital. In theory, a patient would check in at the reception area for a scheduled procedure and pay the secretary, who would immediately attach the payment along with an accompanying receipt to the appropriate procedure form and record the transaction on a daily report. The secretary kept all payments, receipts, and forms in a small lock box for temporary safekeeping.

"At the end of the day, either the doctor, his nurse, or his receptionist would submit all paperwork and payments — easily totaling tens of thousands of dollars — to the clinic cashier across the hall," explained Leclaire. "If it was late in the day, the doctor would sometimes lock the box in his desk drawer until the following day." For procedures performed at an affiliated hospital, the patient paid in advance and the clinic relied on someone from the doctor's office to submit the completed paperwork to the head cashier, allowing the clinic to declare its cut.

But even the best-laid plans often fail in their execution, noted Leclaire. The case that finally nailed the plastic surgeon was that of Rita Mae Givens, a rhinoplasty patient. The clinic offices were arranged so that when a patient stepped off the elevator, they could turn right and enter the clinic's main reception area or they could turn left and walk down the hall and enter Lee's office reception area. Getting off the elevator on to the fifth floor, Givens proceeded to her left as Lee had earlier instructed. Givens gained admittance via Lee's private office door, bypassing the clinic secretary and receptionist down the hall on the right. As planned, the unsuspecting clinic staff never knew that Lee made the appointment with Givens, nor that he performed surgery to correct her deviated septum and trim her proboscis. Givens had paid the doctor by check.

During her recovery, Givens reviewed her insurance policy, which stated that rhinoplasty may be covered under certain circumstances, or at least may count toward meeting the yearly deductible. She decided to file an insurance claim. But Givens realized she had never received a billing statement to attach to her claim form, which was mandated by her carrier. So Givens made an unplanned call to the clinic's office to request a copy of her bill, which then set off a series of spontaneous reactions. Lee's clinic's cashier located the patient's file, but it showed no charges for the procedure performed. The cashier thought this quite odd. Givens assured the cashier that the procedure had been performed and that she had paid for the surgery with a personal check.

The cashier in turn checked with the office manager of the clinic for the corresponding record of Givens' payment. Of course the office manager failed to find the record and called the clinic administrator in on the search. Knowing that doctors sometimes forgot to immediately reconcile procedures performed at other facilities, the clinic administrator suggested they look at the doctor's surgery log, under the time and date that Givens had provided, for any clues. Meanwhile, the office manager asked the patient to provide a copy of her canceled check, which they later discovered had been endorsed and deposited in the doctor's personal bank account.

The clinic administrator verified that Lee had performed the surgery but had never submitted the payment to the head cashier. When confronted, the doctor admitted his wrongdoing. The administrator alerted the board, who then hired Leclaire to investigate.

The private eye interviewed Lee several times over the course of the investigation. Leclaire described Lee as very apologetic and helpful in reviewing his misdeeds. The doctor only stole payments from elective surgery patients, he explained, so as not to alert any insurance providers who may have requested additional documentation from the clinic. Sometimes Lee helped himself to payments in his secretary's lock box before turning it in to the head cashier. Sometimes he swiped a payment directly from a patient with a surreptitious appointment. He preferred cash, but often took checks made payable to "Dr. Lee." The doctor often held checks in his desk drawer for a few weeks before depositing them into his personal bank account or cashing the checks. Lee simply destroyed the receipts that were to accompany payments, he told Leclaire. Out of a sense of professional duty, Lee scrupulously maintained all patient medical files, though.

Because the perpetrator cooperated so fully, Leclaire called this case "fun and easy." The doctor kept meticulous records of all his actions, whether or not they were legitimate. With Lee's help, Leclaire compared the doctor's detailed "Daytimer" personal organizer against the clinic's records and readily identified the missing payments. He even turned over his bank statements so Leclaire could match the deposits to the booty. Lee also opened up his investment portfolio to Leclaire to quash any doubts over additional unreported revenue.

"The doctor didn't try to hide anything," said Leclaire, who has spent 20 years conducting criminal investigations. "I was able to document everything." In all his talks with the doctor, "Everything he told us was pretty much on the up and up."

After spending so much time with the doctor, Leclaire finally asked Lee the one question that everyone puzzled over — Why? Greed, he said. With all his money, he still craved more. Driven like his father and brother, who are also successful, Lee had little time to enjoy sports and recreation. Wealth was the family obsession, one-upmanship the family game. "It grew to be a serious competition," said Leclaire. "Who could amass the most? Who had the best car?"

To win the game, Lee resorted to grand larceny, which carried an enormous risk of punishment should the fraud be detected. "I kind of felt sorry for the doctor. A guy in that position could have lost everything," Leclaire said.

After weeks of work, the law firm and its private investigator brought their findings to the board and made recommendations as requested. He prefaced his report with lessons that were learned from this case. "Weak internal controls tempt all employees, even those earning over $100,000. If given the opportunity, means, and a very slim chance for detection, there are employees who will justify the commission of a fraud in their own minds."

Leclaire suggested they revamp their entire payment system, setting up a central billing area, posting signs to educate the patients, and assigning and spreading out distinct tasks to several office workers during the payment process. "They had no oversight," said the investigator. He told them they needed to reconcile all steps along the way and perform routine internal audits.

This fraud escaped detection for more than four years, Leclaire told his attentive audience. Bottom line by his audit, Lee had embezzled about $200,000.

Much discussion and a question-and-answer period followed. Some board members insisted Lee be terminated immediately. "Others showed real sympathy for one of their brethren," said Leclaire.

"Their biggest concern was the clinic's income tax liability." Leclaire, who had been a special agent with the IRS's criminal investigations department for nine years, assured them the clinic held no liability for uncollected income. No one wanted an IRS audit, given the clinic's history of scant oversight and the doctors' uncertainty over their own culpability, said Leclaire. They feared federal agents would snoop around and perhaps find other instances of unreported income or questionable activity. He warned that taxes would definitely be due upon restitution, however.

"The doctors had worked out an agreement among themselves." They decided not to prosecute or terminate Lee. Of course the doctors expected Lee to make immediate and full restitution of $200,000, plus interest. (For the first installment, Leclaire picked up $15,000 in cash the doctor had lying around his modest abode.) They also insisted that Lee place another $200,000 in escrow to cover any contingencies. And naturally, the doctor would foot the bill for both the lawyers and the private investigator involved in the case.

His fellow physicians agreed to let their top moneymaker continue to practice at the clinic, provided Lee went for professional counseling to correct his aberration. They would help him any way they could, they said. Encouraged to show Lee there were other things in life besides work, from then on the doctors invited him along on their fishing and hunting trips. On the advice of his psychiatrist, Lee eagerly accepted. The reformed loner even enjoyed himself.

To curb temptations, the clinic immediately instituted new policies on payment procedures. Good thing, said Leclaire. The good doctor later told him that if given a chance, "I would probably do it again."

*****

Overview

Skimming, as illustrated in the previous case, is the removal of cash from a victim entity prior to its entry in an accounting system.[1] Employees who skim from their companies steal sales or receivables before they are recorded in the company books. Because of this aspect of their nature, skimming schemes are known as "off-book" frauds; they leave no direct audit trail. The fact that the funds have not yet been recorded means that the victim company may not be aware that the cash was received. Consequently, it may be very difficult to detect that the money has been stolen. This is the prime advantage of a skimming scheme to the fraudster.

Skimming was the most common scheme type in our study, making up 20.75% of the cases we reviewed (see chart 1-6). Skimming schemes cost their victims $142,904,482, in total, with a median loss of $50,000 (see charts 1-4 and 1-5, respectively). We have classified skimming schemes as either *sales skimming* or *receivables skimming*. Chart 3-2 demonstrates that the majority of skimming schemes appear to involve sales rather than receivables. This is probably due to the fact that skimmed sales can be completely unrecorded whereas skimmed receivables appear on the victim company's books as aging accounts. This distinction will be discussed more later.

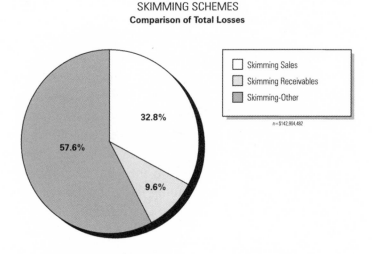

SKIMMING SCHEMES
Comparison of Total Losses

Skimming Sales
Skimming Receivables
Skimming-Other

n=$142,904,482

32.8%

57.6%

9.6%

Chart 3-1: Comparison of Total Losses

The data in charts 3-1 and 3-3 indicate that most of the losses in our skimming schemes came in the "other category." This is mainly attributable to a few cases where very large refunds and other types of revenues were taken by employees. In general, the majority of skimming cases involve sales or receivables. We believe the median losses for these two categories are more in line with the true cost of skimming.

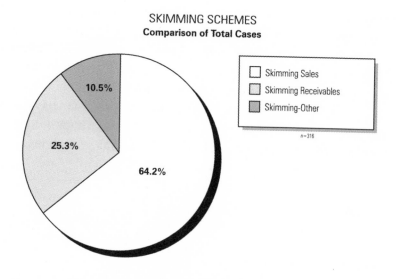

Chart 3-2: Comparison of Total Cases

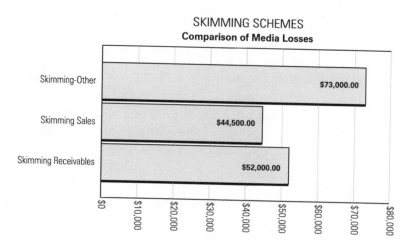

Chart 3-3: Comparison of Median Losses

The distinction between sales and receivables helps illustrate where skimming occurs and who is involved, but the methods used by fraudsters are basically the same regardless of what kinds of funds they are skimming. Therefore, we will discuss all skimming frauds as a whole.

Skimming can occur at any point where funds enter a business, so almost anyone who deals with the process of receiving cash may be in a position to skim money. This includes salespeople, tellers, waitpersons, and others who receive cash directly from customers. In addition, many skimming schemes are perpetrated by employees whose duties include receiving and logging payments made by customers through the mail. These employees are able to slip checks out of the incoming mail for their own use rather than posting the checks to the proper revenue or customer accounts. Those who deal directly with customers or who handle customer payments are obviously the most likely candidates to skim funds. Skimming schemes generally fall into one of the following categories:

Unrecorded Sales	Understated Sales and Receivables	Theft of Checks Through the Mail	Short Term Skimming

Unrecorded Sales

The most basic skimming scheme occurs when an employee sells goods or services to a customer, collects the customer's payment, but makes no record of the sale. The employee pockets the money received from the customer instead of turning it over to his employer (see flowchart 3-2). This was the method used by Dr. Brian Lee in the case study discussed above. He was performing work and collecting money that his partners knew nothing about. As a result he was able to take approximately $200,000 without leaving any indications of his wrongdoings on the books. Had a patient not made an unexpected call for a copy of a billing statement, Lee's crime could have gone on indefinitely. The case of Dr. Lee illustrates why unrecorded sales schemes are perhaps the most dangerous of all skimming frauds.

In order to discuss unrecorded sales schemes more completely, let us consider one of the simplest and most common sales transactions, a sale of goods at the cash register. In a normal transaction, a customer purchases an item and an employee enters the sale on the register. The register tape reflects that the sale has been made and shows that a certain amount of cash (the purchase price of the item) should have been placed in the register. By comparing the register tape to the amount of money on hand, it may be possible to detect thefts. For instance, if there were $500 worth of sales recorded on a particular register on a given day, but only $400 cash in the register, it would be obvious that someone had stolen $100 (assuming no beginning cash balance).

When an employee skims money by making off-book sales of merchandise, however, it is impossible to detect theft by comparing the register tape to the cash drawer because the sale is not recorded on the register (that is why it is "off-book"). Instead, an employee pockets the customer's money. In order to create the appearance that the sale is being entered in the register, the fraudster might ring a "no sale" or some other noncash transaction. In Case 1655, two employees in a midsize retail organization skimmed sales using this method.

Return to the example above where we compared the register tape to the cash on hand. Let's assume that a fraudster wants to make off with $100. Through the course of the day, there are $500 worth of sales at his register; one sale is for $100. When the $100 sale is made, the employee does not record the transaction on his register. The customer pays $100 and takes his merchandise home, but instead of placing the $100 in the cash drawer, the employee pockets it. Since the employee did not record the sale, at the end of the day the register tape will only reflect $400 in sales. There will be $400 on hand in the register ($500 in total sales minus the $100 that the employee stole) so the register will balance. Therefore, by not recording the sale the employee is able to steal money without the missing funds appearing on the books.

The most difficult part in a skimming scheme at the register is that the employee must commit the overt act of taking money. If the employee takes the customer's money and shoves it into his pocket without entering the transaction on the register, the customer may suspect that something is wrong and report the conduct to another employee or manager. It is also possible that a manager, a fellow employee, or a surveillance camera will spot the illegal conduct.

REGISTER MANIPULATION

As we said, some employees might ring a "no sale" or other noncash transaction to mask the theft of sales. The false transaction is entered on the register so that it appears a sale is being rung up, when in fact the employee is stealing the customer's payment. To the casual observer it looks as though the sale is being properly recorded.

In other cases employees have rigged their registers so that sales are not recorded on their register tapes. As we have stated, the amount of cash on hand in a register may be compared to the amount showing on the register tape in order to detect employee theft. It is therefore not important to the fraudster what is keyed into the register, but rather what shows up on the tape. If an employee can rig his register so that sales do not print, he can enter a sale that he intends to skim, yet assure that the sale never appears on the books. Anyone observing the employee will see the sale entered, see the cash drawer open, etc., yet the register tape will not reflect the transaction. How is this accomplished? In Case 1740, a service station employee hid stolen gasoline sales by simply lifting the ribbon from the printer. He then collected and pocketed the sales which were not recorded on the register tape. The fraudster would then roll back the tape to the point where the next transaction should appear and replace the ribbon. The next transaction would be printed without leaving any blank space on the tape, apparently leaving no trace of the fraud. However, the fraudster in this case overlooked the fact that the transactions on his register were pre-numbered. Even though he was careful in replacing the register tape, he failed to realize that he was creating a break in the sequence of transactions. For instance, if the perpetrator skimmed sale #155, then the register tape would only show transactions #153, #154, #156, #157 and so on. The missing transaction numbers, omitted because the ribbon was lifted when they took place, indicated fraud.

Special circumstances can lead to more creative methods for skimming at the register. In Case 2230, for instance, a movie theater manager figured out a way around the theater's automatic ticket dispenser. In order to reduce payroll hours this manager sometimes worked as a cashier selling tickets. He made sure at these times there was no one checking patrons' tickets outside the theaters. When a sale was made, the ticket dispenser would feed out the appropriate number of tickets, but the manager withheld tickets from some patrons, and allowed them to enter the theater without them. When the next customer made a purchase, the manager sold them one of the excess tickets instead of using the automatic dispenser. Thus, a portion of the ticket sales were not recorded. At the end of the night, there was a surplus of cash which the manager removed and kept for himself. Although the actual loss was impossible to measure, it was estimated that this manager stole over $30,000 from his employer.

SKIMMING DURING NONBUSINESS HOURS

Another way to skim unrecorded sales is to conduct sales during nonbusiness hours. For instance, some employees have been caught running their employers' stores on weekends or after hours without the knowledge of the owners. They were able to pocket the proceeds of these sales because the owners had no idea that their stores were even open. One manager of a retail facility in Case 2103 went to work two hours early every day, opening his store at 8:00 a.m. instead of 10:00 a.m., and pocketed all the sales made during these two hours. Talk about dedication! He rang up sales on the register as if it was business as usual, but then removed the register tape and all the cash he had accumulated. The manager then started from scratch at 10:00 as if the store was just opening. The tape was destroyed so there was no record of the before-hours revenue.

Though we have discussed skimming so far in the context of cash register transactions, skimming does not have to occur at a register or even involve hard currency. Some of the most costly skimming schemes are perpetrated by employees who work at remote locations or without close supervision. This can include on-site sales persons who do not deal with registers, independent salesmen who operate off-site, and employees who work at branches or satellite offices. These employees have a high level of autonomy in their jobs, which often translates into poor supervision and in turn to fraud.

SKIMMING OF OFF-SITE SALES

Several cases in our study involved the skimming of sales by off-site employees. Some of the best examples of this type of fraud occurred in the apartment rental industry, where apartment managers handle the day-to-day operations without much oversight. A common scheme, as evidenced by a bookkeeper in Case 250, is for an on-site employee to identify the tenants who pay in currency and remove them from the books. This causes a particular apartment to appear as vacant on the records when, in fact, it is occupied. Once the currency-paying tenants are removed from the records, the manager can skim their rental payments without late notices being sent to the tenants. As long as no one physically checks the apartment, the fraudster can continue skimming indefinitely.

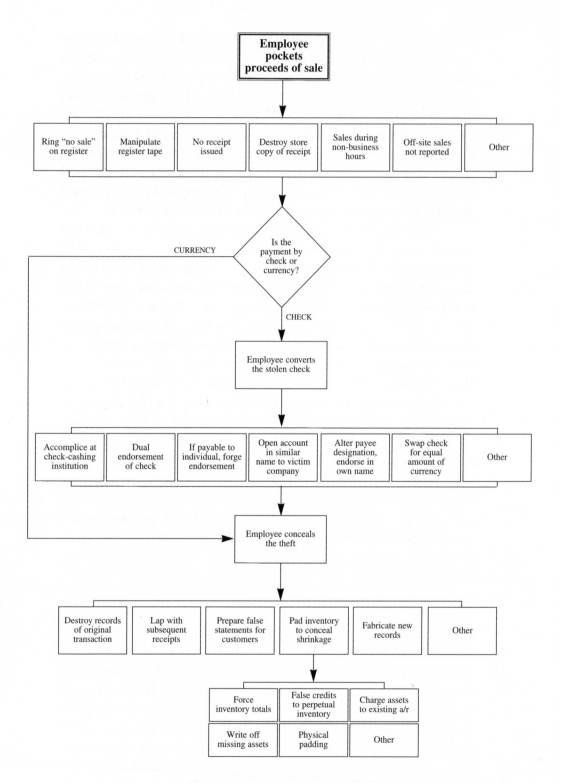

Flowchart 3-2: Unrecorded sales

Another rental-skimming scheme occurs when apartments are rented out but no lease is signed. On the books, the apartment will still appear to be vacant, even though there are rent-paying tenants on the premises. The fraudster can then steal the rent payments, which will not be missed. Sometimes the employees in these schemes work in conjunction with the renters and give a "special rate" to these people. In return, the renter's payments are made directly to the employee and any complaints or maintenance requests are directed only to that employee so the renter's presence remains hidden.

Instead of skimming rent, the property manager in Case 1381 skimmed payments made by tenants for application fees and late fees. Revenue sources such as these are less predictable than rental payments, and their absence may therefore be harder to detect. The central office in Case 1381, for instance, knew when rent was due and how many apartments were occupied, but had no control in place to track the number of people who filled out rental applications or how many tenants paid their rent a day or two late. Stealing only these "nickel and dime" payments, the property manager in this case was able to make off with approximately $10,000 of her employer's money.

A similar revenue source that is unpredictable and therefore difficult to account for is parking-lot-collection revenue. In Case 2045, a parking lot attendant skimmed approximately $20,000 from his employer by simply not preparing tickets for customers who entered the lot. He would take the customers' money and waive them into the lot, but because no receipts were prepared by the fraudster, there was no way for the victim company to compare tickets sold to actual customers at this remote location. Revenue sources which are hard to monitor and predict, such as late fees and parking fees in the examples above, are prime targets for skimming schemes.

Another off-site person in a good position to skim sales is the independent salesman. A prime example is the insurance agent who sells policies but does not file them with the carrier. Most customers do not want to file claims on a policy, especially early in the term, for fear that their premiums will rise. Knowing this, the agent keeps all documentation on the policies instead of turning it in to the carrier. The agent can then collect and keep the payments made on the policy because the carrier does not know the policy exists. The customer continues to make his payments, thinking that he is insured, when in fact the policy is a ruse. Should a claim eventually be filed by the customer, some agents are able to backdate the false policies and submit them to the carrier, then file the claim so that the fraud will remain hidden.

POOR COLLECTION PROCEDURES

Poor collection and recording procedures can make it easy for an employee to skim sales or receivables. In Case 1679, for instance, a governmental authority which dealt with public housing was victimized because it failed to itemize daily receipts. This agency received payments from several public housing tenants, but at the end of the day, "money" received from tenants was listed as a whole. Receipt numbers were not used to itemize the payments made by tenants, so there was no way to pinpoint which tenant had paid how much. Consequently, the employee in charge of collecting money from tenants was able to skim a portion of their payments. She simply did not record the receipt of over $10,000. Her actions caused certain accounts receivable to be overstated where tenant payments were not properly recorded.

Understated Sales And Receivables

The cases discussed above deal with purely off-book sales. Understated sales work differently in that the transaction is posted to the books, but for a lower amount than the perpetrator collected from the customer (see flowchart 3-3). For instance, in Case 2210 an employee wrote receipts to customers for their purchases, but she removed the carbon paper backing on the receipts so that they did not produce a company copy. The employee then used a pencil to prepare company copies which showed lower purchase prices. For example, if the customer had paid $100, the company copy might reflect a payment of $80. The employee skimmed the difference between the actual amount of revenue and the amount reflected on the fraudulent receipt. This can also be accomplished at the register when the fraudster underrings a sale, entering a sales total which is lower than the amount actually paid by the customer. The employee skims the difference between the actual purchase price of the item and the sales figure recorded on the register. Rather than reduce the price of an item, an employee might record the sale of fewer items. If 100 units are sold, for instance, a fraudster might only record the sale of 50 units and skim the excess receipts.

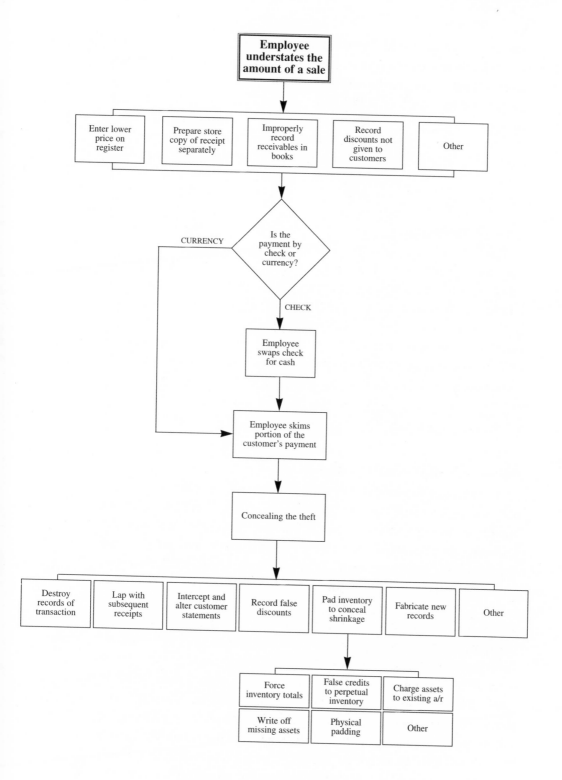

Flowchart 3-3: Understated Sales

A similar method is used when sales are made on account. The bill to the customer reflects the true amount of the sale, but the receivable is understated in the company books. For instance, a company might be owed $1,000, but the receivable is recorded as $800. (Sales will also be understated by $200.) When the customer makes payment on the account, the fraudster can skim $200 and post the $800 to the account. The books will reflect that the account has been paid in full.

FALSE DISCOUNTS

Finally, sales or receivables might be understated by the use of false discounts. Employees with the authority to grant discounts may use this authority to skim revenues. In a false discount skimming scheme, an employee accepts full payment for an item, but records the transaction as if the customer had been given a discount. It therefore appears that the customer paid less than full price for the item. The fraudster skims the amount of the discount. For example, on a $100 purchase, if an employee granted a false discount of 20%, he could skim $20 and leave the company's books in balance. The key to this scheme is to give the customer a receipt reflecting the full price he paid, and provide a different (usually altered) receipt for bookkeeping purposes.

Theft of Checks Through the Mail

Checks received through the mail are a frequent target of employees seeking illicit gains. Theft of incoming checks usually occurs when a single employee is in charge of opening the mail and recording the receipt of payments. This employee simply takes one or more of the incoming checks, and since these checks are not logged as received, the payment is not posted to the customer account (see flowchart 3-4). It appears as if the check had never arrived. When the task of receiving and recording incoming payments is left to a single person, it is all too easy for that employee to slip an occasional check into his pocket.

An example of a check theft scheme occurred in Case 2052, where a mail room employee stole over $2 million in government checks arriving through the mail. This employee simply identified and removed envelopes delivered from a government agency known to send checks to the company. Using a group of accomplices acting under the names of fictitious persons and companies, this individual was able to launder the checks and divide the proceeds with his cronies.

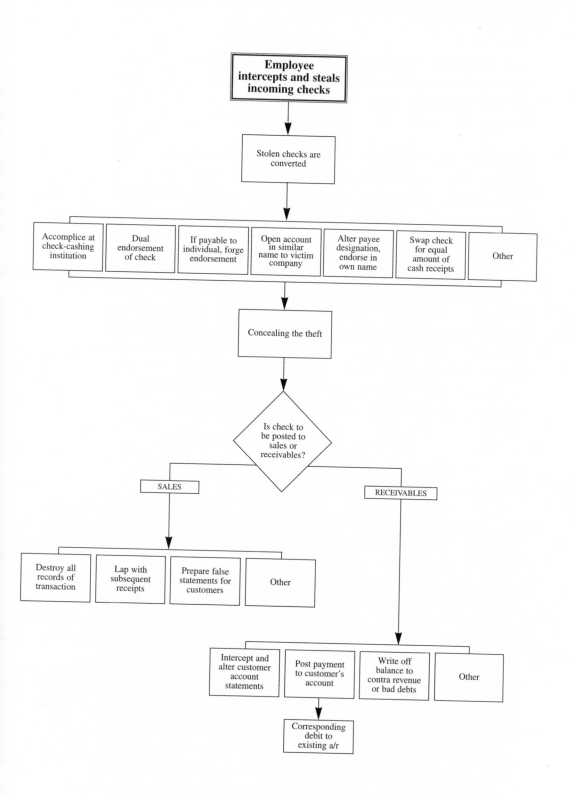

Flowchart 3-4: Theft of Incoming Checks

While the theft of checks is not usually complicated, it may be more difficult to conceal a check theft scheme than other forms of skimming. If the stolen checks were payments on the victim company's receivables, then these payments were expected. As receivables become past due, the victim company will send notices of nonpayment to its customers. A customer is likely to complain when he receives a second bill for a payment he has already made. In addition, the cashed check will serve as evidence that the customer made his payment. In other forms of skimming, such as unrecorded sales schemes, there is no such evidence that cash has been received. We will discuss the methods used to conceal check thefts later in this chapter.

The following case study is an example of one person's check theft scheme. Stefan Winkler skimmed money by taking checks received in the mail, failing to record these checks, and substituting them for collections of currency. Winkler's control over his company's revenue streams allowed him to skim hundreds of thousands of dollars before he was eventually caught. The case also describes how CFE Don Stine unraveled the specifics of Winkler's fraud.

*****

Case Study: Beverage Man Takes the Plunge

* Some names have been changed to preserve anonymity

For most people, Florida shines brightly from postcards and televisions, as brilliant as it must have seemed to the first Europeans who hoped to find the Fountain of Youth and El Dorado there. The contemporary image is a little gaudier than ancient myth, but still going strong. And when most people go to Florida, the vacation schedule and the tourist industry can make it seem like the postcard image lives and breathes. There really is something for the entire family: a tropical paradise for Mom and Dad, lots of noise and colors for the kiddies. But televisions switch off, and tourists go home. The land remains a place where people work, where they live and breathe and raise their families, and the hardest rush they ever feel is a MonsterCup soda pop on a drowsy afternoon. This is the story of one of those people.

Stefan Winkler worked for a beverage company in Pompano Beach, Florida. As director of accounting and controller, Stefan touched the flow of money into and out of the company at every point, though he was particularly focused on how money came in.

The beverage company — call it Mogel's, Inc. — collected from customers in two ways. Either the delivery drivers brought in cash or checks from their route customers, or credit customers sent checks in the mail. The cash and checks from drivers were counted and put in the bank as Route Deposits; the checks arriving by mail from credit customers were filed as Office Deposits. Drivers gave their daily collections to a cashier who made out the Route Deposit slip and sent it to Stefan Winkler. Any checks from office mail came directly to Winkler, who verified the money according to the payment schedule — 30 days for some customers, 60 for others, and so on. Winkler's job was to combine Office Deposits and Route Deposits for the final accounting before bank deposit. Theoretically then, Mogel's had two revenue streams, both of which converged at Winkler's desk and poured smoothly into the bank.

But Winkler had other plans. He siphoned off the cash from the Route Deposits through a lapping operation, covering the money he lifted from one account with funds from another. Winkler took large amounts of cash from the Route Deposits and replaced each cash amount with checks from the credit customers. He might filch $3,000 in cash from the transportation bags and put in $3,000 worth of checks from the mail. That way, the Route total matched the amount listed by the cashier on the deposit slip. There was no gap in Office Deposits, because he never listed the check as received. Instead, he would extend the customer's payment schedule outward, sometimes indefinitely. He occasionally covered the amount later with other embezzlements. Like a kiting operation, lapping takes a continual replenishment of money, forcing the perpetrator to extend the circles of deception wider if the scheme is to continue to produce. And like kiting, lapping is destined to crumble, unless the person can find a way to replace the original funds and casually walk away. Winkler probably told himself he'd replace the money sometime, preferably sooner than later. Maybe he figured he'd make a killing in the stock market or win big at the tracks and set everything right again. Only he knows what he was thinking; he never in fact admitted to taking anything at all. Acting as his own lawyer, he announced at trial, "There are other people besides me who could have taken that money." The prosecution had to prove that Winkler, and not those other people, had actually stolen the money. How that happened is, as they say, the rest of the story.

Mogel's operated in Pompano Beach as a subsidiary of a larger company from Delaware. Oversight was casual; auditors generally prepared their reports by dispatches from the local office. This gave Winkler as accounting director lots of room to maneuver. But maybe there was too much room. Over the course of a year and a half, Winkler's superiors became increasingly dissatisfied with his performance. Winkler was, fatefully enough, fired on the Friday morning before auditors were to arrive the following Monday. He didn't have the money to replace what he'd stolen, so he used the time to rearrange what he could of his misdealings and throw the rest into disarray. He took cash receipts journals, copies of customer checks, deposit slips, and other financial records from the office and removed his personnel file. He altered electronic files, too, backdating accounts receivables lines to make them current and increasing customer discounts. Examiners would eventually discover "an extremely unusual general ledger adjustment of $303,970.25" made just before Winkler was fired. As the prosecuting attorney, Tony Carriuolo, puts its, "He attempted, through computers and other manipulations, to alter history."

When the auditors arrived on Monday, they started the long haul of reconstructing what had actually happened. This was, as Carriuolo and Certified Fraud Examiner Don Stine put it, "the fun part, even though it was exhausting, of piecing together what happened and who did it, with documents missing and nothing that we could use to point directly at Winkler and say, 'There it is, he did it.'" Auditors for Mogul's set about evaluating the mess Winkler had left behind, working through bank statements, total deposit schedules, accounting records, and reports from delivery drivers.

They caught on to Winkler's method during the first efforts to reconstruct the previous two years' activity. An auditor found two checks totaling $60,000 on a Route Deposit slip but no entry in the accounts receivable brought forward for that month. (This was for July, a little over a month before Winkler was fired.) The deposit slip, someone pointed out, was not in the cashier's handwriting but Winkler's. Still, making the case would not be as simple as locating Route Deposits with checks in them. Some customers paid with checks, and the company's cashier routinely used route money to cash employees' paychecks. Thus, deposits regularly contained checks as well as cash. Examiners would have to cover each deposit and its constituent parts, and compare this against what actually hit the bank and the accounts receivable entries in the Office Deposits. Carriuolo says, "I can't tell you how many times we had to compare the deposit slips from the cashier — some of which we had, and some we didn't — with the actual composition going to the bank." Because Winkler had removed so much from the office, sometimes the only way to verify what had come through the mail was to go to customers and reconstruct payments based on their records.

Once the auditors had gone through the material, they hired Don Stine to confirm their findings and help Carriuolo make the case against Winkler. Reviewing their work, Stine agreed that approximately $350,000 had been taken and that Winkler was the man. Mogel's left themselves wide open for this hit because they had no controls covering what happened with the checks that came in the mail, in effect giving Winkler "total authority" to manipulate the accounts. Stine says the situation at Mogel's is all too common, with managers and employees not recognizing a financial crime in progress until it's too late. "There are plenty of things to alert people — missing deposit slips, cash and credit reconciliations between a company and a customer that don't match. There are signs, but it doesn't hit them in the head, and then when something comes out, they say, 'How did this happen?'" Auditors did ask by phone why customers were paying later and later, but they took Winkler's word for it when he put the delays down to computer systems and reorganizations inside the companies.

First contacts with Winkler didn't pan out. He skipped meetings, stonewalled, acted sullen and defiant. "I didn't do it," he said. "Trust me. Other people had access, they could have done it too." But Stine and Carriuolo were ready for this. Winkler admitted that several clerks and cashiers had worked at Mogel's during a two-year period, but that losses had occurred continually. Unless the company was consistently hiring crooks in those positions, Carriuolo argued, the answer lay elsewhere. Besides, the manipulations required someone with accounting skills above the level of the average clerk. The one constant, it turns out, was Stefan Winkler. Two other workers had actually been there during the entire time period, but they had neither the access nor the skills necessary to redirect cash flow on the scale that had occurred.

And there was the physical evidence. When he came to Mogel's, Winkler was in a bind. He had lost his house and his finances were a mess. But his tenure at the beverage company brought a wave of prosperity. He bought luxury watches, expensive clothing and several cars, among them a $40,000 Corvette paid for in cash. Winkler set up several businesses, including a limousine service, a jewelry distributorship, and facilities for a daycare center he planned to establish with his wife. He spent lots of money gambling, which he used as an explanation for his Rich and Famous mode of living. "I gamble a lot. I win a lot," he said. "The pit bosses in the Bahamas taught me how to play, so I win almost all the time. Simple as that. Just lucky, I guess." Stine knew this was bunk. Nobody was that lucky, not over two years. Winkler's wave of wealth pushed the "Lifestyle Changes, You Lose" button in the game of fraud examination. "You see this in many of these employee defalcation, or employee fraud, cases," comments Stine. "Someone is making $50,000 a year, but they're buying a $500,000 home, driving a $75,000 car. And unless someone died and left them an inheritance, it doesn't add up."

In the civil trial for fraud and negligence, Winkler maintained his innocence and his arrogance. Carriuolo and Stine presented evidence to show how the Route Deposits cash had been embezzled and covered for by the Office Deposits, explaining to the jury with charts and graphs and crash-course accounting presentations what crimes had occurred. The employee records and the broad authority necessary to pull the scheme off pointed the finger at Winkler. No one else, Carriuolo maintained, had the "unique access to, and knowledge of Mogel Inc.'s computerized accounting systems" besides Winkler. Winkler's response? He dismissed (or lost) his attorney and declared he would represent himself. Little or no legal expertise was necessary for his defense: "It wasn't me, it must have been one of those other guys." When he cross-examined Don Stine, who has 12 years in litigation consulting, Winkler announced he had only one question. "Mr. Stine, do you know for certain who took the money?" Stine answered, "No," not with absolute, unconditional, ontological certainty. Happy to show there was no smoking gun, Winkler rested his case.

But the jury was unconvinced by Winkler's tactics. After a brief recess, they returned a guilty verdict for the $353,000 lost by Mogel's, plus treble damages, for a total judgment of over a million dollars. And it seems that Winkler remains unreconstructed, since he was recently named in a complaint filed by the company he worked for after Mogel's. His high life keeps seeking new lows.

*****

Short-Term Skimming

Short-term skimming is not a distinct method for stealing sales and receivables, but rather a distinct way of using skimmed money. Any of the methods discussed above — unrecorded sales, understated sales, or theft of incoming checks — could be used in a short-term skimming scheme (see flowchart 3-5). The peculiar aspect to short-term skimming is that the fraudster only keeps the stolen money for a short while before eventually passing the payment on to his employer. The employee merely delays the posting.

In a short-term skimming scheme, an employee steals an incoming payment and then places the skimmed funds in an interest bearing account or in a short-term security. The employee earns interest on the skimmed payments while they remain under his control. Eventually, he withdraws the principle and applies it to the customer's account, but retains the interest for himself.

It should also be noted that payments from several sources can be routed through the employee's personal interest-bearing account where they will earn a return for the perpetrator. The proceeds from these schemes, over time, can be quite large. In Case 968 in our study, an employee made approximately $10,000 in prohibited gains by using a short-term skimming scheme.

The employees who engage in short-term schemes often do not view their activity as fraudulent because the stolen payments are eventually returned to the victim company. Everyone gets their money in the end, they believe, and the employee simply makes a little profit in between. In truth, of course, the employee is stealing the time value of the money, interest which could have been earned for his employer. The fraud is in depriving the company of the use of its money.

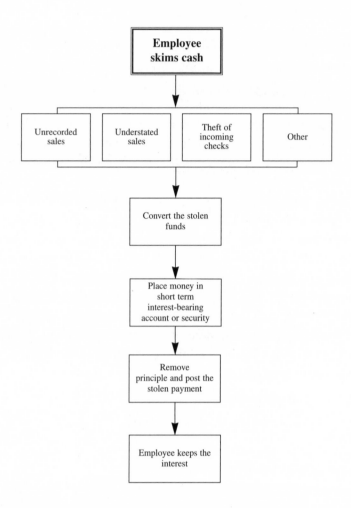

Flowchart 3-5: Short Term Skim

Converting Stolen Checks

As we have mentioned, the intelligent fraudster will generally prefer to steal currency rather than checks if given the opportunity, and the reasons why are obvious. Currency is harder to trace than a check. A cashed check eventually returns to the person who wrote it and may provide evidence of who cashed it or where it was spent. Endorsements, bank stamps and so forth may indicate the identity of the thief. Currency, on the other hand, disappears into the economy once it is stolen. One twenty dollar bill is as good as another, and unless the victim has recorded the serial numbers of his money, there is no way to determine where it has gone once someone steals it.

The second reason that currency is preferable to a check is the difficulty in converting the check. When currency is stolen it can immediately be spent. A check, on the other hand, must be endorsed and cashed or deposited before the thief can put his hands on the funds it represents. How does a fraudster go about converting a check he has skimmed?

Dual Endorsements

When checks are payable to a business, they can be endorsed by simply writing the company's name on the back of the check. The fraudster does not have to forge the signature of another person the way he would if the stolen check were payable to an individual. The problem for the employee is that this endorsement, by itself, is not sufficient for him to convert the check. The company's endorsement only provides for the check to be deposited into a company account — something that does the perpetrator no good. A second endorsement will be required if the employee is to cash the check or deposit it into an account he controls.

The problem of a second endorsement can be overcome if the fraudster has an accomplice at a check-cashing institution. In Case 1914, for instance, a trusted secretary stole over $50,000 from her employer with the aid of an accomplice in a local bank. In this case, checks were sometimes made payable to the secretary's boss individually, rather than to the partnership of which he was a part. When these checks arrived, the boss would endorse the checks and instruct his secretary to deliver them to the partnership's bookkeeper. Instead, the secretary took several of the checks to her boss's bank.

There she was able to cash the checks with the assistance of her accomplice.

In the absence of an accomplice at a check-cashing institution, however, the perpetrator will have to make a second endorsement on the back of the check, making the check payable to himself, an accomplice, or another entity. Once this is done, the employee can cash the check or deposit it into an account he controls. In Case 673, a manager skimmed checks intended for a state agency and deposited them into his own account by signing his own name as the second endorser. Because the funds in this case were not very predictable, they were not likely to be missed if stolen. Consequently, the fraudster was able to continue his scheme for approximately three years and misappropriate over $1 million.

Generally, the fraudster prefers not to endorse a stolen check in his own name. If a victim company investigates the whereabouts of missing payments, a canceled check bearing the fraudster's endorsement will leave little doubt as to his guilt. Obviously, then, it is beneficial for a fraudster to endorse stolen checks in a false name. This simple tactic leaves a gap in the audit trail between the employee and the conversion of the stolen check. We have already alluded to Case 2052, in which a mail room employee stole over $2 million in checks and used several accomplices, acting under fake names, to "launder" the check. This is an excellent example of how an employee can convert a stolen check and simultaneously conceal his identity. In that case, the stolen checks were converted by several different people, all acting under false names and using false addresses.

The trick with this sort of scheme, of course, is in opening the accounts necessary to launder the funds. Personal identification such as a driver's license and social security card in the name of the fictitious individual are usually required. When a shell company is used to launder funds, the fraudster may also need to produce articles of incorporation or an assumed name certificate for his "company." If these false documents can be obtained, the fraudster can distance himself from his crime.

It should be noted that if an employee works for a sole proprietor, incoming checks may be made out in the personal name of that proprietor. In these instances, the perpetrator will likely be able to convert stolen checks by forging that person's name (though fake i.d. in the payee's name will probably still be required).

FALSE COMPANY ACCOUNTS

Some cases involve the use of "similar name" accounts to launder skimmed funds. A similar name account is one that is opened independently of the company by the fraudster. As an illustration, suppose ABC Company, Inc.'s account is maintained at Bank A. An employee goes to Bank B and opens an account in the name of ABC Corporation, Inc. The employee would typically provide false documents to Bank B to open the account. When the employee steals checks from ABC Company, Inc., he can deposit them in his ABC Corporation, Inc. account at Bank B because of the similarity of names. Bank B will not usually question the deposit. When the check is returned to the victim company, the fraudster relies on no one noticing the difference in the endorsement.

An example of the false account method was found in Case 1224, where an employee of a hospital laboratory opened a company account at a local bank in the name of her employer. She intercepted over $180,000 worth of incoming checks and deposited them into this account. The employee was able to write checks on this "company" account to withdraw the stolen money. Canceled checks eventually revealed the existence of the fake account which the employee had opened in her own name.

A twist to the practice of converting checks through the use of fake company accounts occurred in Case 2367, where an employee discovered a seldom-used company account which management thought had been closed. No one in the company was monitoring this forgotten account. The perpetrator of the scheme, an accounts receivable employee, managed to obtain signatory authority on the forgotten account. She then stole incoming checks and deposited them into the hidden account, from which she wrote checks to extract the stolen funds.

ALTERED PAYEE DESIGNATION

A more direct way for an employee to convert a stolen check, if feasible, is to alter the check so that it is payable to that employee or one of his accomplices. In most cases, it is not possible to change the payee designation without defacing the stolen check. However, some employees in our study did manage to add their own names to stolen checks. When this is accomplished, converting the check is easy. No fake identification or hidden accounts are required; the fraudster can deposit the check directly into his own bank account. In Case 571, a credit manager picked up checks from customers and typed his own name on the face of the check above the company name. He was able to convert six checks through this method, amounting to nearly $90,000 in stolen proceeds. Eventually, however, a bank teller noticed the alteration of one of the checks and the scheme was uncovered.

Other than typing his own name on the face of stolen checks, a fraudster might "tack on" additional information to the payee designation, or simply write a new name over the existing payee. Depending on the quality of the alteration, these checks may or may not pass muster when the fraudster attempts to convert them. Most alterations to the faces of checks are noticeable and will prevent a stolen check from being converted. As a result, employees do not usually prefer this method. A more detailed discussion of alterations can be found in the Check Tampering chapter of this book.

CHECK FOR CURRENCY SUBSTITUTIONS

As the preceding discussion should illustrate, it can be quite difficult for an employee to convert a stolen check. Even when a stolen check is successfully converted, the canceled check may remain as evidence of the perpetrator's identity. As we said earlier, if possible a fraudster will usually attempt to steal currency rather than checks. Currency is instantly liquid and therefore allows the employee to forgo much of the messiness we have been discussing.

A common skimming scheme is to take unrecorded checks which the perpetrator has stolen and substitute them for receipted currency. We saw this method used by Stefan Winkler in the Mogel's case study above. Another example of a check for cash substitution was found in Case 1120, where an employee responsible for receipting ticket and fine payments on behalf of a municipality abused her position and stole incoming revenues for nearly two years. When payments in currency were received by this individual, she issued receipts, but when checks were received she did not. The check payments were therefore unrecorded revenues — ripe for skimming. These unrecorded checks were then placed in the days' receipts and an equal amount of cash was removed. The receipts matched the amount of money on hand except that payments in currency had been replaced with checks.

The check for currency substitution was very common among skimming schemes in our study. While these substitutions make it easier for a fraudster to convert stolen payments, the problem of concealing the theft still remains. The stolen checks which were not posted mean that some customers' accounts are in danger of becoming past due. If this happens, the fraudster's scheme is in danger because these customers will almost surely complain about the misapplication of their payments. The methods used by employees to deal with this and other problems are discussed below.

Concealing the Fraud

Skimming schemes are generally easier to conceal than most other types of occupational fraud. Sales skimming schemes, particularly unrecorded sales, are easily hidden because the stolen money and the transaction which generated the payment were never on the books. Therefore, there is no direct audit trail. In many skimming schemes, fraudsters take no action at all to conceal their crimes.

DESTROYING OR ALTERING RECORDS OF THE TRANSACTION

When the perpetrator does take affirmative steps to cover his tracks, one method often used is to destroy the records of the original transaction. For instance, we have already discussed the need for a salesperson to destroy the store's copy of a receipt in order for the sale to go undetected. Similarly, cash register tapes may be destroyed to hide an off-book sale. In Case 788, two management-level employees skimmed approximately $250,000 from their company over a four-year period. These employees tampered with cash register tapes that reflected transactions in which sales revenues had been skimmed. The perpetrators either destroyed entire register tapes or cut off large portions where the fraudulent transactions were recorded. In some circumstances, the employees then fabricated new tapes to match the cash on hand and make their registers appear to balance.

Discarding register tapes may signal fraud by raising suspicions that they were destroyed to conceal fraudulent transactions. Nevertheless, without the tapes it may be very difficult to reconstruct the missing transactions and prove that someone actually skimmed money. Furthermore, it may be difficult to prove who was involved in the scheme.

The fraudsters in Case 788 operated a more refined scheme than simply destroying records. By fabricating completely new tapes, the culprits were able to conceal not only their identities, but also the fraud itself. Not knowing that it was being robbed, the victim company took no action to shore up controls and prevent future thefts. Therefore, the scheme was able to continue for an extended time. It is obviously favorable for a fraudster, if possible, to keep his employer unaware that thefts are occurring. Most of the high-dollar loss schemes in our study owed their profitability, at least in part, to the quality of the concealment efforts of their perpetrators.

CONCEALING RECEIVABLES SKIMMING SCHEMES

We have alluded to the fact that skimming receivables may be more difficult to conceal than skimming sales because receivables payments are expected. The victim company knows the customer owes money and is waiting for the payment. In a revenue skimming scheme where a sale goes unrecorded, it is as though the sale never existed. Receivables skimming, by contrast, may raise questions about missing payments. When a customer's monthly payment is skimmed, the absence of the payment appears on the books as a delinquent account. In order to conceal a skimmed receivable, then, a fraudster must somehow account for the payment that was due to the company but never received.

Lapping

Lapping customer payments is one of the most common methods of concealing skimming, and may be particularly useful to employees who skim receivables. Lapping is the crediting of one account through the abstraction of money from another account. It is the fraudster's version of "robbing Peter to pay Paul." Suppose a company has three customers, A, B, and C. When A's payment is received, the fraudster takes it for himself instead of posting it to A's account. Customer A expects that his account will be credited with the payment he has made, but this payment has actually been stolen. When A's next statement arrives, he will see that his check was not applied to his account and will complain. To avoid this, some action must be taken to make it appear that the payment was posted.

When B's check arrives, the fraudster takes this money and posts it to A's account. Payments now appear to be up-to-date on A's account, but B's account is short. When C's payment is received, the perpetrator applies it to B's account. This process continues indefinitely until one of three things happens: (1) someone discovers the scheme, 2) restitution is made to the accounts, or (3) some concealing entry is made to adjust the accounts receivable balances.

In the Mogel's case study, we saw that one of the ways Stefan Winkler concealed his thefts was to lap payments on customer accounts. Lapping was perhaps the most common concealment technique for skimming schemes in our study. It should be noted that, while more commonly used to conceal skimmed receivables, lapping can also be used to disguise the skimming of sales. In Case 2128, for instance, a store manager stole daily receipts and replaced them with the following day's incoming cash. She progressively delayed the banking as more and more money was taken. Each time a day's receipts were stolen, it took an extra day of collections to cover the missing money. Eventually, the banking irregularities became so great that an investigation was commenced. It was discovered that the manager had stolen nearly $30,000 and concealed the theft by lapping her store's sales.

Because lapping schemes can become very intricate, fraudsters sometimes keep a second set of books on hand detailing the true nature of the payments received. In many skimming cases, a search of the fraudster's work area will reveal a set of records tracking the actual payments made and how they have been misapplied to conceal the theft. It may seem odd that someone would keep records of their illegal activity on hand, but many lapping schemes become complicated as more and more payments are misapplied. The second set of records helps the perpetrator keep track of what funds he has stolen and what accounts need to be credited to conceal the fraud. Uncovering these records, if they exist, will greatly aid the investigation of a lapping scheme.

The most extreme version of how to conceal a lapping scheme I ever investigated involved an employee of a data processing company. Nelson was his name. The company he worked for essentially acted as in-house data processors for a variety of banks and other financial institutions.

Nelson was one of the original employees of this now multibillion-dollar firm with three initials. He had been with the company for nearly 10 years when he began stealing. The company, it seems, wanted to promote Nelson from their Dallas office to be the chief programmer for one of their largest clients, a bank in New Orleans.

The company provided Nelson a $15,000 advance to make the move. It was supposed to be repaid after he sold his house in Dallas. But the company didn't know that Nelson was in debt up to his eyeballs, with creditors calling him constantly. So he took the money from the sale of his house in Dallas and paid as many debts as he could.

When the company didn't get back their money on time, they began applying pressure to Nelson. He agreed to pay out the loan on an installment basis, then promptly gave them a rubber check for his first payment. His manager called him in and said, "Nelson, Dallas has called again about this loan. Let me put it in terms you can understand: you have 30 days to pay off this loan or the company is going to make me fire you." Nelson understood.

The first thing he did was open a checking account under the name of an uncle at his client bank in New Orleans. Once that was done, he started engaging in a series of programming tricks to move money into and out of the uncle's account, over which he had signature authority. The money ultimately came out of the accounts of real bank customers.

The programming trick was to remove money, not directly from the checking account itself, but from one of the fields on the customer's account statement. More specifically, Nelson programmed his computer to debit the ending balance field of the individual account statement the day after the customer's monthly statement was mailed to him. That gave Nelson exactly 29 days to reverse the entry before the next statement would be mailed.

Nelson chose the ending balance field on the statement because it did not leave a trail on the customer's statement the following month—provided he moved the money back to the account on the 29th day. If he had simply debited the customer's checking account itself, the computer would automatically print the transaction on the depositor's statement, thereby causing suspicion.

The scheme itself was made possible by the fact that the bank's computers were programmed to close and mail a portion of the customers' monthly statement each business day of the month. While customer Adams would get his statement on the first of the month, customer Zane would receive his the last of the month.

So Nelson wrote his own little program to track the movement of money in and out of customer accounts. His computer would tell him when it was time to move money from the Adams account to the Zane account. This is complicated enough when one is only dealing with one transaction. But how about hundreds? Nelson didn't stop with "borrowing" enough money to pay back the company, he eventually "lent" himself money from customer accounts to bail him out of debt.

Nelson's downfall came when it was inadvertently discovered that his "how-to-move-money-around" program had some sort of logic error embedded in it. As a result, a customer received a statement for May with an ending balance of $1,300. But her June statement reflected a beginning balance of $500. The bank, assuming the problem was a programming error by the data processing servicing company, gave the statement to Nelson's boss. The boss also assumed it was a programming error, and gave the statements to Nelson. His face went white right in front of the boss.

The following days, many more customers started receiving nonsensical checking account statements, and Nelson's boss finally figured out what was going on. I was called in as a private fraud examiner to document the case and work with the lawyers and authorities. Nelson fully confessed, and helped me gather the documentary evidence to convict him. Because of the way the money was bouncing around from account to account, it would have taken me weeks to figure it out by myself. He had stolen about $150,000 in total.

Nelson's cooperation in documenting the losses didn't cut much soap with the judge, who sent the family man to prison for a year or two. The last I heard—and this crime occurred in the mid eighties—was that Nelson had been released from the joint and was working as an accountant for the Jimmy Swaggart Ministries. I kid you not.

Stolen Statements

Another method used by employees to conceal the misapplication of customer payments is the theft or alteration of account statements. If a customer's payments are stolen and not posted, his account will become delinquent. When this happens, he should receive late notices or statements which reflect that his account is past due. The purpose of altering a customer's statements is to keep him from complaining about the misapplication of his payments.

To keep a customer unaware about the true status of his account, some fraudsters will intercept his account statements or late notices. This might be accomplished, for instance, by changing the customer's address in the billing system. The statements will be sent directly to the employee's home or to an address where he can retrieve them. In other cases the address is changed so that the statement is undeliverable, which causes the statements to be returned to the fraudster's desk. In either situation, once the employee has access to the statements, he can do one of two things. The first option is to throw the statements away. This is not particularly effective, since at some point the customer is likely to request information on his account if he does not receive a statement.

Therefore, the fraudster usually alters the statements or produces counterfeit statements to make it appear that the customer's payments have been properly posted. The employee then sends these fake statements to the customer. The false statements lead the customer to believe that his account is up-to-date and keep him from complaining about stolen payments.

False Account Entries

Intercepting the customer's statements will keep him in the dark as to the status of his account, but the problem still remains that as long as the customer's payments are being skimmed, his account is slipping further and further past due. The fraudster must find some way to bring the account back up-to-date in order to conceal his crime. As we have discussed, lapping is one way to keep accounts current as the employee skims from them. Another way is to make false entries in the victim company's accounting system.

Debit Accounts

An employee might conceal the skimming of funds by making unsupported entries in the victim company's books. If a payment is made on a receivable, for instance, the proper entry is a debit to cash and a credit to the receivable. Instead of debiting cash, the fraudster might choose to debit an expense account. This transaction still keeps the company's books in balance, but the incoming cash is never recorded. In addition, the customer's receivable account is credited, so it will not become delinquent.

Debiting Existing or Fictitious Accounts

The same method discussed above is used when fraudsters debit existing or fictitious accounts receivable in order to conceal skimmed cash. In Case 1996, for example, an office manager in a health care facility took payments from patients for herself. To conceal her activity, the office manager added the amounts taken to the accounts of other patients which she knew would soon be written off as uncollectible. The employees who use this method generally add the skimmed balances to accounts which are either very large or which are aging and about to be written off. Increases in the balances of these accounts are not as noticeable as in other accounts. In the case above, once the old accounts were written off, the stolen funds would be written off along with them.

Rather than existing accounts, some fraudsters set up completely fictitious accounts and debit them for the cost of skimmed receivables. The employees then simply wait for the fictitious receivables to age and be written off, knowing that they are uncollectable. In the meantime, they carry the cost of a skimming scheme where it will not be detected.

Writing Off Account Balances

In Case 2435, an employee skimmed cash collections and wrote off the related receivables as "bad debts." Similarly, in Case 442, a billing manager was authorized to write off certain patient balances as hardship allowances. This employee accepted payments from patients, then instructed billing personnel to write off the balance in question. The payments were never posted; they were intercepted by the billing manager. She covered approximately $30,000 in stolen funds by using her authority to write off patients' balances.

Instead of writing off accounts as bad debts, some employees cover their skimming by posting entries to contra revenue accounts such as "discounts and allowances." If, for instance, an employee intercepts a $1,000 payment, he would create a $1,000 "discount" on the account to compensate for the missing money.

INVENTORY PADDING

A major concealment problem for fraudsters is a company's inventory, if it has one. Off-book sales of goods will always leave an inventory shortage and a corresponding rise in the cost of goods sold. When a sale of goods is made, the physical inventory is reduced by the amount of merchandise sold. If a retailer sells a pair of shoes, for instance, it has one less pair of shoes in the stock room. However, if this sale is unrecorded, the shoes remain on the inventory records.

Thus, there is one less pair of shoes on hand than the records indicate. Such a reduction in the physical inventory without a corresponding reduction in the perpetual inventory is known as "shrinkage."

When an employee skims sales of services there is no shrinkage (because there is no inventory for services), but when sales of goods are skimmed, shrinkage always occurs. Some amounts of shrinkage are expected due to customer theft, faulty products, and spoilage, but high levels of shrinkage serve as a warning that a company could be a victim of occupational fraud. The general methods used to conceal inventory shrinkage are discussed in detail in the Inventory and Other Assets chapter of this book.

Conclusion
DETECTION
The following are some detection methods that may be effective in detecting skimming schemes.

Receipt or Sales Level Detection
- Key analytical procedures, such as vertical and horizontal analysis of sales accounts, can be used for skimming detection on a grand scale. These procedures analyze changes in the accounts and can possibly point to skimming problems including understated sales.
- Ratio analysis can also provide keys to the detection of skimming schemes. These procedures are discussed in detail in the fraudulent financial statement section of the book.
- Detailed inventory control procedures can also be utilized to detect inventory shrinkage due to unrecorded sales. Inventory detection methods include statistical sampling, trend analysis, reviews of receiving reports and inventory records, and verification of material requisition and shipping documentation as well as actual physical inventory counts. These procedures are reviewed in the chapter on inventory and other asset schemes.

Check Conversion Detection

Red flags may arise when an employee attempts to convert a stolen check.

- A bank or check cashing institution employee questions the validity of the check.
- A dual endorsement is not allowed or causes check verification at the cashing institution.
- Canceled checks with dual endorsements should be scrutinized.
- A forged endorsement is discovered.
- It is discovered that an employee has opened a bank account with a name similar to the victim company.
- An alteration of the check payee or endorsement is discovered.
- Additional conversion detection techniques are found in the check-tampering chapter.

Journal Entry Review

Skimming frauds can sometimes be detected by reviewing and analyzing all journal entries made to the cash and inventory accounts. Journal entries involving the following topics should be examined:

- False credits to inventory to conceal unrecorded or understated sales
- Other write-offs of inventory for reason of lost, stolen, or obsolete product
- Write-offs of accounts receivable accounts
- Irregular entries to cash accounts

PREVENTION

Receipt of Sales Level Control

As with most fraud schemes, internal control procedures are a key to prevention of skimming schemes. An essential part of developing control procedures is management's communication to employees. Controlling whether or not an employee will not record a sale, understate a sale, or steal incoming payments is extremely difficult.

Check Conversion Controls

Banks and other financial institutions have stepped up detection and prevention methods. But as with most things, the criminal element is usually one step ahead. Companies should work in a cooperative effort with banks to prevent check fraud. Additional check conversion and tampering controls are detailed in the chapter on check tampering.

General Controls

Sales entries and general ledger access controls should include documented policies and procedures, which are communicated directly from management. The control procedures will generally cover the following subjects:

- Appropriate segregation of duties and access control procedures regarding who makes ledger transactions will be followed.
- Transactions must be properly recorded as to amount, date of occurrence, and ledger account.
- Proper safeguard measures will be adopted to insure physical access to the account systems. Additional measures should insure the security of company assets.
- Independent reconciliations as well as internal verification of accounts will be performed on ledger accounts.[2]

Skimming Controls

The discovery of thefts of checks and cash involves proper controls on the receipt process. Deficiencies in the answers to these typical audit-program questions may be red flags.

- Is mail opened by someone independent of cashier, accounts receivable bookkeeper, or other accounting employees who may initiate or post journal entries?
- Is the delivery of unopened business mail prohibited to employees having access to the accounting records?
- Does the employee who opens the mail:
    Place restrictive endorsements ("For Deposit Only") on all checks received?
    Prepare a list of the money, checks, and other receipts?
    Forward all remittances to the person responsible for preparing and making the daily bank deposit?
    Forward the total of all remittances to the person re-

sponsible for comparing it to the authenticated deposit ticket and amount recorded?

- Is a lock box used?
- Do cash sales occur? If yes:
     Are cash receipts prenumbered?
     Is an independent check of prenumbered receipts done daily and reconciled to cash collections?
     Do cash refunds require approval?
- Are cash receipts deposited intact daily?
- Are employees who handle receipts bonded?
- Is the accounts receivable bookkeeper restricted from:
     Preparing the bank deposit?
     Obtaining access to the cash receipts book?
     Having access to collections from customers?
- Are banks instructed not to cash checks drawn to the order of the company?
- Is the cashier restricted from gaining access to the accounts receivable records and bank and customer statements?
- Are areas where physical handling of cash takes place reasonably safeguarded?
- Is the person make postings to the general ledger independent of the cash receipts and accounts receivable functions?
- Does a person independent of the cashier or accounts receivable functions handle customer complaints?[3]

[1] Association of Certified Fraud Examiners, Fraud Examiners' Manual (Austin: ACFE, 1996).

[2] George Georgiades, Audit Procedures (New York: Harcourt Brace Professional Publishing, 1995).

[3] Georgiades.

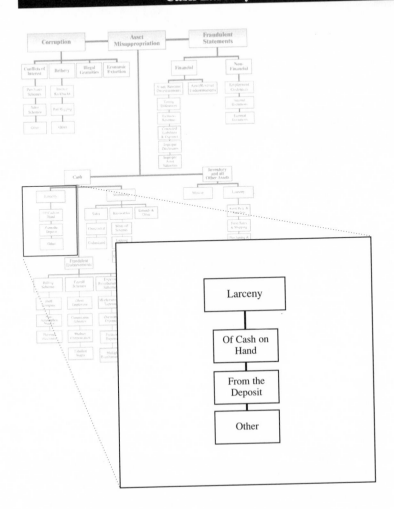

Larceny

Of Cash on Hand

From the Deposit

Other

4. CASH LARCENY

*****

Case Study: Bank Teller Gets Nabbed For Theft

*Several names have been changed to preserve anonymity

Laura Grove worked at Rocky Mountain Bank in Nashville, Tennessee, for five years. As a teller, she thought to herself, she wasn't getting any richer. She and her husband owed about $14,000 in credit card bills, which seemed to get higher and higher each month, especially after adopting a five-year-old girl the year before.

When she transferred to a branch bank in Cheetboro, Tennessee, the bank promoted her to head teller. In this new position, Laura had authority to open the night depository vault with another teller. For security reasons, the bank allowed each teller to possess only half of the combination to the vault.

Every morning, Laura saw the bank night deposit vault door open and close, after the removal of all customer night deposit bags. The bank placed only one camera on the night vault, which was turned on at 8:00 a.m. when the bank opened for business.

Laura thought it would be easy to get into the night depository and take the bags. These thoughts were reinforced when a customer reported his bag missing and the bank quickly paid his money without a thorough investigation. So one Friday morning, Laura made up her mind that she could take about $15,000 with little risk of being identified. But before she actually took the money, she observed. When she opened the night vault with her coworker Frank Geffen, she saw him dial the first half of the combination and was careful to memorize the numbers. After entering the second half of the combination, they opened it as usual, removed and listed each night deposit bag, and shut the vault behind them. This time, however, Laura did not lock the vault.

Here, Laura made her first mistake. She thought she could leave the vault door open and return Monday to take the money. But just before the bank closed and employees prepared to leave, teller Melissa Derkstein checked the vault one more time. Seeing that the vault was open, she spun the dial, shaking the handle to ensure the door was locked.

Laura and the other bank employees punched their security codes on the outside door and left for the day. During the weekend, Laura considered her plot. Should she enter the combination by herself this time and place the money into a personal tote bag? Should she stay at work all day with the goods underneath her feet?

Monday morning, she still was not sure how to pull it off but had resolved to go through with the plan anyway. Arriving at 7:15 a.m., Laura was the first person in the bank that morning. After punching in her security code, she placed her tote bag and personal belongings on her chair. Immediately, she went to the night vault and dialed the full combination. Nothing happened. Her mind raced. "Maybe this won't work; this is too risky." Her fingers tried the combination again, and once again, until she heard a click and the vault opened.

Inside, Laura removed the two customer deposit bags, ones that she knew contained large sums of cash. She placed both bags in her tote bag and walked back to her teller window. She stuffed her Weight Watchers book and purse inside the tote bag, on top of the deposit bags. She then hung her bag on the door of the storage room and returned to the teller window, straightening up her work area.

Fifteen minutes later, the branch manager, Harvey Lebrand, entered, looking startled that Laura was already at her desk. He asked Laura why she had come into work so early this Monday.

"Oh, I just needed to get organized early, because I need to take my Bronco into the shop later today and knew I wouldn't have much time," Laura said.

"You need to get your truck repaired?" Mr. Lebrand asked. "Why don't you go now?"

"Okay, I can get my mother to give me a ride back," Laura said. "See you soon, Mr. Lebrand."

Laura rushed to the storage area, grabbed the tote bag and left the bank. She drove directly to her home and emptied the contents of the bag, watching the many bills and checks spill onto her bed. She lit up with uneasy excitement. Sorting the checks into a separate pile, she gathered the money into a large heap and did a quick count. She estimated she had taken about $15,000. Placing the bills into manila envelopes, she hid them in the headboard storage compartment of the bed. The checks were placed in a small plastic bag. She then phoned her mother and asked her to meet her at the Sears Auto Center.

Laura knew there was an apartment complex next to Sears that had a large blue dumpster. After the checks had been deposited in the dumpster, Laura drove to Sears. Her mother arrived a little later to take her back to work.

A day later, Rocky Mountain Bank Audit Investigator Stacy Boone received a call from Laura's manager, informing her that two customers had not gotten credit for the deposits they'd made the night before. Each deposit was for $8,000.

Boone's investigation quickly led her to suspect Grove. The first one in the bank that morning, Grove also came in before the surveillance cameras turned on. As head teller, she had one-half of the combination to the night depository. Other employees said they "didn't trust her." But when the investigators questioned her, Grove strongly denied any knowledge of the theft.

"During our interview with her, she broke out in a red rash," which suggested stress. "I have seen innocent people break out into a red rash, but she was the only one we interviewed that day who did," Boone said.

Boone also suspected Grove because the branch bank from which she'd transfered "had a lot of unexplained shortages, and she was a suspect there, but we could never pin down that she took the money. She had bought a lot of new jewelry, wore a lot of expensive clothes, but had filed bankruptcy at one point that year."

The investigation came to a swift conclusion, however, when Boone received a call on her answering machine from Grove's husband, a former neighbor. "I was afraid he wanted to know why we were investigating his wife, and hesitated to call him right back," Boone said.

Boone decided she "might as well get this over with and tell him I could not talk about it [the investigation]. When I called him, he told me he found the bank's money in his attic and suspected his wife. His wife had told him of the bank's investigation, but had not admitted any theft.

"Their daughter had overheard a conversation they had the day of the theft" in which Laura had expressed anxiety to her husband about the bank's investigation, Boone said. "His daughter had told him that she saw [Laura] put something in the attic. So, when she wasn't there, the husband went up in the attic and looked, and found two bags of money."

Boone said the husband was also suspicious because his wife had lied to him before. "He told me that his mother-in-law, her mother, always won all these prizes. She had even won a car through a contest. One night, he came home and found a TV-VCR sitting on a table, and asked his wife where it came from. She said 'Oh, mom won that.' At the time, he really didn't think anything about it. But a couple days later, Kirby's Electronics, where the TV came from, called in regards to her credit application. They told him that she charged that TV and VCR."

Faced with this evidence, Laura and her husband delivered the $16,000 in cash as restitution. The bank dismissed Grove and she was prosecuted for the crime but received probation in lieu of prison time.

A year later, Boone received a call from one of the bank's tellers who saw Grove working at another bank in a small city outside of Nashville. Boone called one of the personnel employees there and talked with her. "They were a bank that did not do fingerprint checks, so they had no knowledge that she had been convicted. She did get into another bank to work, but not for very long."

Boone said the bank reviewed its operational procedures and internal controls after the incident. "One of the procedures they stressed [with bank employees] is not letting anyone stand over you when you are entering your combination," she said. Also, the bank issued a new requirement that the first employee to enter in the morning must give an "all clear" signal to a co-worker before entering.

*****

Overview

In the occupational fraud setting, a *cash larceny* may be defined as the intentional taking away of an employer's cash (the term *cash* includes both currency and checks) without the consent and against the will of the employer. In the case study above, Laura Grove's theft of approximately $16,000 from her employer is an example of a cash larceny.

How do cash larceny schemes differ from other cash frauds? In order to understand the distinction in our classifications, it is helpful first to break down the cash schemes into two broad groups, the first being *the fraudulent disbursement schemes* and the second being what we will loosely term the *theft schemes*. Fraudulent disbursement schemes are those in which a distribution of funds is made from some company account in what appears to be a normal manner. The method for obtaining the funds may be the forging of a check, the submission of a false invoice, the doctoring of a timecard and so forth. The key is that the money is removed from the company in what appears to be a legitimate disbursement of funds. Fraudulent disbursements will be discussed later in this book.

Theft schemes, on the other hand, are what we typically think of as the outright stealing of cash. The perpetrator does not rely on the submission of phony documents or the forging of signatures; he simply grabs the cash and takes it. The theft schemes fall into two categories: *skimming*, which we have already discussed, and *larceny schemes*. Remember that skimming was defined as the theft of off-book funds. Cash larceny schemes, on the other hand, involve the theft of money that has already appeared on a victim company's books.

Because the cash stolen by an employee in a larceny scheme has already been recorded, its absence ought to be more easily detectable than the off-book funds taken in a skimming scheme. Consequently, we would expect larceny schemes to be less common and less successful than skimming schemes. This assumption is validated by the results of our study, in which cash larceny schemes comprised only 2.95% of the cases (see chart 1-6). These cases comprised less than 1% of the total losses reported (see chart 1-4), with a median loss of $22,000 (see chart 1-5), which is the third lowest among all the fraud types we have identified.

A cash larceny scheme can take place in any circumstance in which an employee has access to cash. Every company must deal with the receipt, deposit, and distribution of cash (if not, it certainly won't be a very long-lived company!) so every company is potentially vulnerable to a cash larceny scheme. While the circumstances in which an employee might steal cash are nearly limitless, most larceny schemes involve the theft of incoming cash, currency on hand (in a cash register, cash box, etc.), or theft of cash from the victim company's bank deposits.

Theft of Cash from the Register	Other Larceny of Sales and Receivables	Cash Larceny from the Deposit

Incoming Cash

THEFT OF CASH FROM THE REGISTER

A large percentage of the cash larceny schemes in our survey occurred at the cash register, and for good reason — the register is where the currency is. The register (or similar cash collection points like cash drawers or cash boxes) is usually the most common point of access to ready cash for employees, so it is understandable that the register is where larceny schemes frequently occur. Furthermore, there is often a great deal of activity at the register and multiple transactions requiring the handling of cash by employees. This activity can serve as a cover for the theft of cash. In a flurry of activity, with cash being passed back and forth between customer and employee, a fraudster is more likely to be able to slip currency out of the register and into his pocket without getting caught.

This is the most straightforward scheme; open the register up and remove currency (see flowchart 4-2). It might be done as a sale is being conducted to make the theft appear to be part of the transaction, or perhaps when no one is around to notice the perpetrator digging into the cash drawer. In Case 1252, for instance, a teller simply signed onto a register, rang a "no sale" and took currency from the drawer. Over a period of time, the teller took approximately $6,000 through this simple method.

Recall that the benefit of a skimming scheme is that the transaction is unrecorded and the stolen funds are never entered on company books. The employee who is skimming either underrings the register transaction so that a portion of the sale is unrecorded, or he completely omits the sale by failing to enter it at all on his register. This makes the skimming scheme difficult to detect because the register tape does not reflect the presence of the funds which have been taken. In a larceny scheme, on the other hand, the funds which the perpetrator steals are already reflected on the register tape. As a result, an imbalance will result between the register tape and the cash drawer. This imbalance should be a signal that alerts a victim company to the theft.

The actual method for taking money at the register — opening the register and removing currency — rarely varies. It is the methods used by fraudsters to avoid getting caught that distinguish larceny schemes. Oddly, in many instances the perpetrator has no plan for avoiding detection. A large part of fraud is rationalizing; the fraudster convinces himself that he is somehow entitled to what he is taking, or that what he is doing is not actually a crime. Register larceny schemes frequently begin when the perpetrator convinces himself that he is only "borrowing" the funds to cover a temporary monetary need. These people might carry the missing currency in their registers for several days, deluding themselves in the belief that they will one day repay the funds and hoping their employers will not perform a surprise cash count on their register until the missing money is replaced.

The employee who does nothing to camouflage his crimes is easily caught; more dangerous is the person taking active steps to hide his misdeeds. One basic way for an employee to disguise the fact that he is stealing currency is to take money from someone else's register. In some retail organizations, employees are assigned to certain registers. Alternatively, one register is used and each employee has an access code. When cash is missing from a cashier's register, the most likely suspect for the theft is obviously that cashier. Therefore, by stealing from another's register, or by using someone else's access code, the fraudster makes sure that another employee will be the prime suspect in the theft. In Case 1252 discussed above, for example, the employee who stole money did so by waiting until another teller was on break, then logging onto that teller's register, ringing a "no sale" and taking the cash. The resulting cash shortage therefore appeared in the register of an honest employee, deflecting attention from the true thief. In another case we reviewed, Case 2127, a cash office manager stole over $8,000, in part by taking money from cash registers and making it appear that the cashiers were stealing.

A very unsophisticated way to avoid detection is to steal currency in very small amounts over an extended period of time. This is the "death by a thousand cuts" larceny scheme. Fifteen dollars here, twenty dollars there, and slowly, as in Case 709, the culprit bleeds his company. Because the missing amounts are small, the shortages may be credited to errors rather than theft. Typically, the employee becomes dependent on the extra money he is pilfering and his thefts increase in scale or become more frequent, which causes the scheme to be uncovered. Most retail organizations track overages or shortages by employee, making this method largely ineffectual.

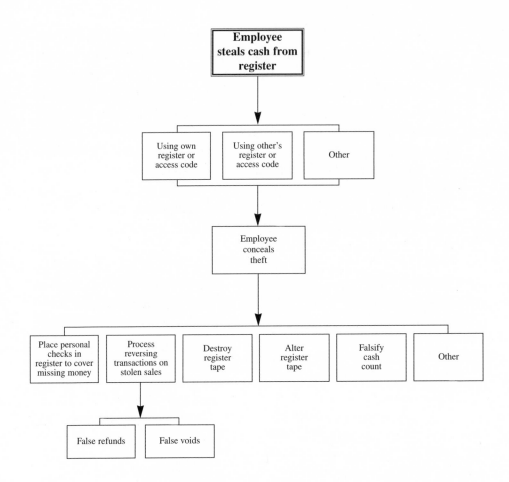

Flowchart 4-2: Cash Larceny from the Register

A register is balanced by comparing the transactions on the register tape to the amount of cash on hand. Starting at a known balance, sales, returns, and other register transactions are added to or subtracted from the balance to arrive at a total for the period in question. The actual cash is then counted and the two totals are compared. If the register tape shows that there should be more cash in the register than what is present, it may be because of larceny.

Personal Checks

One way for employees to conceal larceny schemes is to leave personal checks in their registers to cover the amount of money they have stolen. The employee writes a personal check for the missing amount and places it in his cash drawer so that the register is always in balance. This method is used to avoid the danger of a larceny scheme being discovered during a surprise cash count. (Of course, the presence of the employee's personal check in the register might itself raise concerns of theft). The employee obviously never allows his check to be deposited, so the "balance" on the register is really an illusion.

In Case 1177, a bank teller used a similar concealment method, but instead of a personal check she used a transfer ticket to cover the cash she had stolen. A transfer ticket is a document in a teller's cash drawer which shows that a certain amount of money was transferred to another location. It is a debit to the drawer of the teller who holds the ticket, and a credit to the teller who receives the cash in exchange for the ticket. The teller in the aforementioned case stole over $57,000 and was not detected for a little more than a year as she carried a transfer ticket in her drawer for the amount which she had embezzled. Though her cash was counted quarterly by management, the fraudulent transfer ticket was not validated. In other words, no one traced the offsetting credit on the ticket to another teller. Had they done so, the fraud would have easily been discovered.

Reversing Transactions

Another way to conceal a cash larceny is to use reversing transactions, which cause the register tape to reconcile to the amount of cash on hand after the theft. By processing false voids or refunds, an employee can reduce the amount of cash reflected on the register tape. For instance, in Case 2147, a cashier received payments from a customer and recorded the transactions on her system. She stole the payments from the customers, then destroyed the company's receipts which reflected the transactions. To complete the cover-up, the cashier went back and voided the transactions which she had entered at the time the payments were received. The reversing entries brought the receipt totals into balance with the cash on hand. (These schemes will be discussed in more detail in the Register Disbursement Schemes chapter of this book.)

Instead of using reversing entries, some employees manually alter the register tape or the cash count. Again, the purpose of this activity is to force a balance between the cash on hand and the actual cash received over the period. An employee might use white-out to cover up a sale whose proceeds were stolen, or simply cross out or alter the numbers on the tape so that the register total and the cash drawer balance. A department manager altered and destroyed cash register tapes in Case 788 to help conceal a fraud scheme that went on for four years.

Altering Cash Counts

Instead of falsifying the company's record of receipts, some fraudsters alter the cash counts on their registers. An employee in Case 1806, for example, not only discarded register tapes to conceal her thefts, but also erased and rewrote cash counts for the registers from which she pilfered. The new totals on the cash count envelopes were overstated by the amount of money she had stolen, reflecting the actual receipts for the period and balancing with the cash register tapes. Under the victim company's controls, this employee was not supposed to have access to cash. Ironically, coworkers praised her dedication for helping them count cash when it was not one of her official duties.

Destroying Register Tapes

If the fraudster cannot make the cash and the tape balance, the next best thing is to prevent others from computing the totals and discovering the imbalance. Employees who are stealing from the register sometimes destroy detail tapes which would implicate them in a crime. When detail tapes are missing or defaced, it may be because someone does not want the information on them to be known.

OTHER LARCENY OF SALES AND RECEIVABLES

Not all receipts arrive via the cash register. Though most of the larceny schemes in our study involved the theft of cash from the register, there is no reason that employees cannot steal money received at other points. One of the more common methods for those stealing incoming money is to post the customer's payment to the accounting system but take the cash (see flowchart 4-3). In Case 2758, for example, an employee posted all records of customer payments to date, but stole the money received. In a four month period, this employee took over $200,000 in incoming payments. Consequently, the cash account was significantly out of balance, which led to discovery of the fraud. This was one of the cases in our study, incidentally, in which the employee justified the theft by saying she planned to pay the money back. This case illustrates the central weakness of cash larceny schemes — the resulting imbalances in company accounts. One may notice that the previous case is very similar to many of the skimming schemes discussed in the skimming chapter of this book, except that in those frauds the stolen receipts were not posted to the cash receipts journal.

The problem of out-of-balance accounts can be overcome by those fraudsters who have total control of a company's accounting system. In Case 1663, an employee stole customer payments and posted them to the accounts receivable journal in the same manner as the fraudster discussed in Case 2758 above. As in the previous case, this employee's fraud resulted in an imbalance in the victim company's cash account. The difference between the two frauds is that the perpetrator of Case 1663 had control over the company's deposits and all its ledgers. She was therefore able to conceal her crime by making unsupported entries in the company's books which produced a fictitious balance between receipts and ledgers. This case illustrates how poor separation of duties can allow the perpetuation of a fraud which, ordinarily, would be easy to detect.

In circumstances in which payments are stolen but nonetheless posted to the cash receipts journal, reversing entries can be used to balance the victim company's accounts. For instance, in Case 1886, an office manager stole approximately $75,000 in customer payments from her employer. Her method in a number of these cases was to post the payment to the customer's account, then later reverse the entry on the books with unauthorized adjustments such as "courtesy discounts."

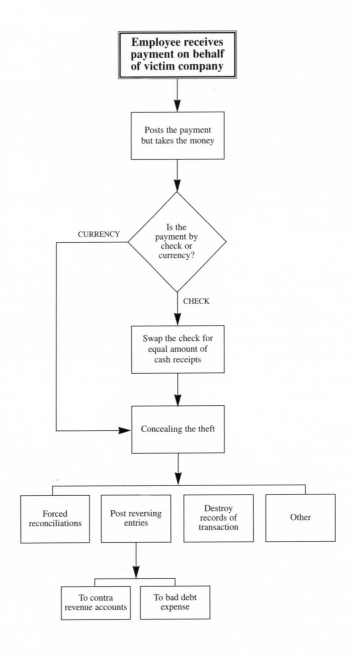

Flowchart 4-3: Other Cash Larceny

A less elegant way to hide a crime is to simply destroy all records which might prove that the perpetrator has been stealing. Destroying records en masse does not prevent the victim company from realizing that it is being robbed, but it may help conceal the identity of the thief. This "slash and burn" concealment strategy was used by a controller in Case 1550. The controller, who had complete control over the books of her employer, stole approximately $100,000. When it became evident that her superiors were suspicious of her activities, the perpetrator entered her office one night after work, stole all the cash on hand, destroyed all records, including her personnel file, and left town.

Cash Larceny from The Deposit

At some point in every revenue-generating business, someone must physically take the company's currency and checks to the bank. This person or persons, left alone literally holding the bag, will have an opportunity to take a portion of the money prior to depositing it into the company's accounts.

Typically, when cash is received by a company, someone is assigned to tabulate the receipts, list the form of payment (currency or check), and prepare a deposit slip for the bank. Then another employee, preferably one who was not involved in the preparing of the deposit slip, takes the cash and deposits it in the bank. One copy of the slip is generally retained by the person who made out the deposit. This copy is matched to a receipted copy of the slip stamped by the bank when the deposit is made.

This procedure is designed to prevent theft of funds from the deposit, but thefts still occur, often because the process is not adhered to (see flowchart 4-4). In Case 1277, for example, an employee in a small company was responsible for preparing and making the deposits, recording the deposits in the company's books, and reconciling the bank statements. This employee took several thousand dollars from the company deposits and concealed it by making false entries in the books which corresponded to falsely prepared deposit slips. Similarly, in a retail store where cash registers were not used — in Case 2833 — sales were recorded on prenumbered invoices. The controller of this organization was responsible for collecting cash receipts and making the bank deposits. This controller was also the only person who reconciled the totals on the prenumbered receipts to the bank deposit. Therefore, he was able to steal a portion of the deposit with the knowledge that the discrepancy between the deposit and the day's receipts would not be detected.

Another oversight in procedure is failure to reconcile the bank copy of the deposit slip with the office copy. When the person making the deposit knows his company does not reconcile the two copies, he can steal cash from the deposit on the way to the bank and alter the deposit slip so that it reflects a lesser amount. In some cases sales records will also be altered to match the diminished deposit.

When cash is stolen from the deposit, the receipted deposit slip will of course be out of balance with the company's copy of the deposit slip (unless the perpetrator also prepared the deposit). To correct this problem, some fraudsters alter the bank copy of the deposit slip after it has been validated. This brings the two copies back into balance. In Case 1446, for example, an employee altered 24 deposit slips and validated bank receipts in the course of a year to conceal the theft of over $15,000. These documents were altered with white-out or ball point pen to match the company's cash reports. Of course, cash having been stolen, the company's book balance will not match its actual bank balance. If the checking account is regularly balanced by another employee, this theft should be easily detected.

Another mistake which can be made in the deposit function, one that is a departure from common sense, is entrusting the deposit to the wrong person. For instance, in Case 693, a bookkeeper who had been employed for only one month was put in charge of making the deposit. She promptly diverted the funds to her own use. This is not to say that all new employees are untrustworthy, but it is advisable to have some sense of a person's character before handing that person a bag full of money.

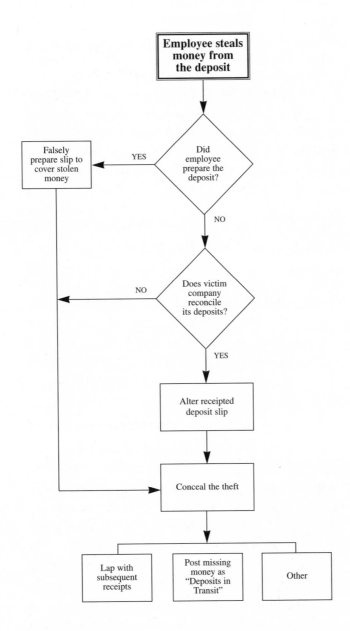

Flowchart 4-4: Cash Larceny from the Deposit

Still another common sense issue is the handling of the deposit on the way to the bank. Once prepared, the deposit should immediately be put in a safe place until it is taken to the bank. In a few of the cases we studied, the deposit was left carelessly unattended. In Case 2232, for example, a part-time employee learned that it was the bookkeeper's habit to leave the bank bag in her desk overnight before depositing it the following morning. For approximately six months, this employee pilfered checks from the deposit and got away with it. He was able to endorse the checks at a local establishment, without using his own signature, in the name of the victim company. The owner of the check cashing institution did not question the fact that this individual was cashing company checks because, as a pastor of a sizable church in the community, the fraudster's integrity was thought to be above reproach.

As with all cash larceny schemes, stealing from the company deposit can be rather difficult to conceal. In most cases these schemes are only successful for a long term when the person who counts the cash also makes the deposit. In any other circumstance the success of the scheme depends primarily on the inattentiveness of those charged with preparing and reconciling the deposit.

Deposit Lapping

One method we have identified which in some cases is successfully used to evade detection is the lapping method. Lapping occurs when an employee steals the deposit from day one, then replaces it with day two's deposit. Day two is replaced with day three, and so on. The perpetrator is always one day behind, but as long as no one demands an up-to-the minute reconciliation of the deposits to the bank statement and if the size of the deposits does not drop precipitously, he may be able to avoid detection for a period of time. In Case 1993, a company officer stole cash receipts from the company deposit and withheld the deposit for a time. Eventually the deposit was made and the missing cash was replaced with a check received at a later day. Lapping is discussed in more detail in the skimming chapter of this book.

Deposits in Transit

A final concealment strategy with stolen deposits is to carry the missing money as deposits in transit. In Case 1716, an employee was responsible for receiving collections, issuing receipts, posting transactions, reconciling accounts, and making deposits. Such a lack of separation of duties leaves a company extremely vulnerable to fraud. This employee took over $20,000 in collections from her employer over a five-month period. To hide her theft, the perpetrator carried the missing money as deposits in transit, meaning that the missing money would appear on the next month's bank statement. Of course, it never did. The balance was carried for several months as "d.i.t." until an auditor recognized the discrepancy and put a halt to the fraud.

The following case study has been selected as an example of how an employee stole cash from his company's bank deposits. Bill Gurado, a branch manager for a consumer-loan finance company, took his branch's deposits to the bank himself, where he placed the money into his own account rather than his employer's. CFE Harry Smith audited Gurado's branch to determine the scope of his scheme. This case provides an excellent example of how an employee's perception of his company's controls can be valuable in preventing and detecting fraud.

✶✶✶✶✶

CASE STUDY: THE OL' FAKE SURPRISE AUDIT GETS 'EM EVERY TIME

Several names have been changed to preserve anonymity

Some people would argue that auditors have no sense of humor, that they are a straight-laced, straight-faced bunch. Bill Gurado knows better.

Gurado worked as a branch manager for Newfund, a consumer-loan finance company in New Orleans. He was the highly respected leader of the company's oldest, largest, and most successful branch. With such a high profile, Gurado commanded a lot of respect. Other managers wanted to be like him. Employees respected him. Everyone in the company considered him a good guy.

For reasons not entirely clear, Gurado began stealing from the company. He did not take a lot of money. His scheme was less than brilliant. And because he did not appreciate an auditor's sense of humor, his fraud was brought to light just weeks after it began.

Newfund employed good controls, both from an accounting as well as a management standpoint. One control on which Barry Ecker, the company's internal auditor, relied was the surprise audit.

He normally sprang surprise audits at least once and sometimes twice a year on each of Newfund's 30 branches. Due to the size of Gurado's branch, Ecker could not perform a surprise audit by himself. He would have to coordinate with the external audit staff.

During these surprise audits, Ecker came in and took control from the start. He was extremely thorough. Harry J. Smith, one of the external auditors whose team would accompany him, describes Ecker as "your typical old-time sleuth-type auditor. A little bitty, short, pudgy guy who got a lot of psychic pleasure out of scaring the hell out of branch people. He'd come in and he'd be quiet and very secure about his papers and his area. He'd stare people down. He'd stare at ledger cards looking for irregularities. He'd just make people quake." Adds Smith, " He was really fun to watch. When he was in his character, he was one for the books."

Having been through several surprise audits, Gurado knew the extent of Ecker's investigating. He probably had that in the back of his mind when he ran into Ecker at a store by chance over the weekend.

They had a brief conversation, and as might be expected from someone like Ecker, who enjoyed putting a little fear into people, he mentioned he was about to launch a surprise audit at Gurado's branch. "Well, I'll see you Monday," he said without cracking a smile. "Harry and I are going to pull an audit on your branch on Monday morning." Of course, he had no plans to audit the branch any time in the near future. As they parted, Gurado said, "Great. See you then."

But Gurado was not looking forward to seeing Ecker at all. He knew that Ecker, with all his searching and checking, would find some irregularities. He would piece together Gurado's fraud without much trouble at all. It would not take much effort to learn Gurado had diverted company money into his own bank account. Newfund's clientele was such that they received a lot of cash. For about a week Gurado took the daily deposits to the bank himself and deposited the money in his personal account. He made certain all the daily reports were sent to headquarters as usual — except, of course, the receipted bank deposit slips. It was only a few thousand dollars. But he had not yet had a chance to replace any of the money (if he had ever intended to), and he would not have time to cover his tracks before the "surprise" audit.

"He was absolutely convinced that had we audited his branch, we would find it," says Smith. "And we probably would have. Barry

Ecker did an old-style audit where you go in and seal the file cabinets and take immediate control of the cash drawers and the ledger tubs. It's a complete instantaneous control and tie-out. I'm pretty sure we'd have found it. I know the branch manager was convinced his boat was sunk."

Gurado did some deep soul searching that weekend. On Sunday night, he called the president of the company, a man with a reputation of being a hard-driving, authoritarian individual. "I know it was a giant step for the branch manager to call him up that night," Smith says.

At the president's house that Sunday evening, Gurado came clean. "I know the auditors are coming tomorrow morning," he said. Then he confessed to taking money from the company. He was immediately fired.

On Monday morning, Ecker called Smith at the accounting firm. He told Smith what had transpired, then said, "Look, we gotta go audit the branch." Smith and Ecker pulled out all the stops to get an audit team over to the branch to make sure there was nothing else going on.

They found exactly what Gurado had reported and nothing else. Looking back on this case, Smith feels certain the fraud would have been detected even without the misunderstood joke. Newfund practiced a control procedure that probably would have turned up the missing money within fifteen days. Because of that fact, he surmises that Gurado might have been covering some kind of short-term debt with the intent of repaying it.

Since Gurado returned the funds immediately and because he had confessed, the company did not pursue any criminal or civil action against him. They felt it a better course of action to keep it out of the public eye.

Word did travel quickly around the company, though. Upper management made sure of that. The fact that this esteemed branch manager tripped himself up and immediately got caught went a long way toward reinforcing the importance of following proper procedures.

"People commonly measure auditing's benefit by the substance of its findings and recommendations," Smith says. "Auditing's role in preventing abuse is hard to observe and measure and is often unappreciated. But, this case clearly shows that the specter of having an audit certainly affects peoples' behavior."

*****

Miscellaneous Larceny Schemes

Obviously, as the Gurado case illustrates, there are numerous ways to steal cash from one's employer. The method used to do so will depend, to a large extent, on the circumstances existing at the victim company. A few of the more interesting cases in our study will be discussed in order to illustrate the variety of methods we have encountered.

A large number of cash larceny schemes we analyzed came from the banking industry, which is no great surprise considering the vast amounts of currency present at most banks. One notable example is Case 976, in which a bank encoding clerk stole a check for nearly $400,000, which had been deposited into the account of a customer. The check had been validated and sent to the proof area for posting when the clerk took it and mailed it to an accomplice in another state. The accomplice opened an account in the depositor's name and attempted to deposit the check in this new account. Fortunately, the error was detected before the culprits were able to make off with the money.

As with other types of occupational fraud, cash larceny schemes often flourish where controls are weak or nonexistent. A perfect example of this was found in Case 807, in which an employee stole over $100,000 worth of checks from his employer. The checks, each of which was endorsed with the company's name and account number, were simply left unattended in a basket marked "cashier."

Cash schemes are usually, but not always, orchestrated by a single person. In some cases a group of employees conspire to rob their company, and in other instances an employee might enlist outside help. Such was the situation in Case 386, where a manager allowed her store to accumulate approximately $150,000 in cash and food stamps, then arranged for a group of accomplices to rob the store.

While cash larceny schemes on the whole are perhaps the most varied of all the classifications in our study, within a particular business they should be among the easiest to prevent and detect. This is true primarily because the employee can only attack the business in these schemes at a few discrete points, those places where money is physically received or distributed. Proper observation of separation of duties and account management, along with ordinary monitoring of the cash handling process should prevent the bulk of these offenses.

Conclusion

DETECTION

Receipt Recording

In-depth analysis of the cash receipts and recording process is the key to detecting a cash larceny scheme. Areas of analysis may include:

- Mail and register receipt points
- Journalizing and recording of the receipts
- The security of the cash from receipt to deposit

In analyzing the cash receipt process, it is important to meet several control objectives:

- Cash receipts must be complete. Each day's receipts must be promptly collected and deposited in full.
- It must be assured that each receivable transaction recorded is legitimate and has supporting documentation.
- All information included in the transaction must be correctly verified as to amount, date, account coding, and descriptions.
- The cash must be safeguarded while in the physical possession of the company.
- There must be appropriate personnel responsible for overseeing cash control processes.
- Cash register tape totals should be reconciled to the amount of cash in drawer.
- An independent listing of cash receipts should be prepared before the receipts are submitted to the cashier or accounts receivable bookkeeper.
- An independent person should verify the listing against the deposit slips.
- Are authenticated deposit slips retained and reconciled to the corresponding amounts in the cash receipts records?
- Is the bank deposit made by someone other than the cashier or the accounts receivable bookkeeper?
- Does a person independent of the cash receipts and accounts receivable functions compare entries to the cash receipts journal with:
    - Authenticated bank deposit slips?
    - Deposit per the bank statements?
- Are areas where physical handling of cash takes place reasonably safeguarded?

Analytical Review

Analyzing the relationship between sales, cost of sales, and the returns and allowances can detect inappropriate refunds and discounts.

- If a large cash fraud is suspected, a thorough review of these accounts may enlighten the examiner as to the magnitude of the suspected fraud.
- An analysis of refunds and returns and allowances with the actual flow of inventory may reveal some fraud schemes. The refund should cause an entry to inventory, even if it is damaged inventory. Likewise, a return will cause a corresponding entry to an inventory account.
- There should be a linear relationship between sales and returns and allowances over a relevant range. Any change in this relationship may point to a fraud scheme unless there is another valid explanation such as a change in the manufacturing process, change in product line, or change in price.

Register Detection

- As cash is received, whether at a register or through the mail, it is important to ensure that the employees responsible for completing these important tasks are informed of their responsibility and properly supervised.
- Access to the register must be closely monitored and access codes must be kept secure.
- An employee other than the register worker should be responsible for preparing register count sheets and agreeing them to register totals.
- Popular concealment methods must be watched for. These methods, discussed earlier, include checks for cash, reversing transactions, register tape destruction or alteration, and sales cash counts.
- Complete register documentation and cash must be delivered to the appropriate personnel in a timely manner.
- Cash thefts sometimes are revealed by customers who have either paid money on an account and have not received credit, or in some cases, when they notice that the credit they have been given does not agree with the payment they have made. Complaints and inquiries also are received frequently from banks.

Cash Account Analysis

Cash larceny can be detected by reviewing and analyzing all journal entries made to the cash accounts. This review and analysis should be performed on a regular basis. If an employee is unable to conceal the fraud through altering the source documents, such as the cash register tape, then he may resort to making a journal entry directly to cash. In general (and except in financial institutions), there are very few instances in everyday business activity where an independent journal entry is necessary for cash. One of these exceptions is the recording of the bank service charge. However, this is an easy journal entry to trace to its source documentation, namely the bank statement. Therefore, all other entries directly to cash are suspect and should be traced to their source documentation or explanation. Suspect entries will generally credit the cash account and correspondingly debit various other accounts such as a sales contra-account or bad debt expenses.

PREVENTION
Segregation of Duties

The primary prevention to cash larceny is segregation of duties. Whenever one individual has control over the entire accounting transaction (e.g., authorization, recording, and custody), the opportunity is present for cash fraud. Each of the following duties and responsibilities should ideally be segregated:
- cash receipts
- cash counts
- bank deposits
- deposit receipt reconciliation
- bank reconciliations
- posting of deposits
- cash disbursements

If any one person has the authority to collect the cash, deposit the receipts, record that collection, and disburse company funds, the risk is high that fraud can occur.

Assignment Rotation and Mandatory Vacations

Many internal fraud schemes are continuous in nature and require ongoing efforts by the employee to conceal defalcations. Mandatory job rotation is an excellent method of detecting cash fraud. By establishing a mandatory job or assignment rotation, the concealment element is interrupted. If mandatory vacations are within the company's policies, it is important that during the employee's absence, the normal workload of that employee be performed by another individual. The purpose of mandatory vacations is lost if the work is allowed to remain undone during the employee's time off.

Surprise Cash Counts and Procedure Supervision

Surprise cash counts and supervisory observations are a useful fraud prevention method if properly used. It is important that employees know that cash will be counted on a sporadic and unscheduled basis. These surprise counts must be made at all steps of the process from receiving the check to deposit.

Physical Security of Cash

- Ensure proper segregation of duties of key personnel
- Review the check and cash composition of the daily bank deposit during unannounced cash counts and during substantive audit tests of cash receipts
- Review the entity's records of the numerical series of printed prenumbered receipts, and verify that these receipts are used sequentially (including voided documents)
- Review the timeliness of deposits from locations to the central treasurer function
- Observe cash receipting operations of locations
- Prepare and review a schedule of all cash receipting functions from a review of revenue reports, from cash receipt forms at the central treasurer function, and from discussion with knowledgeable employees
- Prepare and analyze an inventory of all imprest and change funds by purpose, amount, custodian, date, and location
- Audit all revenue sources on a cycle
- Periodically use comparative analytical reviews to determine which functions have unfavorable trends
- Determine reason(s) why revenue has changed from previous reporting periods
- Confirm responses obtained from managers by using alternative records or through substantive audit tests
- Adhere to a communicated policy of unannounced cash counts

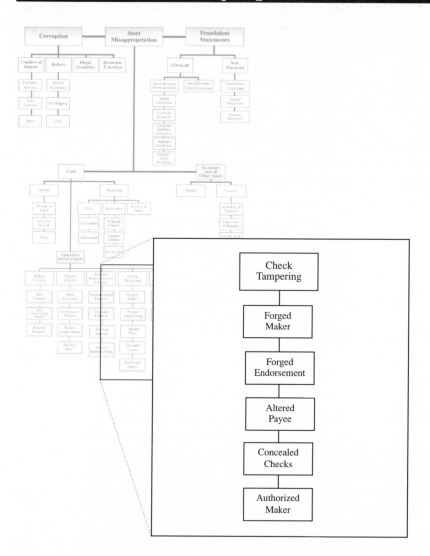

5. CHECK TAMPERING

*****

Case Study: A Wolf in Sheep's Clothing

*Several names have been changed to preserve anonymity.

Melissa Robinson was a devoted wife with two adorable children. She was very active at her children's school and had been known as a charitable person, giving both her time and money to various organizations throughout the community. She spent a good portion of her time working for a world-wide charitable organization chapter in Nashville as the executive secretary. In fact, her fellow employees and club members perceived Robinson's donation of time and hard work as nothing less than a godsend. "Even if somebody had told [the board of directors] that this lady was stealing," recalls Certified Fraud Examiner and CPA David Mensel, who is also a member of the organization, "they would have said 'Impossible, she'd never do it.'"

However, all these accolades could not obscure one cold fact: Melissa Robinson was a thief. Unfortunately, as executive secretary, she was one of two people in the organization allowed to sign checks on its bank accounts. As a result, the club was bilked out of more than $60,000 over five years, until club members put an end to Robinson's scam.

The Nashville chapter of the organization was very much like other charitable entities—they would engage in fundraising activities, such as selling peanuts or candy bars on street corners around the holiday seasons. Although a percentage came in check form, most of the fundraising revenue was naturally cash.

"There was no oversight in those currency collections," says Mensel. "If I had gone out on a collecting route, I'd come back with a bag of money and drop it on the secretary's desk and be gone."

Mensel suspects that Robinson stole far more than the $60,800 that the audit team ultimately established, because the amount of currency that flowed through her office was undocumented. "It is just a supposition, given her behavior with the checking accounts," Mensel explains. "As well, we saw a basic decline in collections from some activities that the organization had been involved in for many years."

Robinson's fraudulent activities were made possible by the relaxed operations of the Nashville chapter's board of directors. The organization's charter mandated that an independent audit be performed annually. However, during Robinson's tenure as executive secretary, not one yearly audit was completed. Mensel describes the board of directors during that tenure as "lackadaisical."

Robinson arrived at the executive secretary's desk through hard work. Starting in 1985, she was one of the most dedicated employees the company had, giving as much time as she could to help out. Once she earned the executive secretary position, Robinson apparently began pilfering from the organization's three bank accounts a little at a time. Although the accounts required two signatures per check, Robinson was able to write checks to herself and others by signing her own name and forging the second signature. Mensel says she would usually write a check to herself or to cash and record the transaction in the organization's books as a check to a legitimate source. If anyone glanced at the books, they would see plenty of hotels and office supply stores, names that were expected to show up in the ledger.

"The club meetings were regularly held in a hotel in town or at one of these executive meeting clubs," Mensel recalls, "and those bills would run from two to four thousand dollars a month. The executive secretary would . . . post in the checkbook that she had paid the hotel, but the actual check would be made out to someone else."

Mensel also remembers that Robinson repeatedly refused to convert her manual checking system into the elaborate computer system the organization wanted her to use. "Now we know why," says Mensel.

Mensel and another associate were very involved in a fundraising operation when Robinson began her reign as executive secretary. Mensel observed that whenever he asked for any financial information from Robinson, she would stonewall him or make excuses.

Mensel became suspicious and took the matter up with the board of directors. But when he told the board that he thought it was very peculiar that he couldn't get much financial data from Robinson, the board quite definitely sided with the executive secretary.

"The officers of the board essentially jumped down my throat, told me I was wrong and that I was being unreasonable," Mensel says. "And since I had no substantiation, just a bad feeling . . . I let it pass."

Mensel felt that the current treasurer was personally offended by his inquiry, as though he were suggesting that the treasurer was not doing his job properly. The treasurer acted defensively and did not check into Robinson's dealings.

As a result, the organization, which Mensel describes as previously "financially very sound," began to feel some financial strain. There simply wasn't as much money to run the organization as in the past, and it was at this point Robinson made what was perhaps her most ingenious maneuver. She convinced the board of directors that because the organization was experiencing some economic troubles, they ought to close the office space rented out for the executive secretary. This office was considered the financial center of the organization. Supposedly out of the goodness of her heart, Robinson told the board members that she would be happy to relinquish her precious space and run the financial matters of the club from her home. The board members agreed.

This allowed Robinson to carry out her embezzlement in small doses; Mensel recalls that Robinson wrote several checks for only $200 to $300. All this time, the board did nothing to impede Robinson's progress, even when she would not divulge financial information upon request. When she came to club meetings, board members would sometimes ask her for information about the finances or ask to look at her books. Robinson would apologize and explain that she had forgotten them.

However, during the last year of the embezzlement, a new group of officers was elected, including a new treasurer. The first thing the treasurer did was ask Robinson for the books. Robinson repeatedly denied his requests, until the new chapter president went to Robinson's house and demanded them. "[The president] stood on her doorstep until she gave the books to him. He said he wouldn't leave until she gave them to him," Mensel recalls. "Once [the board] got their hands on the books . . . they could see that something was very definitely wrong."

In comparing the books with many of the returned checks, the organization could immediately see that not only had some checks been altered or forged, but many of the checks were simply missing. At that point, the board of directors assigned Mensel and two other club members, one a CPA, to investigate Robinson's alleged wrong-doings. As Mensel and the other audit committee members looked at the checks, they realized that Robinson hardly attempted to cover up her scams at all.

"She did physically erase some checks and sometimes even used white-out to rewrite the name of the payee that was in the check-book after the check had cleared," Mensel laughs. "But of course, on the back of the check was her name, as the depositor of the check."

The peculiar thing, in Mensel's mind, was the varying nature of Robinson's check writing. Although Mensel says several of the checks were written to casinos such as the Trump Taj Mahal and weekend getaway spots like the Mountain View Chalet, many more of the checks were written to other charities and the school Robinson's children attended. She apparently didn't use the embezzled moneys to substantially improve her lifestyle, which Mensel describes as "a very standard middle-class life here in Nashville. She and her husband were not wealthy people by any means."

Robinson was immediately excused from her executive secretary position. She was indicted by a grand jury and was tried and found guilty. She was ordered to pay restitution to the club and its insurance company. At last notice, she was still paying back the money. The court will "wipe her slate clean" when she completes her restitution.

Robinson appeared to be one of the most dedicated volunteers in a charitable organization, giving of her time and efforts. The workers around her praised her generosity and work ethic yet all the while she was stealing from them. If there is a lesson to be learned here, it is that audit functions are in place for a reason and should never be overlooked. Unfortunately for the charitable organization, they were reminded of this lesson the hard way.

*****

Overview

Among the asset misappropriation schemes, fraudulent disbursements of cash make up by far the greatest portion (see charts 2-4 and 2-5). *Fraudulent disbursements* are those schemes in which the perpetrator causes his company to issue a payment through some trick or device. The story of Melissa Robinson is an example of one of the most common forms of asset misappropriation, the *check tampering* scheme. Check tampering is a type of fraudulent disbursement scheme in which an employee either (1) prepares a fraudulent check for his own benefit, or (2) intercepts a check intended for a third party and converts the check to his own benefit. Check tampering schemes accounted for 14.62% of the asset misappropriation cases in our study (see chart 2-10), and 8.17%% of the losses (see chart 2-11). Losses due to check tampering schemes in our study totaled $48,908,776, which placed them ninth among all scheme types (see chart 1-4).

Check tampering is unique among the disbursement frauds because it is the one group of schemes in which the perpetrator physically prepares the fraudulent check. In most fraudulent disbursement schemes, the culprit generates a payment to himself by submitting some false document to the victim company such as an invoice or a timecard. The false document represents a claim for payment and causes the victim company to issue a check which the perpetrator then converts. These frauds essentially amount to trickery; the perpetrator fools the company into handing over its money.

Check tampering schemes are fundamentally different. Like in the case of Melissa Robinson, the fraudster takes physical control of a check and makes it payable to himself through one of several methods. Check tampering frauds depend upon factors such as access to the company checkbook, access to bank statements, and the ability to forge signatures or alter other information on the face of the check. The methods used to commit check tampering frauds are:

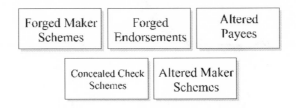

Because of their apparent simplicity, there is a tendency to think of forgeries and other check tampering schemes as inexpensive crimes. The fact is that these schemes can be very damaging to a company's bottom line. In fact, the median loss associated with check tampering schemes in our study was $96,432 (see chart 1-5). This is all the more disturbing given the fact that most of the check tampering schemes in our study might easily have been prevented by the observance of basic control procedures.

From the results of our study it appears that forged maker schemes are the most common of all check tampering frauds, accounting for over 50% of the total losses and total cases we reviewed (see charts 5-1 and 5-2, respectively). The median losses for check tampering schemes range from a low of $25,000 for forged endorsement schemes to a high of $130,000 for authorized maker schemes (see chart 5-3). The mechanics of each of these schemes will be discussed in detail below.

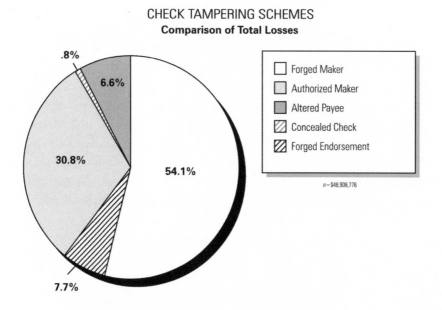

Chart 5-1: Comparison of Total Losses

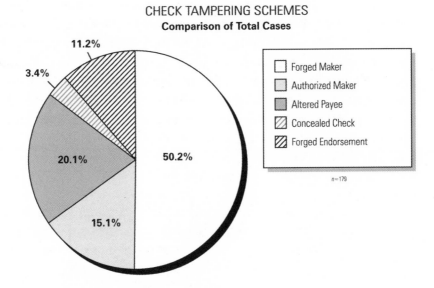

Chart 5.2: Comparison of Total Cases

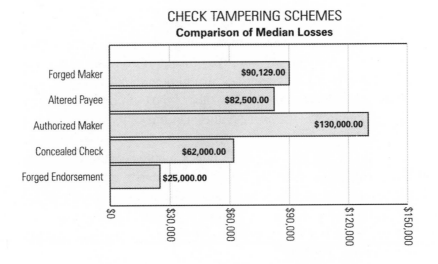

Chart 5.3: Comparison of Median Losses

Forged Maker Schemes

The legal definition of forgery includes not only the *signing of another person's name* to a document (such as a check) with a fraudulent intent, but also the fraudulent *alteration* of a genuine instrument.[1] This definition is so broad that it would encompass all check tampering schemes, so we have narrowed the term to fit our needs. Because we are interested in distinguishing the various methods used by individuals to tamper with checks, we will constrain the concept of "forgeries" to those cases in which an individual signs another person's name on a check.

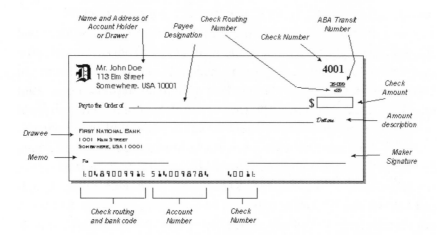

The person who signs a check is known as the "maker" of the check. A forged maker scheme, then, may be defined as a check tampering scheme in which an employee misappropriates a check and fraudulently affixes the signature of an authorized maker thereon (see flowchart 5-2). Frauds that involve other types of check tampering, such as the alteration of the payee or the changing of the dollar amount, are classified separately.

As one might expect, forged check schemes are usually committed by employees who lack signature authority on company accounts. Melissa Robinson's case is something of an exception because, although she did have signature authority, her organization's checks required two signatures. Robinson therefore had to forge another person's signature.

In order to forge a check, an employee must have access to a blank check, he must be able to produce a convincing forgery of an authorized signature, and he must be able to conceal his crime. If the fraudster cannot hide his crime from his employer, his scheme is sure to be short-lived. Concealment is a universal problem in check tampering schemes; the methods used are basically the same whether one is dealing with a forged maker scheme, an intercepted check scheme, a concealed check scheme, or an authorized maker scheme. Therefore, concealment issues will be discussed as a group at the end of the chapter.

OBTAINING THE CHECK
Employees with Access to Company Checks
One cannot forge a company check unless one first possesses a company check. The first hurdle that a fraudster must overcome in committing a forgery scheme is to figure out how to get his hands on a blank check. The results of our study indicate that most forgery schemes are committed by accounts payable clerks, office managers, bookkeepers, or other employees whose duties typically include the preparation of company checks. Like Melissa Robinson, these are people who have access to the company checkbook on a regular basis and are therefore in the best position to steal blank checks. If an employee spends his workday preparing checks on behalf of his company, and if that employee has some personal financial difficulty, it takes only a small leap in logic (and a big leap in ethics) to see that his financial troubles can be solved by writing fraudulent checks for his own benefit. Time and again we see that employees tailor their fraud to the circumstances of their jobs. It stands to reason that those who work around the checkbook would be prone to committing forgery schemes.

Employees Lacking Access to Company Checks
If the perpetrator does not have access to the company checkbook through his work duties, he will have to find other means of misappropriating a check. The way a person steals a check depends largely on how the checkbook is handled within a particular company. In some circumstances the checkbook is poorly guarded, left in unattended areas where anyone can get to it. In other companies the checkbook may be kept in a restricted area, but the perpetrator may have obtained a key or combination to this area, or may know where an employee with access to the checks keeps his own copy of the key or combination. An accomplice may provide blank checks for the fraudster in return for a portion of the stolen funds. Perhaps a

secretary sees the checkbook left on a manager's desk or a custodian comes across blank checks in an unlocked desk drawer.

In some companies, checks are computer generated. When this is the case an employee who knows the password that allows checks to be prepared and issued can usually obtain as many unsigned checks as he desires. There are an unlimited number of ways to steal a check, each dependent on the way in which a particular company guards its blank checks.

A fraudster may also be able to obtain a blank check when the company fails to properly dispose of unused checks. In Case 669, for example, a company used voided checks to line up the printer that ran payroll checks. These voided checks were not mutilated. A payroll clerk collected the voided checks after the printer was aligned and used them to issue herself extra disbursements through the payroll account.

An unusual method of obtaining blank checks was used by an employee in Case 1460. This person had an accomplice who worked for a check-printing company and who printed blank checks with the account number of the perpetrator's company. The perpetrator then wrote over $100,000 worth of forgeries on these counterfeit checks. This case illustrates the creativity and intricacy of some schemes. Considering the amount of illegal gain that the fraudster in Case 1460 realized, it should not be surprising that an employee would go to such trouble to obtain a blank check.

To Whom is the Check Made Payable?

To the Perpetrator

Once a blank check has been obtained, the fraudster must decide to whom it should be made payable. He can write the check to anyone, though in most instances forged checks are payable to the perpetrator himself so that they are easier to convert. A check made payable to a third person, or to a fictitious person or business, may be difficult to convert without false identification. The tendency to make forged checks payable to oneself seems to be a result of fraudsters' laziness rather than a decision based on the successful operation of their schemes. Checks payable to an employee are obviously more likely to be recognized as fraudulent than checks made out to other persons or entities.

If the fraudster owns his own business or has established a shell company, he will usually write fraudulent checks to these entities rather than himself. When the payee on a forged check is a "vendor" rather than an employee of the victim company, the checks are not as obviously fraudulent on their faces. At the same time, these checks are easy to convert because the fraudster owns the entity to which the checks are payable.

To an Accomplice

If a fraudster is working with an accomplice, he can make the forged check payable to that person. The accomplice then cashes the check and splits the money with the employee-fraudster. Because the check is payable to the accomplice in his true identity, it is easily converted. An additional benefit to using an accomplice is that a canceled check payable to a third-party accomplice is not as likely to raise suspicion as a canceled check to an employee. The obvious drawback to using an accomplice in a scheme is that the employee-fraudster usually has to share the proceeds of the scheme.

In some circumstances, however, the accomplice may be unaware that he is involved in a fraud. An example of how this can occur was found in Case 729, in which a bookkeeper wrote several fraudulent checks on company accounts, then convinced a friend to allow her to deposit the checks in the friend's account. The fraudster claimed the money was revenue from a side business she owned and the subterfuge was necessary to prevent creditors from seizing the funds. After the checks were deposited, the friend withdrew the money and gave it to the fraudster.

Payable to "Cash"

The fraudster may also write checks payable to "cash" in order to avoid listing himself as the payee. Checks made payable to cash, however, must still be endorsed. The fraudster will have to sign his own name or forge the name of another in order to convert the check. In addition, checks payable to "cash" are usually viewed more skeptically than checks payable to persons or businesses. Some check-cashing institutions may refuse to cash checks made payable to "cash."

Payable to Vendors

The employee who forges company checks may do so not to obtain currency, but to purchase goods or services for his own benefit. When this is the case, forged checks are made payable to third-party vendors who are uninvolved in the fraud. For instance, we saw in the case study at the beginning of this chapter how several of Melissa Robinson's checks were written to casinos and hotels, apparently for personal vacations.

FORGING THE SIGNATURE

After the employee has obtained and prepared a blank check, he must forge an authorized signature in order to convert the check. The most obvious method, and the one that comes to mind when we think of the word "forgery," is to simply take pen in hand and sign the name of an authorized maker.

Free-hand Forgery

The difficulty a fraudster encounters when physically signing the authorized maker's name is in creating a reasonable approximation of the true signature. If the forgery appears authentic, the perpetrator will probably have no problem cashing the check. In truth, the forged signature may not have to be particularly accurate. Many fraudsters cash forged checks at liquor stores, grocery stores, or other institutions which are known to be less than diligent in verifying the accuracy of signatures and identification. A poorly forged signature can be a clear red flag. The maker's signature on canceled checks should be reviewed for forgeries during the reconciliation process.

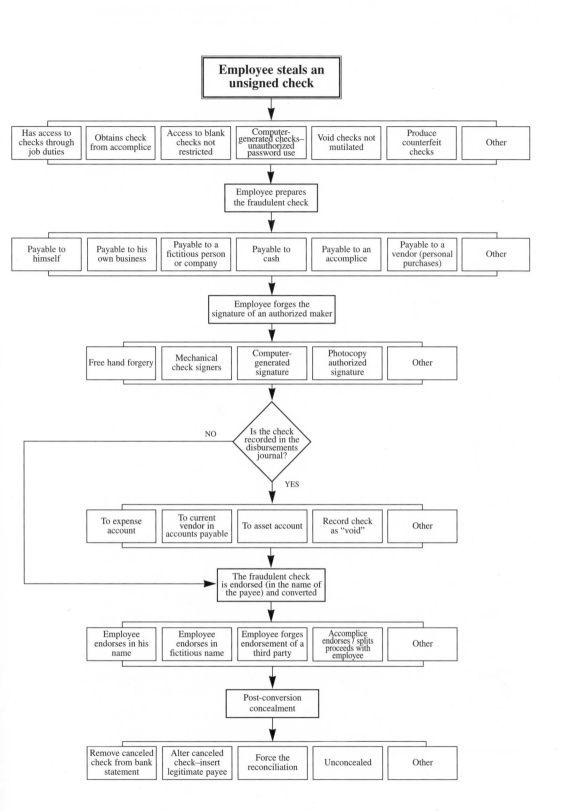

Flowchart 5-2: Forged Maker Schemes

Photocopied Forgeries

To guarantee an accurate forgery, some employees make photocopies of legitimate signatures and affix them to company checks. The fraudster is thus assured that the signature appears authentic. This method was used by a bookkeeper in Case 2514 to steal over $100,000 from her employer. Using her boss's business correspondence and the company Xerox machine, she made transparencies of his signature. These transparencies were then placed in the copy machine so that when she ran checks through the machine the boss's signature was copied onto the maker line of the check. The bookkeeper now had a signed check in hand. She made the fraudulent checks payable to herself, but falsified the check register so that the checks appeared to have been written to legitimate payees.

Automatic Check-signing Instruments

Companies that issue a large number of checks sometimes utilize automatic check-signing instruments in lieu of signing each check by hand. Automated signatures are either produced with manual instruments like signature stamps or they are printed by computer. Obviously, a fraudster who gains access to an automatic check-signing instrument will have no trouble forging the signatures of authorized makers. Even the most rudimentary control procedures should severely limit access to these instruments. Nevertheless, several of the forged maker schemes we reviewed were accomplished through use of a signature stamp. In Case 838, for instance, a fiscal officer maintained a set of manual checks which were unknown to other persons in the company. The company used an automated check signer and the custodian of the signer let the officer have uncontrolled access to it. Using the manual checks and the company's check signer, the fiscal officer was able to write over $90,000 worth of fraudulent checks to himself over a period of approximately four years.

The same principle applies to computer-generated signatures. Access to the password or program which prints signed checks should be restricted, specifically excluding those who prepare checks and those who reconcile the bank statement. The fraudster in Case 2342, for example, was in charge of preparing checks. The fraudster managed to obtain the issuance password from her boss, then used this password to issue checks to a company she owned on the side. She was able to bilk her employer out of approximately $100,000 using this method.

The beauty of automated check signers, from the fraudster's perspective, is that they produce perfect "forgeries." Nothing about the physical appearance of the check will indicate that it is fraudulent. Of course, forged checks are written for illegitimate purposes, so they may be detectable when the bank statement is reconciled or when accounts are reviewed. The ways in which fraudsters avoid detection through these measures will be discussed later in this chapter.

MIS-CODING FRAUDULENT CHECKS

Mis-coding a check is actually a form of concealment, a means of hiding the fraudulent nature of the check. We will discuss the ways fraudsters code their forged checks in the concealment section at the end of this chapter. It should be noted here, however, that mis-coding is typically used as a concealment method only by those employees with access to the checkbook. If a forged maker scheme is undertaken by an employee without access to the checkbook, he usually makes no entry whatsoever in the disbursements journal.

CONVERTING THE CHECK

In order to convert the forged check, the perpetrator must endorse it. The endorsement is typically made in the name of the payee on the check. Since identification is typically required when one seeks to convert a check, the fraudster usually needs fake identification if he forges checks to real or fictitious third persons. As discussed earlier, checks payable to "cash" require the endorsement of the person converting them. Without fake i.d., the fraudster will likely have to endorse these checks in his own name. An employee's endorsement on a cancelled check can obviously be a red flag.

Intercepted Checks

Instead of forging a maker's signature on a check, some fraudsters wait until legitimate checks are prepared and signed, then steal these checks before they are delivered to their proper payees. These schemes are classified as intercepted check schemes. When a fraudster has intercepted a signed check, he can do one of two things in order to cash it: he can endorse the check by forging the true payee's signature, or he can alter the payee designation of the check. These schemes are typically more complicated than forgery schemes and create more concealment problems for the fraudster.

Forged Endorsement Schemes

Forged endorsement frauds are those check tampering schemes in which an employee intercepts a company check intended for a third party and converts the check by signing the third party's name on the endorsement line of the check (see flowchart 5-3). In some instances the fraudster also signs his own name as a second endorser. The term forged endorsement schemes would seem to imply that these frauds should be categorized along with the forged maker schemes discussed in the previous section. It is true that both kinds of fraud involve the false signing of another person's name on a check, but there are certain distinctions which cause forged endorsement schemes to be categorized here rather than with the other forgeries.

In classifying fraud types, we look to the heart of the scheme. What is the crucial point in the commission of the crime? In a forged maker scheme, the perpetrator is normally working with a blank check. The trick to this kind of scheme is in gaining access to blank checks and producing a signature that appears authentic.

In a forged endorsement scheme, on the other hand, the perpetrator is tampering with a check that has already been written, so the issues involved in the fraud are different. The key to these schemes is obtaining the checks after they are signed but before they are properly delivered. If this is accomplished, the actual forging of the endorsement is somewhat secondary. For this reason, forged endorsements are classified as intercepted check schemes.

A fraudster's main dilemma in a forged endorsement case (and in all intercepted check cases, for that matter) is gaining access to a check after it has been written and signed. The fraudster must either steal the check between the point where it is signed and the point where it is delivered, or he must re-route the check, causing it to be mailed to a location where he can retrieve it. The manner used to steal a check depends largely upon the way the company handles outgoing disbursements. Anyone who is allowed to handle signed checks may be in a good position to intercept them.

INTERCEPTING CHECKS BEFORE DELIVERY

Employees Involved in Delivery of Checks

Obviously, the employees in the best position to intercept signed checks are those whose duties include the handling and delivery of signed checks. The most obvious example would be a mailroom employee who opens outgoing mail containing signed checks and steals the checks. Other personnel with access to outgoing checks might include accounts payable employees, payroll clerks, secretaries, etc.

Poor Control of Signed Checks

Unfortunately, fraudsters are often able to intercept signed checks because of poor internal controls. For instance, in Case 1000, signed checks were left overnight on the desks of some employees because processing on the checks was not complete. One of the janitors on the overnight cleaning crew found these checks and took them, forged the endorsements of the payees, and cashed them at a liquor store. Another example of poor observance of internal controls appeared in Case 933. In this scheme a high-level manager with authority to disburse employee benefits instructed accounts payable personnel to return signed benefits checks to him instead of immediately delivering them to their intended recipients. These instructions were not questioned, despite the fact that they presented a clear violation of the separation-of-duties concept, due to the manager's level of authority within the company. The perpetrator simply took the checks that were returned to him and deposited them into his personal bank account, forging the endorsements of the intended payees.

Case 933 represents what seems to be the most common breakdown of controls in forged endorsement frauds. We have seen repeated occurrences of signed checks being returned to the employee who prepared the check. This typically occurs when a supervisor signs a check and hands it back to a clerk or secretary who presented it to the supervisor; it is done either through negligence or because the employee is highly trusted and thought to be above theft. Adequate internal controls should prevent the person who prepares company disbursements from having access to signed checks. This separation of duties is elemental; its purpose is to break the disbursement chain so that no one person controls the entire payment process.

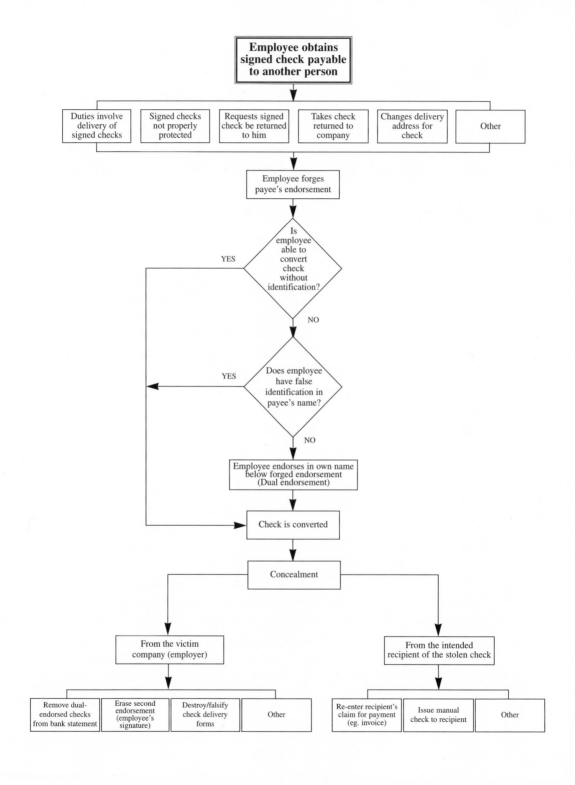

Flowchart 5-3: Forged Endorsement Schemes

Theft of Returned Checks

Another way to obtain signed checks is to steal checks which have been mailed, but have been returned to the victim company for some reason such as an incorrect address. Employees with access to incoming mail may be able to intercept these returned checks from the mail and convert them by forging the endorsement of the intended payee. In Case 2288, for example, a manager took and converted approximately $130,000 worth of checks which were returned due to noncurrent addresses. (He also stole outgoing checks, cashed them, then declared them lost.) The fraudster was well known at his bank and was able to convert the checks by claiming that he was doing it as a favor to the real payees, who were "too busy to come to the bank." The fraudster was able to continue with his scheme because the nature of his company's business was such that the recipients of the misdelivered checks were often not aware that the victim company owed them money. Therefore, they did not complain when their checks failed to arrive. In addition, the perpetrator had complete control over the bank reconciliation, so he could issue new checks to those payees who did complain, then "force" the reconciliation, making it appear that the bank balance and book balance matched when in fact they did not. Stealing returned checks is obviously not as common as other methods for intercepting checks, and it is more difficult for a fraudster to plan and carry out on a long-term basis. However, it is also very difficult to detect and can lead to large scale fraud, as the previous case illustrates.

Re-routing the Delivery of Checks

The other way an employee can go about misappropriating a signed check is to alter the address to which the check is to be mailed. The check is either delivered to a place where the fraudster can retrieve it, or it is purposely misaddressed so that he can steal it when it is returned as discussed above. As we have said before, proper separation of duties should preclude anyone who prepares disbursements from being involved in their delivery. Nevertheless, this control is often overlooked, allowing the person who prepares a check to address and mail it as well.

In some instances where proper controls are in place, fraudsters are still able to cause the misdelivery of checks. In Case 1470, for instance, the fraudster was a clerk in the customer service department of a mortgage company where her duties included changing the mailing addresses of property owners. She was assigned a password which gave her access to make address changes. The clerk was transferred to a new department where one of her duties was the issuance of checks to property owners. Unfortunately, her supervisor forgot to cancel her old password. When the clerk realized this oversight, she would request a check for a certain property owner, then sign onto the system with her old password and change the address of that property owner. The check would be sent to her. The next day the employee would use her old password to re-enter the system and replace the proper address so that there would be no record of where the check had been sent. This fraudster's scheme resulted in a loss of over $250,000 to the victim company.

CONVERTING THE STOLEN CHECK

Once the check has been intercepted, the perpetrator can cash it by forging the payee's signature, hence the term forged endorsement scheme. Depending on where he tries to cash the check, the perpetrator may or may not need fake identification at this stage. As we alluded to earlier, many fraudsters cash their stolen checks at places where they are not required to show an i.d.

If a fraudster is required to show identification in order to cash his stolen check, and if he does not have a fake i.d. in the payee's name, he may use a dual endorsement to cash or deposit the check. In other words, the fraudster forges the payee's signature as though the payee had transferred the check to him, then the fraudster endorses the check in his own name and converts it. When the bank statement is reconciled, double endorsements on checks should always raise suspicions, particularly when the second signer is an employee of the company.

Altered Payee Schemes

The second type of intercepted check scheme is the altered payee scheme. This is a type of check tampering fraud in which an employee intercepts a company check intended for a third party and alters the payee designation so that the check can be converted by the employee or an accomplice (see flowchart 5-4). The fraudster inserts his own name, the name of a fictitious entity, or some other name on the payee line of the check. Altering the payee designation eliminates many of the problems associated with converting the check which would be encountered in a forged endorsement fraud. The alteration essentially makes the check payable to the fraudster (or an accomplice), so there is no need to forge an endorsement and no need to obtain false identification. The fraudster or his accomplice can endorse the check in his own name and convert it.

Of course, if canceled checks are reviewed during reconciliation of the bank statement, a check made payable to an employee is likely to cause suspicion, especially if the alteration to the payee designation is obvious. This is the main obstacle that must be overcome by fraudsters in altered payee schemes.

ALTERING CHECKS PREPARED BY OTHERS: INSERTING A NEW PAYEE

The method used to alter the payee designation on a check depends largely on how that check is prepared and intercepted. (Incidentally, the amount of the check may also be altered at the same time and by the same method as the payee designation.) Checks prepared by others can be intercepted by any of the methods discussed in the forged endorsements section above. When the fraudster intercepts a check which has been prepared by someone else, there are basically two methods which may be employed. The first is to insert the false payee's name in place of the true payee's. This is usually done by rather unsophisticated means. The true name might be scratched out with a pen or whited-out. Another name is then entered on the payee designation. These kinds of alterations are usually simple to detect.

A more intricate method occurs when the perpetrator of the fraud enters the accounts payable system and changes the names of payees, which occurred in Case 1112. An accounts payable employee in this case was so trusted that her manager allowed her to use his computer password in his absence. The password permitted access to the accounts payable address file. This employee waited until the manager was absent, then selected a legitimate vendor with whom her company did a lot of business. She held up the vendor's invoices for the day, and after work used the manager's log-on code to change the vendor name and address to that of a fictitious company. The new name and address were run through the accounts payable cycle with an old invoice number, causing a fraudulent check to be issued. The victim company had an automated duplicate invoice test, but the fraudster circumvented it substituting "1" for "I" and "0" (zero) for capital "O." The next day, the employee would replace the true vendor's name and address, and mutilate the check register so that the check payable to the fictitious vendor was concealed. Approximately $300,000 in false checks were issued using this method.

ALTERING CHECKS PREPARED BY OTHERS: "TACKING ON"

The other method that can be used by fraudsters to alter checks prepared by others is "tacking on" additional letters or words to the end of the real payee designation. This rather unusual approach to check tampering occurred in Case 153, in which an employee took checks payable to "ABC" company and altered them to read "A.B. Collins." She then deposited these checks in an account which had been established in the name of A.B. Collins. The simple inclusion of a filler line after the payee designation would have prevented the loss of over $60,000 in this case. In addition to altering the payee designation, the amount of the check can be altered by tacking on extra numbers if the person preparing the check is careless and leaves space for extra numbers in the "Amount" portion of the check.

ALTERING CHECKS PREPARED BY THE FRAUDSTER: ERASABLE INK

When the fraudster prepares the check which is to be altered, the schemes tend to be a bit more sophisticated. The reason for this is obvious: When the perpetrator is able to prepare the check himself, he can prepare it with the thought of how the payee designation will be altered. But if the perpetrator is preparing the check himself, why not make the check payable to himself or an accomplice to begin with? In order to get an authorized maker to sign the check, the fraudster must make it appear that the check is made out to a legitimate payee. Only after a legitimate signature is obtained does the fraudster in an altered payee scheme set about tampering with the check.

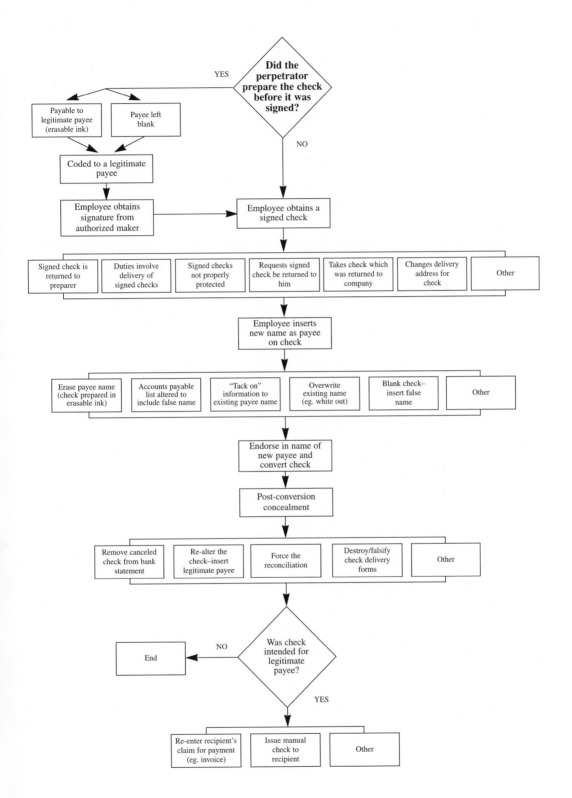

Flowchart 5-4: Altered Payee Schemes

One of the most common ways to prepare a check for alteration is to write or type the payee's name (and possibly the amount) in erasable ink. After the check is signed by an authorized maker, the perpetrator retrieves the check, erases the payee's name, and inserts his own. One example of this type of fraud was found in Case 2212, in which a bookkeeper typed out small checks to a local supplier and had the owner of the company sign them. The bookkeeper then used her erasing typewriter to lift the payee designation and amount from the check. She entered her own name as the payee and raised the amount precipitously. For instance, the owner might sign a $10 check that later became a $10,000 check. These checks were entered in the disbursements journal as payments for aggregate inventory to the company's largest supplier, who received several large checks each month. The bookkeeper stole over $300,000 from her employer in this scheme. The same type of fraud can be undertaken using an erasable pen. In some cases fraudsters have even obtained signatures on checks written in pencil!

We have already discussed how, with a proper separation of duties, a person who prepares a check should not be permitted to handle the check after it has been signed. Nevertheless, this is exactly what happens in most altered payee schemes. When fraudsters prepare checks with the intent of altering them later, those fraudsters obviously have a plan for re-obtaining the checks once they have been signed. Usually, the fraudster knows that there is no effective separation of controls in place. He knows that the maker of the check will return it to him.

ALTERING CHECKS PREPARED BY THE FRAUDSTER: BLANK CHECKS

The most egregious example of poor controls in the handling of signed checks is one in which the perpetrator prepares a check, leaves the payee designation blank, and submits it to an authorized maker who signs the check and returns it to the employee. Obviously, it is quite easy for the fraudster to designate himself or an accomplice as the payee when this line has been left blank. Common sense tells us that one should not give a signed, blank check to another person. Nevertheless, this happened in several cases in our study, usually when the fraudster was a long-time, trusted employee. In Case 1616, for example, an employee gained the confidence of the owner of his company, whom he convinced to sign blank checks for office use while the owner was out of town. The employee would then fill in his own name as the payee on one of the checks, cash it, and alter the check when it was returned along with the bank statement. The owner's blind trust in his employee cost him nearly $200,000.

Converting Altered Checks

As with all other types of fraudulent checks, conversion is accomplished by endorsing the checks in the name of the payee. Conversion of fraudulent checks has already been discussed in previous sections and will not be re-examined here.

Concealed Check Schemes

Another scheme that requires a significant breakdown in controls and common sense is the concealed check scheme. These are check tampering frauds in which an employee prepares a fraudulent check and submits it usually along with legitimate checks to an authorized maker who signs it without a proper review (see flowchart 5-5). Although not nearly as common as the other check tampering methods, it is worth mentioning for its simplicity, its uniqueness and the ease with which it could be prevented.

The perpetrator of a concealed check scheme is almost always a person responsible for preparing checks. The steps involved in a concealed check scheme are similar to those in a forged maker scheme, except for the way in which the employee gets the fraudulent check signed. These schemes work as follows: The perpetrator prepares a check made out to himself, an accomplice, a fictitious person, etc. Instead of forging the signature of an authorized maker, the employee takes the check to the authorized maker, usually concealed in a stack of legitimate checks awaiting signatures. The checks are typically delivered to the signer during a busy time of day when he is rushed and will be less likely to pay close attention to them. Generally, the checks are fanned out on the signer's desk so that the signature lines are exposed but the names of the payees are concealed. If a particular authorized maker is known to be inattentive, the checks are given to him.

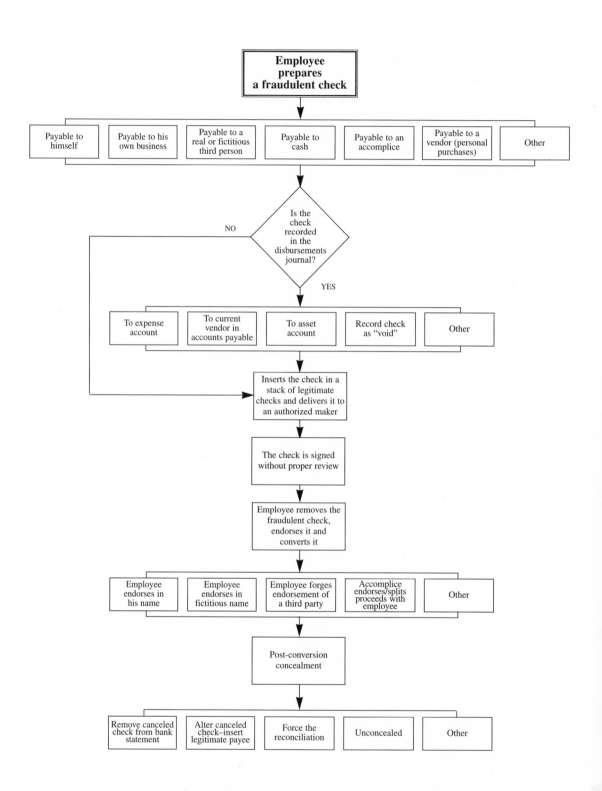

Flowchart 5-5: Concealed Check Schemes

The maker signs the checks quickly and without adequate review. Because he is busy or generally inattentive or both, he simply does not look at what he is signing. He does not demand to see supporting documentation for the checks, and does nothing to verify their legitimacy. Once the checks have been signed they are returned to the employee, who removes his check and converts it. This appears to be one of the methods used by Ernie Philips in the case study at the end of this chapter. Philips slipped several checks payable to himself into a stack of company checks, then took them to the operations manager, who was designated to sign checks when the business's owner was out of town. The operations manager apparently did not check the names of the payees and unknowingly signed several company checks to Philips.

A similar example of the concealed check method took place in Case 2474, where a bookkeeper took advantage of the owner of her company by inserting checks payable to herself into batches of checks given to the owner for signature. The owner simply never looked at who he was paying when he signed the checks.

The perpetrator of a concealed check scheme banks on the inattentiveness of the check signer. If the signer were to review the checks he was signing, he would certainly discover the fraud. It should be noted that the fraudster in these cases could make the fraudulent check payable to an accomplice, a fictitious person or a fictitious business instead of payable to himself. This is more common and certainly a lot less dangerous for the employee (but not nearly as exciting).

Authorized Maker Schemes

The final check tampering scheme, the authorized maker scheme, may be the most difficult to defend against. An authorized maker scheme is a type of check tampering fraud in which an employee with signature authority on a company account writes fraudulent checks for his own benefit and signs his own name as the maker (see flowchart 5-6). The perpetrator in these schemes can write and sign fraudulent checks himself. He does not have to alter a pre-prepared instrument or forge the maker's signature.

OVERRIDING CONTROLS THROUGH INTIMIDATION

When a person is authorized to sign company checks, preparing the checks is easy. The employee simply writes and signs the instruments the same way he would with any legitimate check. In most situations, check signers are owners, officers, or otherwise high-ranking employees, and thus have or can obtain access to all the blank checks they need. Even if company policy prohibits check signers from handling blank checks, the perpetrator's influence can normally be used to overcome this impediment. What employee is going to tell the CEO that he can't have a blank check?

The most basic way an employee accomplishes an authorized maker scheme is to override controls designed to prevent fraud. We have already stated that most authorized signatories have high levels of influence within their companies. This influence may be used by the perpetrator to deflect questions about fraudulent transactions. The most common example is one in which a majority owner or sole shareholder uses his company as a sort of alter ego, paying personal expenses directly out of company accounts. If this arrangement is disclosed and agreed to by other owners, there may be nothing illegal about it. After all, one cannot steal from oneself. On the other hand, in the absence of an agreement between all owners, these disbursements amount to embezzlement. Instead of paying personal expenses, the fraudster might cut checks directly to himself, his friends or family. Using fear of job security as a weapon, the owner can maintain a work environment in which employees are afraid to question these transactions.

High-level managers or officers may also use their authority to override controls in those companies whose ownership is either absent or inattentive. Intimidation can play a large part in the commission and concealment of any type of occupational fraud where powerful individuals are involved. In Case 878, for example, the manager of a sales office stole approximately $150,000 from his employers over a two-year period. This manager had primary check-signing authority and abused this power by writing company checks to pay his personal expenses. The manager's fraudulent activities were well known by certain members of his staff, but these employees' careers were controlled by the perpetrator. Fear of losing their jobs combined with lack of a proper whistleblowing structure prevented the manager's employees from reporting his fraud.

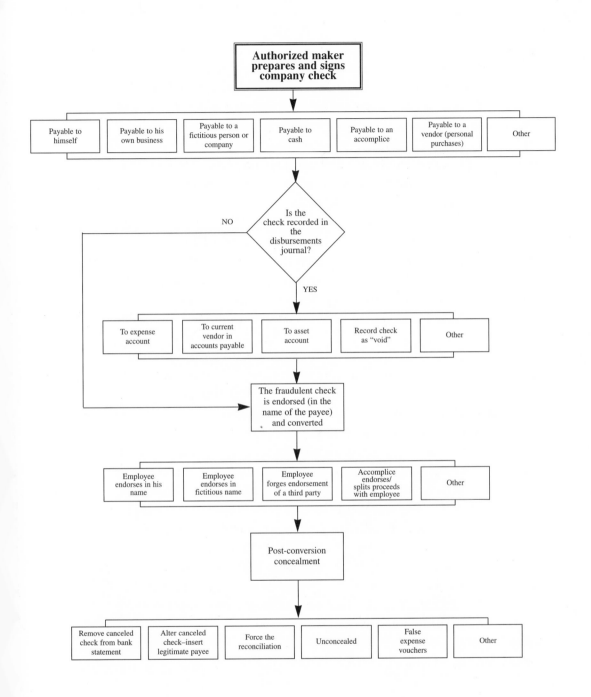

Flowchart 5-6: Authorized Maker Schemes

Poor Controls

Although overriding controls is the most blatant way to execute an authorized maker scheme, it is not the most common. Far more of these schemes occur because no one is paying attention to the accounts and few controls are present to prevent fraud. In Case 740, for example, a manager of a small business wrote company checks to purchase assets for his own business. He took approximately $800,000 from his employer, hiding the missing money in accounts receivable because he knew that those accounts were only reviewed once a year. Before audits, the manager would borrow money from the bank to replace the missing funds, then begin the whole process again when the books were closed. This unfortunate scheme ended in tragedy as the manager and his wife committed suicide when the fraud came to light. Setting aside the personal catastrophe that occurred in this case, it is obvious that if the books had been more closely monitored, or if there had been a threat of surprise audits in addition to the regularly scheduled reviews, this fraud may not have gotten so far out of hand.

The failure to closely monitor accounts is supplemented by lack of internal controls, specifically the absence of separation of duties in the cash disbursements process. In Case 2802, for instance, the perpetrator was in charge of signing all company checks, as well as reconciling the bank accounts for a small business. This put the fraudster in perfect position to write fraudulent checks to herself and her husband. Similarly, in Case 196 the bookkeeper of a medium-sized company was charged with paying all bills and preparing the company payroll. She had access to an automatic check signer and total control over company bank accounts. The bookkeeper wrote extra checks to herself, coded the expenditures to payroll, and destroyed the canceled checks when they were returned with the bank statement. Had the duties of preparing checks and reconciling accounts been separated, as they should be, the fraudster would not have been able to complete her scheme.

Special Project Accounts

Sometimes employees are given signature authority on limited project accounts rather than on company accounts in general. These project accounts are funded based on expected costs, and the employee in question has limited authority to disburse the funds as necessary for the completion of the project. In Case 1335, an employee was in charge of project accounts and succeeded in taking almost $150,000 for his personal use. He accomplished this by charging the cost of supplies for his projects to regular departmental accounts rather than the specially funded project accounts. This left excess money in the project accounts, which the perpetrator removed by writing fraudulent checks under his own signature authority.

TAMPERING WITH THE SIGNATURE CARD

The preceding discussion has centered on cases where the perpetrator is authorized by the company to sign checks. In a few schemes we reviewed, such as Case 1377, employees were able to secretly add their names to the signature card of a company bank account. This allowed the perpetrators to write checks on the company account for their own benefit.

As one might expect, the presence of an unauthorized employee's signature on a check might set off alarms during reconciliation. In Case 2490, an employee avoided this problem by adding a fictitious name to the signature card of a staff fund account. The addition of a fictitious maker to the signature card would assure that, even if someone discovered the fraudulent checks, they would not know who had actually written them. Unfortunately for the victim company, this was not an issue because they did not perform an audit on the account until after the perpetrator retired, eight years later and $120,000 richer.

Concealment

Since most check tampering schemes do not consist of a single occurrence but instead continue over a period of time, concealing the fraud is arguably the most important aspect of the scheme. If a fraudster intended to steal a large sum of money and skip to South America, hiding the fraud might not be so important. But the vast majority of occupational fraudsters remain employees of their companies as they continue to steal from them. Therefore, hiding the fraud is extremely important. Concealment of the fraud means not only hiding the identity of the criminal, but in most cases hiding the fact of the fraud. The most successful frauds are those in which the victim company is unaware that it is being robbed. Obviously, once a business learns that it is being victimized it will take steps to staunch its bleeding and the end of the fraudster's scheme will be at hand.

Check tampering schemes can present especially tricky concealment problems for fraudsters. In other types of fraudulent disbursements such as invoice or payroll schemes, the fraudulent payment is entered in the books as a legitimate transaction by someone other than the fraudster. Remember that the payments in those schemes are generated by the production of false documents which cause accounts payable personnel to think that money is owed to a particular person or vendor. When accounts payable issues a disbursement for a bogus invoice, it does so because it believes the invoice to be genuine. The payment is then entered in the books as a legitimate payment. In other words, the perpetrator generally does not have to worry about concealing the payment in the books, because someone else unwittingly does it for him.

Check tampering schemes do not always afford this luxury to the fraudster. In forgery and authorized maker schemes the perpetrator is the one writing the check, and he is usually the one coding the check in the disbursements journal. He must "explain" the check on the books. Forged endorsement schemes and altered payee schemes are different because they involve the alteration of checks which were already prepared and coded by someone else. Nevertheless, they create a problem for the fraudster because the intercepted check was intended for a legitimate recipient. In short, someone is out there waiting for the check which the fraudster has taken. The culprit in these schemes must worry not only about hiding the fraud from his employer, but also about appeasing the intended payee. If the intended recipient of the check does not receive his payment, he will complain to the fraudster's employer about the nonpayment. This could trigger an investigation into the whereabouts of the missing check, something the fraudster definitely wants to avoid.

The Fraudster Reconciling the Bank Statement

A large portion of those who perpetrate check tampering frauds are involved in reconciling the company's bank statement. The bank statement which a company receives normally includes the canceled checks which have been cashed in the preceding period. A person who reconciles the accounts is therefore in a position to hide the existence of any fraudulent checks which he has written to himself. He can remove the fraudulent checks or doctor the bank statement or both.

We said earlier that in forged maker and authorized maker schemes, the perpetrator usually has to code the check in the disbursements journal. The most fundamental way to hide the check is to code it as "void" or to include no listing at all in the journal. Then, when the bank statement arrives, the perpetrator removes the fraudulent check from the stack of returned checks and destroys it. Now there is no record of the payment in the journal and no physical evidence of the check on hand. Of course, the bank will have a copy of the check, but unless someone questions the missing check there will be little chance that the company will routinely discover the problem. And since the perpetrator is the one who reconciles the account, it is unlikely that anyone will even notice that the check is missing.

The problem with simply omitting the fraudulent check from the disbursements journal is that the bank balance will not reconcile to the book balance. For instance, if the fraudster wrote a $25,000 check to himself and did not record it, then the book balance will be $25,000 higher than the bank balance ($25,000 was taken out of the bank account by the fraudster, but was not credited out of the company's cash account). Fraudsters usually omit their illicit checks from the disbursement journal only in situations where they personally reconcile the bank statement and no one reviews their work. This allows the fraudster to "force" the reconciliation. In other words, the fraudster reports that the bank balance and book balance match, when in fact they do not. These are circumstances in which the employer basically takes the perpetrator's word that the book balance and bank balance reconcile.

Some of the victim companies in our study simply did not reconcile their accounts regularly. Because no one was reconciling the book balance and the bank balance, the fraudster was able to write checks without recording them. In a system where controls are so lax, almost any concealment method will be effective to disguise fraud. In fact, no effort to conceal the crime may even be necessary in these circumstances.

Fraudsters might physically alter the bank statement to cause it to match the company's book balance. For instance, a person engaging in a forged maker scheme may decide to steal blank checks from the back of the checkbook. These checks are out of sequence and therefore will be listed last on the bank statement. The employee then deletes this clump of checks and alters the final total to match the victim company's books. We will see this method of conceal-ment used in the case study below.

In some cases, an employee's duties do not include reconcil-ing the bank accounts, but he is nevertheless able to intercept bank statements and alter them to hide his crimes. In the following case study, Ernie Philips was able to persuade his company's bank to send the bank statements directly to him instead of his boss. Philips then altered the bank statements to conceal his fraudulent activities. This case describes how CFE James Sell put an end to Philips' scheme.

*****

Case Study: What are Friends For?
Several names have been changed to preserve anonymity

Ernie Philips had fallen on hard times. Several back opera-tions left him barely able to move around. He became addicted to the pills that made the pain bearable. His CPA practice was going under. He and his wife had six adopted children to support. Not surprisingly, he suffered from depression and chronic anxiety. But Ernie's luck changed when he ran into his old friend, James Sell. The two men had worked together at a federal agency and known each other over 20 years. Ernie talked about the trouble he was hav-ing and James said he could help. At the time, Ernie was in a reha-bilitation program for his substance abuse, so James told him, "Let me know when you're finished with that, and I'll have some work for you."

James rented Ernie an office and started sending a few small projects his way. "I wanted to try him out, see how he would do," Sell remarks. "He seemed like he was trying to get himself together." Ernie completed the work on time, and performed well, so when James got a big account with the Arizona and Nevada governments, he brought his friend into the main office. They agreed on a salary just over $38,000 a year, which James upped to $42,000 after six months.

Sell was appointed receiver for CSC Financial Services in Arizona and Nevada. CSC owners had been caught diverting $5.5 million of customer escrow funds from its operations in Arizona and Nevada. The computer equipment used in the operation dated from the 1960s, and a lack of supervision and proper controls had obviously allowed the embezzlement to take place. The company didn't use a double-entry system, so management could alter ending totals with a wide latitude. Even after a regulatory audit discovered that things were in disarray at CSC, the Arizona administrators had allowed the offending owners to continue operating for a year and a half. So when Sell finally took over, he found a rather large mess. That's part of the game, he says. "When you get a company as receiver, you try to survive with what you inherit." The receivership involved more than 15,000 active accounts, with about $285 million in-house payments each year, and over 30,000 transactions a month. Sorting out the trouble wouldn't be easy. Sell knew Ernie had experience, and so tapped him for the job. "One of the reasons I brought him in," Sell says, "was to establish controls where there were none before."

But Ernie had little respect for controls. When James asked the mailroom clerk about the bank statements for a particular month, he told him that Ernie had them. "Why is that?" James asked. "He knows those are supposed to come to me unopened. He shouldn't have them." The clerk said Ernie needed the statements for a reconciliation. James didn't want to overreact, but he was nervous. "There's limited control over any position and even less over a key financial position," he says, "and any time you lose a control point, you're in jeopardy. So you have to take a strong position in order to restore the process." He discussed the matter with Ernie and thought they had an understanding.

Ernie was having problems with other people in the company too. He and the operations manager had a heated exchange when the manager retrieved some account papers from Ernie's desk. Ernie had been out and the papers were needed right away. When Ernie aired his grievance, James sided with the operations manager. There shouldn't be any problem, James said. It wasn't like anyone was rifling Ernie's desk. Besides that, Sell traveled frequently, and spent a lot of time in the Nevada office, so having open access in the Arizona office allowed for informal oversight. Sell muses, "One of the best controls in the world is to create an atmosphere of uncertainty. Usually embezzlement doesn't occur unless the person thinks he can hide what he's doing. So I figured this would be a way to keep things on the up and up."

The uncertainty didn't prevent the fraud, but it did help detect what was going on. The operations manager discovered Ernie's sting during a search for accounting records. He brought Sell a company check from Ernie's desk, made out in the name of Ernie Philips for $2,315. It wasn't Ernie's payroll check, so what was it? The check hadn't been cashed, but Sell's signature had been forged. Not sure yet about the situation, Sell arranged to meet Ernie away from the main office.

Sell had been out of town and needed some updates on the escrow operations, so he dropped by Ernie's private office one afternoon. After they finished their discussion, James said, "There's one more thing I wanted to ask you about." He pulled a copy of the check from his briefcase and told Ernie, "I was hoping you could explain this."

There was a long silence. Ernie stared at the check, pursing his lips and scratching his hands across the desktop. The pause stretched into what seemed like minutes. Finally he confessed, "I've been taking money."

"I could tell from the look on his face this was trouble," Sell reports. The worst was confirmed. He had been hoping there was an explanation, an innocuous one, despite all the signs. Still, he had come prepared. "I wanted to confront him away from the main office so if there was anything he could get to and destroy, I'd be protected." James had also brought a copy of the check so it wouldn't be apparent when he showed the check to Ernie that it wasn't cashed. "I wanted to make him believe I knew more than I did. Nailing down this operation would have meant reviewing pages and pages of bank statements, verifying checks and payments. Before I went to that trouble, I wanted to know there was a reason to look."

Sell barred Ernie from both his offices, and began tracing his friend's activities over the past seven months. In some cases, Sell's name was forged onto the checks in handwriting that wasn't his and which bore a resemblance to Ernie's. Others were marked with the signature stamp that was supposed to remain locked in a clerk's office except when she was using it for a very limited set of transactions. Somehow, Ernie had been able to slip the stamp away and mark his checks.

He covered his tracks by taking checks out of sequence so they would show up at the end of the bank statement. Then he'd intercept the statement, and alter the report at the end, returning a copy of the statement to the clerk for filing. After the clerk told Sell about Ernie having the statement, Ernie arranged with the bank for the statements to come addressed to his attention. Without getting authorization, the bank agreed; Ernie could then doctor the statement, copy it, and send it down the line. If someone did ask about an unidentified disbursement, Ernie told them the money went to a supply vendor and, since he was the controller, he was taken at his word. He even managed on a couple of occasions to slip checks made out to himself into a regular batch, which the operations manager — who was authorized to sign checks in Sell's absence — signed.

Sell was, to put it mildly, chagrined. He had believed that his office was set up to avoid the kind of flagrant defalcation he was facing now. But, he admits, "No matter how good a system you design, one knowledgeable person can circumvent it . . . . The trick is to make sure the procedures you set up are followed. I don't know if there's a system in the world that's immune. The key is to limit and control the extent of any one person's action, so you can at least detect when things go awry."

Sell figured his losses at about $109,000. He got a complete run of the bank statements from Ernie's tenure, identified checks out of sequence, or gaps in issued checks, and then verified to whom they were payable and the stated purpose. The scheme had required some footwork, but wasn't terribly sophisticated. The checks were written in odd-number amounts, $4,994.16 for example, but Ernie had made the payments in his own name. He had left behind some of his personal bank statements, which showed deposits correlated with the money he'd taken from Sell. (The amounts didn't always match, because Ernie would take cash back from the deposit, but they were close enough to link the transactions.)

Ernie's brief era of good feelings had ended. He had used the proceeds from his finagling for a lavish family vacation, a new car, a new computer, and improvements on the house where he lived with his wife and their adopted family, but in the fallout of his dismissal Ernie's house went into foreclosure. He was charged around the same time with Driving Under the Influence. The CPA board revoked his license and fined him for ethics violations. He made no defense at his civil trial, where a judgment was rendered against him for the $109,000 he took plus treble damages. While he was out on bail for the criminal charges against him, Ernie took his family and fled. Sell was able to locate him through an Internet search service. Ernie died in May of 1996. "He threw everything away," Sell laments. "For $109,000 he fouled up his life, and his family."

Sell takes the matter philosophically. There are plenty of cases that echo Ernie's. For example, Sell just investigated a paralegal who not only wrote company checks to herself, but also sent one to the County Attorney's office — to pay the fine she owed for writing bad checks. "Typically, these people don't take the time to set up a new identity or a dummy company," James says. "They just want the money fast and grab it the easiest way they can."

"And often enough," he adds, "they want to get caught . . . . Ernie knew he was out of control, that we had been friends for so long. He knew he was doing more than just breaking the law. During one of our conversations after this he told me, 'You know, the first check was real hard to write. But I had clients I had borrowed from, I owed money all over the place, I had a family. As it went on, writing the checks just got easier.'"

*****

RE-ALTERATION OF CHECKS

In altered payee schemes, remember that it is common for the perpetrator to take a check intended for a legitimate recipient, then doctor the instrument so that he is designated as the payee. A company check payable to an employee will obviously raise suspicions of fraud when the canceled check is reconciled with the bank statement. To prevent this, some employees re-alter their fraudulent checks when the bank statement arrives. We have already discussed how some fraudsters alter checks by writing the payee's name in erasable ink or type when the check is prepared. These employees obtain a signature for the check, then erase the true payee's name and insert their own. When these checks return with the statement, the employee erases his own name and re-enters the name of the proper payee. Thus there will be no appearance of mischief. The fraudster in Case 1616 used the re-alteration method to hide over $185,000 in fraudulent checks.

The re-alteration method is not limited to altered payee schemes. The concealment will be equally effective in forged maker schemes, authorized maker schemes, and concealed check schemes. Re-altered checks will match the names of legitimate payees listed in the disbursements journal.

ENTERING FALSE INFORMATION IN THE DISBURSEMENTS JOURNAL

Rather than omit a fraudulent check from the disbursements journal or list it as void, the perpetrator might write a check payable to himself but list a different person as the payee on the books. Usually, the fake payee is a regular vendor a person or business that receives numerous checks from the victim company.   Employees tend to pick known vendors for these schemes because one extra disbursement to a regular payee is less likely to stand out.

The false entry is usually made at the time the fraudulent check is written, but in some cases the fraudster makes alterations to existing information on the book. In the opening case study in this chapter, for instance, Melissa Robinson used white-out and an eraser to change the payee names in her company's checkbook. Obviously, alterations found in a company's books should be carefully scrutinized to make sure they are legitimate.

The fraudster can also conceal a fraudulent check by falsely entering the amounts of legitimate checks in the disbursements journal. He overstates the amounts of legitimate disbursements in order to absorb the cost of a fraudulent check. For instance, assume that a company owes $10,000 to a particular vendor. The fraudster would write a check to the vendor for $10,000, but enter the check in the disbursements journal as a $15,000 payment. The company's disbursements are now overstated by $5,000. The fraudster can write a $5,000 check to himself and list that check as void in the disbursements journal. The bank balance and the book balance will still match, because the cost of the fraudulent check was absorbed by overstating the amount of the legitimate check. Of course, the fact that the canceled checks do not match the entries in the journal should indicate potential fraud. This type of concealment is really only effective when the bank accounts are not closely monitored or where the employee is in charge of reconciling the accounts.

CODING THE FRAUDULENT CHECKS

If possible, fraudsters will try to code their fraudulent checks to existing accounts that are rarely reviewed or to accounts that are very active. In Case 804, for instance, the perpetrator charged his checks to an intercompany payables account because it was only reviewed at the end of the year, and not in great detail. The perpetrator in this case might also have coded his checks to an account with extensive activity in the hopes that his fraudulent check would be lost in the crowd of transactions on the account. In the cases we reviewed, most checks were coded to expense accounts or liability accounts (see chart 5-4).

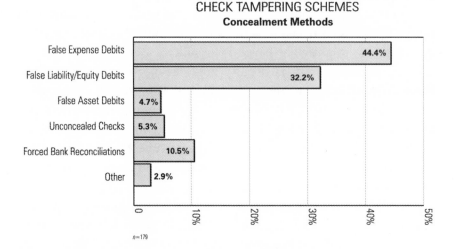

CHECK TAMPERING SCHEMES
Concealment Methods

- False Expense Debits — 44.4%
- False Liability/Equity Debits — 32.2%
- False Asset Debits — 4.7%
- Unconcealed Checks — 5.3%
- Forced Bank Reconciliations — 10.5%
- Other — 2.9%

$n=179$

Chart 5-4: Concealment Methods

This particular method can be very effective in concealing fraudulent checks, particularly when the victim company is not diligent in reconciling its bank accounts. For instance, in Case 1761, the victim company reconciled its accounts by verifying the amount of the checks with the check numbers, but did not verify that the payee on the actual check matched the payee listed in the disbursements journal. As a result, the company was unable to detect that the checks had been miscoded in the disbursements journal. As we discussed in the previous section, the fraudster might also intercept the bank statement before it is reconciled and alter the payee name on the fraudulent check to match the entry he made in the disbursements journal.

RE-ISSUING INTERCEPTED CHECKS

We mentioned before that in intercepted check schemes, the employee faces detection not only through his employer's normal control procedures, but also from the intended recipients of the checks he steals. After all, when these people do not receive their payments from the victim company they are likely to complain. These complaints, in turn, could trigger a fraud investigation.

Some employees head this problem off by issuing new checks to the people whose initial checks they stole. In Case 579, for instance, an employee would steal checks intended for vendors and deposit them into her own checking account. She would then take the invoices from these vendors and re-enter them in the company's accounts payable system, adding a number or letter to avoid the computerized system's duplicate check controls. This assured that the vendors received their due payment, and therefore would not blow the whistle on her scheme, which netted approximately $200,000.

Another example of re-issuance was provided by an accounts payable troubleshooter in Case 1328. The employee in this case was in charge of auditing payments to all suppliers, reviewing supporting documents, and mailing checks. Every once in a while, she would purposely fail to mail a check to a vendor. The vendor, of course, would call accounts payable about the late payment and would be told that his invoice had been paid on a certain date. Since accounts payable did not have a copy of the canceled check (because the fraudster was still holding it), they would call the trouble shooter to research the problem. Unfortunately for the company, the trouble-shooter was the one who had stolen the check. She would tell accounts payable to issue another check to the vendor while she stopped payment on the first check. Thus the vendor received his payment. Meanwhile, instead of stopping payment on the first check, the troubleshooter deposited it into her own account.

The difference between these two schemes is that in the latter, two checks were issued for a single invoice. The trouble shooter in Case 1328 did not have to worry about this problem because she performed the bank reconciliations for her company and was able to "force" the totals. Once again we see how access to the bank statement is a key to concealing a check tampering scheme.

BOGUS SUPPORTING DOCUMENTS

While some fraudsters attempt to wipe out all traces of their fraudulent disbursements by destroying the checks, forcing the bank reconciliation and so on, others opt to justify their checks by manufacturing fake support for them. These fraudsters prepare false payment vouchers, including false invoices, purchase orders, and/or receiving reports to create an appearance of authenticity. This concealment strategy is only practical when the employee writes checks payable to someone other than himself (e.g., an accomplice or a shell company). A check made payable to an employee may raise suspicions regardless of any supporting documents he manufactures.

Conceptually, the idea of producing false payment vouchers may seem confusing in a chapter on check tampering. If the fraudster is using fake vouchers, shouldn't the crime be classified as a billing scheme? Not necessarily. In a check tampering scheme, the fraudster generates the disbursement by writing the check himself. He may create fake support to justify the check, but the support — the voucher — had nothing to do with the disbursement being made. Had the fraudster not created a fake invoice, he would still have had a fraudulent check.

In a billing scheme, on the other hand, the fraudster uses the false voucher to *cause a payment to be generated.* Without a fake voucher in these schemes, there would be no fraudulent disbursement at all, because the employee depends on someone else to actually cut the check. In other words, the false voucher is a means of creating the unwarranted payment in these schemes, rather than an attempt to hide it.

Conclusion

DETECTION

Account Analysis through Cut-off Statements

Bank cut-off statements should be requested for 10 to 15 days after the closing date of the balance sheet. These statements may be used to detect cash fraud during periods between monthly bank statements. Cut-off statements are often used by auditors to ensure that income and expenses are reported in the proper period. If the employees know that at any time during the month a cut-off statement may be ordered and reviewed independently, cash fraud will be less likely.

A cut-off statement generally is ordered from the bank, delivered unopened to the auditor (or outsider), and reconciled. It can be ordered at any time during the accounting cycle.

If cut-off bank statements are not ordered or received, obtain the following period bank statement and perform account analysis and investigation.[2]

Bank Reconciliations

Copies of the bank reconciliations and account analysis should be obtained along with the complete set of bank statements on all checking and savings accounts, as well as certificates of deposit and other interest-bearing and non-interest-bearing accounts. From the reconciliations perform the following tests:

- Confirm the mathematical accuracy of the reconciliation.
- Examine the bank statement for possible alterations.
- Trace the balance on the statement back to the bank cut-off and bank confirmation statements.
- Foot the balance to the company's ledger.
- Trace the deposits in transit to the bank cut-off statement to ensure recording in proper period
- Examine canceled checks and compare to the list of outstanding checks.
- Sample supporting documentation of checks written for a material amount.
- Verify supporting documentation on outstanding checks written for a material amount.
- Verify accuracy of nonoperational cash or cash-equivalent accounts (CDs and other investment accounts). Analysis should include the verification of the institution holding the funds, interest rate, maturity date, beginning and ending balances, and current period activity. Book and bank balances should be compared and any accruals of interest analyzed.[3]

Bank Confirmation

Another method related to the cut-off statement is the bank confirmation request. Unlike the cutoff statement, this detection method is merely a report of the balance in the account as of the date requested. This balance should be requested to confirm the statement balance as well as any other necessary balance date. If the fraud is occurring at the bank reconciliation stage, this independent confirmation may prove to be very helpful.

Check-Tampering Red Flags

The following irregularities may indicate fraud:

- *Voided checks* may indicate employees have embezzled cash and charged the embezzlement to expense accounts. When the expense is paid (from accounts payable), fraudulent checks are marked and entered as void and removed from distribution points. An account-balancing journal entry is then made. The list of voided checks should be verified against physical copies of the checks. Bank statements should be reviewed to ensure that voided checks have not been processed.

- *Missing checks* may indicate lax control over the physical safekeeping of checks. Stop payments should be issued for all missing checks.
- *Checks payable to employees,* with the exception of regular payroll checks, should be closely scrutinized. Such an examination may indicate other schemes such as conflicts of interest, fictitious vendors, or duplicate expense reimbursements.
- *Altered endorsements or dual endorsements* of returned checks may indicate possible tampering.
- *Returned checks* with obviously forged or questionable signature endorsements should be verified with original payee.
- *Altered payees* on returned checks should be verified with intended payee.
- *Duplicate or counterfeit checks* indicate fraud. These checks may be traceable to depositor through bank check coding.
- *Questionable deposit dates* should be matched to the corresponding customer accounts.
- An examination of all *cash advances* may reveal that not all advances are properly documented and, therefore, inappropriate payments have been made to employees.
- *Customer complaints* regarding payments not being applied to their accounts should be investigated.
- *A questionable payee or payee address* on a check should trigger review of the corresponding check and support documentation.

PREVENTION
Check Disbursement Controls

The following list of activities will help tighten controls and possibly deter employees from giving in to the temptation to commit check fraud.

- Check "cutting" and preparation is not done by a signatory on the account.
- Checks are mailed immediately after signing.

- Theft control procedures are adhered to (see below).
- Accounts payable records and addresses are secure from possible tampering. Changes in vendor information should be verified.
- Banks statements should be reviewed diligently ensuring that amounts and signatures have not been altered.
- Bank reconciliations should be completed immediately after monthly statements are received. The Uniform Commercial Code states that discrepancies must be presented within 30 days from the bank statement in order to hold the bank liable.
- Bank reconciliations are not made by signatories on the account.
- Bank statements should be reconciled and reviewed by more than one person.
- Appropriate separation of duties should be documented and adhered to.
- Detailed comparisons are routinely made between check payees and the payees listed in the cash disbursement journal.
- Personnel responsible for handling and coding checks are periodically rotated, keeping total personnel involved to a minimum.

Bank-Assisted Controls

Companies should work in a cooperative effort with banks to prevent check fraud. Consider the following control measures that may be taken in regard to a firm's checking accounts.

- Establish maximum dollar amounts above which the company's bank will not accept checks drawn against the account.
- Use positive pay banking controls. Positive pay allows a company and its bank to work together to detect fraudulent items presented for payment. The company provides the bank with a list of checks and amounts that are written each day. The bank verifies items presented for payment against the company's list. The bank rejects items that are not on the list. Investigations are conducted as to the origin of "nonlist" items.

Physical Tampering Prevention

The following list details check-tampering prevention techniques that are being used today, by some institutions, to secure business's check integrity. These methods can be used individually or in combination.

- *Signature Line Void Safety Band*—The word VOID appears on the check when photocopied.
- *Rainbow Foil Bar*—A horizontal, colored bar placed on the check fades and is shaded from one bar to the next. Photocopied foil bars appear solid.
- *Holographic Safety Border*—Holographic images are created in a way that reflect light to reveal a three dimensional graphic.
- *Embossed Pearlescent Numbering*—Checks are numbered using a new technique that is revealed by a colored highlighter pen or by a bright light held behind the check.
- *Other Chemical Voids*—Checks reveal an image or the word VOID when treated with an eradicator chemical.
- *Micro Line Printing*—Extremely small print is too small to read with the naked eye and becomes distorted when photocopied.
- *High Resolution Microprinting*—Images are produced on the check in high resolution, 2400 dots per inch or higher. This technique is very difficult to reproduce.
- *Security Inks*—Checks contain inks which react with eradication chemicals reducing a forger's ability to modify the check.
- *Chrome Coloring*—The use of chrome-like coloring deters photocopying even with color copiers. The chrome pattern or numbering develops solid black.
- *Watermark Backers*—Hidden images can only be seen when the check is held at an angle. This image is very difficult to reproduce.
- *Ultraviolet Ink*—This ink displays an image or message when held under ultraviolet lighting.

Check Theft Control Procedures

It is very important to provide internal controls which will minimize the possibility of check tampering and theft. Below is a list of items that should be incorporated into company's policies and procedures to help deter check tampering.

- New checks should be purchased from reputable, well established check producers.
- Unused checks should be stored in a secure area such as a safe, vault, or other locked area. Security to this area should be restricted to authorized personnel only. Routinely change keys and access codes to storage areas.
- Review all hiring procedures. One of the most important means of fighting fraud is to not hire people with questionable backgrounds. Develop a distinct separation of duties in the accounts payable department, including written policies and procedures for all personnel who have the opportunity to handle checks, from mailroom clerks to the CEO.
- Use electronic payment services to handle large vendor and financing payments, eliminating the use of paper checks.
- Report lost or stolen checks immediately.
- Properly and securely store canceled checks.
- Destroy unused checks for accounts that have been closed.
- Printed and signed checks should be mailed immediately after signing.

[1] Henry Campbell Black, *Black's Law Dictionary*, Fifth Edition (St. Paul: West Publishing Co., 1979), p. 585.

[2] George Georgiades, *Audit Procedures* (New York: Harcourt Brace Professional Publishing, 1995).

[3] Georgiades.

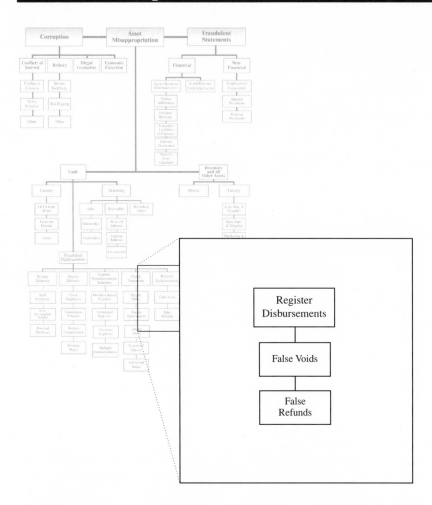

Flowchart 6-1

6. REGISTER DISBURSEMENT SCHEMES

*****

Case Study: Demotion Sets Fraud in Motion
* Several names have been changed to preserve anonymity.

Following a demotion and consequent paycut, Bob Walker silently vowed to even the score with his employer. In six months Walker racked up $10,000 in ill-gotten cash; his employer, caught completely off-guard, lost $10,000 before someone blew the whistle.

The whistleblower was Emily Schlitz, who worked weekends as a backup bookkeeper at a unit of Thrifty PayLess, a chain of 1,000 discount drugstores crossing ten Western states.

One October, while reviewing her store's refund log, Schlitz noticed an unusually large number of policy overrides by the head cashier — one Bob Walker — who naturally handled most refunds. In issuing cash refunds for big-ticket items, for instance, Walker frequently failed to record the customer's phone number. Often, he neglected to attach sales receipts to the refund log, noting that the customers wanted to keep their receipts. Schlitz questioned the high proportion of these irregularities and notified the store manager, who in turn called the asset protection (security) department at headquarters to investigate what he termed "strange entries."

Thrifty PayLess pays serious attention to such phone calls, according to its director of asset protection, James Hansen, who celebrated his 13th anniversary with the retailer that year. In 57% of the fraud cases for that year, Hansen reported, investigators received their first alert directly from store managers, as in this case.

The strange entries that Schlitz found called for immediate action. Hansen dispatched a field investigator, Raymond Willis, to review the findings and conduct a brief background check of Walker

— a 32-year-old single male who had been employed by Thrifty PayLess for five years.

Willis soon learned that six months earlier the store manager, citing poor performance, had demoted Walker from a management position to head cashier, which meant he experienced a $300 a month paycut. For Willis, that information alone raised one of the three red flags that signal potential fraud by employees: personal or financial problems, lifestyle changes or pressures, and low morale or feelings of resentment.

Further inquiry revealed Walker blamed management for the demotion.

But those red flags paled next to the wealth of evidence Willis uncovered during his investigation. He began by calling customers listed in the refund log to politely inquire about the service they received at the drugstore, discreetly looking for verification or vilification. Next, he compared the number of refunds for food processors — by far the most popular merchandise Walker accepted for return — to the number originally received in shipment minus those sold. These numbers were in turn compared to the food processors actually in stock. The investigator discovered major discrepancies.

Willis brought the case to a conclusion in just three days. "He stayed awake nights working on this one because he quickly saw the enormity of the take," recalled boss Hansen. "It just fueled his fire."

"The perpetrator had really gotten carried away with his activity. As will often happen, over time he got greedy. And once Walker got greedy, he got careless and sloppy," said Hansen.

Although aggressive in his investigation, Willis kept it quiet. He limited his interviews to just two or three of Walker's fellow employees. "Several coworkers had previously told managers that Walker seemed disgruntled and somewhat upset. But outwardly, his frustration never peaked enough to warrant the need for management to keep an eye on this guy," explained Hansen.

At the end of Willis' third day in the field, it was time to interview Walker. Initially, Willis asked general questions about store policies and procedures. He went on to focus more on cashiering methods. Walker seemed at ease in the beginning, helpful and responsive. At one point, Walker even offered the suggestion that "more controls should be placed on refunds."

As the interview progressed; however, Walker got more and more nervous. The smooth talker began to stutter and stammer. Willis asked Walker if he knew the definition of shrinkage. He haltingly replied, "for one, loss of cash or inventory due to customer or employee theft."

Willis then asked, "What have you personally done to cause shrinkage?" Walker became very quiet. After a long pause, he asked in a hushed tone, "Well, what if I did do it?" Willis laid out the consequences and continued to query the formerly-trusted employee.

Walker vented his anger toward the managers who had "unjustly" demoted him. He confessed to writing fake cash refunds in retaliation. While the fraud began in May as an occasional act, it soon increased in frequency and flagrancy. At first, to fulfill the blanks on the customer information part of the refund log, he pulled names at random from the phone book. Later he simply made up names and phone numbers, he said. As his greed escalated, he altered legitimate refunds that he had issued earlier in the day, adding merchandise to inflate their monetary value and pocketing the difference.

Although store policy dictated that management approval was required for refunds totaling more than $25 or in the absence of a sales receipt, Walker deliberately thumbed his nose at those rules and others. No one ever questioned the signature authority of this recently-defrocked member of the management team.

To further justify his actions, Walker detailed his previous financial problems, which he said were exacerbated by the $300 monthly paycut.

Proceeds from the fraud initially went toward his two mortgage payments, which equaled $800 a month. His ongoing booty subsequently financed his insurance premiums and living expenses, which were now mounting. He easily paid off his credit cards. The single guy also used the cash for fancy dinners out on the town.

During the two-hour-long confrontation, Walker claimed ignorance about the exact amount he'd filched, saying he had never tallied the score. He did admit, however, that he played this lucrative game with a growing ardor and intensity.

As it turned out, all three refunds Walker had issued the day of the interview proved fraudulent. Yet he still seemed shocked that his fraud totaled upwards of $10,000 — more than 25 times the $300 paycut he had endured over the past six months.

In a store that generates $4 million in annual sales, $10,000 over six months represents a small percentage of loss. In the retailing industry, such shrinkage may be explained away by shoplifting, bad checks, accounting or paperwork errors, breakage or spoilage, shipping shortages, or numerous other reasons. Employee theft, of course, is also a significant factor in shrinkage, said Hansen, who began his career as a store detective and became a CFE in 1991.

"In my mind, a comprehensive loss prevention program is well balanced between preventive and investigative efforts." He said Thrifty PayLess maintains an outstanding educational program for all employees. They attend mandated training classes in both the prevention and detection of fraud. Crucial to its success, employees are always made to feel like an integral part of Thrifty PayLess's whole loss prevention effort. Hansen and his asset protection staff regularly visit the stores to introduce themselves, become familiar to employees, form an ongoing rapport, and build a level of trust in confidentiality. To further encourage communication, the retailer established a hot line that employees can call with anonymous tips about suspected fraud or abuse.

As evidenced by the part-time bookkeeper's suspicions and subsequent actions in this case, Thrifty's efforts obviously work, said the head of security. "It's not that our controls were in any way inadequate; it's that a local manager was not properly enforcing those controls. Generally, he got lax with a 'trusted' employee." (Needless to say, the store manager suffered some repercussions as a result of this case.)

As a result of the Walker experience, manager approval is now required for all refunds over $5. A sales receipt must also accompany all refunds, said Hansen. Thrifty PayLess's internal audit and asset protection departments perform audits regularly, checking for compliance.

"Proper implementation is the key." Hansen continued, "You cannot prevent fraud 100%. The best you can do is to limit it through your proactive educational, awareness, and audit programs. Of course, aggressively investigating all red flags or tips as well." Hansen's asset protection department concludes over 1,400 employee theft and fraud cases and 30,000 customer shoplifting cases annually.

Owing to the grand scale of theft in this case, Walker was arrested immediately after his interview, booked on felony charges of embezzlement, and held pending bail. He faced criminal and civil prosecution. Walker made bail within hours, then disappeared without a trace. All investigative efforts to locate him thus far have failed. To this day Bob Walker remains a fugitive of justice.

*****

Overview

We have so far discussed two ways in which fraud is committed at the cash register — skimming and cash larceny. These schemes are what we commonly think of as theft. They involve the surreptitious removal of money from a cash register. When money is taken from a register in a skimming or larceny scheme, there is no record of the transaction; the money is simply missing.

In this chapter we will discuss fraudulent disbursements at the cash register. These schemes differ from the other register frauds in that, when money is taken from the register, the removal of money is recorded on the register tape. A false transaction is recorded as though it were a legitimate disbursement to justify the removal of money. Bob Walker's fraudulent refunds were an example of such a false transaction.

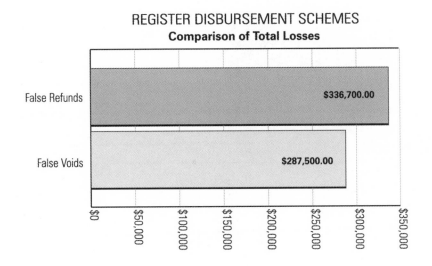

Chart 6-1: Comparison of Total Losses

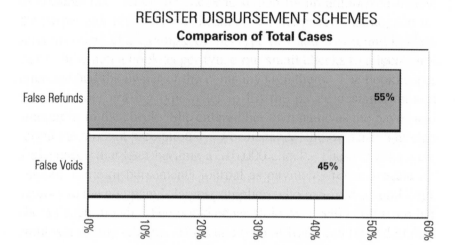

Chart 6-2: Comparison of Total Cases

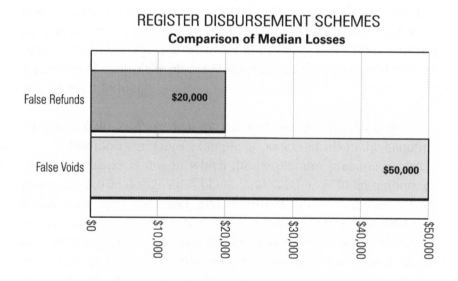

Chart 6-3: Comparison of Median Losses

Register disbursements are among the least costly of all the schemes we have identified. The median loss for register disbursement schemes in our study was $22,500, which was the fourth lowest of all the scheme types (see chart 1-5). It should be remembered, however, that these can be expensive schemes. One register disbursement case in our study caused a loss of $100,000 to a victim company over a two-year period. Register disbursement schemes were the least common of all the asset misappropriations in our study, accounting for less than 2% of those cases (see chart 2-11). However, it should be noted that typically only the more costly frauds are included in the data presented; register schemes are present primarily in the retail sector.

There are two basic fraudulent disbursements schemes which take place at the register: *false refunds* and *false voids*. The total losses and total number of cases for these two categories in our study were fairly comparable (see charts 6-1 and 6-2, respectively), a fact that is probably due to the strong similarities in the mechanics of the two schemes. The median loss associated with false voids schemes, however, was more than twice the median loss for false refunds schemes (see chart 6-3).

While the schemes are largely similar, there are a few differences between the two that merit discussing them separately.

False Refunds

A refund is processed at the register when a customer returns an item of merchandise purchased from that store. The transaction that is entered on the register indicates the merchandise is being replaced in the store's inventory and the purchase price is being returned to the customer. In other words, a refund shows a disbursement of money from the register as the customer gets his money back (see flowchart 6-2).

FICTITIOUS REFUNDS

In a fictitious refund scheme, a fraudster processes a transaction as if a customer were returning merchandise, even though there is no actual return. Two things result from this fraudulent transaction. The first is that the fraudster takes cash from the register in the amount of the false return. Since the register tape shows that a merchandise return has been made, it appears that the disbursement is legitimate. The register tape balances with the amount of money in the register because the money that was taken by the fraudster was supposed to have been removed and given to a customer as a refund. These were the kinds of fraudulent transactions utilized by Bob Walker in the case study at the beginning of this chapter.

As we also saw in that case study, the second thing that happens in a fictitious refund scheme is that a debit is made to the inventory system showing that the merchandise has been returned to the inventory. Since the transaction is fictitious, no merchandise is actually returned. The result is that the company's inventory is overstated. For instance, in Case 1583, a manager created $5,500 worth of false returns, resulting in a large shortage in the company's inventory. He was able to carry his scheme on for several months, however, because (1) inventory was not counted regularly, and (2) the perpetrator, a manager, was one of the people who performed inventory counts.

OVERSTATED REFUNDS

Rather than create an entirely fictitious refund, some fraudsters merely overstate the amount of a legitimate refund and skim the excess money. This occurred in Case 1875, where an employee sought to supplement his income through the processing of fraudulent refunds. In some cases he rang up completely fictitious refunds, making up names and phone numbers for his customers. In other instances he added to the value of legitimate refunds. He would overstate the value of a real customer's refund, pay the customer the actual amount owed for the returned merchandise, then keep the excess portion of the return for himself.

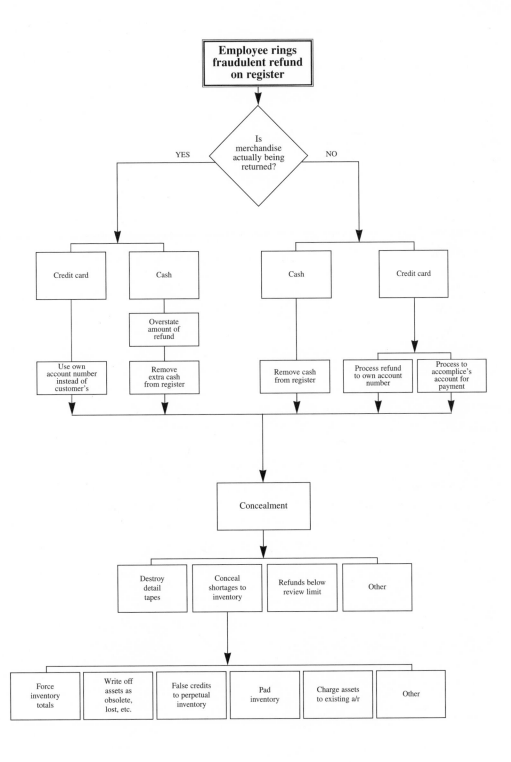

Flowchart 6-2: False Refunds

CREDIT CARD REFUNDS

When purchases are made with a credit card rather than cash, refunds appear as credits to the customer's credit card rather than as cash disbursements. Some fraudsters process false refunds on credit card sales in lieu of processing a normal cash transaction. One benefit of the credit card method is that the perpetrator does not have to physically take cash from the register and carry it out of the store. This is the most dangerous part of a typical register scheme because managers, coworkers, or security cameras may detect the culprit in the process of removing the cash. By processing the refunds to a credit card account, a fraudster reaps an unwarranted financial gain and avoids the potential embarrassment of being caught red-handed taking cash.

In a typical credit card refund scheme, the fraudster rings up a refund on a credit card sale, though the merchandise is not actually being returned. Rather than use the customer's credit card number on the refund, the employee inserts his own. The result is that the cost of the item is credited to the perpetrator's credit card account. A more creative and wide-ranging application of the credit card refund scheme was used by Joe Anderson in the following case study. Anderson processed merchandise refunds to the accounts of other people, and in return received a portion of the refund as a kickback. CFE Russ Rooker discovered Anderson's scheme, which cost Greene's department store at least $150,000. This case is also a bribery scheme because Anderson took illicit payments in exchange for creating fraudulent transactions. It serves as an excellent example of how the cash register can be used as a tool for theft.

*****

Case Study: A Silent Crime

* Several names have been changed to preserve anonymity

"A silent crime" — that's the way Russ Rooker refers to the theft he uncovered at a Detroit-area Greene's department store. "It takes only about 30 seconds, and you can have a thousand bucks," explains the regional investigation specialist.

Joe Anderson, a 15-hour a week employee in that store's shoe department, was an expert at that silent crime — ringing up fictitious returns and crediting credit cards for the cash.

During his five-year tenure with the store, Anderson did this time and time again. Rooker documented at least $150,000 in losses, but believes it was closer to $500,000, and wouldn't be surprised if the fraud exceeded $1 million. "We're scared to even know," he says.

This was a scam that was right up Rooker's analytical alley. At the time of the investigation, he had worked in retail security for about a decade — first as a credit fraud investigator checking the external, or customer, side of credit card fraud. Then he went into internal investigation, searching out employee theft and fraud.

At Greene's store, records showed that the store's shoe department was losing money because it had an exceedingly high rate of returns on its shoes. Rooker decided to investigate by using his "FTM" formula — Follow the Money.

He ordered up five months of sales data for the department from ten sales terminals. Rooker had returns divided into categories of cash, proprietary credit cards (i.e. Greene's cards), and third-party credit cards such as Visa and MasterCard.

And he saw a trend. Around the 28th of each month, certain credit card numbers would be credited for a return of approximately $300. "Two hundred ninety-seven dollars and sixty cents to be exact," says Rooker. There was never a corresponding sale recorded for the returns. And each month, each credit card number was credited only once. Thus, if Rooker had chosen to study only one month's data, the crime would not have been discovered.

He eventually found that more than 200 credit cards belonging to 110 persons were being credited by one part-time employee, Joe Anderson. Each week, Anderson credited $2,000 to $3,000 in returns to his friends', neighbors', and relatives' accounts. In return (no pun intended), Anderson was paid up to 50% of the credit. For instance, if a friend was running $300 short at the end of the month and still needed to make his house payment, he'd phone Anderson. According to Rooker, the word around Detroit was if you needed money, "Call Joe. Give him $150 and he'll double your money."

The friend might contact Anderson at the home he shared with his girlfriend. Or he might meet Anderson at the local bar, in the back of his souped-up van, or page him on his beeper. In the case of a page, he punched his credit card number, rather than his phone number, into the paging system.

Either way, the friend gave Anderson his credit card number and promised to pay him $150 for the money. Then, Anderson, in 30-second increments at the cash register, would punch in the credit. Next, just as rapidly, he'd phone the friend and tell him the deal was done. And finally, the friend would go to the nearest ATM cash machine, swipe through his credit card, and — knowing that he had a $300 credit to his account — get $300 in cash.

"So it was basically turning the money right into cash," says Rooker. "You can see the drug connection here." Yet, a drug connection was never actually proven. What was proven was that a man who "worked 15 hours a week at Greene's was living the high life. He dressed like a million bucks," to quote Rooker. "He ate at fancy restaurants." He wore lots of gold jewelry. And he drove that "fully decked out" conversion van.

And the majority of his "customers" looked as though they lived an upper middle class life, too. Appearances can be deceiving, however. Most of them were in the lower income bracket. Anderson helped them move up. Sometimes he would give them a $300 pair of shoes to go along with their $300 credit. That way, they could then go to another Greene's location, return the shoes, and get an additional $300. One customer was credited $30,000 in one year, says Rooker.

Another regular customer was Anderson's girlfriend. She owned the house they lived in. And she worked as a branch manager for a major bank in Detroit. She, however, was not prosecuted.

The Secret Service and the U.S. Attorney decided who was prosecuted. Rooker called them into the investigation upon his discovery of the perpetrator. In fact, Anderson was well known by many. He had friends and acquaintances just about everywhere.

The 15-hour-a-week employee with the big, illegal income was a mover-and-a-shaker of sorts. Rooker thinks that was part of Anderson's motive — he "hung out" with the upper middle class, was well accepted in their stratum and wanted to stay in that social group. The only way he could find to do that was to commit fraud.

Rooker also believes that Anderson simply got "caught up in it" because people came to expect it of him. In fact, they came into the store and asked for Anderson. Only he could wait on them. Those were often the ones to whom he gave a pair of shoes, too.

The Secret Service told Rooker that if he would document a minimum of $10,000 in returns via video surveillance, they would go from there. So, Rooker had video surveillance equipment installed throughout the shoe department and at the point-of-sale registers. The first day the equipment was up-and-running, Anderson was up-and-running. $5,000 he credited that day.

According to Rooker, Anderson simply reached into the inside pocket of his expensive suit jacket, pulled out a list, and started ringing up credits. One day, he gave one customer a $300 cash refund, a $300 credit refund, and a pair of $300 shoes.

This wreaked havoc on the Greene's inventory. Let's say the store's inventory reports showed there were ten pairs of style 8730 in stock. Then along came Anderson, ringing up a return for style 8730. Suddenly the inventory reports said there were eleven pairs of style 8730 in stock. In reality, though, there were still only the original ten pairs.

Five thousand dollars of returns in one day would cause inventory to be overstated by approximately 17 pairs of shoes. Seventeen pairs of shoes times five work days a week, times 4.3 weeks a month, and Greene's had a lot of invisible shoes in stock.

Six weeks after the start of in-store surveillance, $30,000 in losses was on videotape — that's 100 pairs of shoes reported in stock that weren't in stock.

And most of those losses were documented at the end of each month simply because, by then, Anderson's customers were in a typical end-of-the-month money crunch. "They came to really depend on this money," explains Rooker.

The Certified Fraud Examiner next started matching customers to credit card numbers. That was easy to do with the Greene's cards. But it was a slightly harder task for the third-party cards, and third-party cards were responsible for the majority of the returns.

So, as a member of the International Association of Credit Card Investigators, Rooker was able to contact fraud investigators at various banks to find out informally "what was going on" from the banks' perspectives. That's how he learned that some of Anderson's customers were friends and relatives.

Ironically, the part-time employee never carried a credit card. He was a cash customer only. His only known asset was his conversion van. The house he shared with his girlfriend was in her name.

The Secret Service put Anderson under surveillance. Over two weeks, they discovered how he was making his contacts. All day long, friends, relatives, and neighbors streamed in and out of the home he shared with his banker girlfriend. In essence, his 15-hour-a-week job demanded more than 15 hours a week. And often, the same people who were observed going into his home received credits that very same day.

Anderson had apparently started his "side" job as a bit of a lark and charged as his fee only 10% of the fictitious refund. As the scam and his renown grew, he upped his percentage to 25, then 50%. Everyone in town, everyone in his shoe department knew he was doing something fishy, reports Rooker, but they were scared to report him. Anderson allegedly carried a gun. As many people as there were who liked Anderson, there were as many who were frightened of him.

That, though, did not deter Rooker and the Secret Service. "The Secret Service was very aggressive," says Rooker. They promised to pursue any co-conspirator who had earned at least $5,000 in returns over two years. That led them to Ohio where they interviewed a middle-aged couple. (Most of Anderson's customers were between the ages of 30 and 50.)

This couple had once lived in the Detroit area. Getting them to turn state's evidence, as the Secret Service did on numerous occasions during this investigation, the law enforcement officers learned Anderson's entire scam.

Soon thereafter, four armed U.S. Secret Service agents entered the store, grabbed Anderson, pulled him through the stock room, and arrested him. When confronted with the crime, Anderson told the agents and Rooker, "Pound sand." He had $5,000 in cash stuffed into his socks. In his coat pocket, he had a list of 15 third-party credit card numbers with dollar amounts to credit.

Having those 15 numbers on his person, says Rooker, was enough to charge the perpetrator. Eventually, though, Rooker learned that $60,000 in refunds had been credited to those 15 numbers over the previous two years.

Anderson was led through the mall, in handcuffs, by the Secret Service. As he exited, mall store manager after store manager stood at their doors and yelled, "Hey, Joe, what's going on?"

They were worried. They were losing one of their best cash customers.

Local and federal charges for embezzlement and financial transaction card fraud against Anderson and 27 co-conspirators are pending.

Not pending are new internal controls at Greene's. Rooker implemented them immediately. Over time, another 50 to 60 employees were determined to be pulling off the same scam at losses of $10,000 to $30,000 to Greene's. The only difference was that these employees were crediting their own charge cards. Anderson only credited other persons' charge cards, silently, in 30 second increments.

*****

False Voids

Fictitious voids are similar to refund schemes in that they generate a disbursement from the register. When a sale is voided on a register, a copy of the customer's receipt is usually attached to a void slip, along with the signature or initials of a manager which indicate that the transaction has been approved (see flowchart 6-3). In order to process a false void, then, the first thing the fraudster needs is the customer's copy of the sales receipt. Typically, when an employee sets about processing a fictitious void, he simply withholds the customer's receipt at the time of the sale. If the customer requests the receipt the clerk can produce it, but in many cases customers simply do not notice that they didn't receive a receipt.

With the customer copy of the receipt in hand, the culprit rings a voided sale. Whatever money the customer paid for the item is removed from the register as though it were being returned to a customer. The copy of the customer's receipt is attached to the void slip to verify the authenticity of the transaction.

Before the voided sale will be perceived as valid, it generally must be approved by a manager. In many of the cases in our study, the manager in question simply neglected to verify the authenticity of the voided sale. These managers signed most anything presented to them and thus left themselves vulnerable to a voided sales scheme. An example of this kind of managerial nonchalance occurred in Case 1753. In this case a retail clerk kept customer receipts and "voided" their sales after the customers left the store. The store manager signed the void slips on these transactions without taking any action to verify their authenticity. A similar breakdown in review was detected in Case 1787, where an employee processed fraudulent voids, kept customer receipts, and presented them to her supervisors for review at the end of her shift, long after the alleged transactions had taken place. Her supervisors approved the voided sales and the accounts receivable department failed to notice the excessive number of voided sales processed by this employee.

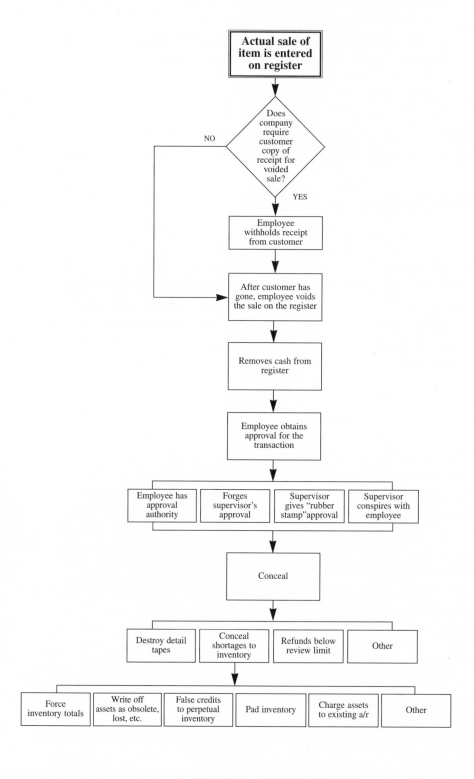

Flowchart 6-3: False Voids

It was not a coincidence that the perpetrators of these crimes presented their void slips to a manager who happened to be lackadaisical about authorizing them. Rather, it is generally the case that these kinds of managers are essential to the employee's schemes.

Since not all managers are willing to provide rubber stamp approval of voided sales, some employees take affirmative steps to get their voided sales "approved." This usually amounts to forgery, as in Case 1753 (noted above) where the fraudster eventually began forging his supervisor's signature as his false voids became more and more frequent.

Finally, it is possible that a manager will conspire with a register employee and approve false voids in return for a share of the proceeds. While we did not encounter any cases like this in our study, we did come across several examples of managers helping employees to falsify timecards or expense reimbursement requests. There is no logical reason why the same kind of scheme would not work with false voids.

Concealing Register Disbursements

As we discussed above, when a false refund or void is entered into the register, two things happen. The first is that the employee committing the fraud removes cash from the register, and the second is that the item allegedly being returned is debited back into the inventory. This leads to a situation in which there is less inventory actually on hand than the inventory records reflect. A certain amount of shrinkage is expected in any retail industry, but too much of it raises concerns of fraud. It is therefore in the fraudster's best interests to conceal the appearance of shrinkage on the books.

Inventory, remember, is essentially accounted for by a two-step process. The first part of the process is the perpetual inventory, which is essentially a running tabulation of how much inventory *should be on hand*. When a sale of merchandise is made, the perpetual inventory is credited to remove this merchandise from the records. The amount of merchandise that should be on hand is reduced. Periodically, someone from the company takes a physical count of the inventory, going through the stockroom or warehouse and counting the amount of inventory that *is actually on hand*. The two figures are then compared to see if there is a discrepancy between the perpetual inventory (what should be on hand) and the physical inventory (what is on hand).

In register disbursement schemes, shrinkage is often concealed by overstating inventory during the physical count, especially if taking inventory is one of the fraudster's duties. The fraudster simply overstates the amount of inventory on hand so it matches the perpetual inventory. For a more detailed analysis of methods used to conceal inventory shrinkage, please see the Inventory and Other Assets chapter of this book.

SMALL DISBURSEMENTS

Another way for employees to avoid detection in a refund scheme is to keep the sizes of the disbursements low. Many companies set limits below which management review of a refund is not required. Where this is the case, fraudsters simply process copious numbers of small refunds which are small enough that they do not have to be reviewed. In Case 791, for example, an employee created over 1,000 false refunds, all under the review limit of $15. He was eventually caught because he began processing refunds before store hours and another employee noticed that refunds were appearing on the system before the store opened. Nevertheless, before his scheme was detected the man made off with over $11,000 of his employer's money.

DESTROYING RECORDS

One final means of concealing a register scheme, as with many kinds of fraud, is to destroy all records of the transaction. Most concealment methods are concerned with keeping management from realizing that fraud has occurred. When an employee resorts to destroying records, however, he typically has conceded that management will discover his theft. The purpose of destroying records is usually to prevent management from determining who the thief is. In Case 2728, for example, a woman was creating false inventory vouchers which were reflected on the register tape. She then discarded all refund vouchers, both legitimate and fraudulent. Because documentation was missing on all transactions, it was extremely difficult to distinguish the good from the bad. Thus it was hard to determine who was stealing.

Conclusion

Detection

Fictitious Refunds or Voided Sales

Fictitious refunds or voided sales often can be detected when closely examining the documentation submitted with the cash receipts.

- One detection method is to evaluate the refunds or discounts given by each cashier or salesperson. This analysis may point out that a single employee or group of employees has a higher incidence of refunds or discounts than others. Further examination is then necessary to determine if the refunds are appropriate and properly documented.
- Signs in the register area asking customers to ask for and examine their receipts employ the customer as part of the internal control system. This helps ensure that the cashier or salesperson is properly accounting for the sale and prevents employees from using customer receipts as support for false void or refunds.
- Random service calls to customers who have returned merchandise or voided sales can be used to verify the legitimacy of transactions.

Register Scheme Red Flags

- Inappropriate employee segregation of duties. For example, register counting and reconciling should not be done by the cashier.
- Cashiers, rather than supervisors, have access to the control keys which are necessary for refunds and voids.
- Register employee has authority to void own transactions.
- Register refunds are not methodically reviewed.
- Multiple cashiers operate from a single cash drawer without separate access codes.
- Personal checks from cashier found in register.
- Voided transactions are not properly documented or not approved by a supervisor.
- Voided cash receipt forms (manual systems) or supporting documents for voided transactions (cash register systems) are not retained on file.
- Missing or obviously altered register tapes.

- Gaps in the sequence of transactions on register tape.
- An inordinate number of refunds, voids, or no-sales on register tape.
- Inventory totals appear forced.
- Multiple refunds or voids for amounts just under the review limit.

PREVENTION

- Review the segregation of duties of key employees who staff the register as well as the duties of their supervisors.
- As cash is received it is important to ensure that the employees responsible for completing these important tasks are informed of their responsibilities and properly supervised.
- An employee other than the register worker should be responsible for preparing register count sheets and agreeing them to register totals.
- Complete register documentation and cash must be delivered to the appropriate personnel in a timely manner.
- Cash thefts sometimes are revealed by customers who have paid money on an account and have not received credit, or in some cases, who have been credited for an amount that does not agree with the payment they have made. Complaints and inquiries also are received frequently from banks.
- Access to the register must be closely monitored and access codes must be kept secure.
- Quantity of refunds should be analyzed to detect multiple small refunds.
- Communicate and adhere to company policy of performing unannounced cash counts.
- Maintain the presence of a manager or supervisor near the area of the cash register as a deterent to theft.
- Review supporting documents for voided and refunded transactions for propriety (i.e., legitimacy and approvals).
- Review the numerical sequence and completeness of cash register tapes.

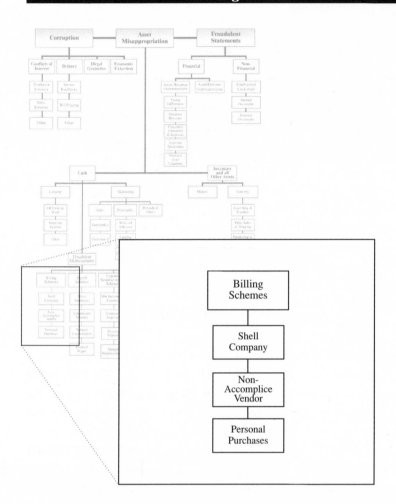

7. BILLING SCHEMES

*****

Case Study: Medical School Treats Fraud and Abuse
* Several names have been changed to preserve anonymity.

Fraud seemed to plague a certain Southeastern medical college, with one bad case erupting after another. One supervisor's minor transgression opened a Pandora's box of fraud perpetrated by his assistant.

It all began when Bruce Livingstone, a married supervisor at the college's three-person business office, took his girlfriend on a business trip using school funds drawn from a suspense account (a temporary account in which entries of credits or charges are made until their proper disposition can be determined). Livingstone did not submit an expense report to offset the charges that month, a violation of a policy governing the college's extensive travel budget.

Once officials realized that employees had grown lax about submitting timely expense reports, they attempted to reconcile the suspense account by requiring employees to settle their own accounts before receiving their paychecks.

Not wanting his indiscretion revealed, Livingstone had to disguise the additional expense of taking his girlfriend on a business trip. He submitted a phony expense report in which he unwisely named a female senior auditor at the college as his traveling partner. He forged the auditor's signature on a letter which stated she had participated.

As luck would have it, the unsuspecting auditor herself reviewed the bogus report. She was quite surprised to find she'd taken a trip with Livingstone. She immediately informed Harold Dore, the director of internal audit for the institution, of the forgery. Dore alerted others.

Following a short interview with college officials, Livingstone admitted his wrongdoing and was promptly terminated. The executive vice president authorized Dore to conduct a full fraud examination. As they were soon to find out, they had not seen the worst of it yet. Livingston's amorous business trip was just the tip of the iceberg.

"Whenever there's fraud found here," said Dore, "I automatically conduct what I call a 'magnitude investigation'." He has learned that perpetrators rarely limit themselves to the fraud initially uncovered. "Chances are, they did something else."

As part of the information-gathering portion of his investigation, Dore decided to interview Cheryl Brown, the 30-year-old administrative assistant who had worked under Livingstone for three years. The interview was to be conducted with the dean of the dental school president, so Dore headed across campus toward the business office.

But Brown left before Dore arrived. She told coworkers that her uncle had been shot and that she had to depart for California immediately. In her haste to get away, she even left her paycheck behind.

Taking that as a sign, Dore immediately sealed the empty office Brown and Livingstone shared and began searching its contents. The search uncovered bags of expensive dental tools and prostheses, which it turned out he had been illegally selling to dental students for years.

Knowing vendor kickbacks are common and since one of the main functions of the business office was to process invoices submitted by vendors, Dore started by reviewing the master file. The list had never been purged and contained tens of thousands of names—all the vendors who had ever supplied goods and services as part of the college's annual budget of $55 million. He selected 50 vendors, deliberately choosing those without a phone number or street address.

Then Dore took his list to the next stop in the payment process, the accounts payable department. After methodically pulling all corresponding documentation, he quickly focused on one vendor: Armstrong Supply Company. It regularly billed two or three times a month for strange items named but unknown by Dore, and always for amounts under $4,500, thus eliminating the necessity of two authorized signatures. All of the request-for-funds forms attached to the invoices either bore the signature of Livingstone or the dean of the dental school. Furthermore, Dore could find no vendor application on file for Armstrong Supply. He also failed to find any competitive bidding process in place.

"Once I looked at the actual invoices, that really got me going," said the fraud examiner. All of the invoices had been produced on a typewriter on regular white bond typing paper. A Roman-soldier-head logo graced the top, above the word "INVOICE," which was typed in boldface 12-point font. Some carried invoice numbers, others did not, but they did carry a four-digit post office box number. (Subsequent research revealed that postal authorities had switched to five-digit and six-digit P.O. boxes years earlier.) Billed items included such things as "3 dozen TPM pins" (the identity of which even the long-time stockroom manager was baffled by).

"The invoices just smelled fake," said Dore, who packs more than 20 years of auditing experience. What's more, he later found blank invoices for Armstrong Supply in one of Brown's desk drawers, directly under a suspect typewriter. And, he noticed one completed invoice that had been readied for submission. (Apparently, Brown left in too much of a hurry to dispose of the smoking gun.)

Based on those cheesy invoices, the accounts payable department would issue a check for the stated amount. On the request-for-funds forms attached, Brown always indicated that she would personally present the check to Armstrong Supply. (Due to lax controls, vendors and employees were allowed to pick up checks.) Canceled checks revealed that a man named Claude Armstrong III cashed them at various check-cashing services, which sometimes called Cheryl Brown for additional verification, as noted on the backs of the checks.

Further research showed yet another scam, according to Dore. The office mail contained a Sears gift certificate with a notecard from a vendor to Brown, thanking her for her recent business. The California vendor had billed the college for roughly $12,000 worth of Xerox cartridges — running $1,500 apiece — and Brown had processed the invoices. After a fruitless search for this valuable cache in the school's storerooms and copy centers, Dore called local dealers and discovered that their most expensive cartridge cost only $183. Under his direction, private investigators located the vendor's "corporate headquarters" in a rental unit at Mail Boxes Etc. USA, but the college abandoned their long-distance pursuit of recovery when it proved too costly.

Although Dore tried to keep his three-month-long investigation quiet, the campus buzzed with news of his activities. Brown's many friends, including two in the accounts payable department, kept her abreast of his movements.

Next he pulled in Livingstone for a chat about the new evidence supporting vendor fraud and kickbacks, as well as his backroom sale of orthodontic supplies. According to Dore, it became apparent during the interview that the philanderer knew nothing about the vendor schemes. Brown had perpetrated the $63,000 vendor fraud without Livingstone's help. He seemed quite taken aback that it had occurred under his nose by someone he trusted so much. In some cases, Brown had forged the signatures of her supervisor and the dean of the dental school. In others, the unwitting bosses actually signed the bogus forms.

At the same time the Livingstone interview was being conducted, the school's general counsel received a call from Brown's lawyer. "He asked if we had ever given leniency to an errant employee in the past, if they were to admit to everything," said Dore. Once the general counsel deemed it a possibility, they scheduled a meeting for September. It was to be attended by both attorneys, Dore, the executive vice president of the college, and Brown, who had never returned to work since her hasty departure. Her lawyer also relayed her request to bring along a friend as a character witness, a nurse for whom she had once worked who could attest to the good nature of this unmarried mother supporting three small children.

Brown was quiet and cooperative at the meeting. Dore took her through his voluminous file folder on Armstrong Supply, the sham company she had created. She willingly identified each and every document that detailed her duplicity, which had begun five months after her hire. Dire cash emergencies prompted the first few deceptions, she said. As Brown realized how easy it was in light of the weak controls, her confidence grew and she stepped up her trickery with no signs of stopping. "It became addictive, in her words," recalled Dore.

To illustrate her need, she explained that her husband had developed a drug and alcohol problem and that she had been dragged into drug abuse as well. She claimed that after she had become addicted, her husband abandoned her and the small children. She then broke down and cried, the first of many times during the interview. Brown went on to point out that she was seeing a doctor for her addictive behavior. When Dore asked how long she had been seeing her doctor, "She said her first visit was going to be next week." (Months later, a casual conversation between Dore and a coworker who had once dated Brown raised doubts about her excuses. "He swore she never touched drugs or alcohol," said Dore.)

She said her accomplice, Claude Armstrong III, was a friend with a history of drug abuse. (Background checks showed an arrest and conviction on drug charges for Armstrong; Brown had no prior arrests or convictions and her references proved favorable.) She also admitted that her cover story about the uncle in California was fabricated.

After Brown expressed remorse over the fake invoices, Dore asked her about her relationship with the phony cartridge supply firm. She totally disavowed any knowledge of that scam. She insisted that the invoices were legitimate and the cartridges were stacked in a storeroom. (Note: No one has found the precious cartridges to date.)

Even without owning up to the recent $12,000 cartridge scam, Brown seemed surprised to learn that her Armstrong Supply fraud had netted $63,000 over two years.

Given the small percentage of the annual budget that was pilfered, college officials were not surprised that the fraud went undetected by the Big Six firm that serves as their external auditor. Their contract states that "audit tests are not all-inclusive and not designed to find fraud," a disclaimer auditors rely upon to absolve them from possible culpability. "If they were that detailed, nobody could afford an external audit," said Dore, also a certified internal auditor.

Looking back, he saw that some good stemmed from the frauds. Since then, the college has instituted much stronger controls and makes sure to enforce them. Dore said tales of his dogged investigation enhanced respect for the audit function. "And probably instilled a bit of fear amongst the 1,500 employees, because the college officials did pursue a criminal prosecution against Brown."

During the course of her trial, the district attorney informed Dore that his testimony was not needed, even though it would have shown hell-bent intent on the part of the defendant. With her lawyer acting on her behalf, Brown struck a deal with the prosecutor. She was placed on probation and ordered to pay partial restitution. (Brown was found three-fourths culpable and Armstrong one-fourth. Because half of the stolen funds came from federal grants, $30,000 was charged off to the federal granting authority.)

As part of the deal, Brown was also sentenced to six months house arrest—with exceptions granted for her to attend work and church.

*****

Overview

The asset misappropriation schemes we have discussed up to this point—skimming, larceny, check tampering, and register schemes—all require the perpetrator of the scheme to physically take cash or checks from his employer. In the typical cash larceny, skimming, or register scheme, the perpetrator pockets cash—in the form of currency and checks—and carries it off company premises. In the check-tampering schemes an employee takes a check and prepares it in such a way that he is able to convert his employer's funds to his own use.

In the next two chapters we will discuss a different kind of asset misappropriation scheme, one which allows the perpetrator to misappropriate company funds without ever actually handling cash or checks while at work. These schemes attack the cash disbursements and payables cycle and are loosely termed *bogus claims*, for they succeed by making a false claim for payment upon the victim company. The bogus-claims schemes induce victim companies to unknowingly issue fraudulent payments for goods or services which they have not received. This group consists of *billing schemes* (which assail the purchasing function of a company), *payroll schemes*, and *employee-expense account schemes*. The most common of these is the billing scheme.

Billing schemes were the second most common method of occupational fraud revealed by our study, making up 16.02% of all the cases we examined (see chart 1-6). They caused losses in excess of $191,436,000 (see chart 1-4). One must ask, then, why billing schemes are so popular among employee fraudsters. One reason is that in a billing scheme (as well as in payroll and expense schemes, which will be discussed in the next chapter) the perpetrator does not have to undergo the risk of taking company cash or merchandise himself. It is always a dangerous enterprise to steal items directly from the workplace because one might be caught red-handed, in front of friends and coworkers, and exposed as a thief. In a billing scheme, the perpetrator submits or alters an invoice which causes his employer to willingly issue a check. Though the support for the check is fraudulent, the disbursement itself is facially valid. Remember that in check-tampering schemes the perpetrator may have to forge a signature or alter the face of a check to make it *appear* valid. In billing schemes, the check itself *is* valid, having gone through the normal cash disbursement cycle.

The other reason billing schemes seem to be so popular among fraudsters is that they offer the prospect of large rewards. The median cost of the billing schemes in our study was $250,000, by far the highest among all asset misappropriation classifications (see chart 2-12). Since the majority of most businesses' disbursements are made in the purchasing cycle, larger thefts can be hidden through false-billing schemes than through other kinds of fraudulent disbursements. Employees who utilize billing schemes are just going where the money is.

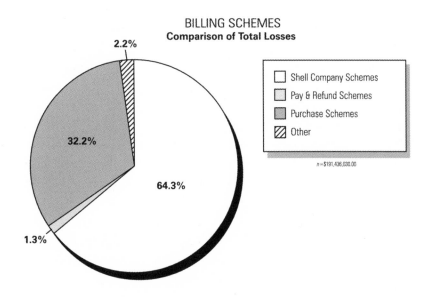

Chart 7-1: Comparison of Total Losses

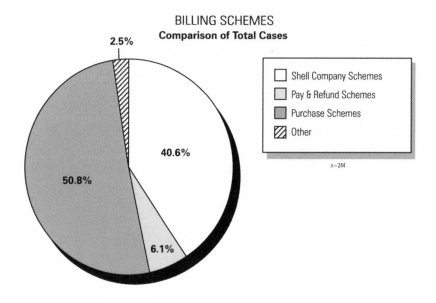

Chart 7-2: Comparison of Total Cases

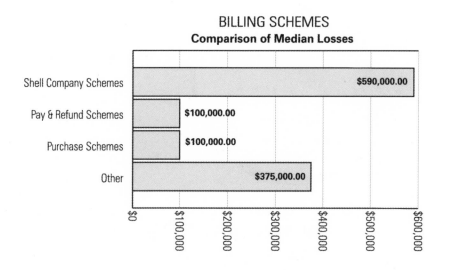

Chart 7-3: Comparison of Median Losses

The majority of losses in the billing schemes we reviewed were the result of false billings by shell companies. These schemes cost their victims over $123,000,000 (see chart 7-1). Purchases schemes were slightly more common than shell company schemes, making up almost 51% of the false billings in our study (see chart 7-2), but their median loss was much lower than that of shell company schemes (see chart 7-3). Notice, however, that the lowest median loss for any billing scheme was $100,000, an indication of just how dangerous all the frauds in this area can be.

Types of Billing Schemes

> Invoicing Via Shell Companies

> Invoicing Via Nonaccomplice Vendors

> Personal Purchases with Company Funds

Cash-Generating Schemes

In a cash-generating scheme, an employee creates false vouchers or submits false invoices to his employer. These false documents cause the employer to issue payments for goods or services which are either completely fictitious or overstated in price. The perpetrator then collects the fraudulent checks and converts them. These schemes are distinct from the purchases schemes (to be discussed at the end of this chapter) in which an employee buys personal goods or services at his company's expense.

A *voucher* is a file that includes the purchase order which was sent to the vendor, the vendor invoice which lists the cost and quantity of items purchased, and the internal receiving reports, which verify that purchased items have been delivered. In the typical purchasing cycle, a completed voucher containing all of these documents is required before the accounts payable department will issue a check to a vendor. Therefore, a billing scheme might necessitate the falsification or alteration of any of these documents.

In general, cash-generating billing schemes are built around invoices from shell companies or employee-owned businesses. In other circumstances, invoices from legitimate vendors may be utilized by a corrupt employee to generate fraudulent disbursements.

Invoicing Via Shell Companies

FORMING A SHELL COMPANY

Shell companies, for the purposes of this book, are fictitious entities created for the sole purpose of committing fraud. As we saw in the case study at the beginning of this chapter, they may be nothing more than a fabricated name and a post office box that an employee uses to collect disbursements from false billings. However, since the checks received will be made out in the name of the shell company, the perpetrator will normally also set up a bank account in his new company's name, listing himself as an authorized signer on the account (see flowchart 7-2).

In order to open a bank account for a shell company, a fraudster will probably have to present the bank with a certificate of incorporation or an assumed-name certificate. These are documents which a company must obtain through a state or local government. These documents can be forged, but it is more likely that the perpetrator will simply file the requisite paperwork and obtain legitimate documents from his state or county. This can usually be accomplished for a small fee, the cost of which can be more than offset by a successful fraud scheme.

If it is discovered that a company is being falsely billed by a vendor, examiners for the victim company may try to trace the ownership of the vendor. The documents used to start a bank account in a shell company's name can sometimes assist examiners in determining who is behind the fraudulent billings. If the corrupt employee formed his shell company under his own name, a search of public records at the local court house may reveal him as the fraudster.

For this reason, the corrupt employee will sometimes form his shell company in the name of someone other than himself. For example, in Case 1737, an employee stole approximately $1 million from his company via false billings submitted from a shell company set up in his wife's name. Using a spouse's name adds a buffer of security to an employee's fraud scheme. When a male employee sets up a shell company, he sometimes does so in his wife's *maiden* name to further distance himself from the fictitious company.

A more effective way for a fraudster to hide his connection to a false company is to form the company under a fictitious name. In Case 1155 an employee used a coworker's identification to form a shell vendor. The fraudster then proceeded to bill his employer for approximately $20,000 in false services. The resulting checks were deposited in the account of the shell company and currency was withdrawn from the account through an ATM.

The other issue involved in forming a shell company is the entity's address — the place where fraudulent checks will be collected. Often, an employee rents a post office box and lists it as the mailing address of his shell company. Some employees list their home address instead. In Case 1434, a department head set up a dummy company using his residence as the mailing address. Over a two-year period, this man submitted over $250,000 worth of false invoices. Eventually, the scheme was detected by a newly hired clerk. The clerk was processing an invoice when she noticed that the address of the vendor was the same as her boss's address. (By a lucky coincidence, the clerk had typed a personal letter for her boss earlier that day and remembered his address.) Had the department head used a p.o. box instead of his home address on the invoices, his scheme might have continued indefinitely.

One reason employees might be hesitant to use p.o. boxes in shell company schemes is that some businesses are especially wary of sending checks to vendors that do not have street addresses. Such an address, as we have already discussed, can signal fraud. For this reason, fraudsters may use the address of a relative, friend, or accomplice as a collection point for fraudulent checks.

SUBMITTING FALSE INVOICES

Once a shell company is formed and a bank account has been opened, the corrupt employee is in a position to begin billing his employer. Invoices can be manufactured by various means such as a professional printer, a personal computer, or a typewriter. As we saw in the case study at the beginning of this chapter, false invoices do not always have to be of professional quality to generate fraudulent disbursements. As illustrated in the previous case study, the typewritten invoices Cheryl Brown used to bill from Armstrong Supply Company "just smelled fake," according to Harold Dore, yet they were sufficient to generate checks.

SELF-APPROVAL OF FRAUDULENT INVOICES

The difficulty in a shell-company scheme is not usually in producing the invoices, but in getting the victim company to pay them. Authorization for the fictitious purchase (and therefore payment of the bill) is the key. In a large percentage of the shell-company cases in our study, the fraudster was in a position to approve payment on the very invoices he was fraudulently submitting. In Case 116, for example, a manager authorized payment of $6 million worth of phony invoices from a dummy company he had formed. Similarly, an employee in Case 982 set up a bogus freight company and personally approved $50,000 worth of bogus invoices it. It is only logical that those with authority to approve purchases would be among the most likely to engage in billing schemes, since they have fewer hurdles to overcome than other employees.

A slight twist to this method was used in Case 1542. The victim organization in this case properly required vouchers to be prepared and approved by different persons. The fraudster in this case had approval authority, but was not allowed to prepare the vouchers which he approved. Therefore, this person created false vouchers and forged a coworker's initials as the preparer. Then the perpetrator approved the voucher for payment under his own authority. It therefore appeared that two employees had signed off on the voucher as mandated by the organization's controls.

Not all companies require the completion of payment vouchers before they will issue checks. In some enterprises, checks are written based on less formal procedures. In Case 1436, for example, the CEO of a nonprofit company simply submitted "check requests" to the accounting department. As the CEO, his "requests" obviously carried great weight in the organization. The company issued checks to whatever company was listed on the request in whatever amount was specified. The CEO used these forms to obtain over $35,000 in payments for fictitious services rendered by a shell company he had formed. In this case, invoices were not even required to authorize the payments. The check request forms simply listed the payee, the amount, and a brief narrative regarding the reason for the check. This made it so easy for the CEO to generate fraudulent disbursements that he eventually had three separate companies billing the victim company at the same time. It is obvious that, as CEO, the fraudster in this case had a wide degree of latitude within the company and was unlikely to be obstructed by one of his subordinates. Nevertheless, this case should illustrate how the failure to require proper support for payments can lead to fraud.

"RUBBER STAMP" SUPERVISORS

If an employee cannot authorize payments himself, the next best thing is if the person who has that authority is inattentive or overly trusting. "Rubber stamp" supervisors like this are destined to be targeted by unethical employees. In Case 1759, for example, an employee set up a fake computer supply company with an accomplice and "sold" parts and services to his employer. The perpetrator's supervisor did not know much about computers and therefore could not accurately gauge whether the invoices from the dummy company were excessive or even necessary. The supervisor was therefore forced to rely on the perpetrator of the scheme to verify the authenticity of the purchases. Consequently, the victim company suffered approximately $20,000 in losses.

RELIANCE ON FALSE DOCUMENTS

When an employee does not have approval authority for purchases and does not have the benefit of a rubber stamp supervisor, he must run his vouchers through the normal accounts payable process. The success of this kind of scheme will depend on the apparent authenticity of the false voucher he creates. If the fraudster can generate purchase orders and receiving reports which corroborate the information on the fraudulent invoice from his shell company, he can fool accounts payable into issuing a check.

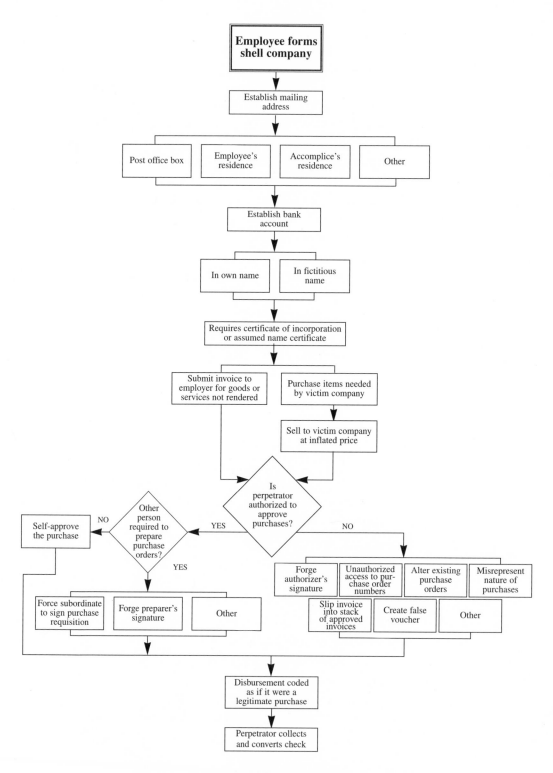

Flowchart 7-2: False Billings From Shell Companies

COLLUSION

Collusion among several employees is sometimes used to overcome well-designed internal controls of a victim company. For example, in a company with proper separation of duties, the functions of purchasing goods or services, authorizing the purchase, receiving the goods or services, and making the payment to the vendor should be separated. Obviously, if this process is strictly adhered to, it will be extremely difficult for any single employee to commit a false-billing scheme. As a result, we have seen several schemes evolve in which several employees conspired to defeat the fraud prevention measures of their employer. In Case 444, for example, a warehouse foreman and a parts ordering clerk conspired to purchase approximately $300,000 of nonexistent supplies. The parts ordering clerk would initiate the false transactions by obtaining approval to place orders for parts he claimed were needed. The orders were then sent to a vendor who, acting in conjunction with the two employee fraudsters, prepared false invoices which were sent to the victim company. Meanwhile, the warehouse foreman verified receipt of the fictitious shipments of incoming supplies. The perpetrators were therefore able to compile complete vouchers for the fraudulent purchases without overstepping their normal duties. Similarly, in Case 1099, three employees set up a shell company to bill their employer for services and supplies. The first employee, a clerk, was in charge of ordering parts and services. The second employee, a purchasing agent, helped authorize these orders by falsifying purchasing reports regarding comparison pricing, etc. The clerk was also responsible for receiving the parts and services, while a third conspirator, a manager in the victim company's accounts payable department, assured that payments were issued on the fraudulent invoices.

The cases above illustrate how collusion among several employees with separate duties in the purchasing process can be very difficult to detect. Even if all controls are followed, at some point a company must rely on its employees to be honest. One of the purposes of separating duties is to prevent any one person from having too much control over a particular business function. It provides a built-in monitoring mechanism where every person's actions are in some way verified by another person. But if *everyone* is corrupt, even proper controls can be overcome.

Purchases of Services Rather than Goods

Most of the shell company schemes in our survey involve the purchase of services rather than goods. Why is this so? The primary reason is that services are not tangible. If an employee sets up a shell company to make fictitious sales of goods to his employer, these goods will obviously never arrive. By comparing its purchases to its inventory levels, the victim company might detect the fraud. It is much more difficult, on the other hand, for the victim company to verify that the services were never rendered. For this reason, many employees involved in shell-company schemes bill their employers for things like "consulting services."

Pass-Through Schemes

In the schemes discussed so far, the victim companies were billed for completely fictitious purchases of goods or services. This is the most common formula for a shell-company fraud, but there is a subcategory of shell company schemes in which actual goods or services are sold to the victim company. These are known as pass-through schemes.

Pass-through schemes are usually undertaken by employees in charge of purchasing on behalf of the victim company. Instead of buying merchandise directly from a vendor, the employee sets up a shell company and purchases the merchandise through that fictitious entity. He then resells the merchandise to his employer from the shell company at an inflated price, thereby making an unauthorized profit on the transaction.

One of the best examples of a pass-through scheme in our study came from Case 1763, in which a department director was in charge of purchasing computer equipment. Because of his expertise on the subject and his high standing within the company, he was unsupervised in this task. The director set up a shell company in another state and bought used computers through the shell company, then turned around and sold them to his employer at a greatly exaggerated price. The money from the victim company's first installment on the computers was used to pay the shell company's debts to the real vendors. Subsequent payments were profits for the bogus company. The scheme cost the victim company over $1 million.

Invoicing Via Nonaccomplice Vendors

PAY-AND-RETURN SCHEMES

Rather than use shell companies as vessels for overbilling schemes, some employees generate fraudulent disbursements by using the invoices of nonaccomplice vendors. In pay-and-return schemes these employees do not prepare and submit the vendor's invoices, rather they intentionally mishandle payments which are owed to the legitimate vendors (see flowchart 7-3). One way to do this is to purposely double-pay an invoice. In Case 1020, for instance, a secretary was responsible for opening mail, processing claims and authorizing payments. She intentionally paid some bills twice, then requested the recipients to return one of the checks. She would intercept these returned checks and deposit them into her own account.

Another way to accomplish a pay-and-return scheme is to intentionally pay the wrong vendor. In Case 756, an accounts payable clerk deliberately put vendor checks in the wrong envelopes. After they had been mailed, she called the vendors to explain the "mistake," and requested that they return the checks to her. She deposited these checks in her own account and ran the vouchers through the accounts payable system a second time to pay the appropriate vendors.

Finally, an employee might pay the proper vendor, but intentionally overpay him. In Case 2649, an employee intentionally caused a check to be issued to a vendor for more than the invoice amount, then requested that the vendor return the excess. This money was taken by the fraudster and deposited into her own account. Similarly, an employee might intentionally purchase excess merchandise, return the excess and pocket the refund.

OVERBILLING WITH A NONACCOMPLICE VENDOR'S INVOICES

In most instances where an employee creates fraudulent invoices to overbill his employer, he uses a shell company. It is rare for an employee to submit the invoice of an existing vendor. Nevertheless, in some instances an employee will undertake such a scheme by altering an existing-vendor invoice. In the following case study, Albert Miano took a copy of a contractor's invoice, deleted the information on it, then used a copy of the blank invoice to print replicas. With the resulting blank invoices he billed his employer for over a million dollars worth of false work. CFE Terence McGrane put a stop to Miano's scheme.

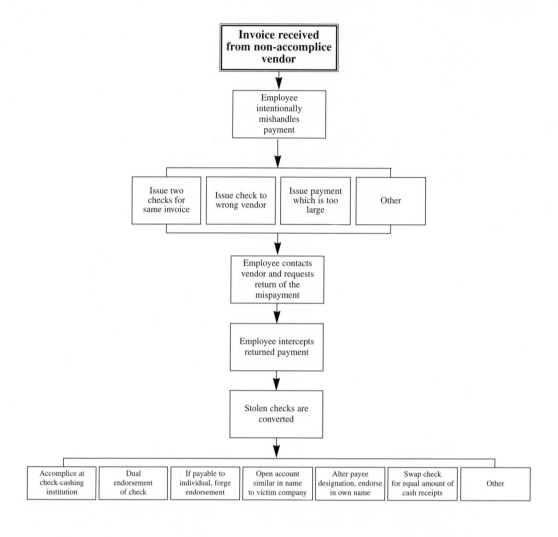

Flowchart 7-3: Pay and Return Schemes

*****

Case Study: For This Magazine, Internal Fraud Proved Hard to Digest

* *Several names have been changed to preserve anonymity*

Sometimes, fraud is discovered by chance instead of deliberate effort. In the $1 million embezzlement fraud by a *Reader's Digest* employee, more than one coincidence brought down the perpetrator.

Reader's Digest is not only a popular magazine, but one of the world's largest direct-mail publishing houses. In the mid 1980s, company officials decided to outsource much of its direct-mail operations to specialized mail vendors. The company began converting its plant in Pleasantville, New York, from a direct-mail-order factory to an office complex. Part of the office complex construction involved building an auditorium. It was to be identical to another auditorium in historic Williamsburg, Virginia.

Terrence McGrane had just begun his third day on the job as chief internal auditor for *Reader's Digest*. In an effort to get to know his new company, he had scheduled a series of interviews with all the vice presidents. His first interview was with the vice president of administrative services, Harold J. Scott, who was in charge of many construction projects and maintenance services. Because of the massive renovation project, it was not unusual for hundreds of invoices to be forwarded to Scott.

Coincidence Number One occurred when McGrane stopped by the accounts payable department and retrieved a series of recently submitted invoices for various trade expenses related to the auditorium construction project. "One of the things I wanted to accomplish was to understand how the accounting codes worked — what was capitalized; what was expensed; how it was recorded, etc." So he grabbed a stack of processed invoices with accounting codes and went up to the construction site to meet with the vice president for an hour-long interview.

As the two walked around the grounds, McGrane asked the vice president if he could explain the accounting codes to him. "He stared at the [top] invoice for approximately 30 seconds and said: 'That is not my signature on the invoice!' As he looked through the stack, he found what appeared to be about three or four other forgeries. He was completely baffled."

The initial investigation revealed that all of the forgeries were in the painting division, budgeted at approximately $500,000 a year. *Reader's Digest* employed only one person to oversee the painting operations in its facilities department: Albert Miano.

Miano, a 35-year-old man from New Fairfield, Connecticut, earned about $30,000 a year. It was his job to coordinate time-and-materials contracts with the scores of painters, carpenters, electricians, and plumbers who toiled daily on the renovation, repair, and construction of the building complex. As facilities supervisor, Miano forwarded invoices to the vice president of administration services for approval regularly.

Miano launched his scheme by crafting false invoices for the jobs done by the painters. He took a copy of a trade invoice from an existing painting contractor, and, using white-out, deleted information on a sample invoice that he had photocopied. He then made a replica of the invoice at a print shop. After work, he would duplicate similar types of services using his home typewriter, but record slightly different hours for the trade contractors' work.

McGrane related a probable scenario of how Miano executed his scheme. "Let's say he knew that during the month of February, as an example," McGrane said, ". . . there were 27 painters on the grounds during the course of one week." Miano also knew the total number of hours and the volume of materials used in that time. "He would type up replicate invoices that were similar in nature, but record only 11 painters on the grounds," McGrane said. Miano would not re-invoice exactly the same work done during a week, but he would make it look so similar that no one's suspicions were ever aroused. Effectively, there were no work orders on the "phantom work" he created on these invoices. Miano always listed fewer painters on the false invoice than the actual number who had worked that week, and he registered less time for their services than they had actually worked.

As part of his job, he regularly brought the trade invoices into the administrative VP's office for signature approval. After delivering a stack of these invoices, he would return to collect them within the next day or two and deliver the approved invoices to the accounts payable department. "It was this opportunity," McGrane said, "that this individual was allowed to go and collect the approved invoices and insert his own replicated fraudulent invoices as approved. This was the first piece of an 'electronic circuit' that allowed him to commit the fraud." The second piece of the circuit for the fraud to ignite,

McGrane said, was allowing this same employee to transport the invoices to the accounts payable department and ultimately to collect the check.

After seeing how easy it was to slip in his own false invoices in the stack of approved ones, Miano became bolder in his scheme. He began calling accounts payable, claiming that a carpenter or painter had arrived on the grounds and needed his check "immediately." To keep the project flowing, the employees in the accounts payable department accommodated him. Many employees knew and liked Miano, who had worked for *Reader's Digest* for nearly 15 years. Eventually, this routine became so familiar to employees in accounts payable that Miano did not even need to make up an excuse to pick up checks. Each time he would collect them, he would stash the check for the false invoice in his pocket. When he returned home to New Fairfield, Connecticut, he took the check to his bank, forged the contractor's name on the back, then endorsed it with his own name and deposited the check.

McGrane explains that Miano was able to pull off the scam due to failure of internal controls and employees not following standard accounting procedures. "For any business transaction, the invoices should be dispatched independently to the approving authority. Once signed, the approved invoices should be sent independently to accounts payable. When the check is prepared by accounts payable, they should mail it directly to the third party. Under a strong internal control system, the employees and/or contractors should not be allowed to come in and collect checks directly. Direct contacts with accounts payable personnel make it too tempting for someone to try to misappropriate funds."

Accounts payable also failed to combine the invoices into a single check — they wrote a check for each invoice. "Had they combined it," McGrane said, "his false invoice would have been added into the legitimate painter's monthly invoice summary, and the money would be mailed to the legitimate contractor," McGrane said. Accounts payable neglected to study the invoice signatures for forgeries, and the accounting department dropped the ball by not perusing processed checks for dual endorsements, another red flag for potentially misappropriated funds.

Miano's first transaction totaled $1,200. His second transaction jumped to $6,000 and his third, $12,000. His largest single transaction came to over $66,000. Miano refined his strategy by pacing, on a parallel basis, a certain amount below the total due the painter. "If the painter submitted an invoice for $20,000 a month," McGrane said, "Miano would submit an invoice for, say, $14,000. If the painter submitted a $6,000 invoice, he'd submit one for $3,000." The individual invoice amounts, because of the continuing construction, would not have alarmed even an auditor.

Miano's behavior at the office was the same as ever. He dressed the same way, drove the same car to work, and shared little of his private life with other workers. He had not taken a vacation in over four years, and his boss thought he should be promoted (a move Miano resisted, for reasons now obvious). After hours, however, Miano was a different person.

Coincidence Number Two in this case was that McGrane's secretary was not only on Miano's bowling team, she was also his neighbor. They saw each other regularly at the local bowling alley. She took notice when Miano's behavior became somewhat extravagant. At first he took to buying the team drinks, a habit most appreciated by his teammates. However, the secretary began wondering where all the money was coming from when he showed up in his new Mercedes (one of five cars he bought) and talked about a new $18,000 boat. He also invested in real estate and purchased a second home costing $416,000.

McGrane's secretary approached Miano one night after he had spent some $800 on drinks for the team. "Did you win the lottery, or what?" she asked. He explained that his father-in-law had recently died and left a substantial inheritance to his wife and him. Miano's father-in-law was actually quite alive, but no one ever bothered to check out the claim. No one suspected Miano of doing anything sinister or criminal. All of his associates considered him "too dumb" to carry out such a scheme. One person described him as "dumb as a box of rocks."

Coincidence Number Three: After four years without a vacation, Miano took what he considered a well-deserved trip to Atlantic City. He wasn't there long, though, before he was called back to Pleasantville. One can imagine his chagrin at having to leave the casinos and boardwalks and head back to the office. Little did he know it was about to get a lot worse.

Upon his return, Miano found himself confronted by the auditor, vice president, and two attorneys from the district attorney's office. He readily admitted guilt. "He said he had expected to get caught," McGrane said. "He did it strictly based on greed. Miano claimed there was no one else involved, and the sum total of his fraud was about $400,000."

The internal audit, however, found that Miano had forged endorsements on more than 50 checks in those four years, the sum of which totaled $1,057,000. Ironically, the auditors could only identify about $380,000 spent on tangible items (boats, cars, down-payment on a home, etc.). The investigators could not account for the other $700,000, although they knew Miano had withdrawn at least that much from the bank.

Miano served only two years of an eight-year sentence in a state penitentiary. At the time of his indictment, his wife filed for divorce, claiming she knew nothing of her husband's crimes. Miano told a reporter in jail that the loss of his family and the public humiliation had taught him his lesson.

"For a nickel or for $5 million, it doesn't pay," Miano said. "You enjoy the money for a while, but you lose your pride and your self-respect. It ends up hurting your family, and no money can ever change that."

*****

Personal Purchases with Company Funds

Instead of undertaking billing schemes to generate cash, many fraudsters simply purchase personal items with their company's money. Company accounts are used to buy items for fraudsters, their businesses, their families, and so on. In Case 649, for instance, a supervisor started a company for his son and directed work to the son's company. In addition to this unethical behavior, the supervisor saw to it that his employer purchased all the materials and supplies necessary for the son's business. In addition, the supervisor purchased materials through his employer that were used to add a room to his own house. All in all, the perpetrator bought nearly $50,000 worth of supplies and materials for himself using company money.

Conceptually, one might wonder why a purchases fraud is not classified as a theft of inventory or other assets rather than a billing scheme. After all, in purchases schemes the fraudster buys something with company money, then takes the purchased item for himself. In Case 649 discussed above, for example, the supervisor took building materials and supplies. How does this differ from those frauds discussed in the "Inventory and Other Assets" chapter, where employees steal supplies and other materials? On first glance, the schemes appear very similar. In fact, the perpetrator of a purchases fraud is stealing inventory just as he would in any other inventory theft scheme. Nevertheless, the heart of the scheme is not the *taking* of the inventory but the *purchasing* of the inventory. In other words, when an employee steals merchandise from a warehouse, he is stealing an asset that the company needs, an asset that it has on hand for a particular reason. The harm to the victim company is not only the cost of the asset, but the loss of the asset itself. In a purchasing scheme, on the other hand, the asset which is taken is superfluous. The perpetrator causes the victim company to order and pay for an asset which it does not really need, so the only damage to the victim company is the money lost in purchasing the particular item. This is why purchasing schemes are categorized as invoice frauds.

PERSONAL PURCHASES THROUGH FALSE INVOICING

Most of the employees in our study who undertook purchases schemes did so by running unsanctioned invoices through the accounts payable system. The fraudster in this type of fraud buys an item and submits the bill to his employer as if it represented a purchase on behalf of the company (see flowchart 7-4). The goal is to have the company pay the invoice. Obviously, the invoice which the employee submits to his company is not legitimate. The main hurdle for a fraudster to overcome, therefore, is to avoid scrutiny of the invalid invoice and obtain authorization for the bill to be paid.

The Fraudster as Authorizer of Invoices

As was the case in the shell company schemes we reviewed, the person who engages in a purchases scheme is often the very person in the company whose duties include *authorizing* purchases. Obviously, proper controls should preclude anyone from approving his own purchases. Such poorly separated functions leave little other than his conscience to dissuade an employee from fraud. Nevertheless, we saw several examples of companies in which this lapse in controls existed. As we continue to point out, fraud arises in part because of a perceived opportunity. An employee who sees that no one is reviewing his actions is more likely to turn to fraud than one who knows that his company diligently works to detect employee theft.

An example of how poor controls can lead to fraud was found in Case 888, where a manager of a remote location of a large, publicly traded company was authorized to both order supplies and approve vendor invoices for payment. For over a year, the manager routinely added personal items and supplies for his own business to orders made on behalf of his employer. The orders often included a strange mix of items; technical supplies and home furnishings might, for instance, be purchased in the same order. Because the manager was in a position to approve his own purchases, he could get away with such blatantly obvious frauds. In addition to ordering personal items, the perpetrator changed the delivery address for certain supplies so that they would be delivered directly to his home or side business. This scheme cost the victim company approximately $300,000 in unnecessary purchases. In a similar case, 770, an employee with complete control of purchasing and storing supplies for his department bought approximately $100,000 worth of unnecessary supplies using company funds. The employee authorized both the orders and the payments. The excess supplies were taken to the perpetrator's home where he used them to manufacture a product for his own business. It should be obvious from the examples cited above that not only do poor controls pave the way for fraud, a lack of oversight regarding the purchasing function can allow an employee to take huge chunks out of his company's bottom line.

In some situations, the perpetrator is authorized to approve purchases, but controls prevent him from also initiating purchase requests. This procedure is meant to prevent the kinds of schemes discussed above. Unfortunately, those with authority to approve purchases are often high-level employees with a good deal of control over their subordinates. These persons can use their influence to force subordinates to assist in purchases scheme. In Case 95, for example, purchases under $1,000 at a certain utility company could be made with limited value purchase orders (LPOs), which required two signatures — the originator of a purchase request and the approver of the request. An LPO, attached to an invoice for less than $1,000 would be paid by the accounts payable department. In this case, a manager bought goods and services on company accounts, and prepared LPOs for the purchases. (In some cases, the LPO would falsely describe the item to conceal the nature of the purchase.) Once the LPO was prepared, the manager forced a clerk in his department to sign the document as the originator of the transaction. The clerk, intimidated by her boss, did not question the authenticity of the LPOs. With two signatures affixed, the LPO appeared to be legitimate and the bills were paid. The scheme cost the victim company at least $25,000.

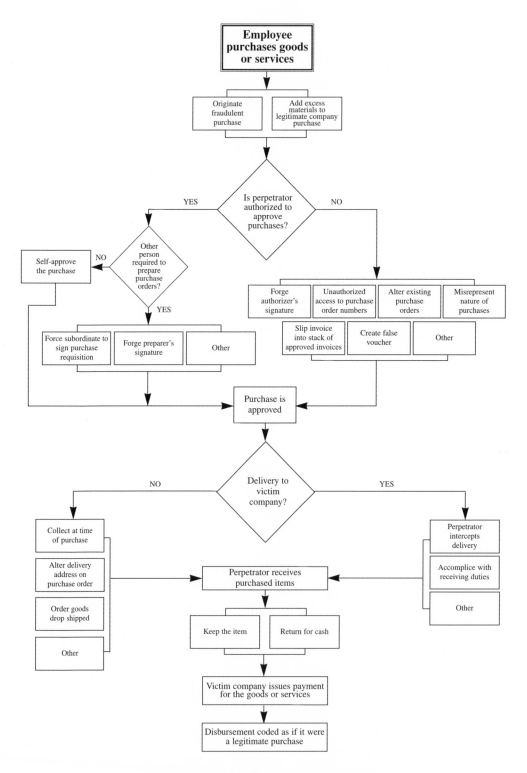

Flowchart 7-4: Invoice Purchasing Schemes

Falsifying Documents to Obtain Authorization

Not all fraudsters are free to approve their own purchases. Those who cannot must rely on other methods to get their personal bills paid by the company. The chief control document in many vouchers is the purchase order. When an employee wants to buy goods or services, he submits a purchase requisition to a superior. If the purchase requisition is approved, a purchase order is sent to a vendor. A copy of this purchase order, retained in the voucher, tells accounts payable that the transaction has been approved. Later, when an invoice and receiving report corresponding to this purchase order are assembled, accounts payable will issue a check.

So in order to make their purchases appear authentic, some fraudsters generate false purchase orders. In Case 634, for example, an employee forged the signature of a division controller on purchase orders. Thus the purchase orders appeared to be authentic and the employee was able to buy approximately $3,000 worth of goods at his company's expense. In another instance, Case 434, a part time employee at an educational institution obtained unused purchase order numbers and used them to order computer equipment under a fictitious name. The employee then intercepted the equipment as it arrived at the school and loaded the items into his car. Eventually, the employee began using fictitious purchase order numbers instead of real ones. The scheme came to light when the perpetrator inadvertently selected the name of a real vendor. After scrutinizing the documents, the school knew that it had been victimized. In the meantime, the employee had bought nearly $8,000 worth of unnecessary equipment.

Altering Existing Purchase Orders

Purchase orders can also be altered by employees who seek to obtain merchandise at their employer's expense. In Case 1334 of our study, several individuals conspired to purchase over $2 million worth of materials for their personal use. The ringleader of the scheme was a low-level supervisor who had access to the computer system which controlled the requisition and receipt of materials. This supervisor entered the system and either initiated orders of materials that exceeded the needs of a particular project or altered existing orders to increase the amount of materials being requisitioned. Because the victim organization had poor controls, it did not compare completed work orders on projects to the amount of materials or-

dered for those projects. This allowed the inflated orders to go undetected. In addition, other employees involved in the scheme were in
charge of receiving deliveries. These employees were able to divert
the excess materials and falsify receiving reports to conceal the missing items. In addition, the victim institution did not enforce a central
delivery point, meaning that employees were allowed to pick up
materials from the vendors in their personal vehicles. This made it
very easy to misappropriate the excess merchandise. The supervisor's
ability to circumvent controls and initiate false orders or alter genuine ones, though, was the real key to the scheme.

False Purchase Requisitions

Another way for an employee to get a false purchase approved
is to misrepresent the nature of the purchase. In many companies,
those with the power to authorize purchases are not always attentive
to their duties. If a trusted subordinate vouches for an acquisition,
for instance, busy supervisors often give rubber stamp approval to
purchase requisitions. Additionally, employees sometimes misrepresent the nature of the items they are purchasing in order to pass a
cursory review by their superiors. For example, in Case 1015, an
engineer bought over $30,000 worth of personal items. The engi-
neer dealt directly with vendors and was also in charge of overseeing
the receipt of the materials he purchased. He was therefore able to
misrepresent the nature of the merchandise he bought, calling it
"maintenance items." Vendor invoices were altered to agree to this
description.

Of course, the problem with lying about what he is buying is
that when delivery occurs, it is the perpetrator's personal items that
arrive, not the business items listed on the purchase requisition. In
the case discussed above, the problem of detection at this stage of
the crime was avoided because the engineer who made the fraudulent purchases was also in charge of receiving the merchandise. He
could therefore falsify receiving reports to perpetuate the fraud. We
have also encountered cases in which fruadsters in the purchasing
department enlisted the aid of employees in the receiving department to conceal their crimes.

Another way to avoid detection at the delivery stage is to
change the delivery address for purchases. Instead of being shipped
to the victim company, the items which the employee buys are sent
directly to his home or business. In a related scenario, an accounts
payable supervisor in Case 592 purchased supplies for her own busi-

ness by entering vouchers in the accounts payable system of her employer. Checks were cut for the expenses during normal daily check runs. To avoid problems with receiving the unauthorized goods, the perpetrator ordered the supplies drop shipped to a client of her side business.

PERSONAL PURCHASES ON CREDIT CARDS OR OTHER COMPANY ACCOUNTS

Instead of running false invoices through accounts payable, some employees make personal purchases on company credit cards or running accounts with vendors (see flowchart 7-5). As with invoicing schemes, the key to getting away with a false credit card purchase is avoiding detection. Unlike invoicing schemes, however, prior approval for purchases is not required. An employee with a company credit card can buy an item merely by signing his name (or forging someone else's) at the time of purchase. Later review of the credit card statement, however, may detect the fraudulent purchase. In invoicing schemes we saw how those who committed the frauds were often in a position to approve their own purchases. The same is often true in credit card schemes. A manager in Case 446, for example, reviewed and approved his own credit card statements. This allowed him to make fraudulent purchases on the company card for approximately two years.

Of course, only certain employees are authorized to use company credit cards. The manager in Case 446 above, for instance, had his own company card. Employees without this privilege can only make fraudulent purchases with a company card if they first manage to get hold of one. To this end, company cards are sometimes stolen or "borrowed" from authorized users. A more novel approach was used by an accountant in Case 1481, who falsely added her name to a list of employees to whom cards were to be issued. She used her card to make fraudulent purchases, but forged the signatures of authorized cardholders to cover her tracks. Since no one knew she even had a company card, she would not be a prime suspect in the fraud even if someone questioned the purchases. For over five years this employee continued her scheme, racking up a six figure bill on her employer's account. In addition, she had control of the credit card statement and was able to code her purchases to various expense accounts, thereby further delaying detection of her crime.

An executive secretary in Case 521 used her access to the statement for a different purpose. After making hundreds of thousands of dollars worth of fraudulent purchases on corporate cards, this employee destroyed both the receipts from her purchases and the monthly credit card statements. Eventually, duplicate statements were requested from the credit card company and the fraud was discovered. The fact that no statements were received by the company therefore led to detection of the scheme. Some fraudsters, having destroyed the real copies of credit card statements, produce counterfeit copies on which their fraudulent purchases are omitted. By taking this extra step, the fraudster is able to keep his employer in the dark about the true activity on the account.

Charge Accounts

Some companies keep charge accounts with vendors with whom they do regular business. Office supply companies are a good example of this kind of vendor. Purchases on charge accounts may require a signature or other form of authorization from a designated company representative. Obviously, that representative is in a position to buy personal items on the company account. Other employees might do the same by forging the signature of an authorized person at the time of a fraudulent purchase. In some informal settings, purchases can be verified by as little as a phone call, making it very easy to make fraudulent purchases.

Returning Merchandise for Cash

The cases we have discussed in the fraudulent purchases section to this point have all involved the false purchase of merchandise for the sake of obtaining the merchandise. In some cases, however, the fraudster buys items and then returns them for cash. The best example of this type of scheme in our survey was Case 1510, in which an employee made fraudulent gains from a business travel account. The employee's scheme began by purchasing tickets for herself and her family through her company's travel budget. Poor separation of duties allowed the fraudster to order the tickets, receive them, prepare claims for payments, and distribute checks. The only review of her activities was made by a busy and rather uninterested supervisor who approved the employee's claims without requiring support documentation. Eventually, the employee's scheme evolved. She began to purchase airline tickets and return them for their cash value. An employee of the travel agency assisted in the scheme by encoding the tickets as though the fraudster had paid for them herself. That caused the airlines to pay refunds directly to the fraudster rather than to her employer. In the course of two years, this employee embezzled over $100,000 through her purchases scheme.

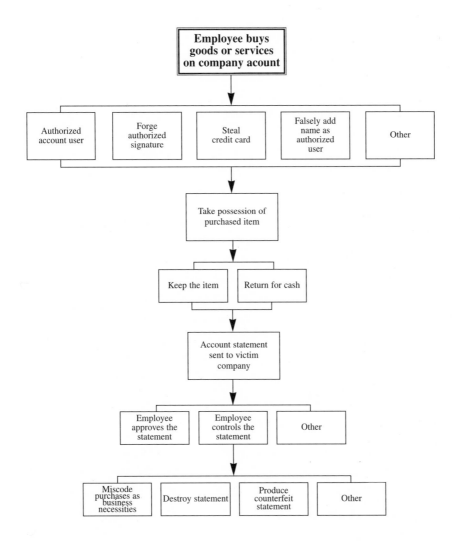

Flowchart 7-5: Purchases on Credit Card or Company Account

Conclusion

DETECTION

The following audit steps may be beneficial in detecting red flags to billing schemes.

- Does the company have a purchasing department? If yes, is it independent of (1) the accounting department, (2) the receiving department, or (3) the shipping department?
- Are purchases made only after the respective department heads sign purchase requisitions?
- Are purchases made by means of purchase orders sent to vendors for all purchases or only for purchases over a predetermined dollar limit?
- Do purchase orders specify a description of items, quantity, price, terms, delivery requirements, and dates?
- Is a list of unfilled purchase orders maintained and reviewed periodically?
- Are purchase order forms prenumbered and is the sequence accounted for periodically?
- Does the client maintain an approved vendors list?
- Are items purchased only after competitive bids are obtained? If so, are competitive bids obtained for all purchases or only for purchases over a predetermined dollar limit?
- Is a log maintained of all receipts?
- Does the receiving department prepare receiving reports for all items received? If yes, are receiving reports (1) prepared for all items, (2) prepared only for items that have purchase orders, or (3) renumbered?
- At the time the items are received, does someone independent of the purchasing department check the merchandise before acceptance as to description, quantity, and condition?
- Are copies of receiving reports (1) furnished to the accounting department, (2) furnished to the purchasing department, or (3) filed in the receiving department?
- Are receipts under blanket purchase orders monitored, and are quantities exceeding authorized total returned to the vendor?
- Are procedures adequate for the proper accounting for partial deliveries of purchase orders?

- Are purchasing and receiving functions separate form invoice processing, accounts payable, and general ledger functions?
- Are vendors' invoices, receiving reports, and purchase orders matched before the related liability is recorded?
- Are invoices checked as to prices, extensions, footings, freight charges, allowances, and credit terms?
- Are controls adequate to ensure that all available discounts are taken?
- Are purchases recorded in a purchase register or voucher register before being processed through cash disbursements?
- Does a responsible employee assign the appropriate general ledger account distribution to which the invoices are to be posted?
- Are procedures adequate to ensure that invoices have been processed before payment and to prevent duplicate payment (e.g., a block stamp)?
- Does a responsible official approve invoices for payment?
- Are procedures adequate to ensure that merchandise purchased for direct delivery to customers is promptly billed to the customers and recorded as both a receivable and a payable?
- Are records of goods returned to vendors matched to vendor credit memos?
- Are unmatched receiving reports, purchase orders, and vendors' invoices periodically reviewed and investigated for proper recording?
- Is the accounts payable ledger or voucher register reconciled monthly to the general ledger control accounts?
- Are statements from vendors regularly reviewed and reconciled against recorded liabilities?
- Do adjustments to accounts payable (e.g., writing off of debit balances) require the approval of a designated official?
- Are budgets used? If yes, are budgets approved by responsible officials, and are actual expenditures compared with budgeted amounts and variances analyzed and explained?

- If excess inventory purchasing is suspected, then verifying that all inventory purchased was received (receiving report) at the proper location might be the attribute tested. Receiving reports or invoices examination might reveal alternate shipping sites.

PREVENTION

The following is a list of billing-scheme-prevention methods that may be helpful in the deterrence of billing fraud.

- Authorization procedures of purchase orders, invoicing, and payments should be documented and adhered to.
- The accounts payable list of vendors should be periodically reviewed for strange vendors and addresses.
- Payment codings should be reviewed for abnormal descriptions.
- Vendor purchases should be analyzed for abnormal levels on both a monthly and yearly basis.
- Purchases and inventory levels should be compared and analyzed. (see "Inventory and Other Assets")
- Control methods to check for duplicate invoices and purchase order numbers should be in place.
- A separation of duties between authorization, purchasing, receiving, shipping, and accounting should be in place.
- Payment of vouchers should be periodically reviewed to ensure integrity of proper documentation.
- Receiving and shipping reports should be reviewed for completeness and accuracy.
- Asset information should include purchasing trails and other information.
- Journal entries to inventory accounts should be strictly scrutinized.
- Appropriate bank reconciliation and review procedures should be periodically performed checking for out-of-place vendors and endorsements.
- Credit card statements should be reviewed often for irregularities.
- The validity of invoices with a post office box address should be verified.
- Proper controls for the receipt and handling of "return to sender" checks should be installed.

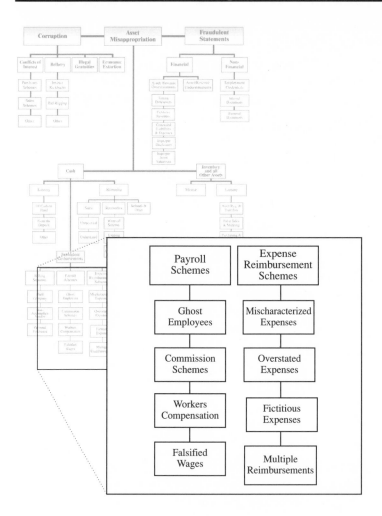

8. PAYROLL AND EXPENSE REIMBURSEMENT SCHEMES

*****

Case Study: Say Cheese!
* Several names have been changed to preserve anonymity

Every once in a while, a person devises a fraud scheme so complex that it is virtually undetectable. Intricate planning allows the person to cheat the company out of millions of dollars with little chance of getting caught.

Jerry Harkanell is no such person.

Harkanell's payroll scheme put only about $1,500 in his pocket before a supervisor detected his fraud less than half a year after it began.

Harkanell worked as a departmental secretary for a unit of a large San Antonio hospital. His duties consisted mostly of administrative tasks, including the recording of payroll for the unit.

An exception report for the month of March listed some unusual activity on Harkanell's time sheet. He had posted eight hours that resulted in overtime wages for a particular pay period. The pay period coincided with a time of low occupancy in Harkanell's unit. During times of low occupancy, there is no need for anyone—especially a secretary—to work overtime.

When his supervisor confronted Harkanell about the eight hours, he confessed. He said he posted the time due to financial problems and threats from his wife to leave him.

He immediately submitted his resignation, a hospital administrator accepted it, and Jerry Harkanell became a former hospital employee.

The hospital administrator shared the specifics of this incident with Oscar Straine, director of internal auditing for the hospital and a Certified Fraud Examiner.

"Nobody leaves for just eight hours," Straine said. "There must be a lot more there."

When Straine delved into the records, he found exactly what he had suspected. Since October of the previous year, Harkanell had been overstating his hours. He had recorded hours which he had not actually worked; he had posted his hours to shifts for which pay was higher; he had reported vacation time as time worked, drawing not only additional pay but extra vacation time, too.

Unfortunately for Harkanell, his method of cheating his employer left a well-marked paper trail. As a department secretary, he submitted the unit's manually prepared time sheets to his supervisor. She would sign the time sheets and make copies to retain for her records. Harkanell would then alter the original time sheets before he delivered them to the payroll department. Amazingly, he marked the time sheets in pencil, allowing him simply to erase the old numbers and make changes.

The audit staff compared the supervisor's copies of time sheets with the time sheets on file in the payroll department. Discrepancies between the two stood out. The investigation lasted less than a month. The results revealed that during a 26-week period, Jerry Harkanell defrauded the hospital out of $1,570.

Interviews conducted with coworkers and supervisors revealed one detail that might have tipped Harkanell's hand even earlier, had anyone recognized a suspicious act for what it was.

One Friday before payday when Harkanell had the day off, he showed up at the hospital anyway. This was more than a minor inconvenience as he didn't own a car. But Harkanell took the bus to work just so he could personally get the time sheet approved and turned in to payroll. At the time, no one questioned why he didn't simply ask someone to cover for him.

At the completion of the investigation, the hospital filed a claim with the district attorney's office. Evidence consisted of copies of the approved time sheets, copies of the altered time sheets, and affidavits from Harkanell's supervisors.

An assistant district attorney in charge of the case called the hospital shortly after receiving the case. She had uncovered some interesting details about Harkanell's past during a routine background check. A computer search revealed he had a criminal past and was currently out on parole. In the 1970s, the assistant district attorney reported, Harkanell had been sentenced to life in prison for armed robbery.

The news that the hospital had unknowingly hired a convicted felon distressed Oscar Straine. He discovered that the hospital's ability to conduct thorough background checks on prospective employees was restricted by money and accessibility to records. The hospital routinely checked criminal records in Bexar County (where the hospital is located) and any counties where an applicant reported having a history. Unfortunately for the hospital, the general public can only access criminal records one county at a time while law enforcement agencies have statewide databases at their disposal. Cost and time prohibit the hospital from checking records in all 254 Texas counties, especially for a low-salaried employee like Harkanell.

The complaint against Harkanell went to the grand jury quickly. Straine testified. The grand jury issued an indictment, and a warrant was issued for Harkanell's arrest.

The Sheriff's department attempted to locate Harkanell several times with no success. He had moved, and not surprisingly, left no forwarding address. The DA's office notified the hospital that Harkanell had disappeared, and that it had no immediate plans to continue the search.

Harkanell remained at large for several months. But luck was on the hospital's side. Or, perhaps more accurately, stupidity was on Harkanell's. Just as he had done with his time-sheet fraud, he left a clue behind, this time concerning his whereabouts. This was no subtle hint, either. He might as well have mailed the hospital an invitation with a map.

The following January, Straine was talking to a woman in the human resources department who had helped on Jerry Harkanell's original case. Straine called this woman to talk about his continuing concerns over the hospital's inability to do a more thorough background check on prospective hires. During the conversation, the woman asked, "By the way, did you happen to see the paper a few weeks ago?"

"I don't know what you're talking about."

"Oh, well, Jerry Harkanell's picture was on the front page of the business section of the *Express*."

"You have to be kidding."

She wasn't.

Straine immediately sent one of his auditors to the library to get a copy of the newspaper. She returned with a half-page article about a nonprofit organization that helps low-income families buy houses with low-interest loans and no down payment.

Right in the middle of the article was a picture, and right in the middle of that picture was Jerry Harkanell. He and his family were sitting on the front porch of the new home the nonprofit group had helped him purchase. The article detailed Harkanell's story, commenting on how hard he had worked to get his house. And though it never mentioned the address, the article contained enough information to pinpoint the location. The Harkanells lived near a new Wal-Mart store and across the street from a park. Theirs was the only new house on the block.

It took Straine ten minutes to find the house from his office. He knew the location of the new Wal-Mart, drove there, then located the park.

Straine said "It was weird driving up the street with the photograph, and there's his house. We could even identify the design on the front door and match it with the photograph in the newspaper as we drove up the street."

As soon as he returned to his office, Straine called the assistant district attorney. Harkanell was arrested the next day.

Harkanell appealed for assistance from the nonprofit organization which had helped him buy his house. They agreed to help him on the condition he promised to come clean. The organization contacted the hospital's community outreach program to request the charge be dropped, or at least decreased from a felony to a misdemeanor.

The hospital declined to drop the charge. The nonprofit group pleaded Harkanell's case, pointing out that he had a wife and a sick child who would have to go on the welfare rolls if he was convicted of a felony.

Straine made it clear that the hospital would pursue a conviction, whether a felony or misdemeanor. The hospital's position was that Harkanell should at least have to face the judge. Later, the assistant district attorney revealed that had Harkanell pleaded guilty to the felony charge, the judge would have sentenced him to 25 years.

While Harkanell continued to try to get the charges dropped, another piece of his past caught up with him. A separate party filed a forgery claim with the district attorney's office. As soon as the nonprofit organization got word of this development, it refused to provide any additional assistance to Harkanell.

A judge sentenced Jerry Harkanell to 35 years in prison. Law enforcement officials escorted him from the courtroom directly to a jail cell. As of the writing of this case, Harkanell is waiting to be transferred to a Texas Department of Corrections facility.

*****

Overview

Payroll and expense reimbursement schemes are similar to billing schemes. The perpetrators of these frauds produce false documents which cause the victim company to unknowingly make a fraudulent disbursement. In the previous chapter, the false document was usually an invoice (coupled, perhaps, with false receiving reports, purchase orders and purchase authorizations). In this chapter, the false documents will be items like timecards, sales orders, and expense reports. In the case study above, for example, Jerry Harkanell turned in false time sheets which caused his employer to overpay his wages. The major difference between these frauds and billing schemes is that payroll and expense frauds involve disbursements to employees rather than external parties.

Payroll Schemes

Payroll schemes made up almost 8% of the cases in our study but accounted for only 1.09% of the total losses (see charts 1-6 and 1-4, respectively). The median loss from a payroll scheme ranks twelfth among the scheme types, but, at $50,000, it is still large enough to merit serious consideration (see chart 1-5). In general, payroll schemes fall into one of the following categories:

Ghost Employees	Falsified Hours and Salary	Commission Schemes	False Workers Compensation Claims

As chart 8-3 illustrates, ghost employee schemes tend to generate the largest losses among payroll frauds. At $275,000 per occurrence, these schemes can be extremely harmful to the financial health of a victim company. Ghost employee schemes, however, made up only 14.2% of the losses among payroll cases in our study (see chart 8-1). By contrast, falsified hours and salary schemes had the lowest median loss of any scheme, but were easily the most common type of payroll fraud (see chart 8-2).

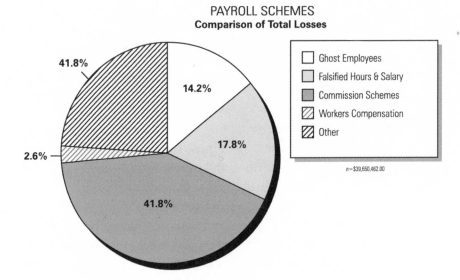

Chart 8-1: Comparison of Total Losses

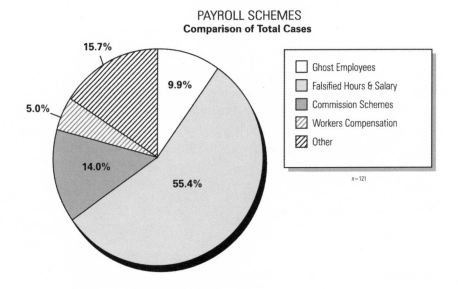

Chart 8-2: Comparison of Total Cases

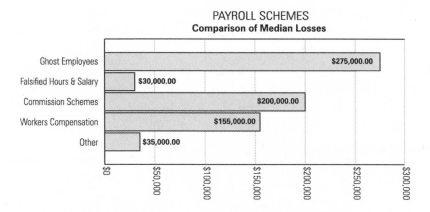

Chart 8-3: Comparison of Median Losses

GHOST EMPLOYEES

The term *ghost employee* refers to someone on the payroll who does not actually work for the victim company. Through the falsification of personnel or payroll records a fraudster causes paychecks to be generated to a ghost. These paychecks are then converted by the fraudster or an accomplice (see flowchart 8-2). Use of a ghost employee scheme by a fraudster can be like adding a second income to his household. The ghost employee may be a fictitious person or a real individual who simply does not work for the victim employer. When the ghost is a real person, it is often a friend or relative of the perpetrator. In some cases the ghost employee is an accomplice of the fraudster who cashes the fraudulent paychecks and splits the money with the perpetrator.

In order for a ghost-employee scheme to work, four things must happen: (1) the ghost must be added to the payroll, (2) timekeeping and wage rate information must be collected, (3) a paycheck must be issued to the ghost, and (4) the check must be delivered to the perpetrator or an accomplice.

Adding the Ghost to the Payroll

The first step in a ghost-employee scheme is entering the ghost on the payroll. In some businesses, all hiring is done through a centralized personnel department, while in others the personnel function is spread over the managerial responsibilities of various departments. Regardless of how hiring of new employees is handled within a business, it is the person or persons with authority to add new employees that are in the best position to put ghosts on the payroll. In Case 2432, for example, a manager who was responsible for hiring and scheduling janitorial work added over 80 ghost employees to his payroll. The ghosts in this case were actual people who worked at other jobs for different companies. The manager filled out time sheets for the fictitious employees and authorized them, then took the resulting paychecks to the ghost employees, who cashed them and split the proceeds with the manager. It was this manager's authority in the hiring and supervision of employees that enabled him to perpetrate this fraud.

Another area where the opportunity to add ghosts is payroll accounting. In a perfect world, every name listed on the payroll would be verified against personnel records to make sure that those persons receiving paychecks actually work for the company, but in practice this does not always happen. Thus, persons in payroll accounting may be able to add fictitious employees to the roll. Access to payroll records is usually restricted, so it may be that only managers have access to make changes to records, making these managers the most likely suspects in a ghost-employee scheme. On the other hand, lower-level employees often gain access to payroll records, either through poor observance of controls or by surreptitious means. In Case 1042, for instance, an employee in the payroll department was given the authority to enter new employees into the payroll system, make corrections to payroll information, and distribute paychecks. This employee's manager gave rubber-stamp approval to the employee's actions because of a trusting relationship between the two. The lack of separation of duties and the absence of review made it simple for the culprit to add a fictitious employee into the payroll system.

One way to help conceal the presence of a ghost on the payroll is to create a fictitious employee with a name very similar to that of a real employee. The name on the fraudulent paycheck, then, will appear to be legitimate to anyone who glances at it. This method was used by the perpetrator of Case 970, a bookkeeper who made off with $35,000 in fraudulent wages.

Instead of adding new names to the payroll, some employees undertake ghost employee schemes by failing to remove the names of terminated employees. Paychecks to the terminated employee continue to be generated even though he no longer works for the victim company. The perpetrator intercepts these fraudulent paychecks and converts them to his own use. For instance, in Case 1738, an accountant delayed the submission of resignation notices of certain employees, then falsified time sheets for these employees to make it appear that they still worked for the victim company. This accountant was in charge of distributing paychecks to all employees of the company, so when the fraudulent checks were generated she simply took them out of the stack of legitimate checks and kept them for herself.

Collecting Timekeeping Information

The second thing that must occur in order for a paycheck to be issued to a ghost employee, at least in the case of hourly employees, is the collection and computation of timekeeping information. The perpetrator must provide payroll accounting with a timecard or other instrument showing how many hours the fictitious employee worked over the most recent pay period. This information, along with the wage rate information contained in personnel or payroll files, will be used to compute the amount of the fraudulent paycheck.

Timekeeping records can be maintained in a variety of ways. Employees might manually record their hours on timecards or punch timeclocks which record the time at which a person starts and finishes his work. In more sophisticated environments, computer systems can track an employee's hours.

When a ghost-employee scheme is in place, someone must create documentation for the ghost's hours. This essentially amounts to preparing a fake timecard showing when the ghost was allegedly present at work. Depending upon the normal procedure for recording hours, a fraudster might write up a fake timecard and sign it in the ghost's name, punch the timeclock for the ghost or so on. The preparing of the timecard is not a great obstacle to the perpetrator. The real key to the timekeeping document is obtaining approval of the timecard.

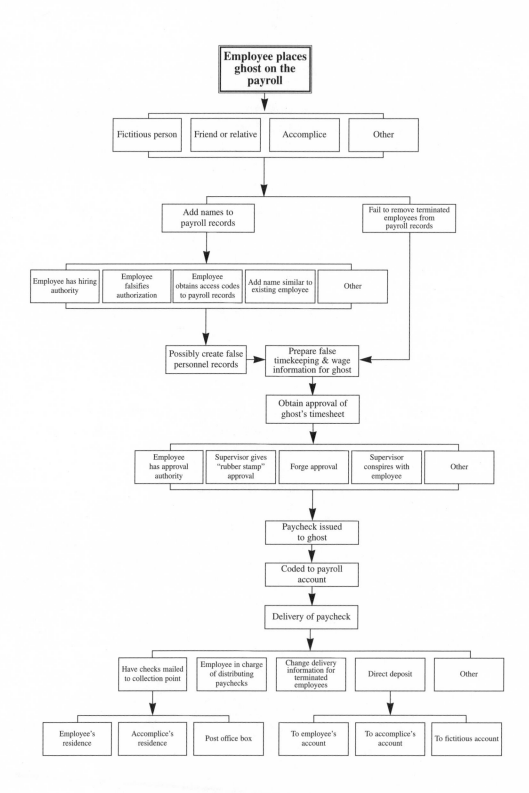

Flowchart 8-2: Ghost Employees

Timecards of hourly employees should be approved by a supervisor. This verifies to the payroll department that the employee actually worked the hours which are claimed on the card. A ghost employee, by definition, does not work for the victim company, so approval will have to be fraudulently obtained. Often, the supervisor himself is the one who creates the ghost. When this is the case, the supervisor fills out a timecard in the name of the ghost, then affixes his approval. The timecard is thereby authenticated and a paycheck will be issued. When a nonsupervisor is committing a ghost-employee scheme, he will typically forge the necessary approval, then forward the bogus timecard directly to payroll accounting, bypassing his supervisor.

In computerized systems, a supervisor's signature might not be required. In lieu of this, the supervisor inputs data into the payroll system and the use of his password serves to authorize the entry. If an employee has access to the supervisor's password, he can input any data he wants, and it arrives in the payroll system with a seal of approval.

If the fraudster creates ghost employees who are salaried rather than hourly employees, it is not necessary to collect timekeeping information. Salaried employees are paid a certain amount each pay period regardless of how many hours they work. Because the timekeeping function can be avoided, it may be more easy for a fraudster to create a ghost employee who works on salary. However, salaried employees typically are fewer and more likely to be members of management. The salaried ghost may therefore be more difficult to conceal.

Issuing the Ghost's Paycheck

Once a ghost is entered on the payroll and his timecard has been approved, the third step in the scheme is the actual issuance of the paycheck. The heart of a ghost-employee scheme is in the falsification of payroll records and timekeeping information. Once this falsification has occurred, the perpetrator does not generally take an active roll in the issuance of the check. The payroll department prints the check—based on the bogus information provided by the fraudster—as it would any other paycheck.

Delivery of the Paycheck

The final step in a ghost employee scheme is the distribution of the checks to the perpetrator. Paychecks might be hand delivered to employees while at work, mailed to employees at their home addresses, or direct deposited into the employees' bank accounts. If employees are paid in currency rather than by check, the distribution is almost always conducted in-person and on-site.

Ideally, those in charge of payroll distribution should not have a hand in any of the other functions of the payroll cycle. For instance, the person who enters new employees in the payroll system should not be allowed to distribute paychecks because, as we saw in Case 1738, this person can include a ghost on the payroll, then simply remove the fraudulent check from the stack of legitimate paychecks which she handles as she disburses pay. Obviously, when the perpetrator of a ghost employee scheme is allowed to mail checks to employees or pass them out at work, he is in the best position to ensure that the ghost's check is delivered to himself.

In most instances the perpetrator does not have the authority to distribute paychecks, and so must make sure that the victim employer sends the checks to a place where he can recover them. When checks are not distributed in the workplace, they are either mailed to employees or deposited directly into those employees' accounts.

If the fictitious employee was added into the payroll or personnel records by the fraudster, the problem of distribution is usually minor. When the ghost's employment information is inputted, the perpetrator simply lists an address or bank account to which the payments can be sent. In the case of purely fictitious ghost employees, the address is often the perpetrator's own (the same goes for bank accounts). The fact that two employees (the perpetrator and the ghost) are receiving payments at the same destination may indicate that fraud is afoot. Some fraudsters avoid this problem by having payments sent to a post office box or a separate bank account. In Case 1042, for example, the perpetrator set up a fake bank account in the name of a fictitious employee and arranged for paychecks to be deposited directly into this account.

As we have said, the ghost is not always a fictitious person. It may, instead, be a real person who is conspiring with the perpetrator to defraud the company. In Case 687, for instance, an employee listed both his wife and his girlfriend on the company payroll. When real persons conspiring with the fraudster are falsely included on the payroll, the perpetrator typically sees to it that checks are sent to the homes or accounts of these persons. In this way, the fraudster avoids the problem of duplicating addresses on the payroll.

Distribution is a more difficult problem when the ghost is a former employee who was simply not removed from the payroll. In Case 146, for instance, a supervisor continued to submit timecards for employees who had been terminated. Payroll records will obviously reflect the bank account number or address of the terminated employee in this situation. The perpetrator, then, has two courses of action.

In companies where paychecks are distributed by hand or are left at a central spot for employees to collect, the perpetrator can ignore the payroll records and simply pick up the fraudulent paychecks. If the paychecks are to be distributed through the mail or by direct deposit, the perpetrator will have to enter the terminated employee's records and change their delivery information.

FALSIFIED HOURS & SALARY

By far the most common method of misappropriating funds from the payroll is the overpayment of wages, accounting for 55.4% of the payroll frauds (see chart 8-3). For hourly employees, the size of a paycheck is based on two essential factors, the number of hours worked and the rate of pay. It is therefore obvious that for an hourly employee to fraudulently increase the size of his paycheck, he must either falsify the number of hours he has worked or change his wage rate (see flowchart 8-3). Since salaried employees do not receive compensation based on their time at work, in most cases these employees generate fraudulent wages by increasing their rates of pay.

When we discuss payroll frauds that involve overstated hours, we must first understand how an employee's time at work is recorded. As we have already discussed, time is generally kept by one of three methods. Timeclocks may be used to mark the time when an employee begins and finishes work. The employee inserts a card into the clock at the beginning and end of work, and the time is imprinted on that card. In more sophisticated systems, computers may track the time employees spend on the job based on login codes or a similar indicator. Finally, timecards showing the number of hours an employee worked on a particular day are often prepared manually by the employee, and approved by his manager.

Manually Prepared Timecards

When hours are recorded manually, an employee typically fills out his timecard to reflect the number of hours he has worked, then presents it to his supervisor for approval. The supervisor verifies the accuracy of the timecard, signs or initials the card to indicate his approval, then forwards it to the payroll department so that a paycheck can be issued. Most of the payroll frauds we encountered in our study stemmed from abuses of this process.

Obviously, if an employee fills out his own timecard, it may be easy to falsify his hours worked. He simply writes down the wrong time, showing that he arrived at work earlier or left later than he actually did. The difficulty is not in falsifying the timecard, but in getting the fraudulent card approved by the employee's supervisor. There are basically three ways for the employee to obtain the authorization he needs.

Forging a Supervisor's Signature

When using this method, an employee typically withholds his timecard from those being sent to the supervisor for approval, forges the supervisor's signature or initials, then adds the timecard to the stack of authorized cards which are sent to payroll. The fraudulent timecard arrives at the payroll department with what appears to be a supervisor's approval and a paycheck is subsequently issued.

Collusion with a Supervisor

The second way to obtain approval of a fraudulent timecard is to collude with a supervisor who authorizes timekeeping information. In these schemes, the supervisor knowingly signs false timecards and usually takes a portion of the fraudulent wages. In some cases, the supervisor may take the entire amount of the overpayment. In Case 2406, for example, a supervisor assigned employees to better work areas or better jobs, but in return she demanded payment. The payment was arranged by the falsification of the employees' timecards, which the supervisor authorized. The employees were compensated for fictitious overtime, which was kicked back to the supervisor. It may be particularly difficult to detect payroll fraud when a supervisor colludes with an employee, because managers are often relied on as a control to assure proper timekeeping.

In payroll collusion schemes, the supervisor does not necessarily take a cut of the overpayment. Case 749, for instance, involved a temporary employee who added fictitious hours to her time sheet. Rather than get the approval of her direct supervisor, the employee obtained approval from an administrator at another site. The employee was related to this administrator, who authorized her overpayment without receiving any compensation for doing so. In another case, 2314, a supervisor needed to enhance the salary of an employee in order to keep him from leaving for another job. The supervisor authorized the payment of $10,000 in fictitious overtime to the employee. Perhaps the most unique case we came across in our study, though, was committed by two part-time employees, who did not even bother to show up for work. One of the fraudsters did not perform any verifiable work for nine months, and the other was apparently absent for *two years!* The timecards for these employees were completed by a timekeeper based on their work schedules, and a supervisor approved the timecards. This supervisor was also a part-time employee who held another job, in which he was supervised by one of the fraudsters. Thus, the supervisor was under pressure to authorize the fraudulent timecards in order to keep his second job.

"Rubber Stamp" Supervisors

The third way to obtain approval of fraudulent timecards is to rely on a supervisor to approve them without reviewing their accuracy. The "lazy manager" method seems risky and one would think that it would be uncommon, but the truth is that it occurs quite frequently. A recurring theme in our study is the reliance of fraudsters on the inattentiveness of others. When an employee sees an opportunity to make a little extra money without getting caught, that employee is more likely to be emboldened to attempt a fraud scheme. The fact that a supervisor is known to "rubber stamp" timecards or even ignore them can be a factor in an employee's decision to begin stealing from his company.

For instance, in Case 1615 a temporary employee noticed that his manager did not reconcile the expense journal monthly. Thus, the manager did not know how much was being paid to the temporary agency. The fraudster completed fictitious time reports which were sent to the temporary agency and which caused the victim company to pay over $30,000 in fraudulent wages. Since the fraudster controlled the mail and the manager did not review the expense journal, this extremely simple scheme went undetected for some time. In another example of poor supervision, Case 503, a bookkeeper whose duties included the preparation of payroll checks inflated her checks by adding fictitious overtime. This person added over $90,000 of unauthorized pay to her wages over a four-year period before an accountant noticed the overpayments.

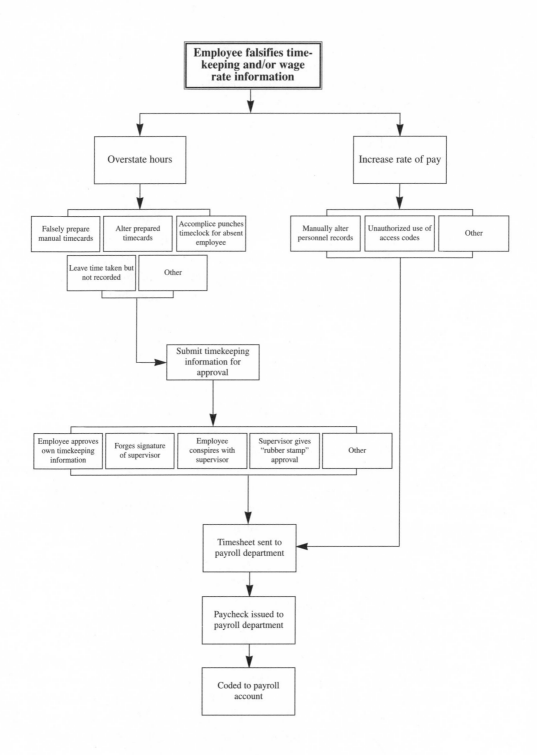

Flowchart 8-3: Falsified Hours and Salary

Poor Custody Procedures

One form of control breakdown that occurred in several cases in our study was the failure to maintain proper control over timecards. In a properly run system, once timecards are authorized by management they should be sent directly to payroll. Those who prepare the timecards should not have access to them after they have been approved. When this procedure is not observed, the person who prepared a timecard can alter it after his supervisor has approved it but before it is delivered to payroll. This is precisely what happened in several cases in our study. In the case study at the beginning of this chapter, for instance, Jerry Harkanell was in charge of compiling weekly timesheets (including his own), obtaining his supervisor's approval on the sheets, and delivering the approved sheets to payroll. As we saw, Harkanell waited until his supervisor signed the unit's time sheets, then overstated his hours or posted hours he had worked to higher-paid shifts. Since the timesheet had been authorized by the supervisor, payroll assumed that the hours were legitimate.

Another way hours are falsified is in the misreporting of leave time. This is not as common as timecard falsification, but can nevertheless be problematic. Incidentally, this is the one instance in which salaried employees commit payroll fraud by falsifying their hours. The way a leave scheme works is very simple. An employee takes a certain amount of time off of work as paid leave or vacation, but does not report this leave time. Employees typically receive a certain amount of paid leave per year. If a person takes a leave of absence but does not report it, those days are not deducted from his allotted days off. In other words, he gets more leave time than he is entitled to. The result is that the employee shows up for work less, yet still receives the same pay. This was another method used by Jerry Harkanell to increase his pay. Another example of this type of scheme was found in Case 1315, where a senior manager allowed certain persons to be absent from work without submitting leave forms to the personnel department. Consequently, these employees were able to take excess leave amounting to approximately $25,000 worth of unearned wages.

Timeclocks and Other Automated Timekeeping Systems

In companies that use timeclocks to collect timekeeping information, payroll fraud is usually uncomplicated. In the typical scenario, the timeclock is located in an unrestricted area, and a timecard for each employee is kept nearby. The employees insert their timecards into the timeclock at the beginning and end of their shifts and the clock imprints the time. The length of time an employee spends at work is thus recorded. Supervisors should be present at the beginning and end of shifts to assure that employees do not punch the timecards of absent coworkers, but this simple control is often overlooked.

We encountered very few timeclock fraud schemes, and those we did come across followed a single, uncomplicated pattern. When one employee is absent, a friend of that person punches his timecard so that it appears the absent employee was at work that day. The absent employee is therefore overcompensated on his next paycheck. This method was used in Case 478 and 2673.

Rates of Pay

While the preceding discussion focused on how employees overstate the number of hours they have worked, it should be remembered that an employee can also receive a larger paycheck by changing his pay rate. An employee's personnel or payroll records reflect his rate of pay. If an employee can gain access to these records, or has an accomplice with access to them, he can adjust them to receive a larger paycheck.

COMMISSION SCHEMES

Commission is a form of compensation calculated as a percentage of the amount of transactions a salesperson or other employee generates. It is a unique form of compensation that is not based on hours worked or a set yearly salary, but rather on an employee's revenue output. A commissioned employee's wages are based on two factors, the amount of sales he generates and the percentage of those sales he is paid. In other words, there are two ways an employee on commission can fraudulently increase his pay: (1) falsify the amount of sales made, or (2) increase his rate of commission (see flowchart 8-4).

Fictitious Sales

An employee can falsify the amount of sales he has made in three ways, the first being the creation of fictitious sales. In Case 531, for example, an unscrupulous insurance agent took advantage of his company's incentive commissions which paid $1.25 for every $1.00 of premiums generated in the first year of a policy. The agent wrote policies to fictitious customers, paid the premiums, and received his commissions, which created an illicit profit on the transaction. For instance, if the fraudster paid $100,000 in premiums, he would receive $125,000 in commissions, a $25,000 profit. No payments were made on the fraudulent policies after the first year.

The way in which fictitious sales are created depends on the industry in which the fraudster operates. A fictitious sale might be constructed by the creation of fraudulent sales orders, purchase orders, credit authorizations, packing slips, invoices and so on. On the other hand, a fraudster might simply ring up a false sale on a cash register. The key is that a fictitious sale is created, that it appears to be legitimate, and that the victim company reacts by issuing a commission check to the fraudster.

Altered Sales

The second way for a fraudster to falsify the value of sales he has made is to alter the prices listed on sales documents. In other words, the fraudster charges one price to a customer, but records a higher price in the company books. This results in the payment of a commission which is larger than the fraudster deserves. Case 1681 provides an example of this type of scheme. In this situation a salesman quoted a certain rate to his customers, billed them at this rate and collected their payments, but overstated his sales reports. The fraudster intercepted and altered the invoices from these transactions to keep his customers from complaining. He also overstated the revenues received from his customers. Since the fraudster's commissions were based on the amount of revenues he billed out, he was overcompensated.

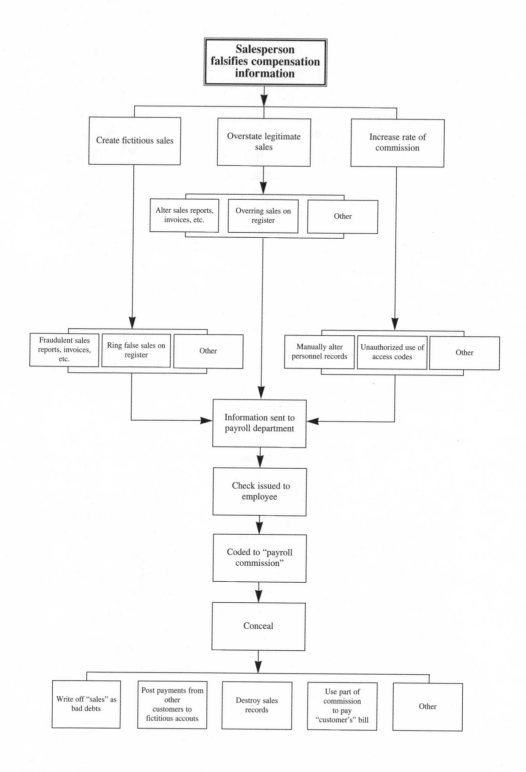

Flowchart 8-4: Commission Schemes

Converting Sales of Others

The third way an employee can overstate his sales is by claiming the sales of another employee as his own. Obviously, this method can only be used in a limited number of circumstances. In most cases, Salesman A cannot take credit for Salesman B's sale, because Salesman B will also claim it. However, the unique circumstances of Case 955 allowed some employees to fraudulently inflate their commissions based on another person's sales. This incident involved a company that sometimes sold merchandise on layaway. Commissions on these sales were not paid until the fulfillment of the layaway contract, meaning that there could be a substantial period of time between the initial sales agreement and the resulting commission. Some layaway sales were initiated by employees who quit or were transferred before the completion of the layaway agreements, meaning that no one was slated to receive a commission on these sales. When customers made their final payments on these contracts, a manager at the location used his authority to cancel the layaway contracts and allowed current salespeople to re-enter the transactions as their own. As a result, the salespeople received commission for the sales, even though they had not generated them. The manager received no benefit from this scheme other than the loyalty of his subordinates.

As mentioned above, the other way to manipulate the commission process is to change the employee's rate of commission. This would likely necessitate the alteration of payroll or personnel records, which should be off-limits to the sales staff.

WORKERS COMPENSATION

Workers compensation is not a payroll account, but rather an insurance expense. Nevertheless, it is essentially an employee benefit, entitling those persons who are injured on the job to compensation while they heal. Therefore, workers compensation schemes are discussed in this chapter.

There was nothing tricky about any of the workers compensation schemes we reviewed in our study. An employee simply fakes an injury and collects payments from the victim company's insurance carrier. Meanwhile, he does not work, even though he is physically able. In some cases, the employee colludes with a doctor who processes bogus claims for unnecessary medical treatments, then splits the payments for these fictitious treatments with the "injured" employee.

The primary victim of a workers compensation scheme is not the employer, rather the insurance carrier for the employer. It is the insurance carrier who pays for the fraudulent medical bills and the unnecessary absences of the perpetrator. Nevertheless, the employer is a tertiary victim of these crimes, as the bogus claims can result in higher premiums for the company in the future.

Expense Schemes

*****

CASE STUDY: FREQUENT FLIER'S FRAUD CRASHES
Several names have been changed to preserve anonymity

In his five years at a regional office of Smith & Carrington, Andrew Worth has spent more time on the road than at home — which means he often whispers good night to his wife over a long-distance phone line. The 35-year-old Ph.D. travels all over North America for his job as a geologist for the privately held firm that specializes in environmental management and engineering services. Its extensive client list represents all types of industries and includes municipalities, construction firms, petroleum companies, and Fortune 500 manufacturers with multimillion-dollar projects. As part of a team assembled by a project manager from Smith & Carrington, Worth was regularly called on to oversee drilling operations, conduct sampling tests, or assist with a formal site analysis.

Going from site to site, the road warrior adheres to the basic rules of business travel: Try to get a room on the top floor, away from the elevators and the ice machine. Request a seat next to an emergency exit on the airplane, which has been declared a child-free zone. Always get documentation for any travel expense. And so on. But Worth broke a basic rule governing ethics: Never ever cheat on your expense report.

His transgression was discovered by Sally Campbell, one of four internal auditors who worked out of Smith & Carrington's East Coast headquarters. During a routine review of the company-sponsored credit card activity reports, Campbell noticed an inordinate number of credits on Worth's credit card account reports, which immediately raised a red flag in her mind. She brought her concern to the attention of Tina Marie Sorrenson, manager of the internal audit department.

"All the credits seemed to be patterned toward one airline," recalled Sorrenson, who was newly accredited as a CFE at the time. The two accountants then took a cursory look at the travel expense reports that Worth had submitted, and found that a couple of the ticket numbers credited by the airline also matched those ticket numbers submitted with the employee's report for business reimbursement. Sorrenson said, "What's going on here?" She intended to find out.

That same day, Sorrenson called Worth's immediate supervisor, whom she knew to be a swift decisionmaker, and laid out the discrepancies. The supervisor gathered together all of Worth's time sheets for the past 18 months and faxed them to Sorrenson forthwith.

Campbell and Sorrenson then mustered all of their documentation for close inspection. They compiled a chronological schedule of his activities. The paperwork they pieced together revealed that for numerous business trips during one four-month period Worth had purchased two airline tickets with a huge cost difference. Out of the more expensive four-part ticket, only the passenger receipt portion accompanied his expense report pegged for reimbursement.

Looking for confirmation of their educated hunch, the auditors placed two phone calls — one to the travel agent who issued the tickets and one to the airline. "All of the outside parties we contacted proved very cooperative," said Sorrenson. Probably because Sorrenson identified herself as an agent of Smith & Carrington and Worth had used a company credit card for the purchase, the airline representative felt free to divulge customer information — the ticket of greater value went unused in each instance.

With the airline supplying the last piece of verification, the auditors had figured out Worth's method of operation. At least 14 days in advance of an upcoming field trip, Worth would purchase an airline ticket to his destination. He purposefully got the lowest fare and most direct route he could find. Edging close to his departure time — sometimes the very same day — Worth bought a second ticket for the same destination, paying a jacked-up fare for a last-minute booking. Sorrenson added, "He deliberately chose a nondirect route in order to further escalate the airfare to his ultimate destination." For a trip to Miami, for instance, he might have stopped in both Charlotte and Greenville, North Carolina, before meandering through Atlanta on yet another leg of his convoluted way to southern Florida, she said. It might have taken five legs to get to Boston. "He used the cheaper ticket for the actual flight and returned the expensive ticket for credit."

But prior to returning the expensive four-part ticket, Worth tore out the passenger receipt coupon, the one part the airlines do not require for a refund, he discovered. Worth retained the coupon so he could later attach it to his company expense report, which did not require full documentation. The project manager, often an engineer but never an accountant, reviews and signs off on any expense reports submitted by team members on the project.

"We do not centralize the approval of our expense reports because of the nature of our business," said Sorrenson. In all fairness, she said, airline tickets are confusing and difficult to decipher to the untrained eye. Sorrenson recognizes that project managers are mostly concerned with meeting their budget goals and billing the correct client for the appropriate hours or procedures, not with searching expense reports for the possibility of fraud.

Armed with indisputable evidence of a $4,100 fraud that seemed to be confined to a four-month time period, Sorrenson moved quickly to bring closure to this case. Still playing by the book, she called the legal department at Smith & Carrington to apprise it of the Worth situation and ask for any advice on procedure. Sorrenson said the legal department put the case under protective privilege.

She then overnighted her collection of evidence along with her detailed analysis of the airfare scheme to Worth's immediate supervisor at the regional office, who in turn showed it to his boss at his earliest availability. Right on time, the two managers scheduled a private meeting with Worth, bright and early on the following Monday morning.

Facing a mountain of evidence, Worth readily admitted his offense. He said he was experiencing temporary financial problems and just needed some money to tide him over. According to Sorrenson, who heard the account second-hand, Worth swore, "I only did it for four months." He swore that he padded his expense account for just a brief period; he urged the managers to check out all the other expense reports he had submitted in his five years at Smith & Carrington. (Sorrenson's detective work backed up his claim.)

The managers then asked Worth to provide his own accounting of his crime. His version closely jibed with Sorrenson's calculation — $4,100. Worth agreed to pay back the stolen money. "He paid us $2,000 in one lump sum initially, then $150 every two months after that," Sorrenson recalled.

Worth was promptly terminated, but Smith & Carrington decided not to prosecute the geologist. Sorrenson said, "It's an unwritten rule in our company." They kept their month-long investigation quiet as well. "No one found out about it except through the grapevine." Even then, others only knew that somebody got in trouble for fudging on an expense report, said Sorrenson.

True to the company's culture of taking decisive action, Sorrenson and her team resolved this case in just under one month from the time of its detection. "This is the smoothest case we've ever had," she admitted.

Sorrenson called this case a real eye-opener. "We discovered that it was a very easy fraud to perpetrate, especially since airline tickets are often confusing to interpret anyway." On behalf of Smith & Carrington, Sorrenson later launched a target audit to uncover other travel scams. And found some. The Worth scam was unfortunately not an isolated incident.

Top management at her company followed her advice and designated one travel agent to handle all travel arrangements for the entire company, including all 50 regional offices. "That makes our auditing lives so much easier. It gives us better control, as well as better cost data," said Sorrenson. "There is no way to prevent this type of fraud from occurring," she stated, "unless you make employees use a corporate credit card."

Although the audit manager also recommended employees use a company credit card to charge all business expenditures, top management declined to issue a mandate. Sorrenson said, "I tried to get that passed years ago and I'm on my bandwagon again." She argues that the billing statement for a company credit card provides a much stronger audit tool and an easy access audit trail.

Sorrenson realizes that Worth's scheme may have gone undetected had he used his personal credit card to charge his business airfare. "This guy was kind of stupid. If you're going to pull something like this, don't use your company credit card." She continued, "One thing you've got to understand about fraud perpetrators is that they'll usually be stupid." Or maybe only the stupid ones get caught.

Sorrenson has one piece of advice for other fraud examiners who face the possibility of this type of crime occurring in their organization. "Always step out of the box and ask the question."

*****

OVERVIEW

Expense reimbursement by the company can be manipulated by employees to generate fraudulent disbursements, like in the previous case. Expense reimbursement schemes are nearly as common as payroll schemes, accounting for 7.16% of the cases in our study (see chart 1-6). But the collective loss from all the expense schemes we have examined accounts for less than one half of one percent of the total losses in our study. The median loss of expense reimbursement schemes is the second lowest of any category in our study, but at $20,000 (see chart 1-5) is still substantial. Although the median cost of an expense scheme is not as high as that of other forms of occupational fraud, it should be noted that, under the proper circumstances, an expense scheme can be devastating. The cases reviewed here ranged as high as $6,000,000 in losses.

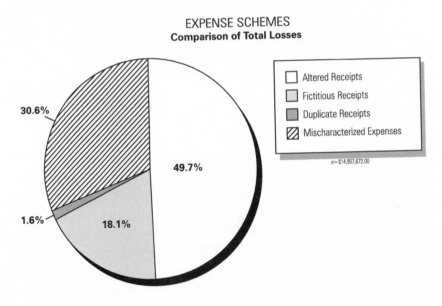

EXPENSE SCHEMES
Comparison of Total Losses

Legend:
- Altered Receipts
- Fictitious Receipts
- Duplicate Receipts
- Mischaracterized Expenses

n = $14,957,672.00

30.6%
49.7%
18.1%
1.6%

Chart 8-4: Comparison of Total Losses - Expenses

The median losses associated with expense schemes ranged from $11,500 for altered receipts schemes to $22,500 for mischaracterized expenses schemes (see chart 8-6). Altered receipts accounted for nearly 50% of the losses in our study (see chart 8-4), but this was largely due to a few high-dollar cases. Overall, mischaracterized expenses schemes seemed to be the most dangerous form of expense scheme, making up the largest percentage of cases in the category (see chart 8-5) as well as having the highest median loss.

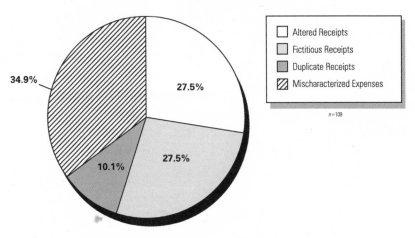

Chart 8-5: Comparison of Total Cases - Expenses

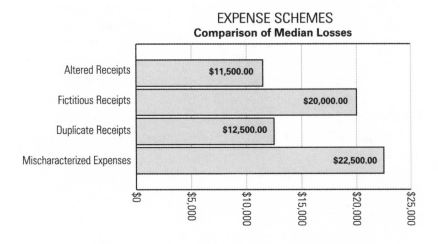

Chart 8-6: Comparison of Median Losses - Expenses

TYPES OF EXPENSE SCHEMES

Expense reimbursements are usually paid by the company in the following manner. An employee submits a report detailing an expense incurred for a business purpose, such as a business lunch with a client, airfare, hotel bills associated with business travel and so on. In preparing an expense report, an employee usually must explain the business purpose for the expense, as well as the time, date and location in which it was incurred. Attached to the report should be support documentation for the expense, typically a receipt. In some cases canceled checks written by the employee or copies of a personal credit card statement showing the expense are allowed. The report usually must be authorized by a supervisor in order for the expense to be reimbursed.

Mischaracterized Expenses	Overstated Expenses	Fictitious Expenses	Multiple Reimbursements

Mischaracterized Expenses

Most companies only reimburse certain expenses of their employees. Which expenses a company will pay depends to an extent upon policy, but in general, business-related travel, lodging, and meals are reimbursed. One of the most basic expense schemes is perpetrated by simply requesting reimbursement for a personal expense, claiming that it is business related (see flowchart 8-5). Examples of mischaracterized expenses include claiming personal travel as a business trip, listing dinner with a friend as "business development," and so on. Fraudsters may submit the receipts from their personal expenses along with their reports and provide business reasons for the incurred costs.

The false expense report induces the victim company to issue a check, reimbursing the perpetrator for his personal expenses. A mischaracterization is a simple scheme, amounting to little more than fibbing. In cases involving airfare and overnight travel, a mischaracterization can sometimes be detected by simply comparing the employee's expense reports to his work schedule. Often, the dates of the so-called "business trip" coincide with a vacation or day off. Detailed expense reports allow a company to make this kind of comparison and are therefore very helpful in preventing expenses schemes.

Requiring detailed information means more than just supporting documents; it should mean precise statements of what was purchased, as well as when and where. In Case 479, a fraudster submitted credit card statements as support for expenses, but he only submitted the top portion of the statements, not the portion that describes what was purchased. Over 95% of his expenses which were reimbursed were of a personal rather than a business nature. Of course, in this particular example the scheme was made easier because the perpetrator was the CEO of the company, making it unlikely that anyone would challenge the validity of his expense reports.

For whatever reason, most of the mischaracterized expense schemes in our study were undertaken by high-level employees, owners, or officers. Many times, the perpetrator actually had authority over the account from which expenses were reimbursed. Another common element was the failure to submit detailed expense reports, or any expense reports at all. Obviously, when a company is willing to reimburse employee expenses without any verifying documentation, it is easy for an employee to take advantage of the system. Nevertheless, there does not seem to be anything inherent in the nature of a mischaracterization scheme that would preclude its use in a system where detailed reports are required. As an example, suppose a traveling salesman goes on a trip and runs up a large bar bill one night in his hotel, saves his receipt, and lists this expense as "business entertainment" on an expense report. Nothing about the time, date, or nature of the expense would readily point to fraud, and the receipt would appear to substantiate the expense. Short of contacting the client who was allegedly entertained, there is little hope of identifying the expense as fraudulent.

One final note is that mischaracterization schemes can be extremely costly. They do not always deal with a free lunch here or there, but instead may involve very large sums of money. In Case 2249, for example, two mid-level managers ran up $1 million in inappropriate expenses over a two-year period. Their travel was not properly overseen and their expense requests were not closely reviewed, allowing them to spend large amounts of company money on international travel, lavish entertainment of friends, and the purchase of expensive gifts. They simply claimed that they incurred these expenses entertaining corporate clients. While this was certainly more costly than the average mischaracterization scheme, it should underscore the potential harm that can occur if the reimbursement process is not carefully tended.

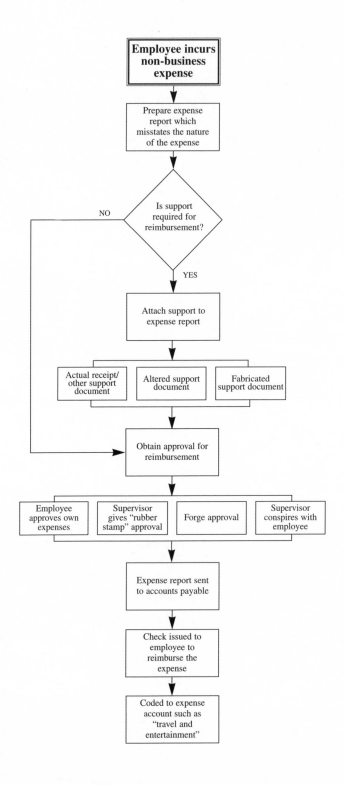

Flowchart 8-5: Mischaracterized Expenses

Overstated Expense Reports

Instead of seeking reimbursement for personal expenses, some employees overstate the cost of actual business expenses (see flowchart 8-6). This can be accomplished in a number of ways.

Altered Receipts

The most fundamental example of overstated expense schemes occurs when an employee doctors a receipt or other supporting documentation to reflect a higher cost than what he actually paid. The employee may use white-out, a ball point pen, or some other method to change the price reflected on the receipt before submitting his expense report. If the company does not require original documents as support, the perpetrator generally attaches a copy of the receipt to his expense report. Alterations are usually less noticeable on a photocopy than on an original document. For precisely this reason, many businesses require original receipts and ink signatures on expense reports.

As with other expense frauds, overstated expense schemes often succeed because of poor controls. In companies where supporting documents are not required, for example, fraudsters simply lie about how much they paid for a business expense. With no support available, it may be very difficult to disprove an employee's false expense claims.

Overpurchasing

The case of Andrew Worth at the beginning of this section illustrated another way to overstate a reimbursement form, the "overpurchasing" of business expenses. As we saw, Worth purchased two tickets for his business travel, one expensive and one cheap. He returned the expensive ticket, but retained the passenger receipt coupon and used it to overstate his expense reports. Meanwhile, he used the cheaper ticket for his trip. In this manner, he was able to be reimbursed for an expense which was larger than what he had actually paid.

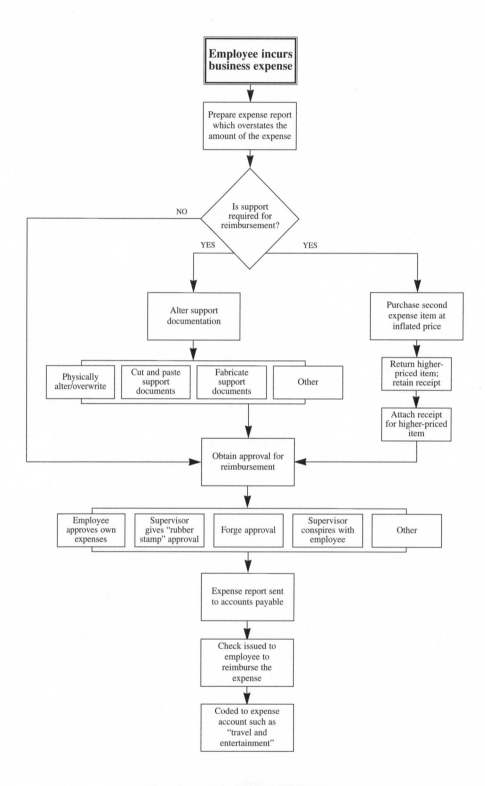

Flowchart 8-6: Overstated Expenses

Overstating Another Employee's Expenses

Overstated expense schemes are not only committed by the person who incurs the expense. Instead, they may be committed by someone else who handles or processes expense reports. An example occurred in Case 2389 where a petty cashier whited-out other employees' requests for travel advances and inserted larger amounts. The cashier then passed on the legitimate travel advances and pocketed the excess. This method can be used for expense reimbursements as well as travel advances.

This kind of scheme is most likely to occur in a system where expenses are reimbursed in currency rather than by a check, since the perpetrator would be unable to extract his "cut" from a single check made out to another employee.

Orders to Overstate Expenses

Finally, we have seen a few cases where employees knowingly falsified their own reports, but did so at the direction of their supervisors. In Case 1971, for instance, a department head forced his subordinates to inflate their expenses and return the proceeds to him. Presumably, the employees went along with this scheme for fear of losing their jobs. The fraud lasted for 10 years and cost the victim company approximately $6 million. Similarly, in Case 1974, a sales executive instructed his salesmen to inflate their expenses in order to generate cash for a slush fund. This fund was used to pay bribes and to provide improper forms of entertainment for clients and customers.

Fictitious Expense Schemes

Expense reimbursements are sometimes sought by employees for wholly fictitious items. Instead of overstating a real business expense or seeking reimbursement for a personal expense, an employee just invents a purchase which needs to be reimbursed (see flowchart 8-7).

Producing Fictitious Receipts

One way to generate a reimbursement for a fictitious expense is to create bogus support documents, such as false receipts. The emergence of personal computers has enabled some employees to create realistic-looking counterfeit receipts at home. Such was the scheme in Case 1275, in which an employee manufactured fake receipts using his computer and laser printer. These counterfeits were very sophisticated, even including the logos of the stores where he had allegedly made business-related purchases.

Computers are not the only means for creating support for a fictitious expense. The fraudster in the case above used several methods for justifying fictitious expenses as his scheme progressed. He began by using calculator printouts to simulate receipts, then advanced to cutting and pasting receipts from suppliers before finally progressing to the use of computer software to generate fictitious receipts.

Obtaining Blank Receipts from Vendors

If receipts are not created by the fraudster, they can be obtained from legitimate suppliers in a number of ways. A manager in Case 2830 simply requested blank receipts from waiters, bartenders, etc. He then filled in these receipts to "create" business expenses, including the names of clients whom he allegedly entertained. The fraudster usually paid all his expenses in cash to prevent an audit trail. One thing that undid this culprit was the fact that the last digit on most of the prices on his receipt was usually a zero or a five. This fact, noted by an astute employee, raised questions about the validity of his expenses.

A similar scheme was found in Case 1980, in which an employee's girlfriend worked at a restaurant near the victim company. This girlfriend validated credit card receipts and gave them to the fraudster so that he could submit them with his expense reports.

Instead of asking for blank receipts, some employees simply steal them. In some cases a fraudster will steal an entire stack of blank receipts and over time submit them to verify fictitious business expenses. This type of fraud should be identifiable by the fact that the perpetrator is submitting consecutively numbered receipts from the same establishment despite the fact that his expense reports are spread out over time.

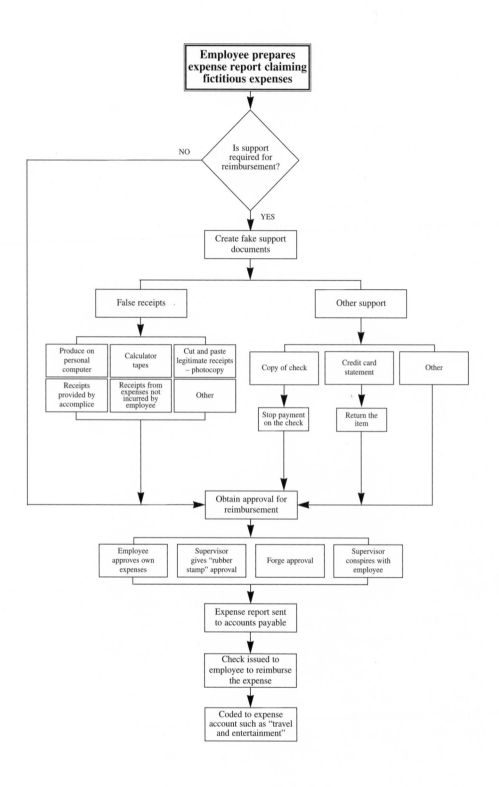

Flowchart 8-7: Fictitious Expenses

Claiming the Expenses of Others

Another way fraudsters use actual receipts to generate unwarranted reimbursements is by submitting expense reports for expenses which were paid by others. For instance, in Case 2619 an employee claimed hotel expenses which had actually been paid by his client. Photocopies of legitimate hotel bills were attached to the expense report as though the employee had paid for his own room.

As we have stated, not all companies require receipts to be attached to expense reports. Checks written by the employee or copies of his personal credit card bill might be allowed as support in lieu of a receipt. In Case 2075 a person wrote personal checks which appeared to be for business expenses, then photocopied these checks and attached them to reimbursement requests. In actuality, nothing was purchased with the checks; they were destroyed after the copies were made. This enabled the fraudster to receive a reimbursement from his employer without ever actually incurring a business expense. The same method can be used with credit cards, where a copy of a statement is used to support a purchase. Once the expense report is filed, the fraudster returns the item and receives a credit to his account.

In many expense schemes the perpetrator is not required to submit any support at all. This makes it much easier to create the appearance of an expense that does not actually exist.

Multiple Reimbursements

The least common of the expense schemes as revealed in our study is the multiple reimbursement. This type of fraud involves the submission of a single expense several times to receive multiple reimbursements. The most frequent example of a duplicate reimbursement scheme is the submission of several types of support for the same expense. An example arose in Case 89, in which an employee used, for example, an airline ticket stub and a travel agency invoice on separate expense reports so that he could be reimbursed twice for the cost of a single flight. The fraudster would have his division president authorize one report and have the vice president approve the other so that neither would see both reports. Additionally, the perpetrator allowed a time lag of about a month between the filing of the two reports so that the duplication would be less noticeable.

In cases where a company does not require original documents as support, some employees even use several copies of the same support document to generate multiple reimbursements.

Rather than file two expense reports, employees may charge an item to the company credit card, save the receipt, and attach it to an expense report as if they paid for the item themselves. The victim company therefore ends up paying twice for the same expense.

Perhaps the most interesting case of duplicated expenses in our study involved a government official who had responsibilities over two distinct budgets. The perpetrator of Case 83 would take a business trip and make expense claims to the travel funds of each of his budgets, thereby receiving a double reimbursement. In some cases the culprit charged the expenses to another budget category and still submitted reports through both budgets, generating a triple reimbursement. Eventually this person began to fabricate trips when he was not even leaving town, which led to the detection of his scheme.

Conclusion

DETECTION OF PAYROLL SCHEMES

Independent Payroll Distribution

Ghost-employee schemes can be uncovered by having personnel (other than the payroll department) distribute the payroll checks, and by requiring positive identification of the payee.

Analysis of Payee Address or Accounts

If payroll checks are either mailed or deposited automatically, then a list of duplicate addresses or deposit accounts may reveal ghost employees or duplicate payments.

Duplicate Social Security Numbers

Because each employee is required to have a Social Security number, a listing of duplicate numbers may reveal ghost employees.

Overtime Authorization

Requiring employees to have overtime authorized by a supervisor, having the supervisor be responsible for the timecards, and having the supervisor refer the timecards directly to payroll will aid in reducing overtime abuses. In addition, the payroll department should scan the time reports, and question obvious abuses such as only one employee working overtime in a department or excessive overtime on a timecard. By examining the source documentation, one may detect unauthorized overtime and falsified hours abuses.

Commissions

- Compare commission expenses to sales figures to verify linear correlation
- Prepare a comparative analysis of commission earned by salesperson verifying rates and calculation accuracy. Inordinately high earnings by an individual could signal fraud.
- Analyze sales by salesperson for uncollected sales amounts.
- Determine proper segregation of duties in calculation of commission amounts. Commissions should be independently provided by personnel outside the sales department.
- Contact a random sample of customers to confirm sales.

Analysis of Deductions from Payroll Checks

An analysis of the payroll withholdings may reveal either ghost employees or trust account abuses. Ghost employees often will have no withholding taxes, insurance, or other normal deductions. Therefore, a listing of any employee without these items may reveal a ghost employee.

An analysis of withholding-tax deposits may reveal that trust account taxes have been "borrowed," even for a short period, before the taxes are deposited. Comparing the disbursement date with the deposit date should reveal if the trust account taxes have been borrowed. Additionally, any delinquent payroll tax notices from the Internal Revenue Service should serve as a red flag to potential trust account tax "borrowings."

DETECTION OF EXPENSE SCHEMES

Detecting personal expense reimbursement fraud involves two basic methods. The first of these is a review and analysis of the expense accounts. The second detection method is a detailed review of the expense reimbursements.

Review and Analysis of Expense Accounts

Generally, expense account review uses one of two methods: historical comparisons or comparisons with budgeted amounts. A historical comparison compares the balance expended this period in relation to the balance spent in prior, similar periods. When performing this review, consider changes to the marketing, servicing, or other company operations.

Budgets are estimates of the money and/or time necessary to complete the task. They are based on past experience with consideration for current and future business conditions. Therefore, when comparing actual and budgeted expenses, determining inordinate expenses or inaccurate budget estimates is important.

Detailed Review of Expense Reimbursements

Overall, the best detection method is a detailed review of employee expense reimbursements. This method requires that the fraud examiner have, at the time of the examination, a calendar and a copy of the employee's schedule for the relevant period. The examiner should be familiar with the travel and entertainment policies of the company. Additionally, the following two steps may help to detect and deter employee expense abuses:

Require employees to submit their expense reimbursements for a detailed review before payment is reimbursed. If an employee knows that his expense reimbursement must be reviewed before payment is made, it is more likely that the expenses submitted will not be fraudulently prepared.

Periodically review employee expense reimbursements. This is particularly effective shortly before employee performance reviews.

PREVENTION OF PAYROLL SCHEMES

There are two basic preventive measures for payroll-related fraud: segregation of duties and periodic payroll review and analysis.

Segregation of Duties

The following duties should be segregated:
- Payroll preparation
- Payroll disbursement (into payroll and withholding tax accounts)
- Payroll distribution

- Payroll bank reconciliations
- Human resource departmental functions

If payroll is prepared by personnel not responsible for its distribution and reconciliation, it will be difficult for anyone to successfully add ghost employees. They also will be prevented from "borrowing" the trust account taxes because they will not have access to the disbursing function. In smaller companies, this function often is handled outside the firm at pennies per employee.

After the payroll checks are prepared, the transfer of funds from the general accounts to the payroll accounts should be handled by accounting. The personnel department should distribute checks and require identification in exchange for the payroll checks. This will curtail the opportunity to add ghost employees to the payroll. A suggested form of identification might be company-issued access passes, if available.

If the bank reconciliation function for the payroll account is assigned to someone other than those in the above described functions, then all the payroll functions have been segregated. No one is able to add ghost employees or "borrow" the withholding taxes without the opportunity for discovery by someone else.

Periodic Review and Analysis of Payroll

Periodically, an independent review of the payroll might reveal that internal controls are not working as designed. Comparing deposit dates with dates of payroll disbursement or transfer may reveal ghost employees. An occasional independent payroll distribution may reveal ghost employees.

A statistical sample of the following may reveal the presence of ghost employees:
- More than one employee with the same address
- More than one employee with the same Social Security number
- More than one employee with the same account number (automatic deposit)
- Employees with no withholding

Indicators of Payroll Fraud

In addition, the following audit program will help spot red flags to payroll distribution fraud and help with installing control procedures:

- Are personnel records maintained independently of payroll and timekeeping functions?
- Is the payroll accounting function independent of the general ledger function?
- Are changes to payroll not made unless the personnel department sends approved notification directly to the payroll department?
- Are references and backgrounds checked for new hires?
- Are all wage rates authorized in writing by a designated official?
- Are signed authorizations on file for employees whose wages are subject to special deductions?
- Are bonuses, commissions, and overtime approved in advance and reviewed for compliance with company policies?
- Are sick leave, vacations, and holidays reviewed for compliance with company policy?
- Are appropriate forms completed and signed by employees to show authorization for payroll deductions and withholding exemptions?
- Is the payroll periodically checked against the personnel records for terminated employees, fictitious employees, etc.?
- Is a time clock used for office employees as well as factory workers?
- If a time clock is used, are timecards (1) punched by employees in the presence of a designated supervisor and (2) signed by a supervisor at the end of the payroll period?
- Are timecards and production reports reviewed and compared with payroll distribution reports and production schedules?
- Are payroll registers reviewed and approved before disbursements are made for (1) names of employees, (2) hours worked, (3) wage rates, (4) deductions, (5) agreement with payroll checks, and (6) unusual items?
- Are all employees paid by check out of a separate bank payroll account?
- Are payroll checks prenumbered and issued in numerical sequence?

- Is access restricted to unissued payroll checks and signature plates?
- Are checks drawn and signed by designated officials who do not (1) prepare payroll, (2) have access to the accounting records, or (3) have custody of cash funds?
- Are payroll checks distributed by someone other than the department head or the person who prepares the payroll?
- Is the distribution of the payroll rotated periodically to different employees without prior notice?
- Is the payroll bank account reconciled by a designated employee who (1) is not involved in the preparing of payroll, (2) does not sign the checks, or (3) does not handle the check distributions?
- Do payroll bank account reconciliations procedures include comparing the paid checks to the payroll, and scrutinizing canceled check endorsements?
- Are the payroll registers reconciled to the general ledger control accounts?
- Is a liability account set up for all wages that have remained unclaimed for a certain period of time? If yes, (1) have these wages been redeposited in a special bank account, and (2) is identification required to be presented at the time of their subsequent distribution?
- Are distributions of hours (direct and indirect) to activity or departments reviewed and approved by supervisory personnel?
- Are actual payroll amounts reviewed and compared to budgeted amounts, and are variances analyzed regularly?
- Do adequate procedures exist for timely and accurate preparation and filing of payroll tax returns and related taxes?
- Are employee benefit plan contributions reconciled to appropriate employee census data?
- Are adequate, detailed records maintained of the entity's liability for vacation pay and sick pay? If yes, are they reconciled to the general ledger control accounts periodically?

PREVENTION OF EXPENSE SCHEMES

Detailed Expense Reports: Submission and Review

- Detailed expense reports should require the following information:
- Receipts or other support documentation
- Explanation of the expense including specific business purpose
- Time period expense occurred
- Place of expenditure
- Amount

It is not enough to have the detailed reports submitted if they are not reviewed. A policy requiring the periodic review of expense reports, coupled with examining the appropriate detail, will help deter employees from submitting personal expenses for reimbursement.

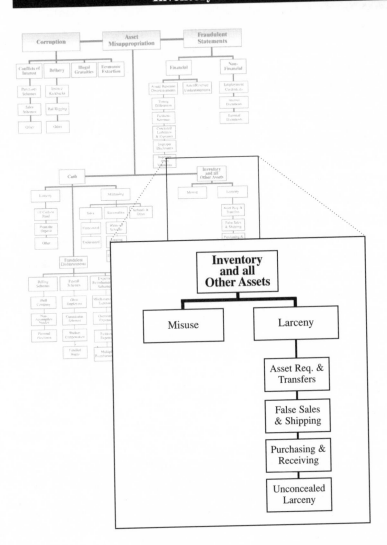

Flowchart 9-1

9. INVENTORY AND OTHER ASSETS

*****

Case Study: Chipping Away at High-Tech Theft
Several names have been changed to preserve anonymity

Nineteen-year-old Larry Gunter didn't know much about computers, but he worked as a shipping clerk in a computer manufacturer's warehouse. Like many other companies in Silicon Valley, this company produced thousands of miniature electronic circuits — microprocessor chips — the building block of personal computers.

Gunter didn't work in the plant's "clean room" building where the chips were manufactured. The company moved the chips next door to the warehouse for processing and inventory, along with other computer components. On the open market, one of these computer chips, which is comprised of millions of transistors, diodes, and capacitors, packed in a space the size of a baby's fingernail, is worth about $40. Over 1,000 chips were packaged in plastic storage tubes inside a company-marked cardboard box.

Gunter knew they were worth something, but didn't know how much. One day, he took a chip from a barrel in the warehouse and gave it to his girlfriend's father, Grant Thurman, because he knew Thurman operated some type of computer-salvage business. He told Thurman that the company had discarded the chip as "scrap."

"I asked him if he knew anyone who would buy scrap chips," Gunter said, and Thurman said he did. "So after about another week or two I stole three boxes of computer chips and brought them to Grant to sell them to his computer guy. Around a week later I got paid by Grant Thurman in the amount of $5,000 in a personal check."

Gunter knew the chips were not scrap, since the boxes, each about the size of a shoe box, bore the marking "SIMMS," signifying that the chips were sound. In fact, the manufacturer maintained a standard procedure for scrap chips, taking them to another warehouse on the company's grounds and sealing the components for shipment to another plant for destruction.

Gunter concealed the boxes from the security guards by placing them on the bottom of his work cart, with empty boxes on top. He pushed the cart out of the warehouse as if he were just taking empty boxes to the trash. Once in the parking lot, where there were no security guards, he loaded the three boxes of chips into his truck.

Shortly after the theft, an inventory manager filling an order noticed that many company chips were missing and immediately went to his supervisor, the warehouse manager. The manager verified they were missing about 10 cartons of chips, worth over $30,000. They contacted the company's director of operations, who accelerated the product inventory process at the plant. Instead of once a month, he began taking product inventory once a week.

Gunter still found it easy to steal, he said, because the security guards didn't pay much attention and because it was easy to evade the stationery surveillance cameras in the warehouse. About two weeks after his first theft, he stole four boxes of new chips for which Thurman paid him $10,000. Excited about his new conquest, Gunter told his young friend and coworker, Larry Spelber, about the easy profit to be made. The two could split $50,000 from a theft of six boxes of chips, he told Spelber — enough to quit work and finance their schooling.

By this time, however, the company had detected the second loss and contacted private investigator and fraud examiner Lee Roberts. Roberts ran his own Roberts Protection & Investigations business and had worked with the company's attorney previously.

"They knew exactly how much of their product they were missing," Roberts said, "because no product was supposed to leave the building unless they had the paper for loading it on the truck to fill a specific order. However, there was a flaw in the system. The company's operation was separated in two buildings, about 300 feet apart . . . . They would receive an extremely valuable product, and it would go from one building to the other, simply by being pushed by employees with carts through this 300-foot parking lot. Consequently, they would end up with an overstock of product that needed to leave the warehouse and be returned to Building One. Of course, that generated no internal paperwork; someone would simply say 'I'm taking this product to Building Two or vice versa, and that was such a common occurrence that the security guards started to think nothing about it."

"My immediate concern was," Roberts said, "if we've got something leaving the building in the ordered process, then we must have supervisors involved, drivers involved, and the like. It would be a fairly massive operation, and maybe that was their concern."

Roberts suspected the thefts occurred between these inter-building transfers. Since the employees who did these transfers were the 30 or so warehouse floor workers, he had many potential suspects.

To catch the thieves, however, a new video surveillance system would need to be set up at the warehouse. "We looked at their video surveillance system and found their cameras were improperly positioned and they were not saving their tapes in the library long enough to go back and look at them." Roberts' firm, which partly specializes in alarms and security protection, set up an additional 16 hidden video cameras inside the warehouse, and extra cameras in the parking lots.

"We agreed to pretend that nothing had happened," Roberts said of the thefts, "which would give the suspects a false sense of security, and the company agreed to restock the computer chips."

The warehouse manager and his assistant began to surreptitiously track inter-building transfers on a daily basis. With access to the paperwork and new video, "we were able to freeze-frame images" in order to look at all sides of an employee's cart. This time, the warehouse manager knew exactly how many boxes an employee was supposed to be taking to the other building.

Unbeknownst to Gunter and Spelber, the video cameras recorded them talking in the aisleways and other areas of the warehouse. Coupled with the daily inventory check, the record showed that the two employees frequently had more than the number of boxes they were supposed to be moving.

About 3:30 one afternoon, Gunter and Spelber removed six boxes from the shelves, placed them on a cart with empty boxes on top, and moved the cart outside. In the parking lot, Spelber loaded the boxes into his truck and returned to work. After work, they drove their own vehicles down the street and transferred the boxes to Gunter's car.

At home, Gunter removed the company labels from the chips and drove to Thurman's house. Thurman promised to pay him $50,000 for this stock.

Gunter and Spelber never did see that money, for the next day company security confronted them with the evidence. They quickly admitted their guilt and identified Thurman as the receiver of the stolen equipment. When police interviewed Thurman at his home, he denied knowing the computer chips were stolen. He admitted to reselling the chips to an acquaintance named Marty for $180,000, paid for with cashier's checks.

Interviews with Marty and check receipts revealed that the amount was actually much more — that Marty had paid out approximately $697,000 to Thurman for the chips (a profit of about 50 cents on the dollar, as compared to the 10 cents on the dollar Gunter received). Although investigators could not uncover any stolen equipment, they believed that Marty had sold the goods to the aerospace industry and possibly federal agencies.

The next day, police arrested Thurman after he attempted to make a large withdrawal from his credit union. Thurman and Gunter both served over a year in the state pen for grand theft and embezzlement; Spelber got nine months in a work furlough program. The police were never able to tag anything on Marty, who made the most money in the open market for the chips. Since none of the product could be found in his store, and since investigators could not prove he knew the property was stolen, they could not criminally prosecute him.

Roberts said the case was unique in that it represented the largest internal theft in the history of this California county — over $1 million. The company, while unable to recover most of the stolen property, learned a valuable lesson from the fraud. Afterwards, managers conducted tighter controls on transfers of property between buildings, produced more frequent inventory audits, and established enhanced physical security. That security included a new chainlink fence between the two buildings.

"I think this fraud was difficult to detect because the audit controls that they set up, and the manner in which they had set them up, were improper," Roberts said. "That's a common thing that we see as fraud examiners or investigators. Often people spend a great deal of money to set up audit controls — they set up physical security; they install alarms — and we often say to them: Simply buying that piece of equipment or putting those procedures into place is not enough. You need a trained, experienced professional to tell you how to do it and how to use them. If you don't do it the right way, it's worthless."

*****

Overview

To this point, our discussion of asset misappropriations has centered on cash schemes. These are much more prevalent than cases involving noncash assets, accounting for approximately 89% of the asset misappropriation losses and 87% of the asset misappropriation cases in our study (see charts 2-1 and 2-2, respectively). While schemes involving the misappropriation of inventory and other assets are not as common as cash schemes, they are nevertheless potentially disastrous. As Larry Gunter's scheme illustrates, thefts of inventory can run into the millions of dollars. The median loss associated with noncash schemes in our study was actually higher than in cash schemes $100,000 to $60,000 (see chart 2-3). In this chapter we will discuss the ways in which inventory, supplies, and other noncash assets are misappropriated by employees.

Inventory and other assets are targeted for theft by employees in a number of ways. These schemes can range from taking a box of pens home from work to the theft of millions of dollars worth of company equipment. We have classified the theft of noncash assets in three groups: inventory schemes, supplies schemes, and other assets schemes. Approximately 67% of the losses due to noncash misappropriations in our survey involved the theft or misuse of company inventory (see chart 9-1). Misappropriation of supplies accounted for another 19% of the losses, while the remaining losses involved various types of fixed assets, equipment, information and so on. The term *inventory and other assets* is meant to encompass the misappropriation schemes involving any assets held by a company other than cash.

For statistical purposes, we classified noncash misappropriation schemes according to the types of assets taken in order to gain a clear picture of what *kinds* of assets are misappropriated. However, for the purpose of describing *how* these assets are misappropriated, all noncash assets will be lumped together, since the methods for miappropriation do not vary much among the different asset types.

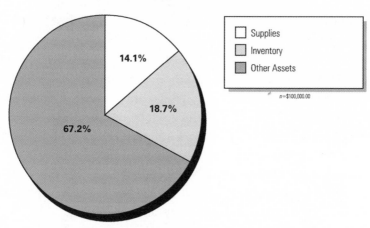

Chart 9-1:   Comparison of Total Losses

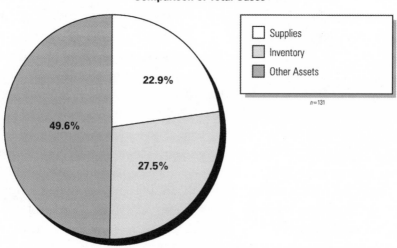

Chart 9-2:   Comparison of Total Cases

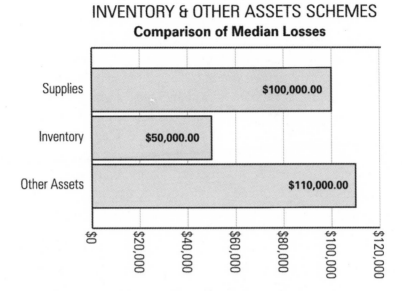

Chart 9.3: Comparison of Median Losses

Misuse of Inventory and Other Assets

There are basically two ways a person can misappropriate a company asset. The asset can be misused (or "borrowed") or it can be stolen. Simple misuse is obviously the less egregious of the two. Assets that are misused but not stolen typically include company vehicles, company supplies, computers, and other office equipment. In Case 1421, for example, an employee made personal use of a company vehicle while on an out-of-town assignment. The employee provided false information, both written and verbal, regarding the nature of his use of the vehicle. The vehicle was returned unharmed and the cost to the perpetrator's company was only a few hundred dollars. Nevertheless, such unauthorized use of a company asset does amount to fraud when a false statement accompanies the use.

Computers, supplies, and other office equipment are also used by some employees to do personal work on company time. For instance, an employee might use his computer at work to write letters, print invoices, or do other work connected with a business he runs on the side. In many instances, these side businesses are of the same nature as the employer's business, so the employee is essentially competing with his employer and using the employer's equipment to do it. An example of how employees misuse company assets to compete with their employers was provided by Case 1406, where a group of employees not only stole company supplies, but used the stolen supplies and their employer's equipment to manufacture their own product. The fraudsters then removed the completed product from their work location and sold it in competition with their employer. In a similar scheme, the perpetrator of Case 2579 used his employer's machinery to run his own snow removal and excavation business for approximately nine months. He generally did his own work on weekends and after hours, falsifying the logs which recorded mileage and usage on the equipment. The employee had formerly owned all the equipment himself, but had sold it in order to avoid bankruptcy. As a term of the sale, he had agreed to go to work for the new owner operating the equipment, but in truth, he never stopped running his old business.

The preceding cases offer a good illustration of how a single scheme can encompass more than one type of fraud. While the perpetrators in these schemes were misusing company materials and equipment—a case of asset misappropriation—they were also competing with their employers for business—a conflict of interest. The categories we have developed for classifying fraud are helpful in that they allow us to track certain types of schemes, noting common elements, victims, methods and so on; but those involved in fraud prevention should remember that every crime will not fall neatly into one category. Frauds often expand as opportunity and need allows, and a scheme that begins as something small may grow into a massive crime that can cripple a business.

THE COSTS OF INVENTORY MISUSE

The costs of inventory misuse are difficult to quantify. To many individuals this type of fraud is not viewed as a crime, but rather as "borrowing." In truth, the cost to a company from this kind of scheme may often be immaterial. When a perpetrator borrows a stapler for the night or takes home some tools to perform a household repair, the cost to his company is negligible, as long as the assets are returned unharmed.

On the other hand, misuse schemes could be very costly. Take, for example, situations discussed above in which an employee uses company equipment to operate a side business during work hours. Since the employee is not performing his work duties, the employer suffers a loss in productivity. If the low productivity continues, the employer might have to hire additional employees to compensate, which means more capital diverted to wages. If the employee's business is similar to the employer's, then lost business could be an additional cost. If the employee had not contracted work for his own company, the business would presumably have gone to his employer. Unauthorized use of equipment can also mean additional wear and tear, causing the equipment to break down sooner than it would have under normal business conditions. Additionally, when an employee "borrows" company property, there is no guarantee that he will bring it back. This is precisely how some theft schemes begin. Despite some opinions to the contrary, asset misuse is not always a harmless crime.

Theft of Inventory and Other Assets

While the misuse of company property might be a problem, the *theft* of company property is obviously of greater concern. As we have seen, losses resulting from larceny of company assets can run into the millions of dollars. The means employed to steal company property range from simple larceny—just walking off with company property—to more complicated schemes involving the falsification of company documents and ledgers.

METHODS FOR STEALING INVENTORY AND OTHER ASSETS

Larceny Schemes	Asset Requisitions and Transfers	Purchasing and Receiving Schemes	False Shipments

Larceny Schemes

The textbook definition of *larceny* is too broad for our purposes, as it would encompass every kind of asset theft. In order to gain a more specific understanding of the methods used to steal inventory and other assets, we have narrowed the definition of larceny. For our purposes, larceny is the most basic type of inventory theft, the schemes in which an employee simply takes inventory from the company premises without attempting to conceal it in the books and records (see flowchart 9-2). In other fraud schemes, employees may create false documentation to justify the shipment of merchandise or tamper with inventory records to conceal missing assets. Larceny schemes are more blunt. The culprit in these crimes takes company assets without trying to "justify" their absence. In the case study at the beginning of this chapter, for instance, Larry Gunter simply walked out of his warehouse with several hundred thousand dollars worth of computer chips.

Most noncash larceny schemes are not very complicated. They are typically committed by employees (such as warehouse personnel, inventory clerks, and shipping clerks) with access to inventory and other assets. A technique representative of the unsophisticated nature of noncash larceny schemes is what may be termed a set-aside scheme. In this type of crime, an employee responsible for loading merchandise for shipment to customers withholds some of the merchandise and sets it aside with the intent of misappropriating it later. The perpetrator of Case 968 used the set-aside method, leaving the targeted inventory in plain sight on the warehouse floor as he went about his duties. Because the inventory was visible rather than hidden, the employee's coworkers did not suspect that it was marked for theft. If someone noticed that a shipment was short, the fact that the merchandise was sitting out in the open made it appear that the omission had been an oversight rather than an intentional removal. In most cases, however, no one noticed that shipments were short, and the excess inventory was available for the perpetrator to take. If customers complained about receiving short shipments, the company sent the missing items without performing any follow-up to see where the missing inventory had gone. The culprit was eventually caught when someone noticed that he was involved in the preparation of an inordinate number of short shipments.

When we speak of asset theft we tend to conjure up images of late-night rendezvous at the warehouse or merchandise stuffed hastily under clothing as a nervous employee beats a path to his car. Sometimes this is how employees go about stealing inventory and other assets, but in many instances fraudsters do not have to go to these extremes. In several of the cases in our study, employees took items openly, during business hours, in plain view of their coworkers. How does this happen? The truth is that people tend to assume that their friends and acquaintances are acting honestly. When they see a trusted coworker taking something out of the office, persons are likely to assume that the culprit has a legitimate reason for removing the asset. In most cases, people just don't assume that fraud is going on around them. Such was the situation in Case 728, where a university faculty member was leaving his offices to take a position at a new school. This person was permitted to take a small number of items to his new job, but certainly exceeded the intentions of the school when he loaded two trucks full of university lab equipment and computers worth several hundred thousand dollars. The perpetrator simply packed up these stolen assets along with his personal items and drove away.

While it is true that employees sometimes misappropriate assets in front of coworkers who do not suspect fraud, it is also true that employees may be fully aware that one of their coworkers is stealing, yet refrain from reporting the crime. There are several reasons that employees might ignore illegal conduct, such as a sense of duty to their friends, a "management vs. labor" mentality, intimidation of honest employees by the thief, poor channels of communication, or where the coworkers are assisting in the theft. When high-ranking personnel are stealing from their companies, employees often overlook the crime because they fear they will lose their jobs if they report it. For example, a school superintendent in Case 2462 was not only pilfering school accounts but was also stealing school assets. A search of his residence revealed a cellar filled with school property. A number of school employees knew or suspected the superintendent was involved in illegal dealings, but he was very powerful and people were afraid to report him for fear of retaliation. As a result, he was able to steal from the school for several years. Similarly, in Case 144, a city manager ordered subordinates to install air conditioners — known to be city property — in the homes of several influential citizens, including his own. Although there was no question that this violated the city's code of ethics, no one reported the manager because of a lack of a proper whistle-blowing procedure in the department.

Ironically, employees who steal inventory are often highly trusted within their organizations. This trust can provide employees with access to restricted areas, safes, supply rooms, or even keys to the business. Such access, in turn, makes it easy for employees to misappropriate company assets. Case 716 provides an example of how an employee abused his position of trust to misappropriate noncash assets. In this case, a long-term employee of a contractor was given keys to the company parts room. It was his job to deliver parts to job sites. This individual used his access to steal high-value items which he then sold to another contractor. The scheme itself was uncomplicated, but because the employee had a long history of service to the company and because he was highly trusted, inventory counts were allowed to lapse and his performance went largely unsupervised. As a result, the scheme continued for over two years and cost the company over $200,000.

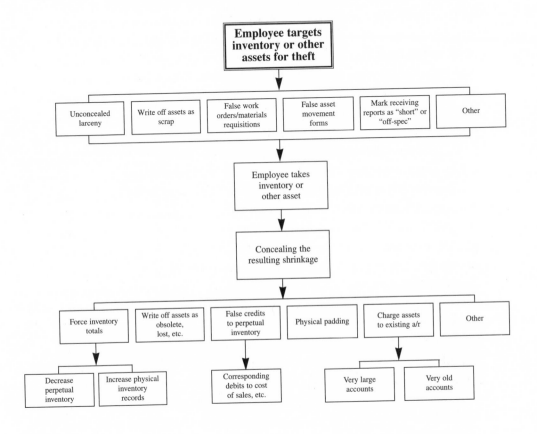

Flowchart 9-2: Non-Cash Larceny

Employees with keys to company buildings are able to misappropriate assets during nonbusiness hours, when they can avoid the prying eyes of their fellow employees as well as management and security personnel. Our study revealed several schemes in which employees entered their places of business to steal assets during weekends, as well as before or after normal working hours. Case 1766 provided an example of this after-hours activity. In this scheme two employees in management positions at a manufacturing plant would set finished items aside at the end of the day, then return the next day an hour before the morning shift and remove the merchandise before other employees arrived. These perpetrators had keys to the plant's security gate, which allowed them to enter the plant before normal hours. Over the course of several years, these two fraudsters removed and sold approximately $300,000 worth of inventory from their company.

It can be unwise for a fraudster to physically carry inventory and other assets off the premises of his company. This practice carries with it the inherent risk and potential embarrassment of being caught red-handed with stolen goods on his person. Some fraudsters avoid this problem by mailing company assets to a location where they can pick them up without having to worry about security, management, or other potential observers. In Case 1465, for instance, a spare-parts custodian took several thousand dollars worth of computer chips and mailed them to a company that had no business dealings with the custodian's employer. He then reclaimed the merchandise as his own. By taking the step of mailing the stolen inventory, the fraudster allowed the postal service to unwittingly do his dirty work for him.

The Fake Sale

Asset misappropriations are not always undertaken solely by employees of the victim company. In many cases, corrupt employees utilize outside accomplices to help steal inventory. The fake sale is one method that depends upon an accomplice for its success. Like most inventory thefts, the fake sale is not difficult. As reflected in Case 1963, a fake sale occurs when the accomplice of the employee-fraudster "buys" merchandise, but the employee does not ring up the sale, and the accomplice takes the merchandise without making any payment. To a casual observer, it will appear that the transaction is a normal sale. The employee bags the merchandise, and may act as though a transaction is being entered on the register, but in fact, the "sale" is not recorded. The accomplice may even pass a nominal amount of money to the employee to complete the illusion. In Case 1963 the perpetrator went along with these fake sales in exchange for gifts from her accomplice, though in other cases the two might split the stolen merchandise.

Accomplices are also sometimes used to return the inventory that an employee has stolen. This is an easy way for the employee to convert the inventory into cash when he does not have a need for the merchandise itself and has no means of reselling it on his own.

Asset Requisitions and Transfers

Asset requisitions and other forms that allow noncash assets to be moved from one location in a company to another can be used to facilitate the misappropriation of those assets. Fraudsters use internal documents to gain access to merchandise which they otherwise might not be able to handle without raising suspicion. Transfer documents do not account for missing merchandise the way false sales do, but they allow a fraudster to move assets from one location to another. In the process of this movement, the fraudster takes the merchandise for himself (see flowchart 9-2).

The most basic scheme occurs when an employee requisitions materials to complete a work-related project, then steals the materials. In some cases the fraudster simply overstates the amount of supplies or equipment it will take to complete his work and pilfers the excess. In more extreme cases the fraudster might completely fabricate a project which necessitates the use of certain assets he intends to steal. In Case 2744, for instance, an employee of a telecommunications company used false project documents to request approximately $100,000 worth of computer chips, allegedly to upgrade company computers. Knowing that this type of requisition required verbal authorization from another source, the employee set up an elaborate phone scheme to get the "project" approved. The fraudster used his knowledge of the company's phone system to forward calls from four different lines to his own desk. When the confirmation call was made, it was the perpetrator who answered the phone and authorized the project.

Dishonest employees sometimes falsify property transfer forms so they can remove inventory or other assets from a warehouse or stockroom. Once the merchandise is in their possession, the fraudsters simply take it home with them. In Case 653, for ex-

ample, a manager requested merchandise from the company warehouse to be displayed on a showroom floor. The pieces he requested
never made it to the showroom, because he loaded them into a pickup
truck and took them home. In some instances he actually took the
items in broad daylight and with the help of another employee. The
obvious problem with this type of scheme is that the person who
orders the merchandise will usually be the primary suspect when it
turns up missing. In many cases the fraudster simply relies on poor
communication between different departments in his company and
hopes no one will piece the crime together. The individual in this
case, however, thought he was immune from detection because the
merchandise was requested via computer using a management level
security code. The code was not specific to any one manager, so
there would be no way of knowing which manager had ordered the
merchandise. Unfortunately for the thief, the company was able to
record the computer terminal from which the request originated. The
manager had used his own computer to make the request, which led
to his undoing.

Where inventory is stored in multiple locations, the transfer
of assets from one building to another can create opportunities for
employees to pilfer. Larry Gunter, in the case study at the beginning
of this chapter, stole over $1 million worth of computer chips by
adding extra merchandise to his cart as he transferred materials between two company buildings or as he took out the trash. He simply
took a detour and loaded the stolen chips in his truck before continuing on his route. As is the case in many businesses, Larry Gunter's
company required no internal paperwork when product was moved
between its two buildings, so it was very difficult to track the movement of assets. Consequently, it was easy for Gunter to steal.

Purchasing and Receiving Schemes

The purchasing and receiving functions of a company can
also be manipulated by dishonest employees to facilitate the theft of
inventory and other assets (see flowchart 9-2). It might at first seem
that any purchasing scheme should fall under the heading of false
billings. There is, however, a distinction between the purchasing
schemes that are classified as false billings and those that are classified as noncash misappropriations. If an employee causes his company to purchase merchandise which the company does not need,

this is a false billing scheme. The harm to the company comes in paying for assets for which it has no use. For instance, in Case 1693 a carpenter was allowed control over the ordering of materials for a small construction project. No one bothered to measure the amount of materials ordered against the size of the carpenter's project. The carpenter was therefore able to order excess, unneeded lumber, which was then delivered to his home in order to build a fence for himself. The essence of the fraud in this case was the *purchase* of unneeded materials.

On the other hand, if the assets were intentionally purchased by the company but simply misappropriated by the fraudster, this is classified as an inventory larceny scheme. In the preceding example, assume that the victim company wanted to keep a certain amount of lumber on hand for odd jobs. If the carpenter took this lumber home, the crime is a theft of lumber. The difference is that, in the second example, the company is deprived not only of the cash it paid for the lumber, but also of the lumber itself. It will now have to purchase more lumber to replace what it is missing. In the first example, the company's only loss was the cash it paid in the fraudulent purchase of the materials it did not need.

Falsifying Incoming Shipments

One of the most common ways for employees to abuse the purchasing and receiving functions is for a person charged with receiving goods on behalf of the victim company — such as a warehouse supervisor or receiving clerk — to falsify the records of incoming shipments. In Case 684, for instance, two employees conspired to misappropriate incoming merchandise by marking shipments as short. If 1,000 units of a particular item were received, for example, the fraudsters would indicate that only 900 were received. They were then able to steal the 100 units which were unaccounted for.

The obvious problem with this kind of scheme is that if the receiving report does not match the vendor's invoice, there will be a problem with payment. In the above example, if the vendor bills for 1,000 units but the accounts payable voucher only shows receipt of 900 units of merchandise, then someone will have to explain where the extra 100 units went. Obviously, the vendor will indicate that a full shipment was made, so the victim company's attention will likely turn to whoever signed the receiving report.

In the preceding case (684), the fraudsters attempted to avoid this problem by altering only one copy of the receiving report. The copy which was sent to accounts payable indicated receipt of a full shipment so the vendor would be paid without any questions. The copy used for inventory records indicated a short shipment so that the assets on hand would equal the assets in the perpetual inventory.

Instead of marking shipments short, the fraudster might reject portions of a shipment as not being up to quality specifications. The perpetrator then keeps the "substandard" merchandise rather than sending it back to the supplier. The result is the same as if the shipment had been marked short.

False Shipments of Inventory and Other Assets

To conceal thefts of inventory and other assets, fraudsters sometimes create false shipping documents and false sales documents to make it appear that missing inventory was not actually stolen but was instead sold (see flowchart 9-3). The document that tells the shipping department to release inventory for delivery is usually the packing slip. By creating a false packing slip, a corrupt employee can cause inventory to be fraudulently delivered to himself or an accomplice. The "sales" reflected in the packing slips are typically made to a fictitious person, a fictitious company, or an accomplice of the perpetrator.   In Case 1598, for instance, an inventory control employee used his position to create fraudulent paperwork which authorized the shipment of over $30,000 worth of inventory to his accomplices. The fraudsters were then able to sell the inventory for their own profit.

One benefit to using false shipping documents to misappropriate inventory or other assets is that the product can be removed from the warehouse or storeroom by someone other than the fraudster. The perpetrator of the scheme does not have to risk being caught stealing company inventory. Instead, the victim company unknowingly delivers the targeted assets to him.

False packing slips allow inventory to be shipped from the victim company to the perpetrator, but alone they do not conceal the fact that inventory has been misappropriated. In order to hide the theft, fraudsters may create a false sale so it appears that the missing inventory was shipped to a customer. In this way the inventory is accounted for. Depending on how the victim organization operates, the fraudster may have to create a false purchase order from the "buyer," a false sales order, and a false invoice along with the packing slip to create the illusion of a sale.

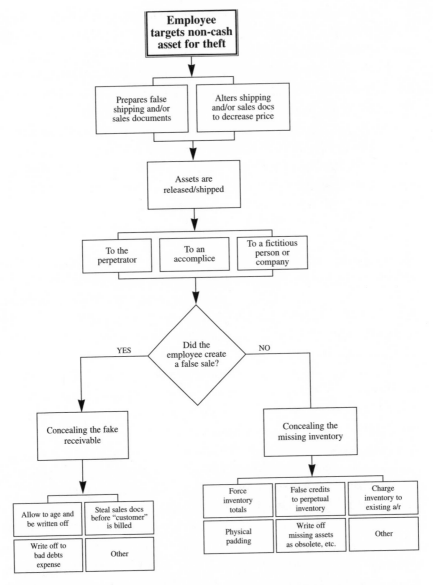

Flowchart 9-3: False Shipments of Inventory and Other Assets

The result is that a fake receivable account goes into the books for the price of the misappropriated inventory. Obviously, the "buyer" of the merchandise will never pay for it. How do fraudsters deal with these fake receivables? In some cases, the fraudster simply lets the receivable age on his company's books until it is eventually written off as uncollectable. In other instances the employee may take steps to remove the sale — and the delinquent receivable that results — from the books. For instance, in Case 1683, the perpetrator generated false invoices and delivered them to the company warehouse for shipping. The invoices were then marked "delivered" and sent to the sales office. The perpetrator removed all copies of the invoices from the files before they were billed to the fictitious customer. In other scenarios the perpetrator might write the receivables off himself, as did a corrupt manager in Case 651. In that five-year scheme, the perpetrator would take company assets and cover up the loss by setting up a fake sale. A few weeks after the fake sale went into the books, the perpetrator would write off the receivable to an account for "lost and stolen assets." More commonly, the fake sale will be written off to discounts and allowances or a bad debt expense account.

Instead of completely fabricated sales, some employees understated legitimate sales so that an accomplice is billed for less than delivered. The result is that a portion of the merchandise is sold at no cost. For instance, in Case 998 a salesman filled out shipping tickets which he forwarded to the warehouse. After the merchandise was delivered he instructed the warehouse employees to return the shipping tickets to him for "extra work" before they went to the invoicing department. The extra work which the salesman did was to alter the shipping tickets, reducing the quantity of merchandise on the ticket so that the buyer (an accomplice of the salesman) was billed for less than he received.

The following case study was selected as an example of a false shipping scheme. In this case, a marketing manager, with the help of a shipping clerk, delivered several computer hard drives to a computer company in return for a substantial cash payment. The victim company in this case had poor controls which allowed merchandise to be shipped without receipts, leaving the company extremely vulnerable to such a scheme. Harry D'Arcy, CFE, investigated this crime and eventually helped bring the culprits to justice.

*****

Case Study: Hard Drives and Bad Luck
Several names have been changed to preserve anonymity

Someone had stolen 1,400 hard drives from a computer warehouse in Toronto. That much was certain. The question remained, though — who took them? The answer was more than academic; it could mean the difference between the distributor's continuing operation and a total crash. Swainler's Technology averaged between $8-9 million dollars a year in sales, but with an 8% profit margin, they didn't have much financial room to maneuver. The company was a joint venture, overseen by a group of investors who were, to put it mildly, nervous. They had theft insurance, but with a particularly sticky clause that said the policy wouldn't cover theft committed by a Swainler's employee. In order to collect on the $600,000 worth of disk drives missing from the warehouse, the investors had to show that the theft was an outside job.

Their report showed just that. Employees and management agreed that the skids bearing the equipment had been safe and sound until the week that a competitor of Swainler's, Hargrove Incorporated, had sent delivery drivers over for an exchange. Evidently, some of Hargrove's people had swiped the equipment during the several days they were working in the Swainler's warehouse. Hargrove and Swainler's worked together when they had to. They were in hot competition though, and at different times each company had lost business and employees to the other. Since all Swainler's employees checked out, management concluded that the theft must have been committed by someone from Hargrove.

Doug Andrews was an independent adjuster hired by Swainler's Technology's insurance company. Besides conducting routine loss estimates, he's also a Certified Fraud Examiner, who's willing, as he puts it, "to see things other people either don't see or choose to ignore." While the Swainler's board assured Andrews this was a simple case, he wasn't convinced. "I wasn't sure it wasn't an inside job. Too many questions left hanging. How did the Hargrove people get the stuff out without being seen? The date management was setting for the loss seemed awfully convenient. It seemed like at the least someone at Swainler's had to be involved," Andrews remembers. He needed some help chasing down these hunches, so Andrews hired Harry D'Arcy to assist. D'Arcy worked for the Canadian Insurance Crime Prevention Bureau as a CFE and investigator. He and Andrews interviewed everyone at the warehouse and on the investors' board, going back two or three times if necessary to ask their questions. They traced serial numbers and possible distribution routes to turn up some sign of the hard drives. D'Arcy says, "We met at least twice a week to come up with a way to solve this. It was like a think tank, bouncing ideas and options off each other. 'What tack should we take now? Should we call out to California?

Do we need to go to that shop in Ottawa?' We knew we were being stymied. We just had to find a way around the blocks they put in front of us."

The main thing bothering Harry D'Arcy was that the board was presenting them with what appeared to be an open and shut case. Everyone's stories matched like precision parts. "It was too good to be true, too neat," D'Arcy says. The board members had seen the material on the Friday before Hargrove came; they noticed it was gone afterward; they had reason to suspect their competitor was behind it. Yes, they knew their insurance policy wouldn't pay if the hit was done by an employee, but that was beside the point. The board trusted its employees. Many of the people at Swainler's, from clerks to warehouse personnel, were either related to, or friends of, the management. D'Arcy and Andrews were encountering what Andrews later described as "an active campaign of misinformation."

Once he got a sense of the operating system at Swainler's, D'Arcy had some material for a new round of questioning. He noticed that as skids of equipment were prepared for shipping, the entire apparatus was wrapped in a thick plastic sealant and moved from the warehouse floor into the shipping dock. "Now," he asked one of the investors, "if those disk drives were ready for shipping on the Friday you say, then they would have already been wrapped, right?"

"Sure."

"Then, how did you know what you were seeing if the wrapping was already on? You can't see through the wrapping."

"I knew that batch was supposed to go out for the next week," the man replied.

"Then the skids should have been moved to the loading dock," D'Arcy interjected.

"I don't see your point."

"You said you saw them in the warehouse," D'Arcy reminded the man. "You couldn't have seen them in the warehouse if they had been moved to the dock for shipping."

The witness, feeling some stymie of his own, shifted and said, "Well, maybe they hadn't been taken over yet."

D'Arcy had a full house of questions for the initially talkative managers. Why would they notice a particular skid of drives on a particular day? Why were their memories so specific on this one shipment? How often did management tour the warehouse for an informal inventory? D'Arcy reports, "Once I had them shaken up, I would ask them point blank, 'Are you parroting something you heard somebody else say?'" The men would declare, No, they'd seen the material themselves.

"Did you discuss this with other board members?" D'Arcy asked.

"We talked about it in board meetings, sure," came the answer.

"And did you all agree on what you would say when you gave a statement?"

"No."

"But your statements all match."

"We agreed that we remembered the drives being there on the same day."

Doug Andrews was feeling fed up. "We were getting this string of non-answers. I felt like we were coming up dry."

Swainler's had hired a private investigator of their own to work the case. Harry D'Arcy talked with the man, who was convinced he had the material to show an outside job. The P.I. had been to Hargrove and spoken with employees there, including a man who had once worked for Swainler's. "I don't know if somebody here took the stuff or not," the man said. "But those guys at Swainler's deserve everything they get." He claimed Swainler's required its employees to work long hours with little pay or benefits, that workers were little more than switches on a processing board. To Swainler's investigator, then, this was a classic case of employee resentment, a common excuse for fraud.

D'Arcy said he disagreed but the investigator persisted. Swainler's Technology was now claiming their expenses for the investigation, finally totaling $125,000. During one week alone, the P.I. billed $45,000 when he conducted a stakeout in another city. An anonymous tip to the executive vice president at Swailer's placed the stolen disks at a storage facility in London, Ontario. The investigator took a team of people and equipment, and after a weekend surveillance, they observed a man opening the unit. When the team approached, they found nothing inside but the man's personal belongings.

Meanwhile, D'Arcy and Andrews pursued their own strategy. They notified the manufacturer's representatives throughout Canada and the United States to be on the lookout for a set of serial numbers. Sure enough, a call came in from a dealer in California; one of the disk drives had shown up for repair. Invoices showed the drive had been shipped from upstate New York and was purchased in Ottawa, Canada. The Ottawa shop had received the drive from a distributor in Montreal. Doug Andrews went to the Montreal warehouse but found it empty. Canvassing the neighborhood, he was told the people renting the warehouse had moved to another area in northern Montreal.

When Andrews got to the new address, he questioned four or five of the workers there about his case. They had never heard of Swainler's and knew nothing about the stolen drives. But when Andrews pressured them to look through their records with him, he found documents matching his serial numbers. Then, one of the missing drives turned up inside the warehouse.

Andrews wasn't ready to celebrate, though. "I was feeling beat. We'd been spending all this time, running back and forth, interviewing and re-interviewing. I said, 'I don't know, we may not get this one.'" The invoices he'd looked at were dated five weeks earlier than the time Swainler's had listed the theft. The discrepancy might help disprove the company's outside perpetrator theory, but could also be used to throw Andrews's largely circumstantial case into further confusion. As he was driving back to Toronto, Andrews got a call from Harry D'Arcy. "I've been doing some work based on what you found there," D'Arcy told him excitedly. "When you get back they'll be in chains."

Since D'Arcy now knew that at least some of the merchandise had gone through the warehouse in Montreal, he had looked for phone calls from that city in the phone logs at Swainler's. The marketing manager, Frederic Boucher, had not only received a large number of calls from Montreal, the calls were coming from the warehouse Andrews had just visited, the one claiming they had never heard of Swainler's. D'Arcy spoke again with people in the warehouse, one of whom admitted that the skids had disappeared much earlier than first reported. He guessed the actual date was about a month earlier than the one management had given. This of course coincided with the invoices Andrews had found in Montreal. At a special meeting, the board of directors reviewed D'Arcy's findings and confronted Frederic Boucher with the evidence pointing toward him. Boucher denied any involvement, and the board supported his story.

The next morning, Boucher told a different story. He had talked with his wife and a lawyer and was ready to come clean. He said he'd met the people from the Montreal warehouse at a conference. Together they worked out a deal in which Boucher would provide them with a supply of hard drives at a sweet price. With the help of a Swainler's shipping clerk, Boucher sent 60 low-end drives to Kingston, halfway between Montreal and Toronto, for $20,000 paid in cash. The atmosphere at Swainler's was ripe for this sort of offense. Harry D'Arcy recalls, "The bookkeeping system wasn't controlled. It was nothing to find things going out with no receipts. The operation was mainly run on trust. The men who headed up the company were all old friends, and they hired people they knew or to whom they were connected in one way or another. It ran on blind trust and nepotism." Encouraged by their first success, Boucher and his accomplices then arranged to make the big sale: 1,400 top-quality hard drives for a $600,000 take. They didn't have to worry about covering their tracks because management was eager to point the finger outside the company and collect on their insurance.

With Boucher's confession, Doug Andrews could make a happy report to his client that they weren't liable for the claim. Boucher was sentenced to make restitution for the theft and two years imprisonment, while the shipping clerk and the Montreal distributor were given one year each. All the sentences were suspended and the defendants placed on probation. The executives at Swainler's were, according to Harry D'Arcy, "cautioned regarding their complicity in the matter." Swainler's survived the loss but was later purchased by a prominent Canadian investment group and now operates under that umbrella.

Doug Andrews, who lectures and writes articles on insurance fraud in addition to conducting investigations, finds that people resist seeing cases like Swainler's as a real crime. "There's a belief that perpetrating fraud against an insurer is a victimless crime." Reports from the KPMG accounting firm and the Canadian Coalition Against Insurance Fraud place the yearly insurance losses in Canada between $1 billion and $2.6 billion a year. Andrews believes you can "take the middle figure of $2 billion and double it." While a significant portion of those losses are related to occupational crimes, an accurate account is not yet available. That's because some of the major acts that occur in business felonies — like supplier and kickback fraud — aren't included in the insurance industry figures. Nevertheless, these crimes are serious and proliferating. "They are frequent," Andrews says, "and often systematic and well-organized. Especially since insurance companies don't advertise as aggressively in Canada as they do in the U.S., people see insurance as a kind of faceless bureaucracy." With the tremendous amounts of money changing hands in this industry every day, "there's a mindset that labels these companies fair game. . . . But people see the difference in the end, when they pay their premiums."

*****

Other Schemes

Because employees tailor their thefts to the security systems, record keeping systems, building layout, and other day-to-day operations of their companies, the methods used to steal inventory and other assets vary. The preceding categories comprised the majority of schemes in our study, but there were a couple of other schemes which did not fit any established category, yet which merit discussion.

Write-offs are often used to conceal the theft of assets after they have been stolen. In some cases, however, assets are written off in order to make them available for theft. In Case 894 a warehouse foreman abused his authority to declare inventory obsolete. He wrote off perfectly good inventory, then "gave" it to a dummy corportation which he secretly owned. This fraudster took over $200,000 worth of merchandise from his employer. Once assets are designated as "scrap," it may be easier to conceal their misappropriation. Fraudsters may be allowed to take the "useless" assets for themselves, buy them or sell them to an accomplice at a greatly reduced price, or simply give the assets away.

One final unique example was presented in Case 2188. In this scheme a low-level manager convinced his supervisor to approve the purchase of new office equipment to replace existing equipment, which was to be retired. When the new equipment was purchased, the perpetrator took it home and left the existing equipment in place. His boss assumed that the equipment in the office was new, even though it was actually the same equipment that had always been there. If nothing else, this case illustrates that sometimes a little bit of attentiveness by management is all it takes to halt fraud.

Concealment

When inventory is stolen, the key concealment issue for the fraudster is shrinkage. Inventory shrinkage is the unaccounted-for reduction in the company's inventory that results from theft. For instance, assume a computer retailer has 1,000 computers in stock.

After work one day, an employee loads ten computers into a truck and takes them home. Now the company only has 990 computers, but since there is no record that the employee took ten computers, the inventory records still show 1,000 units on hand. The company has experienced inventory shrinkage in the amount of 10 computers.

Shrinkage is one of the red flags that signal fraud. When merchandise is missing and unaccounted for, the obvious question to ask is, "Where did it go?" The search for an answer to this question can uncover fraud. The goal of the fraudster is to proceed with his scheme undetected, so it is in his best interest to prevent anyone from looking for missing assets. This means concealing the shrinkage that occurs from asset theft.

Inventory and other assets are typically tracked through a two-step process. The first step, the perpetual inventory, is a running count that records how much should be on hand. When new shipments of supplies are received, for instance, these supplies are entered into the perpetual inventory. Similarly, when goods are sold they are removed from the perpetual inventory records. In this way a company tracks its inventory on a day-to-day basis.

Periodically, a physical count of assets on hand should be made by companies. In this process, someone actually goes through the storeroom or warehouse and counts everything that the company has in stock. This total is then matched to the amount of assets reflected in the perpetual inventory. A variation between the physical inventory and the perpetual inventory totals is shrinkage. While a certain amount of shrinkage may be expected in any business, large shrinkage totals may indicate fraud.

CONCEALING INVENTORY SHRINKAGE

Altered Inventory Records

One of the simplest methods for concealing shrinkage is to change the perpetual inventory record so that it will match the physical inventory count. This is also known as a *forced reconciliation* of the account. Basically, the perpetrator just changes the numbers in the perpetual inventory to make them match the amount of inventory on hand. In Case 1465, a supervisor involved in the theft of inventory credited the perpetual inventory and debited the cost of sales account to bring the perpetual inventory numbers into line with the actual inventory count. Once these adjusting entries were made, a review of inventory would not reveal any shrinkage. Rather than use correcting entries to adjust perpetual inventory, some employees simply alter the numbers by deleting or covering up the correct totals and entering new numbers.

There are two sides to the inventory equation, the perpetual inventory and the physical inventory. Instead of altering the perpetual inventory, a fraudster who has access to the records from a physical inventory count can change those records to match the total of the perpetual inventory. Going back to the computer store example, assume the company counts its inventory every month and matches it to the perpetual inventory. The physical count should come to 990 computers, since that is what is actually on hand. If the perpetrator is someone charged with counting inventory, he can simply write down that there are 1,000 units on hand.

Fictitious Sales and Accounts Receivable

We have already discussed how fraudsters create fake sales to mask the theft of assets. When the perpetrator made an adjusting entry to the perpetual inventory and cost of sales accounts in Case 1465 above, the problem was that there was no sales transaction on the books which corresponded to these entries. Had the perpetrator wished to fix this problem, he would have entered a debit to accounts receivable and a corresponding credit to the sales account to make it appear that the missing goods had been sold.

Of course, the problem of payment then arises, because no one is going to pay for the goods which were "sold" in this transaction. There are two routes which a fraudster might take in this circumstance. The first is to charge the sale to an existing account. In some cases, fraudsters charge fake sales to existing receivables accounts which are so large that the addition of the assets which the fraudster has stolen will not be noticed. Other corrupt employees charge the "sales" to accounts which are already aging and will soon be written off. When these accounts are removed from the books, the fraudster's stolen inventory effectively disappears.

The other adjustment that is typically made is a write-off to discounts and allowances or bad debt expense. In Case 2790, an employee with blanket authority to write off up to $5,000 in uncollectable sales per occurrence used this authority to conceal false sales of inventory to nonexistent companies. The fraudster bilked his company out of nearly $180,000 using this method.

Write off Inventory and Other Assets

We have already discussed Case 894, in which a corrupt employee wrote off inventory as obsolete, then "gave" the inventory to a shell company which he controlled. Writing off inventory and other assets is a relatively common way for fraudsters to remove assets from the books before or after they are stolen. Again, this is beneficial to the fraudster because it eliminates the problem of shrinkage that inherently exists in every case of noncash asset misappropriation. Examples of this method include Case 705, in which a manager wrote supplies off as lost or destroyed, then sold the supplies through his own company; and Case 720, in which a director of maintenance disposed of fixed assets by reporting them as broken, then took the assets for himself.

Physical Padding

Most methods of concealment deal with altering inventory records, either changing the perpetual inventory or miscounting during the physical inventory. In the alternative, some fraudsters try to make it appear that there are more assets present in the warehouse or stockroom than there actually are. Empty boxes, for example, may be stacked on shelves to create the illusion of extra inventory. In Case 5, for example, employees stole liquor from their stockroom and restacked the containers for the missing merchandise. This made it appear that the missing inventory was present when in fact there were really empty boxes on the stockroom shelves. In a period of approximately 18 months, this concealment method allowed employees to steal over $200,000 of liquor.

The most egregious case of inventory padding in our study occurred in Case 1666, where the fraudsters constructed a facade of finished product in a remote location of a warehouse and cordoned off the area to restrict access. Though there should have been a million dollars worth of product on hand, there was actually nothing behind the wall of finished product, which was constructed solely to create the appearance of additional inventory.

Conclusion

DETECTION

Statistical Sampling

Companies with inventory accounts typically have enormous populations of source documents. Statistical sampling allows the fraud examiner to inspect key attributes on a smaller portion (or sample) of those documents. For example, the examiner may select a statistically valid, random sample of purchase requisitions to determine that all requisitions in the sample selected were properly approved. Statistical sampling enables the examiner to predict the occurrence rate for the population and, therefore, determine with some accuracy, the error rate, or the potential for fraud.

Other items which may be sampled on a statistical basis include the following:

- Receiving reports
- Perpetual inventory records
- Raw materials requisitions
- Shipping documents
- Job cost sheets

The attributes tested for on the above-mentioned documents might include a specific date, item or location.

Perpetual Inventory Records

Unexplained entries in the perpetual records might reveal embezzlement losses.

- Are all the reductions to the perpetual inventory records explained by source documents (such as, sales invoices, approvals to remove to scrap inventory, or spoilage)?
- Are all increases in perpetual records explained by source documents such as receiving reports?

Shipping Documents

Inventory theft may be uncovered by answers to questions such as:

- Are all sales properly matched with a shipping document?
- Are any shipping documents not associated with a sale?
- Is inventory disappearing from storage?

Physical Inventory Counts

Physical inventory counts can sometimes give rise to inventory theft detection. However, because other explanations satisfy inventory shortages (such as shrinkage), historical analysis of inventory is usually necessary. Furthermore, if the only method used to detect inventory fraud is the year-end physical count, the perpetrators will have had all year to devise concealment methods to circumvent potential detection.

Analytical Review

By using an analytical review, inventory fraud may be detected because certain trends become immediately clear. For example, if the cost of goods sold increases by a disproportionate amount relative to sales, and no changes occur in the purchase prices, quantities purchased, or quality of products purchased, the cause of the disproportionate increase in cost of goods sold might be one of two things: the ending inventory has been depleted by theft; or inventory has been charged with embezzlement.

An analytical review of all the component parts of the cost of goods sold should indicate to the examiner where to direct further inquiries. For example, assuming that the type of inventory purchased is the same and there is no change in the manufacturing process or purchase price, if sales and cost of sales change from $5,650,987 and $2,542,944 to $6,166,085 and $2,981,880, respectively, what is the data telling the examiner? To begin, sales have increased by 9.12% whereas cost of sales increased by 17.26%. The profit margin has decreased by 3% (from 55% to 52%). Based on this data, the fraud examiner might want to look further at the components of inventory, such as beginning inventory, purchases, and ending inventory. If beginning inventory was $1,207,898, purchases were $2,606,518, and $2,604,972, respectively, and ending inventory was $894,564, then an inventory matrix would look like the following:

	Year 1	Year 2	% Change
Beginning Inventory	$ 1,207,898	$ 1,271,472	5.26%
Purchases	$ 2,606,518	$ 2,604,972	-0.06%
Goods Available for Sale	$ 3,814,416	$ 3,876,444	1.63%
Ending Inventory	$ (1,271,472)	$ (894,564)	-29.64%
Cost of Sales	$ 2,542,944	$ 2,981,880	17.26%

Inventory purchases, as a percentage of sales, have declined from 46.13% to 42.25%. From this example, we can hypothesize that (1) inventory purchases were purposely increased in year one only to be liquidated in year two, (2) the increased sales in year two were unexpected and the purchase of inventory did not keep pace with the sales, or (3) there might be some fraud scheme in inventory. If, by interview, the examiner is unable to ascertain a reasonable explanation such as (1) or (2) above, then further examination of the ending inventory may be warranted.

The fraud examiner may next look at the differences in the physical inventory procedures, to see if that created a more (or less) accurate inventory count at the end of either year one or year two. If there is no other logical explanation, then further investigation into these and other inventory accounts may be necessary to explain the anomalies occurring in inventory.

Computer-Generated Trend Analysis

The computer can be used to facilitate obtaining lists of items with specified attributes. For example, in a lumberyard operation, the computer can be programmed to list all purchases of 4 X 4 cedar fence posts, eight feet in length. Examine all the source documents that are represented by the listing. By examining the source documents for each of these purchases, the examiner can plot trends to determine the occurrence of the following (or other) patterns:

SEARCHES	SCHEMES
Purchases by vendor	If the same vendor is receiving favorable treatment
Inventory levels by types and dates	If inventory is being purchased at its reorder point or if excess inventory is being ordered
Inventory shipped by address	If the vendor's address matches either an employee address or the address of another vendor
Cost per item	If discounts are properly credited to purchases
Direct labor by item	If there are excess labor hours being added to a particular job or item
Direct materials by item	If materials are properly charged to the job (too much or the wrong materials)
Overhead per inventory item	If overhead is being properly applied, and applied only once
Disposals then reorders	If usable inventory is being prematurely designated as scrap
Shortages by inventory item	If there is inventory theft or the reorder system is not functioning
Returns and Allowances	If there are an unusually high incidence of returns and allowances
Sales Allowances	If sales allowances are not properly credited to promotional allowances
Buyer	If the buyer is not acting within scope of authority

Detailed Audit Program

The following audit program will also be helpful in establishing inventory control:

- Do adequate, detailed, written inventory instructions and procedures exist? Do inventory procedures give appropriate consideration to the location and arrangement of inventories?
- Do inventory procedures give appropriate consideration to identification and description of inventories?
- Is the method of determining inventory quantities specified (e.g., weight, count)?
- Is the method used for recording items counted adequate (e.g. count sheets, prenumbered tags)?
- Are inventory tags used? If yes: (1) Are they prenumbered? (2) Is accounting for inventory tags adequate and does it include control with respect to tags used, unused, and voided?
- Are adequate procedures in place to identify inventory counted, ensure that all items have been counted, and prevent double counting?
- Are obsolete, slow-moving, or damaged inventories properly identified and segregated?
- Is the inventory reasonably identifiable for proper classification in the accounting records (e.g., description, stage of completion)?
- Are inventory counts subject to (1) complete recounts by persons independent of the ones involved in the initial counts, (2) recounts only of merchandise having substantial value, or (3) spot checks by supervisory personnel?
- Are counts performed by employees whose functions are independent of the physical custody of inventories and record-keeping functions?
- Do proper accounting controls and procedures exist for the exclusion from inventory of merchandise on-hand which is not property of the client (e.g., customers' merchandise, consignments in)?
- Do proper accounting controls and procedures exist for the inclusion in inventory of merchandise not on-hand, but the property of the client (e.g., merchandise in warehouses, out on repair, consignments out)?

- Will identical inventory items in various areas be accumulated to allow a tie in total counts to a summary listing subsequent to the observation?
- Is the movement of inventory adequately controlled (e.g., shipping and receiving activities suspended) during the physical count to ensure a proper cut-off?
- Are significant differences between physical counts and detailed inventory records investigated before the accounting and inventory records are adjusted to match the physical counts?
- Will inventory at remote locations be counted?
- Will special counting procedures or volume conversions be necessary (e.g., items weighed on scale)?
- How will work-in-process inventory be identified?
- How will the stage of completion of work-in-process inventory be identified?
- Are there any other matters that should be noted for the inventory count?[1]

PREVENTION

There are four basic measures for prevention which, if properly installed and implemented, may help prevent inventory fraud. They are proper documentation, segregation of duties (including approvals), independent checks, and physical safeguards.

Proper Documentation

The following items should be prenumbered and controlled:
- Requisitions
- Receiving reports
- Perpetual records
- Raw materials requisitions
- Shipping documents
- Job cost sheets

However, not all inventory requires the purchasing of raw materials. In these cases, the proper documentation might take the form of prenumbered and controlled tickets and receipts for sales.

Segregation of Duties

The following duties should be handled by different personnel:

- Requisition of inventory
- Receipt of inventory
- Disbursement of inventory
- Conversion of inventory to scrap
- Receipt of proceeds from disposal of scrap

Independent Checks

Someone independent of the purchasing or warehousing functions should conduct physical observation of inventory. The personnel conducting the physical observations also should be knowledgeable about the inventory.

Physical Safeguards

All merchandise should be physically guarded and locked; access should be limited to authorized personnel only. For example, strategic placement of security guards may aid in the detection and deterrence of potential theft schemes. Electronic methods may also be used, such as cameras and surveillance devices. The effectiveness of any device will, however, depend on the employee's knowledge that physical safeguard controls are adhered to and the type of inventory available for misappropriation.

[1] George Georgiades, *Audit Procedures* (New York: Harcourt Brace Professional Publishing, 1995).

PART III - CORRUPTION

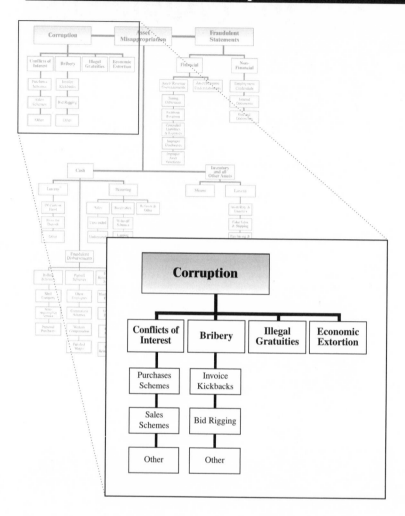

10. CORRUPTION

History of Corruption

Bribery and corruption is one of the oldest white-collar crimes known to mankind. The tradition of the "paying off" of public officials or company insiders for preferential treatment roots itself from the crudest business system developed. Bribery, it could be argued, is mankind's second oldest profession.

Certainly one of the most infamous cases of bribery in early history was that of Judas Iscariot, the disciple who betrayed Jesus Christ. Judas was paid 30 pieces of silver by the chief priests and elders of Jerusalem to disclose the location of Christ during the night so that he could be captured and executed; during the day, Christ was readily visible, but the elders feared a backlash from the Passover pilgrims in Jerusalem if they attempted to apprehend him. Christ was seen by the city elders and political heads as a serious threat to their power and ability to preside over the land.

Judas led an armed guard to the garden of Gethsemane, where Christ prayed with the other disciples. He identified Christ by kissing Jesus on the cheek and whispering "Master." Christ was crucified by the city elders. In most versions of the biblical story, Judas was distraught about betraying Jesus and gave the silver pieces back to the elders and hanged himself shortly after.

In today's society, many turn to the realm of politics when thinking of bribery and corruption. While politicians may not have earned this reputation due to their collective lack of undignified activities, bribery and corruption is not by any stretch of the imagination limited to the political realm. In the world of business, kickbacks, bribes, and other forms of corruption are all prevalent when situations of potential contracts or arrangements are concerned.

Bribery has been associated with government and politics before and after the time of Christ, which is not surprising considering the relative power that politicians yield over the private sector. Because politicians' decisions can have a profound effect on particular private industries, and thus the fortunes of a great many business-men, it is obvious that the private sector will inevitably attempt to influence the politician. However, attempting to influence a politi-cian is one thing; flouting the law is quite another.

An early example of illegal influences can be found in the annals of British royalty. Francis Bacon, the esteemed poet and writer of the late 16th and early 17th century, was also one the most trusted court advisors of King James I. Bacon held the position of king's solicitor general from 1607 to 1613, was England's attorney general from 1613 to 1617, and became lord keeper in 1617. In 1618, Bacon was promoted to the highest position in the king's court, that of Lord Chancellor, in which he served over the entire British court system as well as holding the king's ear on important matters.[1] Bacon, how-ever, abused his position, influencing the Star Chamber to rule in many different cases. A British landowner, John Wrenham, was the first to step forward against Bacon and make an accusation of cor-ruption, an offense which was punishable by death due to Bacon's high ranking in the royal court.[2] Once the king began probing into the complaint, it became soberly obvious that Wrenham's accusa-tions were justified. In fact, it was uncovered that Bacon had taken bribes on many different instances to manipulate the judgments of impending cases. Bacon ultimately conceded that he was guilty of the offenses and was publicly shamed for his actions, resigning his post, but he was not executed.[3]

In a bribery scandal which rocked Washington D.C. in the 1920s, the paper trail of corruption led back to the White House Cabi-net and nearly implicated then-President Warren G. Harding. Known as the Teapot Dome Scandal, the incident surrounded a group of Naval Oil Reserves that were improperly handled by several key members of Harding's staff.

Teapot Dome, an oil reserve in Wyoming, as well as two other California oil fields had been set aside by the government for the use of the U.S. Navy in the case of an emergency. However, Teapot Dome was located near another private oil reserve and the government, fear-ing that the private oil field would drain Teapot Dome, authorized that the oil field could be contracted out to the private sector for limited drilling.

Newly appointed Secretary of the Interior Albert B. Hall, one of President Harding's closest friends and a former New Mexico Senator, seized the opportunity and wrestled control of the oil fields from the Navy by insisting that Harding decree Hall in charge of the oil fields.[4] The Navy superiors objected vigorously in a letter to the President, but the letter mysteriously disappeared in route.[5] Once in control of the fields, Hall contracted the field drilling to Olin Harry Sinclair, one of Hall's old cronies, and Hall and several other Cabinet members received kickbacks from the contract. This was only one of several dozen scams that Hall and company were operating, but the lack of competitive bidding for the rights to the oil fields caught the attention of several U.S. Senators, who spearheaded an investigation into the improprieties.

Hall did not go quietly; the Senators at the forefront of the investigation received numerous death threats and warnings.[6] Hall also refused to admit that he had done anything unethical, claiming that bidding the oil field drilling jobs openly would have been a compromise to national security.

Ultimately, Hall was convicted and President Harding's reputation was thoroughly tarnished. The President surrounded himself with the largest collection of crooks and con men that Washington has seen before or since, save possibly for the scandal-ridden Nixon administration in the 1970s.

The list of corrupt politicians in the late 1800s and early 1900s is numerous and worthy of mention, from Huey Long's Louisiana machine, which marched the portly local politician to a U.S. Senate seat and ultimately to an unsuccessful run at the presidency, to the storied New York machine, the political organization of neighborhood bosses who performed favors of all sort, to the constituency in exchange for votes. Boss Tweed, one of New York's most powerful political machine bosses, was beloved by the citizens of the various burrows he was charged with: every Thanksgiving, his citizens' dinner tables were stuffed with a robust turkey and every Christmas, presents were piled underneath their trees. All the while, Tweed and his "business associates" were bilking the city out of fortunes and forcefully keeping themselves in office. Even former President Lyndon Johnson was accused of rigging elections while serving in the Texas House of Representatives as a young politician and was forced to go to court to keep himself in office.

In a different sort of corruption scheme, several vice presidents and other brass at General Electric, the Westinghouse Electric Corporation, and other companies, were called to the mat in one of the most high-profile collusion cases in history. The crime, which was prosecuted in 1961, is interesting for several reasons: it was one of the first times a group of high corporate officers was tried and convicted of a "white-collar crime," the antitrust violations had been carried out in a manner that Dr. Gil Geis describes as "willful and blatant" in nature, and the fact that a lawyer on the defense team argued in court that his clients should not be put "behind bars with common criminals who have been convicted of embezzlement and other serious crimes."[7]

Serious crimes? All these executives at two of the most powerful electric companies did was irreverently flaunt the Sherman Antitrust Act of 1890, which forbade any companies of price-fixing, price-gouging, or any other scheme to drive up the costs of industry-specific contracts. The General Electric and Westinghouse Company executives apparently agreed with several other large companies to submit identical bids for contracts with government entities such as the Tennessee Valley Authority, the governmental department which ultimately blew the whistle on the scam.[8]

The electric giants worked out an agreement which stipulated that each conspirator company would receive 20% of the contracts bid. The ring allowed one company to bring in the lowest bid on a particular contract and the rest of the companies bid higher. The only problem was that in many cases, the companies agreed on identical bids for "losing" companies and some of the contractors caught on.[9]

When the participating companies' executives went on trial, they routinely dismissed the charges as technically illegal but certainly not immoral. The company heads argued one after another that they had conspired to rig the bidding process, yes, but were not harming the public welfare because they had not stolen any property or embezzled any moneys.

The court found seven of the company executives guilty of breaking the Sherman Antitrust Act and sentenced each to 30 days in jail. The court also fined the companies involved $1,787,000 for the infractions.[10] The light sentences, and the fact that each of the imprisoned executives was released five days early for good behavior, insinuates that the courts found the offenses nearly as acceptable as did the companies who perpetuated them. Since that time, however, both business as well as government regulation have begun to look much less favorably upon business practices such as these.

One recent and infamous example of high-ranking bribery and corruption that also occurred in the political realm was the ABSCAM case. In the late 1970s, the Federal Bureau of Investigation worked in concert with an apprehended con man named Melvin Weinberg to nail several U.S. Senators with bribery charges.[11] The FBI agents posed as wealthy Arabs and videotaped numerous meetings with New Jersey Senator Harrison Williams, in which Williams promised political sway in exchange for shares in an Arab-backed mining project. Senator Williams went so far as to promise the Arabs that he would take a meeting with then President Jimmy Carter to discuss Arab interests and bragged extravagantly of his political muscle.[12]

The federal government was most recently shocked by the improprieties of members of the U.S. Department of Housing and Urban Development. Officials in the department in the late 1980s and early 1990s were discovered diverting resources which were supposed to go to poverty housing projects to wealthy land developers in exchange for kickbacks.[13] The developers and contractors who received the HUD funds were also found to be high-paying contributors to the Reagan administration, well financed and well connected. The investigation also uncovered the improprieties of many former HUD officials, who had repeatedly used their influences to arrange the illicit payments to the wealthy developers.[14]

A succession of bribery and kickback scandals rocked the auto industry in the early 1990s, as several Honda America executives were convicted of accepting lavish "gifts" from needy local dealers. The hint of sprawling wrongdoings within the corporation first reared its head when a New Hampshire Acura dealer, Richard Nault, filed a lawsuit against Honda America. Nault alleged that the company was playing favorites within his town by not supplying his dealership with enough Acura Legend luxury cars, while the cross-town dealership, owned by Thomas Bohlander, received a surplus inventory from Honda. During the course of the lawsuit investigation, the Acura district sales manager for the Northeast U.S., Damien Budnick, admitted to attorneys that he had delivered a $100,000 kickback from a Florida dealer to David Peterson, the zone manager who was also responsible for car deliveries to the New Hampshire dealership.

Armed with the knowledge that Peterson openly accepted kickbacks, Nault's attorneys called Honda America to the mat, forcing the company to admit that it was aware that such corrupt business practices within the company were common. Honda America, wanting no part of a publicly fought boondoggle, settled quickly and quietly with Nault out of court. But the stop-gap maneuverings were too little, too late; the U.S. district attorney's office began an investigation into the allegations. The investigators encountered corruption at every turn, as if the Honda America executives had adopted the Japanese tradition of exchanging small gifts in an obscenely twisted fashion. The bribes dropped at the foot of former senior vice president James Cardiges, who was foolish enough to elaborately document every kickback he ever received in a personal journal. The log detailed the odd variance of "gifts" Cardiges received: a $45,000 kickback from one dealer, a $20,000 laser karaoke machine from another, a $30,000 baby grand piano. Cardiges was one of 16 Honda America executives who have admitted to bribery and corruption charges. Two other notable Honda executives, former vice president of sales John Billmyer and former Western zone manager Dennis Joselyn, were sentenced to 60 months in prison and fined $125,000, and 78 months in prison, respectively. Authorities have not stopped their investigation at the top of the chain, however. The list of those who have been implicated or indicted in the Honda American bribery scandal continues to grow. Rick Hendrick, the nation's largest auto dealer, was indicted on a federal level on charges of conspiracy, mail fraud, and money laundering. Hendrick, notable also for his considerable influence in the NASCAR racing circuit, has adamantly denied allegations that he bribed various Honda America executives for favorable treatment and new dealerships. The court case is still pending.

In the 1990s, bribery schemes have even found their way into cyberspace. In February 1997, the SEC settled an investigation with the publisher of an on-line investment newsletter. Although the publisher, George Chelekis, neither admitted nor denied any wrongdoing, his company was forced to pay over $150,000 in fines. The two newsletters which appeared on the Internet, KGC Inc. and Hot Stocks Review, recommended stock buys to subscribers, but it was revealed that the tips were hardly objective.[15] Chelekis apparently received 275,000 shares of stock and at least $1.1 million as payment from the companies whose stocks he was recommending. The SEC charged that Mr. Chelekis's publications made "false and misleading statements" about six companies that had been listed with Hot Stocks Review and KGC Inc.[16]

Overview

Black's Law Dictionary defines *corrupt* as "spoiled; tainted; vitiated; depraved; debased; morally degenerate. As used as a verb, to change one's morals and principles from good to bad."[17] The authors obviously didn't think highly of those who are corrupt. They further define corruption as "an act done with an intent to give some advantage inconsistent with official duty and the rights of others. The act of an official or fiduciary person who unlawfully and wrongfully uses his station or character to procure some benefit for himself or for another person, contrary to duty and the rights of others."[18]

My first official experience with bribery came when the FBI transferred me from El Paso, Texas, to New York, New York (". . . the town so nice they named it twice . . ."). Sending me to New York was the FBI's cruel joke on someone who grew up in Duncan, Oklahoma. But I eventually learned to love the city. At the time I was transferred, about one out of every seven FBI Agents was assigned to the Manhattan office. As a result, the agents were divided into specialized squads, consisting of about 20 investigators and a supervisor.

Because there was an empty desk on the Bribery and Corruption Squad, that's where I found myself assigned. There was no other reason; I knew absolutely nothing about the topic. But I was about to learn. Over the next several years, I investigated part or all of several hundred cases. The most famous was the government's investigation of former U.S. Attorney John N. Mitchell for his role in Watergate. We sent him to prison. It seemed like a great accomplishment then—he did the crime, and he did the time. But later, after he was released and all the media fury died down, Mitchell died a broken man. My pride in that conviction has since turned to pity. As Lord Acton observed: "Power corrupts. And absolute power corrupts absolutely."   Perhaps many of us placed in the same circumstances as Mitchell would fall victim to temptation.

Although Watergate was my most famous case, it was not my first. And for those of us in the investigative field, the initial time we encounter a situation is frequently our most memorable. My first bribery case involved allegations against a highly placed government civil servant, Herman Klegman. He was with the Immigration and Naturalization Service (INS) and held the title of district director. Klegman's area covered all of New Jersey.

As district director for INS, Klegman had the ultimate authority to issue all "green cards" in his district. For the uninitiated, a green card gives a non-U.S. citizen the right to live and work in the country without becoming a permanent citizen. Green cards are strictly allotted by foreign country, and may be very hard to come by legitimately, depending on the country of residence. Citizens from mainland China at that time were especially likely to have their green card applications rejected, so many of them immigrated illegally. Once in the United States, these illegal immigrants would find their way into the Chinese community. In New York City, many of them would become employed by the numerous restaurants in Chinatown.

Unconfirmed rumors about Klegman's ethics had apparently circulated for years in INS circles. Finally, someone—presumably an employee—wrote the FBI an anonymous letter claiming Klegman was "on the take" from a New York City Chinese restaurateur, Stanley Yee. No details were forthcoming, and I had no idea whatsoever where to start. So I spoke with the Corruption Squad's most experienced agent, Boyd Henry. He was a veteran of at least a thousand bribery cases and really knew how to cut through the fog. I asked Boyd how to prove such a case.

"Joe," Boyd said, "if someone is taking payoffs, then they're doing something they should not officially be doing. Look for what that something is, and you'll find the answer." Boyd was able to sum up the essence of investigating corruption in two sentences, and I have not forgotten it.

In the case of Klegman I reasoned that he must somehow be issuing green cards to Yee's workers in exchange for a kickback. But this theory had an obvious flaw: Klegman's authority was limited to New Jersey only, and Yee's Chinese restaurants—20 of them—were all located in New York.

I discussed the theory with Boyd, who said, "That must be it—Klegman is probably somehow issuing green cards to Chinese restaurant workers in New York City through his office in New Jersey. You need to focus on exactly how he could pull that off." Boyd's approach made perfect sense to me. Sol Saletra, my contact at INS, explained that an application for a green card is filed in the district of the immigrant's residence. So if Klegman issued green cards to workers in New York City, they would show a New Jersey residence. Otherwise, it would look too suspicious to the compliance auditors at INS, who periodically check the procedure for issuing green cards. The first step in proving the address theory was to find the personnel records of all the employees of Yee's 20 eating establishments —

about 400 people in total. We issued subpoenas to all the restaurants for their records. Once we had the names of Yee's Chinese workers, we searched them against INS records in New York and New Jersey.

Lo and behold, we hit paydirt.

The search revealed a mysterious pattern with a dozen or so immigrants. It seemed their original immigration files were initiated in New York. Then, each of these immigrants, at different times, sent letters to the INS stating they had "moved" from New York to New Jersey. Their applications for green cards were thereafter processed in the New Jersey INS office by—you guessed it—Klegman himself. After their green cards were issued, each of these Chinese immigrants sent letters to the New Jersey INS office, stating that they had "moved" back to New York. Interestingly, all the letters looked to the naked eye like they had been prepared on the same typewriter.

I went back to Boyd Henry for more of his sage advice. "Yes, Joe, you're on to something," he said. "But you've still got a long way to go. You haven't quite proved that Klegman has done something he shouldn't have officially done." First, to put a circumstantial case together, Boyd reasoned that a highly placed INS official like Klegman would never personally approve green card applications, even though he had the authority to do so. Sol Saletra of the INS confirmed it would be very unusual for the district director's signature to be on the application, as it was on these dozen or so Chinese immigrants' applications.

But Saletra's observations would have to be confirmed for court purposes. I only knew one way to do that, and so did Sol: Someone would have to examine every immigration file in the District of New Jersey and inspect the approving official's signature. We reluctantly committed the manpower to do just that. Hundreds of hours of tedious labor later, we found exactly what we needed—out of thousands of immigration applications in his district, Klegman's signature appeared only on the dozen Chinese restaurant workers'.

Through Chinese FBI interpreters, we next interviewed the restaurant workers. To a man, they denied paying for their green cards. But during the interview process, we obtained bank account information from them and then subpoenaed those records. In each and every case, the restaurant workers had made a $10,000 cash withdrawal from their respective savings accounts. And each withdrawal closely coincided with the approval date of that immigrant's INS application.

Boyd Henry, my FBI mentor, smiled at my progress in the case. "In order to prove a bribery case, you're going to have to prove that Klegman got a 'thing of value' as required by the statute," he observed. "In most—but not all—cases, the 'thing of value' is going to be money. If you find where Klegman has stashed his bribe money, I think you have enough for a conviction." Finding the location of the stash proved more difficult than Henry thought. "For some inexplicable reason," Boyd said, "most people taking cash deposit some or all of it in their own bank account. Then they spend it. Look at his bank statements first," he suggested. I did. Nothing there. We then piecemealed a financial picture of Klegman indicating he wasn't living ostentatiously—no new homes, cars, or toys as far as we could tell. Then the Assistant United States Attorney, Robert "Bolt" Beller, who was interested in prosecuting the case, pulled Klegman before the grand jury. Klegman didn't take the Fifth—he cooperated fully but denied everything.

Then, as is standard in corruption cases, Bolt offered a deal to Stanley Yee which he couldn't refuse: Cooperate with the government and we'll go easier on you. Eventually, Yee came into the FBI office with his lawyer. In exchange for a reduced sentence, Yee furnished the key information. Yes, he had paid Klegman, he admitted. They had an arrangement—for every green card issued to one of Yee's restaurant workers, the illegal immigrant would pay Yee $10,000. In turn, Yee would pay that money to Klegman. The arrangement had been going on for years, and Yee estimated he had paid Klegman at least a quarter of a million dollars in bribes.

But where did Klegman stash the ill-gotten gain? In Israel, Yee said, in a secret bank account Klegman had set up in Tel Aviv. We were able to confirm that through our international contacts. Klegman was indicted for bribery. A few days before his trial, Herman Simon Klegman entered a guilty plea and drew a modest prison term. Yee walked.

The lesson to be learned from such a difficult corruption case is that they are very hard to prove. And in almost all cases, it is necessary to make a deal with the proverbial "bag man" like Stanley Yee. Making such deals originally grated against me. But one learns in the criminal justice system to take what you can get. Otherwise, people like Klegman will go scot-free.

Statistics

Corruption is broken down into the following four scheme types:

>Bribery Schemes
>Conflicts of Interest Schemes
>Economic Extortion Schemes
>Illegal Gratuities Schemes

As the charts below illustrate, bribery schemes accounted for the majority of cases and losses among in the category of corruption. In addition, with a median loss of $500,000, bribery and conflicts of interest were the two most expensive types of fraud, on average, in our entire study.

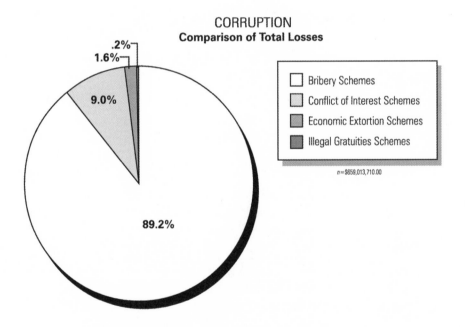

Chart 10-1: Comparison of Total Losses

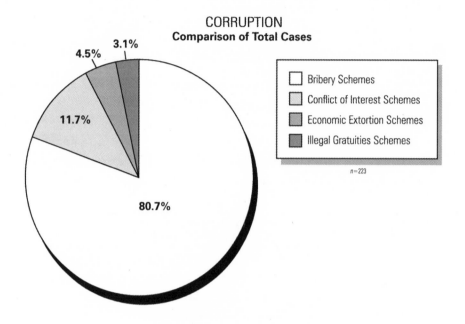

Chart 10-2: Comparison of Total Cases

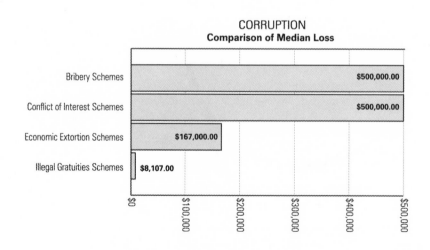

Chart 10-3: Comparison of Median Losses

[1] John T. Noonan, Jr., *Bribes* (New York: Macmillan Publishing Company, 1984).

[2] Noonan.

[3] Noonan.

[4] Bruce Bliven, "The Tempest Over Tepot," *American Heritage*, September-October, 1995.

[5] Charles L. Mee, Jr., *The Ohio Gang: The World of Warren G. Harding* (New York: M. Evan and Company, 1981).

[6] Dale R. Gardner, "Teapot Dome: Civil Legal Cases That Closed the Scandal," *Journal of the West*, October 1989.

[7] Gilbert Geis and Robert F. Meier. *White-Collar Crime, Revised Edition* (New York: The Free Press, 1977).

[8] Geis.

[9] Geis.

[10] Geis

[11] Gerald M. Caplan, *ABSCAM Ethics: Moral Issues & Deception in Law Enforcement,* (Cambridge: Ballinger, 1983).

[12] Caplan.

[13] Larry J. Siegal, *Criminalogy, 4th Edition* (New York: West Publishing Company, 1993).

[14] Seigel.

[15] Paul Beckett. "SEC, Publisher of On-Line Newsletter Settle Fraud Case Involving the Internet," *The Wall Street Journal,* February 26, 1997.

[16] Beckett.

[17] Black, p. 311.

[18] Black, p. 311.

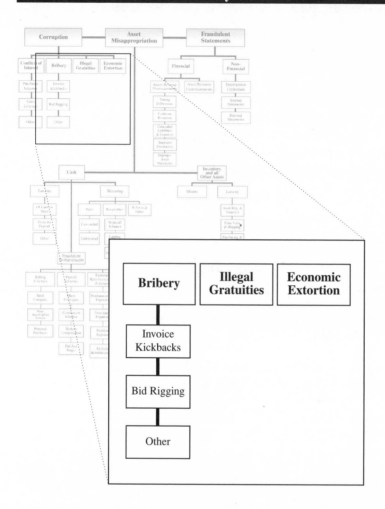

Flowchart 11-1

11. BRIBERY

*****

Case Study: Why Is This Furniture Falling Apart?

* Several names have been changed to preserve anonymity

A number of years ago, the *Washington Post* ran a series of articles detailing charges of waste, fraud, and abuse in the General Services Administration (GSA), the federal government's housekeeping agency. In particular, for more than a decade a furniture manufacturer in New Jersey had churned out $200 million worth of defective and useless furniture which GSA purchased.

Despite years of complaints from GSA's customers about the shoddiness of the furniture and equipment, the GSA had done little to investigate the contractor, Art Metal U.S.A. Government agencies which had been issued the furniture, like the Internal Revenue Service, the Central Intelligence Agency, and the State Department, told horror stories about furniture that fell apart, desks that collapsed, and chairs with one leg shorter than the others.

When federal employees complained to the GSA, they were ignored or rebuffed. "You didn't fill out the right form," GSA would say, or "You have to pay to ship it back to the contractor and wait two years and you might get a replacement."

After several years, this behavior naturally gave rise to the speculation that bribery and corruption were the cause of the problem.

A series of articles in the *Washington Post* led to a congressional investigation. Peter Roman, then chief investigator for a subcommittee of the U.S. Senate Committee on Government Affairs, recalled when Senator Lawton Chiles of Florida, chairman of the subcommittee, called him to his office. "He wanted a full investigation into all the practices of GSA," Roman said. Unlike a private audit, a congressional investigation involves a thorough review of financial and operational records, interviews, and sworn testimony, when necessary. If there is enough evidence to show a crime has been committed, then the U.S. Justice Department prosecutes. Roman said this was "one of the few white-collar fraud investigations the Senate had done in years, with the exception of the Investigation Subcommittee's organized crime inquiries."

The first step in such an analysis involved general oversight hearings for the Subcommittee on Federal Spending Practices and Open Government. At one of the first hearings, Mr. Phillip J. Kurans, president of the Art Metal furniture company, appeared, uninvited, and demanded an opportunity to testify. He told Senator Chiles, that his company produced good quality furniture at bargain prices and challenged the subcommittee to prove otherwise. He invited the senator to the plant in Newark, New Jersey, to inspect their records.

"Chiles had me in his office the next morning," Roman recalls. "He said, 'Tell them we accept their offer. Get up to New Jersey and find out what happened.'"

Roman assembled an investigation team borrowed from other federal agencies. The principals were Dick Polhemus, CFE, from the Treasury Department; and Marvin Doyal, CFE, CPA; and Paul Granetto from the U.S. General Accounting Office. "We agreed that the logical approach was to do a cash flow analysis," Roman recalls. "If the furniture was defective, then someone had to generate cash to bribe somebody else to accept it. All of us had experience in following the money, so we went off to Newark to look for it."

Together, they paid a visit to Art Metal U.S.A. on behalf of the senator. Kurans grudgingly sent them into a large room filled with 30 years of financial records. In the past, the sheer volume of paper had caused two GSA investigations to end without incident and the company's own auditors to find nothing untoward. Half the team began controlling the checks, separating them out into operations and payroll, while the others reviewed the canceled checks to do a pattern analysis.

"Marvin Doyal and I still argue over which one of us first found the checks to a subcontractor which had been cashed rather than deposited," Roman says.

"As we began to review the operational checks," he remembers, "one of the items that stood out were checks made out to one company, but under three different names: I. Spiegel, Spiegel Trucking Company, and Spiegel Trucking, Inc." Were the bookkeepers

careless in writing the wrong name? The investigators discovered
that the checks made out to I. Spiegel (which were folded into threes,
like one would fold a personal check and place in his wallet) were
cashed by one Isador Spiegel, unlike the other accounts. These checks
were not run through any Spiegel Trucking Co. business account and
had been used solely for cash. The checks to Spiegel Trucking Co.,
on the other hand, "looked like they had been used for actual delivery of furniture to various GSA depots or customers," Roman said.

The other item that caught the investigators' eyes involved
checks made out simply to "Auction Expenses" for even sums of
money. Kurans told them that the company bought used machinery
for cash at auctions throughout the East Coast. That was the reason,
he said, that the company spent large amounts of cash money.

Yet when the team called operators of furniture auctions they
found that auctions required the buyer to show up with a certified
check for 10% of the amount bought. The rest was also to be paid
with certified checks. Over four years, Art Metal generated $482,000
in cash through so-called "auction expenses." More than $800,000
flowing to Spiegel was converted into cash. This was enough evidence to garner Kurens a subpoena to appear before the subcommittee. The subpoena enabled investigators to obtain "literally a truck
full of documents" from Art Metal, Roman said, "which filled a whole
room in the basement of the Russell Senate Office Building."

With over $1 million in cash discovered, the next step for the
investigating team was to look for evidence of bribery. They pains-
takingly interviewed every furniture inspector in GSA's Region Two,
eventually focusing on a former regional inspector of the GSA. Over
the past four years, this man had bought 11 race horses at an average
price of $13,000 each—much more money than a GSA furniture in-
spector could afford. At this point, Senator Chiles authorized bringing in a special counsel. This was Charles Intriago, Esq., a former
Miami Strike Force prosecutor. When confronted, the inspector
availed himself of his Fifth Amendment rights and the search for
another witness continued. They found one: Louis Arnold, a retired
bookkeeper at Art Metal. Arnold would testify that Art Metal management was paying off GSA inspectors. Arnold revealed a third
source of cash, a petty cash fund, totaling about $100,000, that was
used to pay for the inspectors' lunches and hotel expenses.

Based on Arnold's testimony, investigators subpoenaed three
banks which had photographed all of their cash transactions. "We

found pictures of the treasurer, the plant manager, and occasionally one of the partners cashing these 'auction expense' checks, and taking the money in twenties."

During the Senate hearings, several senior agency officials testified to the shoddiness of the furniture. Roman, who spent some time on the floor of the plant, saw many examples of shabby workmanship. For example, although plant managers claimed they had bought a quality paint machine to paint filing cabinets, Roman said all he ever saw was a man wearing a gas mask, with a hand-held paint sprayer, wildly spraying at cabinets that darted past him on a conveyor belt. "It was like seeing a little kid playing laser tag, and the target appears for half a second, and he takes a wild shot at it and hopes he hits the target," he said.

Marvin Doyal testified to the generation of $1.3 million in cash, a company official testified that the money had been used to bribe (unnamed) GSA inspectors, and company officials and GSA inspectors availed themselves of their Fifth Amendment rights. Interagency problems between the subcommittee and the Justice Department played a major role in a failed plea bargain with a former GSA official. At this point, Senator Chiles and the staff decided that the subcommittee had gone as far as it could go.

Why did Art Metal not make an attempt to hide their fraud? "In the first place," Roman said, "they thought nobody would ever come. Secondly, they had been the subject of two GSA-appointed investigations" that uncovered nothing.

The result of the investigations proved disappointing to Senator Chiles and the subcommittee staff.

"In the end," however, Senator Chiles later said, "we achieved our legislative mission. We were disappointed that the plea bargain and other subcommittee efforts didn't pay off as fully as it might have, but we sure got GSA's attention."

Embarrassed by the subcommittee disclosures, GSA stopped awarding government furniture contracts to the Art Metal compay. Having lost what amounted to its sole customer, Art Metal soon went bankrupt. Its plant manager and general counsel were convicted of related offenses within two years. The investigations into the GSA prompted a housecleaning of that agency. At the time of the hearings, GSA had 27,000 employees; today, it employs about 9,000. GSA's role as the federal government's chief purchasing agent has been greatly diminished. The Art Metal case showed that centralized purchasing is not always a good idea.

*****

Overview

As the previous case study illustrates, bribery schemes can be difficult and expensive. Though they made up only 11.82% of the cases in our study (chart 1-6), their median cost of $500,000 (chart 1-5) was the highest cash loss of any scheme type (remember that financial statements and non-financial statements schemes reflect the size of misstatements rather than the size of cash losses). While you are less likely to be victimized by a bribery scheme, the potential for high dollar losses is much greater than in asset misappropriation frauds.

Corruption schemes in our study are broken down into four classifications: *bribery*, *economic extortion*, *illegal gratuities*, and *conflicts of interest*. The first three classifications are very similar in nature and will be discussed presently. Conflict of interest schemes will be covered in the next chapter.

Before discussing how corruption schemes work, we must understand the similarities and differences that exist between bribery, extortion, and illegal gratuity cases. Bribery may be defined as the offering, giving, receiving, or soliciting any thing of value to influence an official act.[1] The term *official act* means that traditional bribery statutes only proscribe payments made to influence the decisions of government agents or employees. In the case of Art Metal, U.S.A., this is exactly what happened. The furniture supplier paid off government inspectors to accept substandard merchandise.

Many occupational fraud schemes, however, involve commercial bribery, which is similar to the traditional definition of bribery except that something of value is offered to influence a business decision rather than an official act of government. Of course, payments are made every day to influence business decisions, and these payments are perfectly legal. When two parties sign a contract agreeing that one will deliver merchandise in return for a certain sum of money, this is a business decision that has been influenced by the offer of something of value. Obviously, this transaction is not illegal. In a commercial bribery scheme, the payment is received by an employee without his employer's consent. In other words, commercial bribery cases deal with the acceptance of under-the-table payments in return for the exercise of influence over a business transaction. Notice also that *offering* a payment can constitute a bribe, even if the illicit payment is never actually made.

Illegal gratuities are similar to bribery schemes, except that something of value is given to an employee to *reward* a decision rather than influence it. In an illegal gratuities scheme, a decision is made which happens to benefit a certain person or company. This decision is not influenced by any sort of payment. The party who benefited from the decision then rewards the person who made the decision. For example, in Case 1739 an employee of a utility company awarded a multimillion dollar construction contract to a certain vendor and later received an automobile from that vendor as a reward.

At first glance, it may seem that illegal gratuities schemes are harmless if the business decisions in question are not influenced by the promise of payment. But most company ethics policies forbid employees from accepting unreported gifts from vendors. One reason is that illegal gratuities schemes can (and do) evolve into bribery schemes. Once an employee has been rewarded for an act such as directing business to a particular supplier, an understanding might be reached that future decisions beneficial to the supplier will also be rewarded. Additionally, even though an outright promise of payment has not been made, employees may direct business to certain companies in the hope that they will be rewarded with money or gifts.

Economic extortion cases are the "Pay up or else. . ." corruption schemes. Whereas bribery schemes involve an offer of payment intended to influence a business decision, economic extortion schemes are committed when one person demands payment from another. Refusal to pay the extorter results in some harm such as a loss of business. For instance, in Case 2234, an employee demanded payment from suppliers and in return awarded those suppliers subcontracts on various projects. If the suppliers refused to pay the employee, the subcontracts were awarded to rival suppliers or held back until the fraudster got his money.

Bribery Schemes

At its heart, a bribe is a business transaction, albeit an illegal or unethical one. As in the GSA case discussed above, a person "buys" something with the bribes he pays. What he buys is the influence of the recipient. Bribery schemes generally fall into two broad categories: *kickbacks* and *bid-rigging schemes*.

| Kickback Schemes | Bid-Rigging Schemes |

Kickbacks are undisclosed payments made by vendors to employees of purchasing companies. The purpose of a kickback is usually to enlist the corrupt employee in an overbilling scheme. Sometimes vendors pay kickbacks simply to get extra business from the purchasing company. Bid-rigging schemes occur when an employee fraudulently assists a vendor in winning a contract through the competitive bidding process.

As chart 11-1 illustrates, the bid rigging schemes that we reviewed accounted for over $400,000,000 in losses, almost three times the amount of losses caused by kickback schemes. This occurred despite the fact that there were twice as many kickback schemes as bid rigging schemes in our study (see chart 11-2). A review of the median losses associated with these schemes shows that bid rigging was especially harmful. It's median loss of $2,000,000 was far higher than that of kickback schemes (see chart 11-3). In fact, bid rigging was the single most costly scheme in our study in terms of median cash losses.

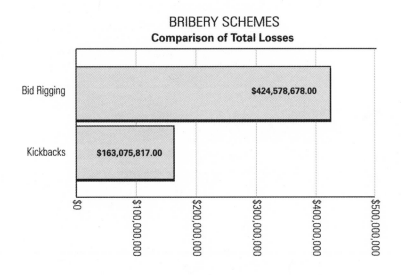

Chart 11-1: Comparison of Total Losses

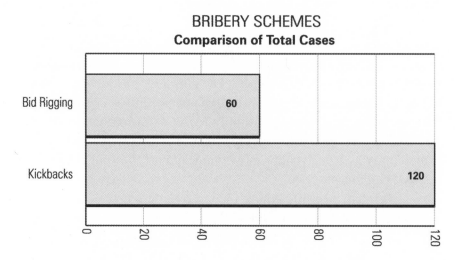

Chart 11-2: Comparison of Total Cases

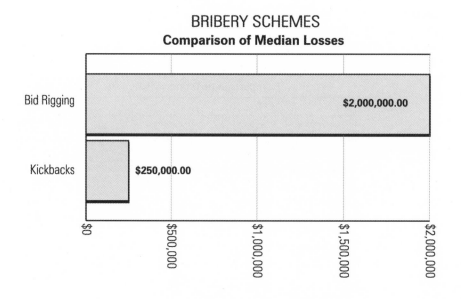

Chart 11-3: Comparison of Median Losses

KICKBACK SCHEMES

Kickback schemes are usually very similar to the billing schemes described in the asset misappropriation section of this book. They involve the submission of invoices for goods and services which are either overpriced or completely fictitious (see flowchart 11-2).

Kickbacks are classified as corruption schemes rather than asset misappropriations because they involve collusion between employees and vendors. In a common type of kickback scheme, a vendor submits a fraudulent or inflated invoice to the victim company and an employee of that company helps make sure that a payment is made on the false invoice. For his assistance, the employee-fraudster receives some form of payment from the vendor. This payment is the kickback.

Kickback schemes almost always attack the purchasing function of the victim company, so it stands to reason that these frauds are often undertaken by employees with purchasing responsibilities. Purchasing employees often have direct contact with vendors and therefore have an opportunity to establish a collusive relationship. In Case 119, for instance, a purchasing agent redirected orders to a company owned by a supplier with whom he was conspiring. In return for the additional business, the supplier paid the purchasing agent over half the profits from the additional orders.

Diverting Business to Vendors

In some instances, an employee-fraudster receives a kickback simply for directing excess business to a vendor. There might be no overbilling involved in these cases; the vendor simply pays the kickbacks to ensure a steady stream of business from the purchasing company. In case 1987, for instance, the president of a software supplier offered a percentage of ownership in his company to an employee of a purchaser in exchange for a major contract. Similarly, a travel agency in Case 1211 provided free travel and entertainment to the purchasing agent of a retail company. In return, the purchasing agent agreed to book all corporate trips through the travel agent.

If no overbilling is involved in a kickback scheme, one might wonder where the harm lies. Assuming the vendor simply wants to get the buyer's business and does not increase his prices or bill for undelivered goods and services, how is the buyer harmed? The problem is that, having bought off an employee of the purchasing company, a vendor is no longer subject to the normal economic pressures of the marketplace. This vendor does not have to compete with other suppliers for the purchasing company's business, and so has no incentive to provide a low price or quality merchandise. In these circumstances the purchasing company almost always ends up overpaying for goods or services, or getting less than it paid for. In Case 1211, described above, the victim company estimated that it paid $10,000 more for airfare over a two-year period by booking through the corrupt travel agency than if it had used a different company.

Once a vendor knows it has an exclusive purchasing arrangement, his incentive is to raise prices to cover the cost of the kickback. Most bribery schemes end up as overbilling schemes even if they do not start that way. This is one reason why most business codes of ethics prohibit employees from accepting undisclosed gifts from vendors. In the long run, the employee's company is sure to pay for his unethical conduct.

Overbilling Schemes

Employees with Approval Authority

In most instances, kickback schemes begin as overbilling schemes in which a vendor submits inflated invoices to the victim company. The false invoices either overstate the cost of actual goods and services, or reflect fictitious sales. In Case 520, an employee with complete authority to approve vouchers from a certain vendor authorized payment on over 100 fraudulent invoices in which the vendor's rates were overstated. Because no one was reviewing her decisions, the employee could approve payments on invoices at above-normal rates without fear of detection.

The ability to authorize purchases (and thus to authorize fraudulent purchases) is usually a key to kickback schemes. The fraudster in Case 520, for example, was a nonmanagement employee who had approval authority for purchases made from the vendor with whom she colluded. She authorized approximately $300,000 worth of inflated billings in less than two years. Similarly, in Case 127, a manager was authorized to purchase fixed assets for his company as part of a leasehold improvement. The assets he ordered were of a cheaper quality and lower price than what was specified, but the contract he negotiated did not reflect this. Therefore, the victim company paid for high-quality materials, but received low-quality materials. The difference in price between what the company paid and what the materials actually cost was diverted back to the manager as a kickback.

The existence of purchasing authority can be critical to the success of kickback schemes. The ability of a fraudster to authorize payments himself means he does not have to submit purchase requisitions to an honest superior who might question the validity of the transaction.

Fraudsters Lacking Approval Authority

While the majority of the kickback schemes we reviewed involved people with authority to approve purchases, this authority is not an absolute necessity. When an employee cannot approve fraudulent purchases himself, he can still orchestrate a kickback scheme if he can circumvent accounts payable controls. In some cases, all that is required is the filing of a false purchase requisition. If a trusted employee tells his superior that the company needs certain materials or services, this is sometimes sufficient to get a false invoice approved for payment. Such schemes are generally successful when the person with approval authority is inattentive or when he is forced to rely on his subordinates' guidance in purchasing matters.

Corrupt employees might also prepare false vouchers to make it appear that fraudulent invoices are legitimate. Where proper controls are in place, a completed voucher is required before accounts payable will pay an invoice. One key is for the fraudster to create a purchase order that corresponds to the vendor's fraudulent invoice. The fraudster might forge the signature of an authorized party on the purchase order to show that the acquisition has been approved. Where the payables system is computerized, an employee with access to a restricted password can enter the system and authorize payments on fraudulent invoices.

In less sophisticated schemes, a corrupt employee might simply take a fraudulent invoice from a vendor and slip it into a stack of prepared invoices before they are input into the accounts payable system. A more detailed description of how false invoices are processed may be found in the Billing Schemes chapter of this book.

Kickback schemes can be very difficult to detect. In a sense, the victim company is being attacked from two directions. Externally, a corrupt vendor submits false invoices which induce the victim company to unknowingly pay for goods or services which it does not receive. Internally, one or more of the victim company's employees waits to corroborate the false information provided by the vendor.

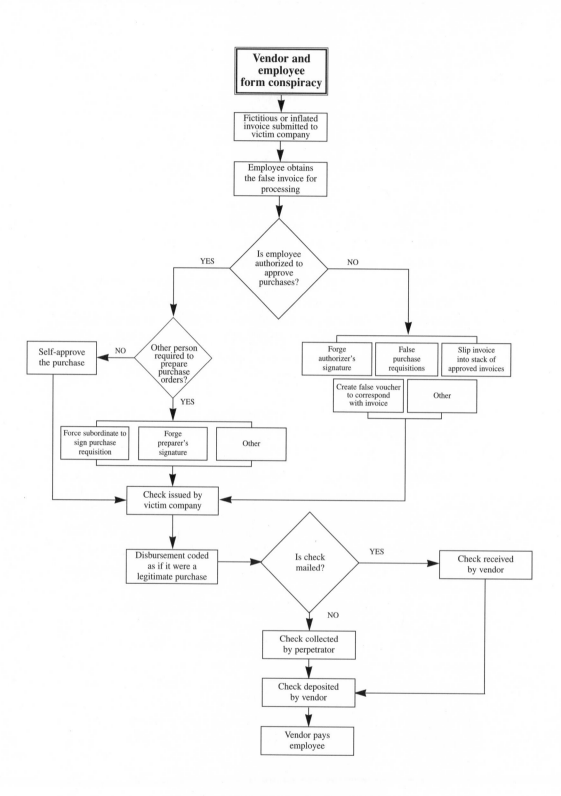

Flowchart 11-2: Kickbacks-Overbilling

Other Kickback Schemes

Bribes are not always paid to employees to process phony invoices. In some circumstances outsiders seek other fraudulent assistance from employees of the victim company. In the case study at the beginning of this chapter, for instance, Art Metal U.S.A. paid huge sums to quality insurance inspectors so that their substandard equipment would be accepted by the General Services Administration. In this case the vendor was not overbilling the agency. He was instead trying to dump substandard products in lieu of providing equipment which met government specifications.

In other cases, bribes come not from vendors who are trying to sell something to the victim company, but rather from potential purchasers who seek a lower price from the victim company. In Case 1866, for instance, an advertising salesman not only sold ads, but was authorized to bill for and collect on advertising accounts. He was also authorized to issue discounts to clients. In return for benefits such as free travel, lodging, and various gifts, this individual either sold ads at greatly reduced rates or gave free ads to those who bought him off. His complete control over advertising and a lack of oversight allowed this employee to "trade away" over $20,000 in advertising revenues. Similarly, in Case 986 the manager of a convention center accepted various gifts from show promoters. In return, he allowed these promoters to rent the convention center at prices below the rates approved by the city which owned the center.

Slush Funds

It should also be noted that every bribe is a two-sided transaction. In every case where a vendor bribes a purchaser, there is someone on the vendor's side of the transaction who is making an illicit payment. It is therefore just as likely that your employees are paying bribes as accepting them.

In order to obtain the funds to make these payments, employees usually divert company money into a slush fund, a noncompany account from which bribes can be made. Assuming that bribes are not authorized by the briber's company, he must find a way to generate the funds necessary to illegally influence someone in another organization. Therefore, the key to the crime from the briber's perspective is the diversion of money into the slush fund. This is a fraudulent disbursement of company funds, which is usually accomplished by the writing of company checks to a fictitious entity or the submitting of false invoices in the name of the false entity. In Case 1605, for example, an officer in a very large healthcare organization created a fund to pay public officials and influence pending legislation. This officer used check requests for several different expense codes to generate payments which went to one of the company's lobbyists, who placed the money in an account from which bribe money could be withdrawn. Most of the checks in this case were coded as "fees" for consulting or other services.

It is common to charge fraudulent disbursements to nebulous accounts like "consulting fees." The purchase of goods can be verified by a check of inventory, but there is no inventory for these kinds of services. It is therefore more difficult to prove that the payments are fraudulent. The discussion of exactly how fraudulent disbursements are made can be found in the chapters on check tampering and invoices.

BID-RIGGING SCHEMES

As we have said, when one person pays a bribe to another, he does so to gain the benefit of the recipient's influence. The competitive bidding process, in which several suppliers or contractors are vying for contracts in what can be a very cutthroat environment, can be tailor-made for bribery. Any advantage one vendor can gain over his competitors in this arena is extremely valuable. The benefit of "inside influence" can ensure that a vendor will win a sought-after contract. Many vendors are willing to pay for this influence.

In the competitive bidding process, all bidders are legally supposed to be placed on the same plane of equality, bidding on the same terms and conditions. Each bidder competes for a contract based on the specifications set forth by the purchasing company. Vendors submit confidential bids stating the price at which they will complete a project in accordance with the purchaser's specifications.

The way competitive bidding is rigged depends largely upon the level of influence of the corrupt employee. The more power a person has over the bidding process, the more likely the person can influence the selection of a supplier. Therefore, employees involved in bid-rigging schemes, like those in kickback schemes, tend to have a good measure of influence or access to the competitive bidding process. Potential targets for accepting bribes include buyers, contracting officials, engineers and technical representatives, quality or product assurance representatives, subcontractor liaison employees, or anyone else with authority over the awarding of contracts.

Bid-rigging schemes can be categorized based on the stage of bidding at which the fraudster exerts his influence. Bid-rigging schemes usually occur in the pre-solicitation phase, the solicitation phase, or the submission phase of the bidding process (see flowchart 11-3)

The Pre-Solicitation Phase

In the pre-solicitation phase of the competitive bidding process — before bids are officially sought for a project — bribery schemes can be broken down into two distinct types. The first is the need recognition scheme, where an employee of a purchasing company is paid to convince his company that a particular project is necessary. The second reason to bribe someone in the pre-solicitation phase is to have the specifications of the contract tailored to the strengths of a particular supplier.

Need Recognition Schemes

The typical fraud in the need recognition phase of the contract negotiation is a conspiracy between the buyer and contractor where an employee of the buyer receives something of value and in return recognizes a "need" for a particular product or service. The result of such a scheme is that the victim company purchases unnecessary goods or services from a supplier at the direction of the corrupt employee.

There are several trends which may indicate a need recognition fraud. Unusually high requirements for stock and inventory levels may reveal a situation in which a corrupt employee is seeking to justify unnecessary purchase activity from a certain supplier.   An employee might also justify unnecessary purchases of inventory by writing off large numbers of surplus items to scrap. As these items leave the inventory, they open up spaces to justify additional purchases. Another indicator of a need recognition scheme is the defining of a "need" that can only be met by a certain supplier or contractor. In addition, the failure to develop a satisfactory list of backup suppliers may reveal an unusually strong attachment to a primary supplier — an attachment that is explainable by the acceptance of bribes from that supplier.

Specifications Schemes

The other type of pre-solicitation fraud is a specifications scheme. The specifications of a contract are a list of the elements, materials, dimensions, and other relevant requirements for completion of the project. Specifications are prepared to assist vendors in the bidding process, telling them what they are required to do and providing a firm basis for making and accepting bids.

One corruption scheme that occurs in this process is the fraudulent tailoring of specifications to a particular vendor. In these cases, the vendor pays off an employee of the buyer who is involved in the preparation of specifications for the contract. In return, the employee sets the specifications of the contract to accommodate that vendor's capabilities. In Case 1063, for instance, a supplier paid an employee of a public utility to write contract specifications which were so proprietary that they effectively eliminated all competition for the project. For four years this supplier won the contract, which was the largest awarded by the utility company. The fraud cost the utility company in excess of $2 million.

The methods used to restrict competition in the bidding process may include the use of "prequalification" procedures which are known to eliminate certain competitors. For instance, the bid may require potential contractors to have a certain percentage of female or minority ownership. There is nothing illegal with such a requirement, but if it is placed in the specifications as a result of a bribe rather than as the result of other factors, then the employee has sold his influence to benefit a dishonest vendor, a clear case of corruption.

Sole-source or noncompetitive procurement justifications may also be used to eliminate competition and steer contracts to a particular vendor. In Case 2015, a requisitioner distorted the requirements of a contract up for bid, claiming the specifications called for a sole-source provider. Based on the requisitioner's information, competitive bidding was disregarded and the contract was awarded to a particular supplier. A review of other bids received at a later date showed that certain materials were available for up to $70,000 less than what the company paid in the sole-source arrangement. The employee had helped divert the job to the contractor in return for a promise of future employment. Competitive bidding was also disregarded in Case 1075, where management staff of a state entity took bribes from vendors to authorize purchases of approximately $200,000 in fixed assets.

Another type of specifications scheme is the deliberate writing of vague specifications. In this type of scheme, a supplier pays an employee of the purchasing company to write specifications which will require amendments at a later date. This will allow the supplier to raise the price of the contract when the amendments are made. As the buyer's needs become more specific or more detailed, the vendor can claim that, had he known what the buyer actually wanted, his bid on the project would have been higher. In order to complete the project as defined by the amended specifications, the supplier will have to charge a higher price.

Another form of specifications fraud is bid splitting. In Case 1797, a manager of a federal employer split a large repair job into several component contracts in order to divert the jobs to his brother-in-law. Federal law required competitive bidding on projects over a certain dollar value. The manager broke the project up so that each sectional project was below the mandatory bidding level. Once the contract was split, the manager hired his brother-in-law to handle each of the component projects. Thus, the brother-in-law got the entire contract while avoiding competitive bidding.

A less egregious but nevertheless unfair form of bid-rigging occurs when a vendor pays an employee of the buyer for the right to see the specifications earlier than his competitors. The employee does not alter the specifications to suit the vendor, but instead simply gives him a head start on planning his bid and preparing for the job. The extra planning time gives the vendor an advantage over his competitors in preparing a bid for the job.

The Solicitation Phase

In the solicitation phase of the competitive bidding process fraudsters attempt to influence the selection of a contractor by restricting the pool of competitors from whom bids are sought. In other words, a corrupt vendor pays an employee of the purchasing company to assure that one or more of the vendor's competitors do not get to bid on the contract. In this manner, the corrupt vendor is able to improve his chances of winning the job.

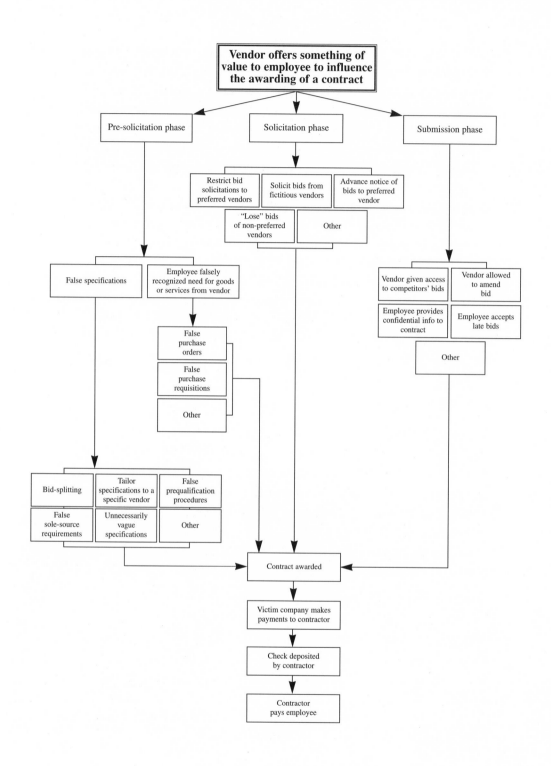

Flowchart 11-3: Bid Rigging (Bribery)

One type of scheme involves the sales representative who deals on behalf of a number of potential bidders. The sales representative bribes a contracting official to rig the solicitation, ensuring that only those companies represented by him get to submit bids. It is not uncommon in some sectors for buyers to "require" bidders to be represented by certain sales or manufacturing representatives. These representatives pay a kickback to the buyer to protect their clients' interests. The result of this transaction is that the purchasing company is deprived of the ability to get the best price on its contract. Typically, the group of "protected" vendors will not actually compete against each other for the purchaser's contracts, but instead engage in "bid pooling."

Bid Pooling

Bid pooling is a process by which several bidders conspire to split contracts up and ensure that each gets a certain amount of work. Instead of submitting confidential bids, the vendors discuss what their bids will be so they can guarantee that each vendor will win a share of the purchasing company's business. For example, if vendors A, B, and C are up for three separate jobs, they may agree that A's bid will be the lowest on the first contract, B's bid will be the lowest on the second contract, and C's bid will be the lowest on the third contract. None of the vendors gets all three jobs, but on the other hand, they are all guaranteed to get at least one. Furthermore, since they plan their bids ahead of time, the vendors can conspire to raise their prices. Thus the purchasing company suffers as a result of the scheme.

Fictitious Suppliers

Another way to eliminate competition in the solicitation phase of the selection process is to solicit bids from fictitious suppliers. In Case 1797 discussed above (the bid-splitting case), the brother-in-law submitted quotes in the names of several different companies and performed work under these various names. Although confidential bidding was avoided in this case, the perpetrator used quotes from several of the brother-in-law's fictitious companies to demonstrate price reasonableness on the final contracts. In other words, the brother-in-law's fictitious price quotes were used to validate his actual prices.

Other Methods

In some cases, competition for a contract can be limited by severely restricting the time for submitting bids. Certain suppliers are given advance notice of contracts before bids are solicited. These suppliers are therefore able to begin preparing their bids ahead of time. With the short time frame for developing bid proposals, the supplier with advance knowledge of the contract will have a decided advantage over his competition.

Bribed purchasing officials can also restrict competition for their co-conspirators by soliciting bids in obscure publications where other vendors are unlikely to see them. Again, this is done to eliminate potential rivals and create an advantage for the corrupt suppliers. Some schemes have also involved the publication of bid solicitations during holiday periods when those suppliers not "in the know" are unlikely to be looking for potential contracts. In more blatant cases, the bids of outsiders are accepted but are "lost" or improperly disqualified by the corrupt employee of the purchaser.

Typically, when a vendor bribes an employee of the purchasing company to assist him in any kind of solicitation scheme, the cost of the bribe is included in the corrupt vendor's bid. Therefore, the purchasing company ends up bearing the cost of the illicit payment in the form of a higher contract price.

The Submission Phase

In the actual submission phase of the process, where bids are proffered to the buyer, several schemes may be used to win a contract for a particular supplier. The principle offense tends to be abuse of the sealed-bid process. Competitive bids are confidential; they are, of course, supposed to remain sealed until a specified date at which all bids are opened and reviewed by the purchasing company. The person or persons who have access to sealed bids are often the targets of unethical vendors seeking an advantage in the process. In Case 1170, for example, gifts and cash payments were given to a majority owner of a company in exchange for preferential treatment during the bidding process. The supplier who paid the bribes was allowed to submit his bids last, knowing what prices his competitors had quoted, or in the alternative, he was allowed to actually see his competitors' bids and adjust his own accordingly.

Vendors also bribe employees of the purchaser for information on how to prepare their bid. In Case 613, the general manager for a purchasing company provided confidential pricing information to a supplier which enabled the supplier to outbid his competitors and win a long-term contract. In return, both the general manager and his daughter received payments from the supplier. Other reasons to bribe employees of the purchaser include to ensure receipt of a late bid or falsify the bid log, to extend the bid opening date, and to control bid openings.

The following case study was selected to illustrate in greater detail a case of bid tampering at the submission phase. The story deals with Thad Ferguson, a corrupt salesman who consistently won bids for his clients because he had the plant manager of a buyer "in his back pocket." In return for cash payments and other gifts, the plant manager provided Ferguson with information which allowed him to narrowly outbid his competition. The study also describes in detail how CFE Gene Earle uncovered the scheme and shut it down.

*****

Case Study: Keep Your Eye on the Salesman
* Several names have been changed to preserve anonymity

CFE Gene Earle thought he was just going to a party. But the small talk was more than he bargained for. The party was thrown by Earle's employer, HydroCo, an air-separation company with over $600 million in annual sales. HydroCo isolates gases like argon, oxygen, and hydrogen from the atmosphere and then distributes them for industrial use. While Gene Earle sampled the hors d'oeuvres and drinks, he talked with the controller of a construction firm that had done several jobs for HydroCo.

"I'm gonna be frank with you," the man told Earle. "Your bid process on this asbestos work isn't fair." "What's the problem?" Earle wondered out loud. "Well, if you'll look into it you'll see that your work follows this one salesman. His name's Thad Ferguson. He's worked for different companies. But no matter who he works for, they end up getting your contracts. Where he goes, HydroCo business follows. Now, that's too wet to plow if you ask me." Besides that, the man said, Ferguson was known by insiders as a "sleazebag." What's a sleazebag in these circumstances? "You can apply any definition you want, and it'll describe this guy. He does it all," said the controller

When Earle got to his office the next day, he started looking at the asbestos abatement projects. A government mandate branded asbestos a health hazard and demanded its immediate removal from all public buildings. Abatement was sensitive, headache-inducing work to say the least. From the outset, Earle learned that whatever he counted on could not be counted on. The purchasing department, a logical place to begin asking questions, had not handled the purchasing for these jobs. That had been deferred to the plant operations office.

Bid files at Operations were in a mess. Earle found precious little documentation of anything. Competitive bids had no verification and safety compliance forms were either missing or incomplete. The papers that were present described work that didn't measure up to the $300,000 and $400,000 contracts. Engineers had designed an overall abatement project amounting to a couple million dollars. The actual removal of the asbestos would be performed in phases at several hundred thousand dollars a phase. The disorganized files didn't tell much of a story; though to Earle, "it looked like the work was being done, but not to the value we were paying for." HydroCo's chief engineer would later estimate that the company was bilked for between $250,000 and $400,000 on the first three phases of the abatement, which was settled with individual contractors. As for the bid-rigging fraud, Earle couldn't tell if his source's accusations were true or not, but he did find Thad Ferguson's name on several key papers.

Actually finding the abatement companies was the next hurdle. Because the work is so sensitive, webbed with regulations, and always a target for lawsuits, Earle had a hard time getting a clear picture of the various companies and their operations. "It's a nightmare trying to sort through the different layers of ownership and subsidiaries to find out where the company actually is, who is authorized to handle bids, approve bids, and oversee the process." Narrowing down the list of targets, Earle called one of Ferguson's old jobs and got nothing. The manager there said he had no idea what Earle was talking about. Ferguson had been there, he was gone, end of story. But the manager's company was still bidding for HydroCo jobs. If he wanted to remain competitive in the bidding, Earle hinted, it would be in everyone's interest for the man to stop talking nonsense. The manager thought for a second and made an offer. If he could be sure there wouldn't be any legal or business repercussions, he'd talk to Earle. He'd show him the paperwork. But the man said they'd have to meet at a hotel. Earle thought this was a bit cloak-and-dagger but agreed to the meeting.

"When Ferguson came to work for us," the manager said bluntly, "he told us he had HydroCo in his back pocket. . . . He was going to be able to get your business regardless of who he worked for."

"Did he tell you how he was going to do this?" Earle asked.

"I didn't really want to know."

"I'm having a hard time believing that," Earle replied. The manager observed that it often pays to keep yourself in the dark. Earle took another approach.

"Ferguson was working for somebody else at the time. What did you have to do to get him on with you?"

"We made concessions on commissions."

"Were those pretty lucrative?"

"They were substantial," the manager said, emphasizing substantial.

The conversation continued. "How did Ferguson say he was going to get our business for you?"

"We were going to have to buy a service, something called a 'travel evaluation report,' from your plant manager. Name of Ben Butler . . . . Butler's sister had some kind of travel agency. We were to purchase this evaluation from her."

"And how much was that?" asked Earle.

"Ten thousand dollars."

"How'd you pay for that?"

"With a check."

"One check?"

"One check, ten thousand dollars."

The manager said he had no idea what a travel evaluation report was. They never got anything from the travel agency. "We got the job," he deadpanned. He didn't like doing business that way. His company had gotten shafted twice on the project, he said. Besides the up-front money, Thad Ferguson's 19-year-old son was put on the construction payroll though he rarely, if ever, showed up for work. Just another perk in exchange for access to Ferguson's lucrative back pocket. At the end of the meeting, the manager gave Earle what he needed—a copy of the canceled check for $10,000 with Ben Butler's signature on the money line. A simple conversation with bank officials about authorized account signatures showed that Sun

& Fun Travel didn't belong to Butler's sister; Butler himself was the primary owner.

Back at the plant, Earle talked with people in the operations office where construction bids were processed. Oh yes, they all knew Ferguson. He dropped by at least once a month, more than that if a construction job was going on. He schmoozed everybody, brought flowers and candy to female workers, sprang for long lunches and drinks. A purchasing clerk told Earle that Ben Butler, as plant manager, handled the nuts and bolts of construction bids himself. "I did some of the paperwork," the woman said, "but that was just him giving me the numbers and I'd prepare the bid sheets . . . . For anything with Thad, Mr. Butler took care of that personally."

And Ferguson took care of Butler. The two of them disappeared for entire afternoons, touring the finest restaurants and topless bars in Houston. And quid pro quo, Ferguson's employers—whoever they happened to be—ended up filing a bid within 1% of the next lowest competitor. The purchasing clerk remembered one project during which she was first astounded, then confounded, then too worried to ask any questions. After a set of bids had been filed, a contractor called to say that he had misread a key requirement; he wanted to submit another version of his bid, and the clerk revised the numbers accordingly. Later, when the bids were unsealed, Ferguson's company had also revised their bid! They were just a little lower than the other contractor's new figure, and Ferguson got the job. As Earle's source declared at the party, this ground was too wet to plow.

Earle set up a meeting with Thad Ferguson. The salesman arrived in a nice suit and good spirits but was suffering from severe amnesia. He couldn't remember anything about Ben Butler or asbestos abatement. "He was slick," Earle says, "smiling, a fast talker, but you felt like you needed to take a bath after you left the room." Earle asked him about arranging for his old employer to buy a travel evaluation from Sun & Fun. Ferguson smirked and shook his head. "I never heard of such a thing. What do *you* think that is?" he asked in return. Earle got itchy as the interview went on, with nothing but smirks and denials from the charming Mr. Ferguson. "He knew I knew he was lying," Earle recalls bitterly, "but there wasn't anything I could do about it."

Ben Butler tried the amnesia track, but without Ferguson's luck. "I know Thad Ferguson, yes," Butler said. "Not very well, though. Just, I see him in the office, talk about jobs."

Earle listened patiently. "I needed for him to show his hand. We knew he had financial problems. Two of his adult children had moved back home, and he was supporting them. He had debts from a ranch he had bought a couple of years before." Plus, Earle had his ace—the contractor's canceled check with Butler's signature. About halfway through the six-hour interview, Earle put the check on the table. "We need to talk about this," he told Butler.

From there, the dam broke. Butler spilled out the whole story. "At first, it was just a business thing. We would go out, have lunch, go to a couple strip joints. Nothing out of line. After a while, we'd be talking and I'd give him a tip on jobs coming around, things like that." Eventually, Butler said, he felt trapped. He knew he was giving Ferguson more information than he should. So he had already crossed ethical lines. He might as well get something for his trouble. Butler and Ferguson set it up. Butler would provide inside information on jobs as they were let out for bids, or adjust Ferguson's price in accordance with the other numbers the company received. Ferguson would see to it that his current employer took advantage of the value of Sun & Fun's multithousand-dollar evaluations.

No one was ever prosecuted. Butler was fired, and forfeited the company contributions to his benefits plan, a substantial penalty since the former plant manager had been accruing funds for nearly thirty years. Thad Ferguson still makes his living in sales, though he has no welcome at HydroCo. Never mind. He keeps smiling and patting his pocket.

*****

Something of Value

Bribery was defined at the beginning of this chapter as "offering, giving, receiving, or soliciting *any thing of value* to influence an official act or business decision." A corrupt employee like Ben Butler helps the briber obtain something of value, and in return the employee is given something of value. There are several ways for a vendor to "pay" an employee to surreptitiously aid the vendor's cause. The most common, of course, is money. In the most basic bribery scheme, the vendor simply gives the employee currency. This is what we think of in the classic bribery scenario — an envelope stuffed with currency being slipped under a table, a roll of bills hastily stuffed into a pocket. These payments are preferably made with currency rather than checks, because the payment is harder to trace. Currency may not be practical, however, when large sums are involved. When this is the case, slush funds are usually set up to finance the illegal payments. In other cases, checks may be drawn directly from company accounts. These disbursements are usually coded as "consulting fees," "referral commissions," or the like. The $10,000 check to Ben Butler's sister in the case study above is an excellent example.

Instead of cash payments, some employees accept promises of future employment as bribes. In Case 1590, for instance, a government employee gave a contractor inside information in order to win a bid on a multimillion dollar contract in return for the promise of a high-paying job. As with money, the promise of employment might be intended to benefit a third party rather than the corrupt employee. In Case 1584, a consultant who worked for a particular university hired the daughter of one of the university's employees.

In Case 1987, we also discussed how a corrupt individual diverted a major purchase commitment to a supplier in return for a percent of ownership in the supplier's business. This is similar to a bribe effected by the promise of employment, but also contains elements of a conflict of interest scheme. The promise of part ownership in the supplier amounts to an undisclosed financial interest in the transaction for the corrupt employee.

Gifts of all kinds may also be used to corrupt an employee. The types of gifts used to sway an employee's influence can include free liquor and meals, free travel and accommodations, cars, other merchandise, and even sexual favors.

Other inducements include the paying off of a corrupt employee's loans or credit card bills, the offering of loans on very favorable terms, and transfers of property at substantially below market value. The list of things that can be given to an employee in return for the exercise of his influence is almost endless. Anything that the employee values is fair game and may be used to sway his loyalty.

Economic Extortion

At stated earlier, economic extortion is basically the flip side of a bribery scheme. Instead of a vendor offering a payment to an employee to influence a decision, the employee demands a payment from a vendor in order to make a decision in that vendor's favor. In

any situation where an employee might accept bribes to favor a particular company or person, the situation could be reversed to a point
where the employee extorts money from a potential purchaser or supplier. In Case 802, for example, a plant manager for a utility company started his own business on the side. Vendors who wanted to do
work for the utility company were forced by the manager to divert
some of their business to his own company. Those that did not "play
ball" lost their business with the utility.

Illegal Gratuities

As stated, illegal gratuities are similar to bribery schemes
except there is not necessarily an intent to influence a particular business decision. An example of an illegal gratuity is Case 2294, where
a city commissioner negotiated a land development deal with a group
of private investors. After the deal was approved, the commissioner
and his wife were rewarded with a free international vacation, all
expenses paid. While the promise of this trip may have influenced
the commissioner's negotiations, this would be difficult to prove.
However, merely accepting such a gift amounts to an illegal gratuity,
an act which is prohibited by most government and private company
codes of ethics.

Conclusion

DETECTION

The following red flags may indicate that employees are involved in a bribery scheme:

General Purchasing

Questions such as the following may reveal that single (sole)
source vendors are being favored, or competitive bidding policies
are not being followed.
- Are materials being ordered at the optimal reorder point?
- Are often made from the same vendor?
- Are the established bidding policies being followed?
- Are the costs of materials out of line?

Pre-Bid Solicitation

Placing any restrictions in the solicitation documents which tend to restrict competition, such as:

- Tailoring specifications and statements of work to fit the products or capabilities of a single contractor
- Using "prequalification" procedures to restrict competition
- Unnecessary sole source or noncompetitive procurement justifications:
    Containing false statements
    Signed by unauthorized officials
    Bypassing necessary review procedures
- The buyer provides to the contractor information or advice on a preferential basis
- Using statements of work, specifications, or sole source justifications developed by, or in consultation with, a contractor who will be permitted to bid
- Permitting consultants who assisted in the preparation of the statements of work, specifications, or design to perform on the contract as subcontractors or consultants
- Splitting costs into separate contracts to avoid review
- Release of information by firms participating in the design and engineering to contractors competing for the prime contract
- Splitting up requirements so contractors can each get a "fair share" and can rotate bids
- Specifications are not consistent with past similar procurement

Bid Solicitation

- Limiting time for submission of bids so only those with advance information have adequate time to prepare bids or proposals
- Revealing information to one contractor which is not revealed to all
- Conducting a bidders' conference which permits improper communications between contractors, who then are in a position to rig bids

- Failure to ensure a sufficient number of potential competitors are aware of the solicitation, such as:
    - Using obscure publications to publish bid solicitations
    - Publishing bid solicitations during holiday periods
- Bid solicitations are vague as to the time, place, or other requirements for submitting acceptable bids
- Inadequate internal controls over the number and destination of bid packages sent to interested bidders
- Improper communication by purchasers with contractors at trade or professional meetings, or improper social contact with contractor representatives
- Financial interest by purchasing agent in the business of the contractor
- Discussions by purchaser of possible employment with the contractor
- Assistance by the purchaser in helping the contractor prepare his or her bid
- Referring a contractor to a specific subcontractor, expert, or source of supply
- Failure to amend solicitation to include necessary changes or clarifications in the bid, such as telling one contractor of changes that can be made after the bid
- Falsification of documents or receipts to get a late bid accepted
- Low bidder withdraws to become subcontractor on the same contract
- Any indications of collusion between bidders
- Falsification of the contractor's qualifications, work history, facilities, equipment, or personnel

Bid or Contract Acceptance

- Restricting procurement to exclude or hamper any qualified contractor
- Improper acceptance of a late bid
- Falsification of documents or receipts to get a late bid accepted
- Change in a bid after other bidders' prices are known. This is sometimes done by mistakes deliberately "planted" in a bid

- Withdrawal of the low bidder who may become a sub-contractor to the higher bidder who gets the contract
- Collusion or bid-rigging between bidders
- Revealing one bidder's price to another
- False certifications by contractor
- Falsification of information concerning contractor qualifications, financial capability, facilities, ownership of equipment and supplies, qualifications of personnel, and successful performance of previous jobs, etc.

Behavior Profile of Bribery Recipient

The behavior profile of employees who are involved in bribery schemes may include the following characteristics:

- A drug and/or alcohol addiction
- Personal financial problems
- A gambling habit
- Extravagant lifestyle
- Loan shark or other private debts
- A girlfriend (or boyfriend) supported by the subject
- Extraordinary medical expenses
- Significant, regular cash expenses for entertainment and/or travel

PREVENTION

Bribery Prevention Policy

The prevention of the use of bribery schemes can be difficult. The traits and characteristics of people who use bribery as a tool are often inherent in the perpetrator. The primary resource for heading off this complex act is a company policy that specifically addresses the problems and illegalities associated with bribery and related offenses. The purpose of the policy is to make the position of the company absolutely clear. The absence of a clear policy leaves an opportunity for a perpetrator to rationalize a bribe or related offense or to claim ignorance to the wrongdoing. Examples of bribery prevention policies are given below:

Gifts

No employee or member of his immediate family shall solicit or accept from an actual or prospective customer or supplier any compensation, advance loans (expect from established financial institutions on the same basis as other customers), gifts, entertainment, or other favors which are of more than token value or which the employee would not normally be in a position to reciprocate under normal expense account procedures.

Under no circumstances should a gift or entertainment be accepted which would influence the employee's judgment. In particular, employees must avoid any interest in or benefit from any supplier that could reasonably cause them to favor that supplier over others. It is a violation of the code for any employee to solicit or encourage a supplier to give any item or service to the employee regardless of its value, no matter how small. Our suppliers will retain their confidence in the objectivity and integrity of our company only if each employee strictly observes this guideline.

Reporting Gifts

An employee who receives, or whose family member receives, an unsolicited gift prohibited by these guidelines, should report it to his supervisor and either return it to the person making the gift or, in the case of a perishable gift, give it to nonprofit charitable organization.

Discounts

An employee may accept discounts on a personal purchase of the supplier's or customer's products only if such discounts do not affect the company's purchase price and are generally offered to others having a similar business relationship with the supplier or customer.

Business Meetings

Entertainment and services offered by a supplier or customer may be accepted by an employee when they are associated with a business meeting and the supplier or customer provides them to others as a normal part of its business. Examples of such entertainment and services are transportation to and from the supplier's or customer's place of business, hospitality suites, golf outings, lodging at the supplier's or customer's place of business, and business lunches and dinners for business visitors to the supplier's or customer's location. The services should generally be of the type normally used by the company's employees and allowable under the applicable company's expense account.

[1] The Association of Certified Fraud Examiners, *Fraud Examiners' Manual, Revised 2nd Edition* (Austin: ACFE, 1996).

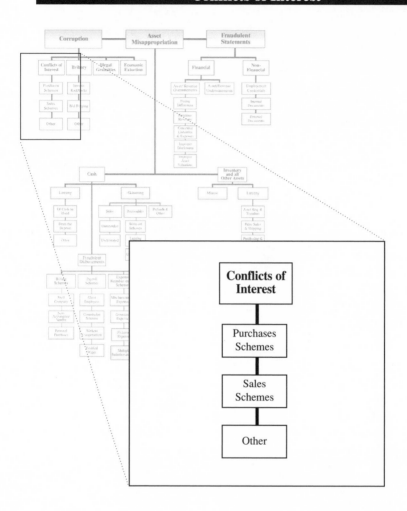

12. CONFLICTS OF INTEREST

*****

Case Study: Working Double Duty
*Several names have been changed to preserve anonymity

After grabbing a quick bite to eat at the mall, Troy Biederman spent the rest of his lunch hour shopping for clothes. He liked to present a professional appearance as a sales manager at ElectroCity, an electronics and appliance chain. While waiting on a charge approval at a small menswear store, Biederman spotted its promotion for a free Lazy-Boy and tossed his business card into the drawing fishbowl on the counter. Suddenly his eye caught a familiar name on top of the pile — Rita Mae King, the full-time purchasing agent at ElectroCity. The card, however, read: Rita Mae King, account executive at Spicewood Travel.

"He put two and two together and it smelled fishy," explained Bill Reed, the vice president of loss prevention at ElectroCity. Biederman knew Spicewood Travel was the agency his company used to book incentive trips for its salesforce, of which he was a member. He also knew King enjoyed close ties with Spicewood. Now he wondered how close. Biederman snatched King's card from the pile and discreetly turned it in to his boss that afternoon.

Within two weeks the business card had made its way up to the executive vice president of ElectroCity, a company which rings up annual sales of $450 million. Not wanting to jump to any conclusions, yet also suspecting that his purchasing agent might be in cahoots with a travel vendor, the EVP handed the card over to Bill Reed "to investigate the extent of the relationship."

Reed immediately requisitioned the accounts payable department for all corporate travel billings for the past three years. Early entries showed that the company had been using Executive Travel for most of its travel needs. In her first year as purchasing agent, however, King had introduced Spicewood and had placed it at the top of the travel vendor list. Reed said that although ElectroCity had never designated any one agency as its sole vendor, under the direction of the corporation's purchaser, Spicewood had squeezed out Executive Travel for the store's business — which now exceeded $200,000.

Corporate fraud examiners then phoned numerous other travel agencies, asking for quotes on similar services for the same period in an effort to compare prices. They found many of the bills were inflated between 10 and 30% over the other agencies' package trips to destinations such as Trump Castle in Atlantic City and Bally's in Las Vegas. Calls to other branches of Spicewood Travel further confirmed significant overcharging by the local office, which King used exclusively.

Six days into his investigation, Reed took a statement from the corporate merchandising buyer at ElectroCity, who had experienced difficulties with King on several occasions about competitively-priced trips. He said King was insistent on using Spicewood. In his written account of a recent episode, the merchandising buyer told of personally shopping for a better price on an incentive vacation to the Cayman Islands. "With this trip, I went to an outside agent first and then gave Rita Mae the information to price this trip. Spicewood came in almost $100 higher per person. Rita Mae did not book the trip through the lower-priced agent, but went back and had Spicewood requote for what was supposed to be the same trip. When I asked to have Spicewood's now lower re-quote spelled out exactly, I found that the airfare included an additional stopover, which lowered the airfare."

In order to establish King's relationship with the travel agency, Reed had one of his investigators call its local office and ask to speak with account executive Rita Mae King. Without missing a beat, the receptionist transferred him to Janet Levy, manager of corporate services. The investigator identified himself as an interested traveler who had King's business card and wanted her to book a good deal to the Bahamas. Levy assured him it would not be a problem since she worked closely with King. Levy then asked him to call King at another phone number. It turned out to be her number at ElectroCity.

"She was essentially running her own travel shop out of her office here," said Reed. Although she had no access to an on-line computer, she jerry-rigged a system for her travel customers. "Apparently, if King fed business to Spicewood, they would add that to her credit arrangement."

King operated out of a beehive of activity littered with paperwork, said Reed. The 51-year-old married woman often kept two or three conversations going in her workplace at the same time. "She was a very take-charge, bossy kind of person — very outgoing, but also caustic in a lot of her interactions with other employees. Also quick to denigrate and complain." On the flip side, "She can be very ingratiating and very nice when she wants." Through her work, King became well-networked in the travel industry, with many friends and lots of contacts.

After having established an outside business link between King and Spicewood, Reed then reviewed personnel records for her travel activity. Working on a hunch, he homed in on a vacation King took the previous December when she and a companion flew to the Caribbean island of Antigua via American Airlines.

Reed, a former police officer, scrutinized King's personal credit card statements from that time. An examination of the statements revealed a MasterCard charge from the Royal Antiguan Hotel. Again, Reed had one of his investigators place a call. Posing as "Mr. Lowell King," the investigator phoned the hotel claiming to need help with his travel records in preparation for an IRS audit. The hotel bookkeeper graciously faxed the "guest" a copy of the King hotel bill.

On the bill, King had listed her occupation as a travel agent, giving her business address as the local office of Spicewood Travel. To receive a 50% discount on her room rate — a savings worth $412 — she furnished the manager with her business card and an Airline Reporting Corporation number, a code issued by an international clearinghouse to identify every travel booking agency. While Reed suspected King may have gone on other company-subsidized trips, "Antigua was the only one we flushed out. We only needed one."

Further analysis of King's credit statements showed that she charged three other airline tickets over a seven-month period and received three corresponding credits that canceled out the price of the trips, saving her $834.

The fraud examiners clearly proved that King had breached her duty to act in the company's best interests in connection with her role as the company's purchasing agent. She had also derived some benefit from a vendor, another violation of corporate policy. ElectroCity's personnel handbook addresses both issues: "Employees must disclose any outside financial interest that might influence their corporate decisions or actions. If the company believes that such activities are in conflict with the company's welfare, the employee will be expected to terminate such interests. Such interests include but are not limited to personal or family ownership or interest in a business deemed a customer, supplier, or competitor."

King broke other rules listed in the personnel handbook as well: "Employees may not use corporate assets for their personal use or gain. Employees and their families must never accept any form of under-the-table payments, kickbacks, or rebates, whether in cash or goods, from suppliers." Contrary to company policy, King had set up an off-site mini-agency using the company's phone, accepted travel discounts from a vendor for continued and increased business, and received an estimated 10% of the agency's billings in kickbacks.

Based on their findings, the examiners also determined that King violated the state's commercial bribery statute and could be liable for civil damages if the company decided to press charges. While Reed said her transgressions warranted immediate termination, the ex-cop recommended against pursuing criminal action, given King's age and the ill-health of her unemployed husband. "When you take someone to court, the only options you have are fines or prison."

He takes full responsibility for the decision not to prosecute King. Like police officers, security professionals must make appropriate assessments based on the circumstances, Reed said. "The bad ones always follow the book, regardless of what's best for the community."

"We made the case, corrected the system within the company, and damaged her professionally," Reed said. ElectroCity now requires all vendors to sign agreements acknowledging prohibitive behavior and gifts to all its employees, who now number 3,200. The errant employee was not required to make restitution.

Reed next brought the results of their fraud examination to the president of Spicewood Travel, who reacted with total silence and stunned disbelief. "The documentation was there. They knew they were going to lose business." The company also made verbal legal threats against the agency in the beginning. They held prolonged negotiations to recover $20,000, an estimate of two years of overcharges, "but another VP dropped that ball," said Reed.

The corporation's director of investigations conducted a corporate interview with King to make a final determination of the nature and extent of her relationship with Spicewood and to elicit evidence of any other kickback arrangements that might have adversely affected the company. Reed suggested that King be asked to furnish investigators with a full written disclosure of her interests and activities in connection with Spicewood and any other suppliers.

During the interview, King composed her thoughts in a hand-written letter to the president of ElectroCity:

> *Dear Mr. Smith:*
>
> *I must say that I am sorry. It never dawned on me that what I did was in conflict of my trusted position here at ElectroCity. I truly f——d up — there is no explanation other than that. There was no consideration on my part that a reduced price was anything other than that. I never even thought about it. I am truly sorry, especially because I feel I have broken a trust that we have built over the years. Please understand that I meant nothing against ElectroCity or anyone. Additionally I didn't even see that special rate as a benefit from a supplier, only as a manner by which I could save some dollars personally.*
>
> *Respectfully,*
> *Rita Mae King*

King had misused her authority as a purchasing agent and had violated her duty to ElectroCity. "She was remorseful in the sense that she was now going to have to bite the bullet," said Reed. "I think she probably kicked herself because she didn't get more out of the scam. She felt that she was a woman who worked very hard at a very difficult job, was unappreciated, and was not compensated properly by a male-dominated class system in corporate America."

*****

Overview

A *conflict of interest* occurs when an employee, manager, or executive has an undisclosed economic or personal interest in a transaction that adversely affects the company.[1] As with other corruption cases, conflict schemes involve the exertion of an employee's influence to the detriment of his company. In the ElectroCity case, for instance, Rita Mae King used her influence to direct the bulk of her employer's travel business to Spicewood Travel. In the schemes discussed in the Bribery chapter, fraudsters were paid to exercise their influence on behalf of a third party. Conflicts cases instead involve self-dealing by an employee. Rita Mae King overbilled ElectroCity to benefit herself and her other employer, Spicewood Travel.

Conflicts of interest were not very common in our study, accounting for only 1.71% of the cases we reviewed (see chart 1-6). Nevertheless, with a median loss of $500,000, they were tied with bribery schemes as the most harmful type of fraud on average (see chart 1-5).

The vast majority of conflicts cases occur because the fraudster has an undisclosed economic interest in a transaction. But the fraudster's hidden interest is not *necessarily* economic. In some scenarios an employee acts in a manner detrimental to his company in order to provide a benefit to a friend or relative, even though the fraudster receives no financial benefit from the transaction himself. In Case 1797, for instance, a manager split a large repair project into several smaller projects to avoid bidding requirements. This allowed the manager to award the contracts to his brother-in-law. Though there was no indication that the manager received any financial gain from this scheme, his actions nevertheless amounted to conflict of interest.

In order to be classified as a conflict of interest scheme, the employee's interest in the transaction must be undisclosed. The crux of a conflict case is that the fraudster takes advantage of his employer; the victim company is unaware that its employee has divided loyalties. If an employer knows of the employee's interest in a business deal or negotiation, there can be no a conflict of interest, no matter how favorable the arrangement is for the employee.

Any bribery scheme we discussed in the previous chapter could be used in the conflict of interest context. The only difference is the fraudster's motive. For instance, if an employee approves payment on a fraudulent invoice submitted by a vendor in return for a kickback, this is bribery. If, on the other hand, an employee approves payment on invoices submitted by his own company (and if his ownership is undisclosed), this is a conflict of interest. This was the situation in Case 1132, where an office service employee recommended his own company to do repairs and maintenance on office equipment for his employer. The fraudster approved invoices for approximately $30,000 in excessive charges.

The distinction between the two schemes is obvious. In the bribery case the fraudster approves the invoice in return for a kickback, while in a conflicts case he approves the invoice because of his own hidden interest in the vendor. Aside from the employee's motive for committing the crime, the mechanics of the two transactions are practically identical. The same duality can be found in bid-rigging cases, where an employee influences the selection of a company in which he has a hidden interest instead of influencing the selection of a vendor who has bribed him.

Conflicts schemes do not always simply mirror bribery schemes, though. There are vast numbers of ways in which an employee can use his influence to benefit a company in which he has a hidden interest. This chapter will discuss some of the more common methods that appeared in our study.

Types of Schemes

The majority of the conflicts schemes in our survey fit into two categories: *purchases schemes* and *sales schemes*.

Purchases Schemes	Sales Schemes	Other Schemes

In other words, most conflicts of interest arise when a victim company unwittingly *buys* something at a high price from a company in which one of its employees has a hidden interest, or unwittingly *sells* something at a low price to a company in which one of its employees has a hidden interest. Most of the other conflicts we have come across involved employees who stole clients or diverted funds from their employer.

PURCHASES SCHEMES

The majority of conflicts schemes in our study were purchase schemes and the most common of these was the overbilling scheme. We have already briefly discussed conflicts schemes involving billings (see reference to Case 1132 above). These schemes are very similar to the billing schemes discussed in the asset misappropriation section of this book, so it will be helpful at this point to discuss the distinction we have drawn between traditional billing schemes and purchasing schemes that are conflicts of interest.

While it is true that any time an employee assists in the overbilling of his company there is probably some conflict of interest (the employee causes harm to his employer because of a hidden financial interest in the transaction), this does not necessarily mean that every false billing will be categorized as a conflict scheme. In order for the scheme to be classified as a conflict of interest, the employee (or a friend or relative of the employee) must have some kind of ownership or employment interest in the vendor that submits the invoice. This distinction is easy to understand if we look at the nature of the fraud. Why does the fraudster overbill his employer? If he engages in the scheme only for the cash, the scheme is a fraudulent disbursement billing scheme. If, on the other hand, he seeks to better the financial condition of his business at the expense of his employer, this is a conflict of interest. In other words, the fraudster's *interests* lie with a company other than his employer. When an employee falsifies the invoices of a third-party vendor to whom he has no relation, this is not a conflict of interest scheme because the employee has no interest in that vendor. The sole purpose of the scheme is to generate a fraudulent disbursement.

One might wonder, then, why shell company schemes are classified as fraudulent disbursements rather than conflicts of interest. After all, the fraudster in a shell company scheme owns the fictitious company and therefore must have an interest in it. Remember, though, that shell companies are created for the sole purpose of defrauding the employer. The company is not so much an entity in the mind of the fraudster as it is a tool. In fact, a shell company is usually little more than a post office box and a bank account. The fraudster has no interest in the shell company, which causes a division of loyalty; he simply uses the shell company to bilk his employer. Shell company schemes are therefore classified as false billing schemes.

A short rule of thumb can be used to distinguish between overbilling schemes that are classified as asset misappropriations and those that are conflicts of interest: if the bill originates from a *real company* in which the fraudster has an economic or personal interest, and if the fraudster's interest in the company is undisclosed to the victim company, then the scheme is a conflict of interest.

Now that we know what kinds of billing schemes are classified as conflicts of interest, the question is, how do these schemes work? After our lengthy discussion about distinguishing between conflicts and fraudulent disbursements, the answer is somewhat anticlimactic. The schemes work the same either way. The distinction between the two kinds of fraud is useful only to distinguish the status and purpose of the fraudster. The mechanics of the billing scheme, whether conflict or fraudulent disbursement, do not change (see flowchart 12-2). In Case 464, for instance, a purchasing superintendent defrauded his employer by purchasing items on behalf of his employer at inflated prices from a certain vendor. The vendor in this case was owned by the purchasing superintendent but established in his wife's name and run by his brother. The perpetrator's interest in the company was undisclosed. The vendor would buy items on the open market, then inflate the prices and resell the items to the victim company. The purchasing superintendent used his influence to ensure that his employer continued doing business with the vendor and paying the exorbitant prices. A more detailed analysis of overbilling frauds can be found in the Billing Schemes chapter of this book.

Fraudsters also engage in bid rigging on behalf of their own companies. The methods used to rig bids are discussed in detail in the Bribery chapter and will not be dealt with in depth here. Briefly stated, an employee of the purchasing company is in a perfect position to rig bids because he has access to the bids of his competitors. Since he can find out what prices other vendors have bid, the fraudster can easily tailor his own company's bid to win the contract. Bid waivers are also sometimes used by fraudsters to avoid competitive bidding outright. In Case 1473, for instance, a manager processed several unsubstantiated bid waivers in order to direct purchases to a vendor in which one of his employees had an interest. The conflict was undisclosed and the scheme cost the victim company over $150,000.

In other cases a fraudster might ignore his employer's purchasing rotation and direct an inordinate number of purchases or contracts to his own company. Any way in which a fraudster exerts his influence to divert business to a company in which he has a hidden interest is a conflict of interest.

Unique Assets

Not all conflicts schemes occur in the traditional vendor-buyer relationship. Several of the cases in our survey involved employees negotiating for the purchase of some unique, typically large asset such as land or a building in which the employee had an undisclosed interest. It is in the process of these negotiations that the fraudster violates his duty of loyalty to his employer. Because he stands to profit from the sale of the asset, the employee does not negotiate in good faith to his employer; he does not attempt to get the best price possible. The fraudster will reap a greater financial benefit if the purchase price is high.

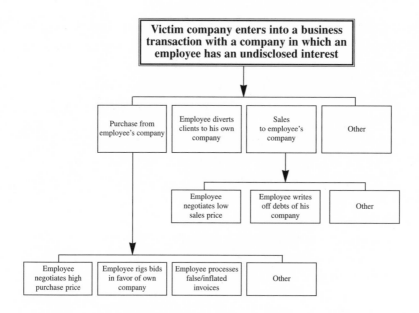

Flowchart 12-2: Conflicts of Interest

An example of this type of scheme was found in Case 2421, where a senior vice president of a utility company was in charge of negotiating and approving mineral leases on behalf of his company. Unbeknownst to his employer, the vice president also owned the property on which the leases were made. The potential harm in this type of relationship is obvious. There was no financial motive for the vice president to negotiate a favorable lease for his employer.

Turnaround Sales

A special kind of purchasing scheme which we have encountered in our study is called the turnaround sale or flip. In this type of scheme an employee knows his employer is seeking to purchase a certain asset and takes advantage of the situation by purchasing the asset himself (usually in the name of an accomplice or shell company). The fraudster then turns around and resells the item to his employer at an inflated price. We have already seen one example of this kind of scheme in Case 464, discussed above, where a purchasing supervisor set up a company in his wife's name to resell merchandise to his employer. Another interesting example of the turnaround method occurred in Case 1379, in which the CEO of a company, conspiring with a former employee, sold an office building to the CEO's company. What made the transaction suspicious was that the building had been purchased by the former employee on the same day that it was resold to the victim company, and for $1.2 million less than the price charged to the CEO's company.

Sales Schemes

Our study has identified two principal types of conflicts schemes associated with the victim company's sales. The first and most harmful is the underselling of goods or services. Just as a corrupt employee can cause his employer to overpay for goods or services sold by a company in which he has a hidden interest, so too can he cause the employer to undersell to a company in which he maintains a hidden interest (see chart 12-2).

Underbillings

The perpetrator underbills the vendor in which he has a hidden interest. The victim company ends up selling its goods or services below fair market value, which results in a diminished profit margin or even a loss on the sale, depending upon the size of the discount. This method was used in Case 2427 by two employees who sold their employer's inventory to their own company at off-spec prices, causing a loss of approximately $100,000. Another example was found in Case 2684, where an employee disposed of his employer's real estate by selling it below fair market value to a company in which he had a hidden interest, causing a loss of approximately $500,000.

Writing off Sales

The other type of sales scheme involves tampering with the books of the victim company to decrease or write off the amount owed by an employee's business. For instance, after an employee's company purchases goods or services from the victim company, credit memos may be issued against the sale, causing it to be written off to contra accounts such as Discounts and Allowances. This method was used by a plant manager in Case 2197. This fraudster assisted favored clients by delaying billing on their purchases for up to 60 days. When the receivable on these clients' accounts became delinquent, the perpetrator issued credit memos against the sales to delete them.

A large number of reversing entries to sales may be a sign that fraud is occurring in an organization. The fraudster in Case 2197 avoided the problem of too many write-offs by issuing new invoices on the sales after the "old" receivables were taken off the books. In this way, the receivables could be carried indefinitely on the books without ever becoming past due.

OTHER SCHEMES

In other cases the perpetrator might not write off the scheme, but simply delay billing. This is sometimes done as a "favor" to a friendly client and is not an outright avoidance of the bill but rather a dilatory tactic. The victim company eventually gets paid, but loses time value on the payment which arrives later than it should.

Business Diversions

In Case 1258, an employee started his own business which would compete directly with his employer. While still employed by the victim company, this employee began siphoning off clients for his own business. This activity clearly violated the employee's duty of loyalty to his employer. There is nothing unscrupulous about free competition, but while a person acts as a representative of his employer it is certainly improper to try to undercut the employer and take his clients. Similarly, the fraudster in Case 2161 steered potential clients away from his employer and toward his own business. There is nothing unethical about pursuing an independent venture (in the absence of restrictive employment covenants such as non-compete agreements) but if the employee fails to act in the best interests of his employer while carrying out his duties, then this employee is violating the standards of business ethics.

Resource Diversions

Finally, some employees divert the funds and other resources of their employers to the development of their own business. In Case 209, for example, a vice president of a company authorized large expenditures to develop a unique type of new equipment used by a certain contractor. Another firm subsequently took over the contractor, as well as the new equipment. Shortly after that, the vice president retired and went to work for the firm that had bought out the contractor. The fraudster had managed to use his employer's money to fund a company in which he eventually developed an interest. This scheme involves elements of bribery, conflicts of interest, and fraudulent disbursements. In this particular case, if the vice president financed the equipment in return for the promise of a job, his actions may have been properly classified as a bribery scheme. Case 209 nevertheless illustrates a potential conflict problem. The fraudster could just as easily have authorized the fraudulent expenditures for a company in which he secretly held an ownership interest.

While these schemes are clearly corruption schemes, the funds are diverted through the use of a fraudulent disbursement. The money could be drained from the victim company through a check tampering scheme, a billing scheme, a payroll scheme, or an expense reimbursement scheme. For a discussion of the methods used to generate fraudulent disbursements, please refer to the asset misappropriation section of this book.

Financial Disclosures

Management has an obligation to disclose to the shareholders significant fraud committed by officers, executives, and others in positions of trust. Management does not have the responsibility of disclosing uncharged criminal conduct of its officers and executives. However, if and when officers, executives, or other persons in trusted positions become subjects of a criminal indictment, disclosure is required.

The inadequate disclosure of conflicts of interests is among the most serious of frauds. Inadequate disclosure of related-party transactions is not limited to any specific industry; it transcends all business types and relationships.

The following case study has been selected to illustrate the actual experience of one CFE in dealing with a conflict of interest fraud. As we will see, James Larken used his influence to pour over a million dollars of his employer's money into a struggling business in which he had a hidden interest. This study not only describes Mr. Larken's scheme, but also shows how CFE Puyler Simonds went about uncovering his fraud.

*****

Case Study: A Parasite Farm

* Several names have been changed to preserve anonymity.

James Larken had it going on. As Chief Financial Officer he arranged for his employer to acquire another company. Then he supported the other company's operations from his employer's till. And because Larken never told his employers that they owned a subsidiary, he reaped all the benefits personally.

Larken worked for a large meat-packing house in the Midwest, for our purposes called Theriot's, Incorporated. Theriot's did in fact consider expanding their business into the supply end of the meat industry, approaching a feedlot operation that was in trouble but had potential. Upon closer inspection, the feedlot, Napa Farms, had nothing to offer but a little land and a lot of trouble, so Theriot's backed out of the deal.

Mr. Larken saw a different story. Since he didn't have to use his own money, Napa Farms was nothing but potential. His authority at Theriot's was beyond question. Theriot's had an audit department but the staff reported to him. And they were scared of him. He had the power to do anything he wanted, or so he thought. "If this guy hadn't gotten greedy," says Puyler Simonds, the CFE who eventually brought down Larken's scheme, "he might have gotten away with it."

Larken exercised a stock option on Napa Farms which he had obtained secretly. Using his position inside Theriot's, he bought up Napa's receivables (money it was owed for livestock sold and services performed) and its inventory. With the help of a Theriot's CPA, the money was tucked away as various credits on the accounting books.

Napa was ailing so badly, however, that the cash from the receivables sale wasn't enough. Larken decided to buy building equipment and vehicles for the feedlot. He ordered a truck, for example, on the Theriot's account, and had it delivered to Napa Farms. Larken had created a financial parasite. A couple months before, Napa was sliding into bankruptcy; now it was drawing new life from the coffers of Theriot's.

But Larken's appetite exceeded his ability to cover his tracks. After a clerk discreetly voiced her suspicions about Larken and his relations with Napa Farms, the CEO started going over the books. He was astounded by the receivables acquired from this company, the same one he had toured and considered buying. The same one that should have been defunct by now. All flags were flying when the CEO saw an invoice showing that Theriot's had bought a truck and sent it to Napa.

Simonds came in on behalf of the accounting firm working for Theriot's to check out the situation. Seizing Larken's files, Simonds' team found titles to equipment, bank records, signature cards, and other business documents, all signed by Larken on behalf of Napa. The people who worked with and under Larken weren't slow about pointing the finger, even if their comments amounted to innuendo and suspicion. They didn't like him. Simonds remembers Larken as loud, aggressive, and harassing, especially to women. "I don't think there was any love lost between this guy and the people he had working for him."

Simonds next went to see the head of Napa Farms. Initially, Blain Fletcher dodged questions and avoided saying anything other than he knew Larken from past business. Fletcher was eventually persuaded to open his files, where Simonds found, "almost by accident," the stock option in Larken's name. From there, it was a matter of following the footprints back to Larken. In eight months, he had funneled over a million dollars into Napa using Theriot's cash. Charges were filed and the case turned over to the police.

Unrepentant and arrogant as always, Larken nevertheless pled guilty and awaits sentencing. Bad news for him, though: you can buy the farm, but you can't take it with you.

*****

Conclusion

Following the old saying of an ounce of prevention being worth a pound of cure, conflict of interest cases are more easily prevented than detected. There are internal controls which make it much more difficult for employees to run this kind of scheme.

Detection

Some of the more common methods that can be used are tips and complaints, comparisons of vendor addresses with employee addresses, review of vendor ownership files, review of exit interviews, and comparisons of vendor addresses to addresses of subsequent employers, and interviews with purchasing personnel for favorable treatment of one or more vendors.

Tips and Complaints

If a particular vendor is being favored, then competing vendors may file complaints. Additionally, employee complaints about the service of a favored vendor may lead to the discovery of a conflict of interest.

Comparison of Vendor Addresses with Employee Addresses

If nominee or related parties are used as owners of vendors, then the business address of the vendor may match that of the employee. Also, look for post office box addresses for vendors. This detection method is similar to that used for locating phony vendors.

Review of Vendor Ownership Files

When a vendor is selected, a complete file of the ownership of that vendor should be kept. This is particularly important for closely held businesses. If the vendor is required to update the file annually then changes in ownership also will be disclosed. A computer comparison of the vendor ownership and the employee file may reveal conflicts of interest.

Review of Exit Interviews and Comparisons of Vendor Addresses to Addresses of Subsequent Employers

If a review of an employee's exit interview yields the name and address of the subsequent employer, then a simple comparison of that name and address with the vendor file may reveal conflicts of interest wherein the employee has obtained employment from a contractor.

Interviews of Purchasing Personnel for Favorable Treatment of One or More Vendors

Employees are generally the first to observe that a vendor is receiving favorable treatment. Therefore, by asking employees if any vendor is receiving favorable treatment, the examiner may discover conflicts of interest that would otherwise have gone unnoticed. Another question which may be asked of employees is whether any vendor's service (or product) has recently become substandard.

PREVENTION

Conflict of interest schemes are variations of the rule that a fiduciary, agent, or employee must act in good faith, with full disclosure, in the best interest of the principal or employer. Most schemes are a violation of the legal maxim that a person cannot serve "two masters." Some of the more common schemes involve an employee's, manager's, or executive's interest in a customer or supplier and receipt of gifts. Often, the employee, manager, or executive is compensated for his interest in the form of "consulting fees."

Seemingly, one of the most arduous occupational frauds most difficult to prevent is the conflict of interest scheme. A policy requiring employees to complete an annual disclosure statement is an excellent proactive approach. Comparing the disclosed names and addresses with the vendor list may reveal real conflicts of interest and the appearance of such. Communication with employees regarding their other business interests is advisable.

[1] Association of Certified Fraud Examiners, *Fraud Examiners' Manual, Revised 2nd Edition* (Austin: ACFE).

PART IV - FRAUDULENT STATEMENTS

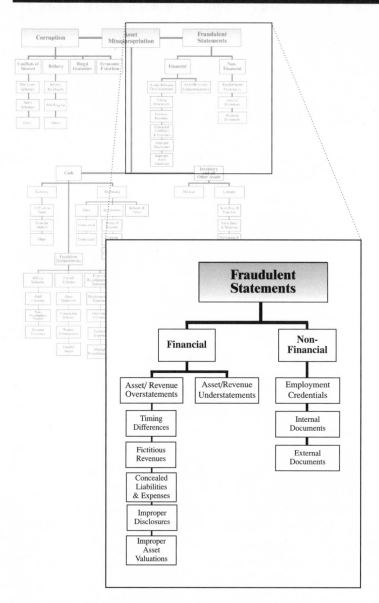

13. FRAUDULENT STATEMENTS

History of Fraudulent Statements

The company which falsifies its financial statements is involved in deceiving the public or its lenders and investors. There is an insidious lineage of companies throughout history which have offered inflated stock to the public, either directly through the company or through Wall Street. These companies all have preyed on investors by using "cooked books"; a statement of financial health is all the naive investors require before handing millions of dollars to well-tailored con artists.

An early, flamboyant practitioner of investment swindles through fraudulent financial statements was a European shyster named John Law. The con man, who had barely escaped Edinborough with his life due to his previous schemes, was able to gain the confidence of the French Duke of Orleans.

When the Duke graduated to become King Louis XV of France in the early 1700s, Law was inexplicably put in charge of reversing the French government's dire financial conditions.[1] Law, rarely an honest man, instead devised a scheme to hoodwink the Paris public. Through the use of fraudulent financial information, he was able to convince national investors to back a fledgling venture know as The Mississippi Company. Law's grand scam was for the company to cultivate the rich French Louisiana territory, plundering the natural resources of the New World for great fortunes and profit.

France's investors went on a spending frenzy, desperate to purchase stocks of the bound-for-success company. Temporarily, Law unintentionally reversed the financial fortunes of France, as a good portion of the Paris economy churned due to the turnover of the Mississippi Company shares from one investor to another.[2] Unfortunately, Law had not taken the first step to form his operation. But the French investors continued to buy stock in the company and sell it at a dramatically higher price. Paris swelled with inflation as the people became wealthy. When word spread that the company was a hoax, the French economy collapsed and the angry public looked to lynch John Law. He fled the country disguised as a beggar, but Law left without the war chest of riches he had accumulated over his tenure as France's monetary maestro. The infamous scheme has become known as "The Mississippi Bubble" and has been copied to various extents in the United States since.[3]

A landmark fraudulent financial statement case occurred in the U.S. in the 1930s, rocking the auditing field to the extent that the accounting profession was forced to change several auditing practices. The McKesson-Robbins case unfolded as McKesson & Robbins, Inc., a pharmaceutical giant, was discovered overstating its physical inventory and sales by $19 million (the company's total inventory was said to be $87 million).[4] When auditors from Price Waterhouse & Co. inspected the McKesson & Robbins books in 1937, they did not take a count of the physical inventory or check out the validity of any of the company's numerous new customers, resulting in the opportunity for the company to pull off the fraud. During this time, the auditing community did not consider accounting for physical inventory a necessity in an auditing situation, instead relying on the records of the company.

Legend has it that the fraud was discovered when one of the Price Waterhouse auditors took a vacation near the supposed location of McKesson & Robbins' warehouse and, curious, stopped by to have a look. However, when the auditor arrived at the supposed location, he was staring at an empty field, discovering the lack of reported inventory firsthand.[5] While this story makes for great folklore within the auditing community, the reality is that the McKesson treasurer and director discovered the overstatement and reported it immediately to the company president. The president ordered a stockholder investigation, resulting in the uncovering of $9 million in fictitious inventory counts and $10 million in fictitious customers on the McKesson & Robbins books. The McKesson stock, as a result, was overstated as well. As the fraud unraveled, it became clear that the company president was actually the person responsible for instigating the fraud, but the president shot himself before he was indicted.[6]

McKesson & Robbins was important because it altered the auditing community's responsibilities in auditing situations. After the case, auditors adopted measures that required them to in engage in a physical inventory count, as well as an investigation of company's new clients.[7]

The Great Salad Oil Swindle was a financial statement fraud which was pulled off by the pure salesmanship of a deceptive entrepreneur. The scam was engineered in the late 1950s and early 1960s by Anthony De Angelis, a man who stood 5'5" but weighed 240 pounds. De Angelis was not physically imposing, but he had a reputation as being a brilliant salesman of salad oil; his New Jersey company, built from the ground up, appeared to be robust.[8] De Angelis began as the only employee of his company, which grew to become a fortress of steel holding drums, largely purchased with the investment money of others, at a plant in New Jersey. The stories of De Angelis' ability to engineer terrifically intricate deals were legendary and the salad oil business was a virtual monetary empire for him.

De Angelis continually obtained loans from large companies and wealthy investors who were eager to profit from the Salad Oil King's good fortunes. He would issue his investors certificates of authenticity from a prestigious subsidiary of the American Express company, whose executives vouched for the massive quantity of salad oil in the De Angelis reserve tanks.[9]

The investors didn't independently investigate, trusting in the good word of De Angelis and AmEx that the salad oil was bountiful. Had they delved into De Angelis' operations, they would have realized that the salad oil shares offered for sale were individually larger than the total amount of salad oil in the entire country.[10] In fact, no one ever thought to check the salad oil reserves for themselves by touring the facility and examining the large holding tanks that De Angelis owned in New Jersey. All the while, De Angelis recorded one amazing sale of a large quantity of salad oil after another, sending the company's stock prices and profit margin soaring. Competitors were envious of the man's ability to pull off sales of mass quantity at prices that seemed impossible; in fact, many questioned how the company was able to stay afloat.

De Angelis' financial background could be described as spotty at best. He had previously run a solvent business into bankruptcy, had attempted to cheat the government on several occasions while carrying out government contracts with a second company, and had been expelled from two New York banks on the suspicion that he was running check kiting schemes. De Angelis couldn't have obtained credit at any bank in New York, and yet everyone took the salad oil salesman at his word every time he announced his latest, greatest salad oil sale.[11]

The reality, of course, was that De Angelis was simply collecting investor checks for millions of dollars to line his own pockets, infusing very little of those dollars into the salad oil business. In November 1963, the company folded without warning and it was revealed that although $175 million in investors' money had been collected, there was nary a drop of salad oil in the reserve tanks.[12] De Angelis had paid off employees of the American Express subsidiary to lie about the amount of salad oil the company possessed, but he steadfastly denied any wrongdoing when confronted with the truth.

In the instance of the Great Salad Oil Swindle, De Angelis' overblown financial statements were relatively easy to keep under wraps. Because of the small number of American Express insiders who fully understood what De Angelis was doing, very few people were aware of the dearth of assets in the company coffers.

In the case of Equity Funding, however, a series of intricate frauds were committed in the late 1960s and early 1970s by not one employee, but nearly the entire Equity Funding top brass. Equity was a giant insurance and investment company, headquartered in Los Angeles, which traded publicly on the New York Stock Exchange. The company was reportedly bursting with profit, boasting a spectacular track record and several subsidiaries with bountiful assets. The company's profit margin grew every year, until the price of its stock had risen in 1973 to $37 a share, doubling the opening stock price when it had debuted only a few years earlier.[13]

As it turned out, however, Equity Funding was a sham. Authorities subsequently discovered that the company had not turned a profit during its existence, instead having lost money in every quarter of every year.[14] Equity Funding was engaged in a company-wide cover-up in which numerous employees, under the supervision of management, altered and massaged the profit line and inflated company holdings to indicate a healthy company. The fraud was so widespread that the company's auditors even had an inadvertent hand in the scheme, continually rubber-stamping Equity Funding with a clean bill of health. The unique angle of the Equity Funding fraud was not that the company had succeeded in hoodwinking investors out of millions of dollars; it was the fact that corruption within the company was so widespread, yet remained a tightly-held secret for so long. It is alarming that the continuous fraudulent activity — conducted over more than a ten year period — could be perpetrated by so many individuals without anyone outside the company discovering it.

Equity's downfall occurred when the corporation fired an employee who had taken a large role in the scheme. The employee, understandably irritated at his former employer, turned over every detail of the cover-up to the authorities. The company, it turns out, fired an employee whose knowledge of improprieties could sink the whole ship. Within the week word had been leaked by several prominent firms around Wall Street that Equity had been deep-sixed and the price of Equity Funding stock plummeted to $14. External auditors Julian Weiner, Solomon Block, and Marvin Lichtig, of the accounting firm Wolfson, Weiner, were held responsible for their auditing oversights and convicted of fraud in the aftermath of the scheme.

Barry Minkow likely studied the moves of Equity Funding with great interest; he certainly understood a thing or two about cooking the books and bamboozling the likes of Wall Street. The former owner of ZZZZ Best carpet cleaning service founded the company in his parents' garage as a high school junior. Minkow originally sold shares of his company at five cents a share, but by the time the company was five years old, he had led ZZZZ Best to a prestigious rise on Wall Street. The lofty business reputation Minkow built only set the fraudster up for a monumental fall, landing the flamboyant entrepreneur in prison.

Minkow built ZZZZ Best into a large carpet cleaning and renovation service in California in the mid 1980s, but the "building" of the business was by and large a pure canard. ZZZZ Best's books were a stew of inflated numbers and bogus accounts, pumped up to impress possible investors and clients. Minkow's books boasted a large backlog of orders and insurance restoration project. Upon closer inspection, it should have been noticed that these numbers were unreasonably high. For instance, the insurance project orders Minkow showed on his books totaled more funds than were available through this type of work in the entire U.S. And one of Minkow's renovation accounts was projected to cost even more than the renovation of the MGM Grand Hotel in Las Vegas. Minkow's company was in reality losing millions of dollars, but the young, self-styled entrepreneur was too proud to admit to anyone that his company was failing. Instead, Minkow dreamed up new schemes to cover the growing ZZZZ Best debt.

Minkow's fraud turned more grand when he offered the company to the public on the New York Stock Exchange in 1986, netting ZZZZ Best more than $13 million in capital. Not surprisingly, very little of the $13 million was infused into the corporation; instead it lined the pockets of the brash owner. Most of the funds were used to pay previous investors and lenders to keep the fraud afloat. But the scheme blew up in the owner's face when the Los Angeles Times ran an article about Minkow, exposing him as a credit card fraudster. The company collapsed quickly as securities investigators delved into ZZZZ Best's fictitious finances. Minkow, convicted of an assortment of offenses and sent to prison, later admitted that much of the reason he continued to commit the frauds was that his ego wouldn't allow him to stop.

I met Minkow in 1992, while he was serving a 25-year federal prison sentence in Colorado. (He was released in 1996 after serving 8 years.) Minkow wrote me while he was institutionalized and told me he wanted to tell his story — something he hadn't even done for *60 Minutes*.

A video crew met me at the prison and we spent the afternoon taping Minkow's story. It was easy to see why he was so successful as a con. He had the natural gift for blarney that all people of his ilk have; Barry is very likable, sincere, and above all, believable.

The fascinating thing about Minkow is how young he developed his skills, almost as if being a con was born in him. Since leaving prison, he has become a minister and self-styled fraud prevention expert. Minkow's new occupation will not impress his critics.

Another large-scale financial statement fraud occurred in the early 1990s, when a small discount drug store called Phar-Mor rose to prominence. Phar-Mor founder and co-owner Mickey Monus was able to get funding for his discount stores from a number of different sources. The conglomeration of nationwide stores grew to 40 in just over four years. Phar-Mor was considered a "white-hot commodity in a sizzling industry," according to PBS's investigative show Frontline, in an episode on the fraudulent chain. Behind closed doors, however, Monus and several other Phar-Mor executives were wringing their hands: Phar-Mor was in reality losing millions of dollars every year, unable to sell its goods at the prices it had promised in promotions and advertisements and still break even.

Too embarrassed to admit the losses and damage the company's blooming status, Monus directed CFO Pat Finn to doctor monthly financial statements to show Phar-Mor to be a thriving business. The duo was able to steer around the auditors year after year because they knew which stores would be audited in advance and made certain that everything appeared in order in those locations.

Meanwhile, Monus had the radical idea of forming a "six feet and under" professional basketball franchise, the World Basketball League (WBL), and the fledgling basketball organization hung like an albatross on the Phar-Mor corporation's neck. Monus directed Finn and other company members to channel Phar-Mor funds to his struggling league. He also upset several Phar-Mor business associates, such as Coca-Cola, by pressuring the corporations to lend support to the WBL.

The fraudulent financial scheme hit a roadblock when the company began withholding checks to various vendors, knowing that if the vendors cashed the checks, they would most certainly bounce. When vendors began to pull their products off of Phar-Mor shelves, CFO Finn began to squirm, fearing that Monus would attempt to shovel the blame onto him. Finn went to the government and unloaded the whole scheme. Monus was subsequently indicted on 129 criminal counts of fraudulent activity, sentenced to 20 years in prison, and barred for life from serving as an officer of any publicly traded company by the Northern District of Ohio. Finn testified against his former boss and was sentenced to a 33-month prison term for his part in the scheme. The accounting firm was also found liable for not discovering the $500 million fraud at the troubled drugstore chain. However, the damage took its toll most directly on Phar-Mor's victims. Phar-Mor's books, upon investigation, had been overstated by $290 million and the company was able to raise some $500 million more in investor money directly from the fraud.

In a high-profile securities fraud scandal, Prudential Securities agreed to pay more than $1.3 billion to investors that the firm misled and deceived for the better part of a decade. Prudential admitted in 1994 to administering a company-wide policy of misleading its clientele through the use of false promises and loaded books. The company, for example, invested the retirement moneys of a large base of elderly clients into high-risk funds, contrary to what Prudential was telling the clients. Prudential was able to escape a federal indictment only by entering a deferred prosecution agreement with the Manhattan U.S. District Attorney and the Securities and Exchange Commission. The admission of guilt not only shook the credibility of the securities arm of the conglomerate, but it was also responsible for an unfavorable reaction to Prudential's lucrative insurance division, which was once referred to as "rock-solid."

Fraudulent financial statements have hardly been used exclusively by American companies. In early 1997, a hotshot commodities trader, Yasuo Hamanaka, pled guilty to fraud and forgery charges. Hamanaka at one point controlled more than 5% of the world's copper market and was the most revered trader at the prestigious Sumitomo Corporation. The flamboyant trader seemingly turned a profit on every trade and thus, according to Hamanaka's prosecutor, had the full confidence of his superiors and clients.

Hamanaka was living a lie, turning to forgeries of documents, fake reports, and inflated numbers to make his deals seem sweet. In reality, Hamanaka's losses piled up to $2.6 billion, resulting in a depression of the world copper market. The trader may not have stood alone in his guilt; while nothing was proven, many skeptics wondered aloud how the Sumitomo Corporation could have possibly overlooked the too-good-to-be-true deals that Hamanaka was able to generate. The company's image has been considerably battered as a result of the illegal transactions.

Financial statement fraud schemes will not disappear anytime soon. In February 1997, Charles O. Huttoe admitted in U.S. District Court that he had bilked investors out of more than $12 million by inflating the financial statements of his Systems of Excellence corporation.[15] Huttoe was able to raise the revenues via the Internet. The SEC determined that the entrepreneur made false claims about the financial health of the videoconferencing hardware company. Huttoe grabbed the investor money and distributed most of the company stock to his family.[16] Because Huttoe cooperated with authorities, he was able to plead guilty and received a relatively light sentence of 46 months in prison, plus a $10,000 fine.

Introduction

When I was in the FBI during the 70s and 80s, the workaday financial statement fraud came from bank borrowers, either individual or corporate. Under the Bank Secrecy Act, financial institutions are required to notify the FBI of possible fraud by their borrowers in connection with a host of activity, most of it loan fraud.

The typical financial statement fraud case did not impress the typical FBI agent. That is because many of us learned the hard way that some banks would attempt to use the government as collection agencies. A common complaint by agents was that the banks would do little due diligence on the borrower before loaning him money. Many of the financial statements in bank loan files I examined would make an accountant laugh. Most of them were unaudited, a clue; and a number of them contained simple math errors in the balance sheet or income statement; in short, they didn't even add up, another clue.

But in order for the financial statement fraud to be a violation of federal statutes, the lender was required to have relied on the false financials to some extent in making the loan. In most instances, the reality was that the numbers were in the bank's loan files only to conform with government regulations. Banks, in general, prefer hard collateral. And if the collateral loses its value or disappears when the loan goes into default, it is very tempting for even good bankers to run to the FBI crying "financial statement fraud."

You can see the obvious advantage, from the bank's point of view, of having an FBI agent show up at the door of a delinquent borrower. Even though the agents don't attempt to collect funds, it is amazing how many borrowers suddenly come up with the money to pay off their loans after being visited by the Federal Bureau of Investigation.

One memorable case, though, wasn't like that. Toward the latter part of my FBI career, I was assigned the investigation of Orange Associates, Inc. It was a start-up company supposedly specializing in a new concept expressly for stress: biofeedback equipment. Such equipment has come a long way since the 70s, and has been integrated into the mainstream of medical and psychological treatment.

The equipment has sensors that are placed on parts of the head, neck, and other areas. These sensors are connected by wire to a computer and screen. When the sensors are placed on strategic parts of a patient's body, it is possible to actually see and hear, in real time, increases and decreases in the level of stress in that person. By seeing and hearing the stress level, the patient is taught exercises which control the stress; hence, biofeedback.

The concept of Orange Associates was actually developed by an educator, who I remember as David Aldridge, or something close to that. At any rate, Aldridge had a vague past as a "consultant" to the medical and psychological community. He eventually met a psychologist, Dr. Wayne Gaffney, who agreed to supply start-up capital for Orange. Their grand plan was to manufacture and distribute various models of biofeedback equipment.

Gaffney was a good choice for Aldridge. The former came from a long line of rice farmers in south Texas, where land holdings are so vast that they are quoted in the nearest thousand acres. Through inheritance of various real estate holdings from his family, Dr. Gaffney was worth millions. He was a gadget freak. Their initial plan was for Dr. Gaffney to be the money partner, and for Aldridge to run the operation. Off they went to Travis Bank, where Gaffney pledged some of his rice land on a note for a million dollars. That money was the initial seed capital. The loan proceeds went to the company checking account at what was then Austin State Bank.

Like so many other start-up operations, the initial seed money quickly proved inadequate; within months, Orange needed additional working capital. Gaffney balked at borrowing more on his inheritance, so Aldridge prepared a loan package on Orange for submission to Austin State Bank.

Since Orange had no net worth, Aldridge, behind Gaffney's back, concocted a series of "contracts" the company had supposedly signed to sell its equipment in bulk to wholesalers. These "contracts" were pledged as accounts receivable on still a second million dollar loan, this time at Austin State Bank. The "contracts" had one major flag that glowed like a neon light, the so-called customers were all Cayman Island corporations.

Aldridge's explanation for the Cayman customers was that they were resellers to the Japanese and Europeans. But Aldridge also said that the Japanese were manufacturing the biofeedback equipment for Orange. In essence, Aldridge claimed, the equipment was manufactured by one Japanese company and sold on paper to a company in the Caymans, and the Cayman company purchased the equipment from Orange. If the bank had really listened to what Aldridge was telling them, they would have noticed his ludicrous story made no sense whatsoever.

But the bank bought Aldridge's story, and so did his partner Gaffney, who still had to sign the Orange note individually as a guarantor before the bank would give them more working capital. Indeed, Orange Associates did get the money and Gaffney was now $2 million in debt.

Still Orange continued to bleed red. Aldridge's headquarters operations consisted of about a dozen administrators. Neither the bank nor Gaffney noticed that there was not one sales or marketing person in the lot. The rent was high. Research and development added to the costs. Soon, Aldridge knew he had to go back to the well for more money or close the operation — an unthinkable option to him by this point.

Aldridge saw the problem coming six months before Orange actually applied for a third working capital loan. That was time enough for him to figure out that he needed to churn the operations checking account at Austin State Bank. After all, Aldridge reasoned, if the bank saw lots of activity, big deposits especially, they would be more likely to believe business at Orange was booming.

So Aldridge began kiting checks in the Austin State Bank demand deposit account. To create legitimate-looking sales, he deposited checks from a Cayman Island bank account into the Orange Associates operating account. Then he wire-transferred funds to a bank in Dallas, ostensibly for payment of equipment manufactured by the Japanese. In truth, the funds were going right back to the Cayman bank account to cover the check he'd deposited at Austin State Bank.

When it came time to apply for a loan, the deposits in the Orange checking account looked pretty good to the bank; several hundred thousand dollars went into the account. But of course, it went right back out. Aldridge told the bank and Dr. Gaffney that business was so good they had to borrow more money to satisfy new orders. They would need about two million this time, Aldridge figured.

After reviewing the corporate accounts and yet another set of fraudulent statements, the bank bit one final time, but on this loan, they made a fatal error. They allowed Orange, who had been paying well on the other loans (albeit with the bank's money), to borrow on the equipment inventory alone. Gaffney didn't even have to guarantee the note individually.

Orange managed to stay afloat, in total, about five years. This turned out to be a remarkable feat, considering the fact that the company never generated a cent of revenue. Instead, Aldridge had relied totally on bank financing to sustain the operations. He had lied to Dr. Gaffney and everyone else in the process. Orange Associates was largely a figment of David Aldridge's imagination.

The scheme came to light the fourth and final time Aldridge tried to go to the bank for still more money. By this time, senior management at Austin State Bank had changed. They wanted Orange to reduce its loan balance, which was over three million. With nowhere else to turn for financing, Orange quickly ran out of money and began missing loan payments not only to Austin State Bank, but also to Travis Bank, where they still owed a million dollars, more or less.

Both banks filed suit against Orange, Aldridge, and Gaffney to foreclose on their collateral. There was none. The combined losses completely wiped out the equity position of both banks. Rather than come up with more money, shareholders of both banks decided to sell. Because of the possibility of fraud, the FBI was contacted. That's where I came in.

I went to the United States Attorney's office and obtained a subpoena for Orange's financial and bank records. Then the real work began. One " Loan Ranger" FBI Agent (me) without a staff or computer, spent the better part of six months simply scheduling debits and credits in and out of Orange's operating accounts.

The numbers told the real story. Four million in loans and five million in expenses over five years. The expenses included a reasonable salary for Aldridge, but nothing outrageous. He had a rather large staff, spent millions on outside contractors for research and development, went on international trips to develop business, and paid lobbyists and other consultants. The expenses turned out to be legitimate.

After doing the financial homework, it was time to interview everyone in the loop. Aldridge's lawyer wouldn't let him talk, but the other people talked. Gaffney, it turned out, was simply naive. For years he would listen to Aldridge but never verified anything for himself. The employees of Orange Associates liked and respected Aldridge; however, they admitted to confusion over the business. The employees said Aldridge was both CEO and de facto chief financial officer. The company bookkeeper, when I interviewed her, was clueless about the big picture.

So in the situation of Orange, the only culprit was Aldridge. I took my evidence to the United States Attorney's office to discuss a possible indictment. The prosecutor quickly honed in on the key question. If Aldridge did not particularly enrich himself, what was his motivation to concoct these patently fraudulent financial statements?

My investigation of Aldridge had turned up a curious contradiction. Aldridge was a good guy. He was well liked and respected by his employees, neighbors, and professional associates. He was as straight as an arrow — married, stable, college educated, a volunteer in the community, and a regular church-goer.

By putting together the financial picture along with his personal profile, I told the prosecutor what I thought happened. When Aldridge first got involved with Gaffney and they borrowed the first million, Aldridge essentially misspent the money. He should have realized then that he was no businessman.

But instead, in order to cover his mistakes, he got Gaffney to borrow another million. Aldridge wasted a great deal of that money, too. By that time, he'd told too many lies to backtrack. He had to go forward and hope that by keeping the company alive long enough, Orange would start turning a profit. If that happened, his fraud would never be discovered.

The main reason Orange failed was because Aldridge was an egghead; he simply didn't know what he was doing. The prosecutor agreed with that theory, and it bothered him. "Joe," he said, "other than his salary, Aldridge has received no personal benefit." I argued that the salary alone was derived principally from fraudulent activity.

"I know you are technically right, Joe," the prosecutor said. "But this doesn't have the jury appeal elements of a good criminal fraud case — someone the jury can hate because he is evil and greedy. This isn't such a man. I think we should decline criminal prosecution in favor of the bank taking civil action."

The prosecutor was right, I knew, but I still tried to sell him on the case. I guess my heart wasn't in it either, really. As I learned quickly working in the criminal justice system, you have to let many people go to concentrate on others. It is simply a question of resources.

Aldridge got off scot-free, without any criminal penalties. Both defrauded banks sued Aldridge and Gaffney, along with the defunct Orange Associates, Inc. I understand they got some money from Gaffney, but not enough to cover the losses. Gaffney was forced into bankruptcy; it seems the millions in real estate he had inherited was tied up mostly in a family trust. His family almost disowned Dr. Wayne Gaffney, I heard, because of the legal trouble he created.

So in some financial statement fraud cases like Orange, the principals do not necessarily directly pocket ill-gotten gain. But like Aldridge, even top executives of major corporations do indeed have the motivation to sometimes cook the books; they look at this activity as vital to keeping their jobs. Unlike Aldridge, some corporate executives frequently are paid millions, the ultimate motivator to lie. For others the opportunity to benefit illegally through statement manipulation is irresistible.

Fraud in Financial Statements

Financial statement frauds like those described above are caused by a number of factors occuring at the same time, the most significant of which is the pressure on upper management to show earnings. Preparing false financial statements is made somewhat easier by the subjective nature of the way books and records are kept. The accounting profession has long recognized that, to a large extent, accounting is a somewhat arbitrary process, subject to wide interpretation. The profession also indirectly recognizes that numbers are subject to manipulation. After all, a debit on a company's books can be recorded as either an expense or an asset. A credit can be a liability or equity. Therefore, there is tremendous temptation — when a strong earnings showing is needed — to classify those expenses as assets, and those liabilities as equity. But that's not all. Over the years, businesses have found numerous ingenious ways to overstate their true earnings and assets. As a result, a number of accounting conventions, or what are termed *generally accepted accounting principles* have developed. Most historic accounting principles have now been codified by the Financial Accounting Standards Board (FASB), an independent public watchdog organization responsible for standard setting.[17]

Major Generally Accepted Accounting Principles

Generally Accepted Accounting Principles include eight major standards. The following is a list of the major principles:

| Materiality | Matching | Conservatism | Going Concern |

| Cost | Objective Evidence | Consistency | Full Disclosure |

MATERIALITY

Financial statements are not meant to be perfect, only reasonable and fair. There are doubtless many small errors in the books of major and minor corporations, but what does it really mean when considering the big picture? The answer is that it depends on who is looking at the financial statements and making decisions based on them. If a company's estimated earnings is $1 million a year on its financial statements, and it turns out that figure is actually $990,000 (or $1,010,000), who cares? Probably not many people. But suppose that $1 million in earnings on the financial statements is actually $500,000 — half what the company showed. Then many people, investors and lenders, principally, would care a great deal.

Materiality, then, according to GAAP, is a user-oriented concept. "If there exists a misstatement so significant that reasonable, prudent users of the financial statements would make a different decision than they would if they had been given correct information, then the misstatement is material and requires correction."[18]

A typical issue involving materiality and fraud would be asset misappropriations. Many of them are quite small, and not material to the financial statements as a whole. But what of the aggregate? If many steal small amounts, the result could indeed be material.

MATCHING

The matching concept requires the books and records and the resultant financial statements to match revenue and expense in the proper accounting period. Fraud can occur when purposeful attempts are made to manipulate the matching concept. For example, through controlling the year-end cut-off in financial figures, many companies boost their current net income by counting revenue from the following year early, and by delaying the posting of this year's expenses until next year.

CONSERVATISM

By conservatism, accountants mean that the financial figures presented by the company are at least as much as reflected in the statements, if not more. There is a saying in accounting: "Anticipate possible losses and omit potential profits." This results in *asymmetrical accounting*, where the expenses are purposefully overstated and the revenues are purposefully understated. Remember, the only time a business's true worth can be determined is when it is sold. Until then, the numbers reflected in the historical financial statements are the best available estimates — but should be on the low side. If a company's financial statements intentionally violate the conservatism principle, they could be fraudulent.

GOING CONCERN

In valuing a firm's assets for financial statement purposes, it is assumed that the business is one which will continue into the future. That is because the worth of the business, if it is any good, will always be higher than the value of its hard assets. For example, if you wanted to buy a business which paid you a 10% return, then you would pay up to a million dollars for an investment that earned $100,000 a year. The value of the actual assets underlying the business, if they were sold at auction, would typically not bring nearly a million dollars. This is the *going concern* concept, which assumes the business will go on indefinitely in the future. If there is serious doubt about whether a business can continue, the accountants must disclose this information as a footnote in the financial statements.

Fraud in the going concern concept will usually result from attempts by an entity to conceal its terminal business condition. For example, assume a company is in the computer parts manufacturing business. Last year, the company earned $100,000 after taxes. This year, management is aware that new technology will make their business totally obsolete, and by next year, the business will likely close. This fact might not be known to the company's auditors. And when they prepare the financial statements for their company, management has the duty to inform the accountants of the business's future ability to earn money. They in turn will insist that the financial statements for the current period reflect this future event.

COST

Generally accepted accounting principles require that assets be carried on the financial statements at cost, as this is generally the most conservative method. However, if the assets are worth less than what they cost, this value is carried on the financial statements. You can easily see that using the lower cost or market value produces the most conservative asset valuations. The cost figure generated for assets, providing they are worth more than they cost, is called historical or acquisition cost. But there are other cost definitions, too.[19]

Price-Level Adjusted Historical Cost

This method of pricing would carry an asset's value on the financial statements as what it would currently cost, considering inflation. At present, it is not acceptable as a method of carrying costs on the balance sheet.

Net Realizable Value

The net realizable value of an asset is the amount of money that would be realized upon the sale of the asset, less the costs to sell it. Because this method deals with a projection, it is not acceptable for costing assets.

Future Profits

The reason businesses acquire assets is to use them to produce goods and services. This method would determine the estimates of future profits the company could earn because it has the asset. This method, like others, is not acceptable for asset costing because of the subjective nature of the information.

Replacement Cost

This method is really the opposite of net realizable value. Instead of determining the value of the item if it is sold, this method assumes the value of the asset if it must be replaced. During inflationary periods, replacement cost would boost assets and equity. Replacement cost is not permitted to determine the value of assets under generally accepted accounting principles.

OBJECTIVE EVIDENCE

Another generally accepted accounting principle that has a fraud impact deals with the subject of objective evidence. Accounting records are designed to be kept on objective, rather than subjective, evidence. That is to say, most everyone can agree on what the asset costs historically, versus what it may be worth at the present time. In valuing assets on the financial statements, the accountant looks for objective evidence of that asset's cost — an invoice, a canceled check, a contract. Built into this assumption of objective evidence, but not specifically stated, is that such evidence can be fraudulently presented; a document can be forged or faked. So the evidence used by the accountant to value assets at their cost does not have to be absolute, only reasonable.

CONSISTENCY

In order for financial information to be presented fairly over a period of time, the method of presentation must be consistent, even if not the most accurate measure from year to year. For example, one easy way for the value of assets and income to be inflated is through the depreciation methods companies use on their books. Assume a valuable piece of equipment was purchased by a company for $99,000 and was expected to last three years. That means under *straight line* depreciation, the write-off in the first year would be $33,000 maximum. Under the *double declining balance* method of depreciation, the write-off would be $66,000 the first year. By switching depreciation methods from one year to the next, the company could influence its net income by as much as $33,000. In reality, this is not income, but a way to compare apples and oranges. So if a company changes the way it keeps its books from one year to the next, and if these changes have a material impact on the financial statements, they must be disclosed in a footnote to the financials. Fraud often occurs when consistency is intentionally avoided to show false profits.

FULL DISCLOSURE

The principle behind full disclosure, like in the last example, is that any material deviation from generally accepted accounting principles must be explained to the reader of the financial information. In addition, any known event that could have a material impact on future earnings must be explained or disclosed. For example, as we discussed earlier, suppose a company is aware that its principal manufacturing method for computer parts is being made obsolete by competitors. Such an event must be disclosed. If the company is being sued and is in danger of a material monetary judgment, that must be disclosed, too. In actuality, any potential adverse event of a material nature must be disclosed in the financials. Many major financial frauds have been caused by the purposeful omission of foot-note disclosures to the statements.

Responsibility for Financial Statements

Financial statements are the responsibility of company man-agement. Therefore, it is hard to imagine that financial statement fraud can be committed without some knowledge or consent of man-agement, although financial statement fraud can be perpetrated by anyone who has the opportunity and the motive to omit or misstate the data presented in furtherance of their purpose.

Fraud is generally instigated by members of management, at the very least, by persons under the direction and control of manage-ment. In the instances where management does not investigate sus-pected frauds, how can management assure itself that fraud will be prevented and, if fraud does occur, that it will be detected?

A company's board of directors and senior management gen-erally set the code of conduct for the company. This code of conduct is often referred to as the company's "ethic." This ethic is the stan-dard by which all other employees will tend to conduct themselves. It stands to reason, therefore, that if the company's ethic is one of high integrity, the employees will tend to be more honest. If, on the other hand, the ethic is corrupt, the employees will view that as a license to also be corrupt. An unimpeachable company ethic does not, in and of itself, ensure that financial statement fraud will not occur. Additional measures are required in order for management to discharge its responsibilities with respect to prevention and detec-tion of fraudulent financial reporting.

Users of Financial Statements

Financial statement fraud schemes are most often perpetrated by management against potential users of the statements. These us-ers of financial statements include company ownership and manage-ment, lending organizations, and investors. Fraudulent statements are used for a number of reasons. The most common is to increase the apparent prosperity of the organization in the eyes of potential and current investors. This not only may induce new investment, but can help keep current investors satisfied. Fraudulent financial state-ments can be used to dispel negative perceptions of an organization in the open market. Company management often uses financial state-ments to judge employee or management performance. Employees are tempted to manipulate statements to ensure continued employment and additional compensation that is potentially tied to performance. Certain internal goals, such as satisfying budgets, contribute added pressure to the manager responsible. The following diagram displays the role of financial information and statements in the decision-making process of the users.

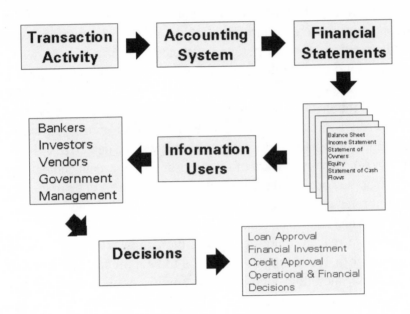

Types of Financial Statements

According to the Statement on Auditing Standards (SAS) No. 62, published by the AICPA Auditing Standards Board, financial statements include presentations of financial data and accompanying notes prepared in conformity with either generally accepted accounting principles or some other comprehensive basis of accounting. The following is a list of such financial statements:

- Balance sheet
- Statement of income or statement of operations
- Statement of retained earnings
- Statement of cash flows
- Statement of changes in owners' equity
- Statement of assets and liabilities that does not include owners' equity accounts

- Statement of revenue and expenses
- Summary of operations
- Statement of operations by product lines
- Statement of cash receipts and disbursements

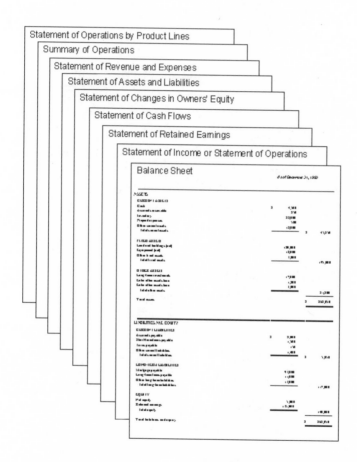

Although not specifically noted in SAS No. 62, financial statements also typically include other financial data presentations, such as:

- Prospective financial information
- Proxy statements
- Interim financial information

- Current value financial representations
- Personal financial statements
- Bankruptcy financial statements
- Registration statement disclosures

Other comprehensive bases of accounting, according to SAS No. 62, include:

- Government or regulatory agency accounting
- Tax basis accounting
- Cash receipts and disbursements, or modified cash receipts and disbursements
- Any other basis with a definite set of criteria applied to all material items such as the price-level basis of accounting

Consequently, the term financial statement includes almost any financial data presentation prepared according to generally accepted accounting principles or in accord with another comprehensive basis of accounting. Throughout this section, the term financial statements will include the above forms of reporting financial data, including the accompanying footnotes and management's discussion. Financial statements are the vehicles through which fraud occurs.

Effect of Fraud on Financial Statements

Fraud in financial statements takes the form of:

Overstated Assets or Revenue	Understated Liabilities or Expenses

Overstated assets and revenues falsely reflect a financially stronger company by inclusion of fictitious asset costs or artificial revenues. Understated liabilities and expenses are shown through exclusion of costs or financial obligations. Both methods result in increased equity and net worth for the company.

Statistics

Fraudulent Statement schemes accounted for 4.01% of the overall cases. Misstatements due to Financial Statement schemes totaled $2,112,756,500.00, which was 58.27% of the total losses and misstatements uncovered by our study. Non-financial misstatements accounted for 6.56% or $237,764,400.00 in total. Median misstatement for Financial Statement and Non-Financial Statement schemes were approximately $5 million and $3 million, respectively.

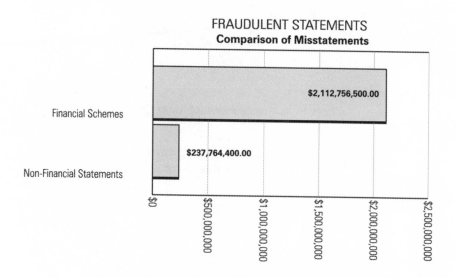

Chart 13-1: Comparison of Total Misstatements

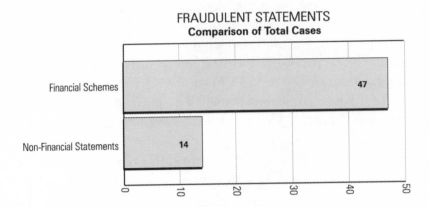

Chart 13-2: Comparison of Total Cases

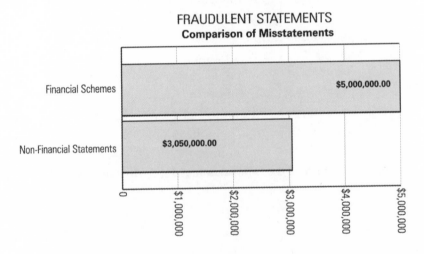

Chart 13-3: Comparison of Median Misstatements

[1] Jay Robert Nash, *Hustlers & Con Men* (New York: Lippincott, 1976).

[2] Nash.

[3] Nash.

[4] W. Steve Albrecht, Gerald W. Wernz and Timothy L. Williams, *Fraud: Bringing Light to the Dark Side of Business* (Burr Ridge, IL: Irwin Professional Publishing, 1995).

[5] Albrecht, et.al.

[6] Albrecht, et.al.

[7] Dale L. Flesher, Paul J. Miranti and Gary John Previts, "The First Century of the CPA," *Journal of Accountancy*, October 1996.

[8] Norman C. Miller, *The Great Salad Oil Swindle* (Baltimore: Penguin Books, 1965).

[9] Miller.

[10] Miller.

[11] Miller.

[12] Miller.

[13] Raymond L. Dirks and Leonard Gross, *The Great Wall Street Scandal* (New York: McGraw-Hill Book Company, 1974).

[14] Lee. J. Seidler, Fredrick Andrews, and Marc J. Epstein, *The Equity Funding Papers* (New York: John Wiley & Sons, 1997).

[15] Associated Press, "*Software Executive Pleads Guilty to Stock Fraud.*" *USA Today*, January 31, 1997.

[16] Associated Press.

[17] Steven A. Finkler, *Finance and Accounting for Nonfinancial Managers* (Prentice-Hall, Englewood Cliffs, N.J. 1996), p32-34.

[18] Finkler, p34.

[19] Finkler, pp45-51.

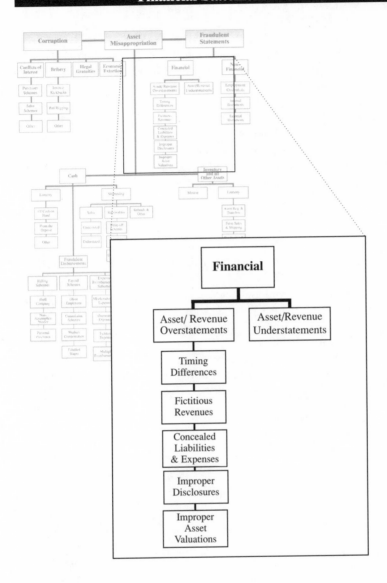

14. FRAUDULENT FINANCIAL STATEMENT SCHEMES

*****

Case Study: That Way Lies Madness

Several names may have been changed to preserve anonymity

"I'm Crazy Eddie!" a goggle-eyed man screams from the television set, pulling at his face with his hands. "My prices are IN-SANE!" Eddie Antar got into the electronics business in 1969, with a modest store called Sight and Sound. Less than 20 years later, he had become Crazy Eddie, a millionaire many times over and an international fugitive from justice. He was shrewd, daring, and self-serving; he was obsessive and greedy. But he was hardly IN-SANE. A U.S. Attorney said, "He was not Crazy Eddie. He was Crooked Eddie."

The man on the screen wasn't Eddie at all. The face so dutifully watched throughout New Jersey, New York, and Connecticut — that was an actor, hired to do a humiliating but effective impersonation. The real Eddie Antar was not the kind of man to yell and rend his clothes. He was busy making money. However, he was making a lot of it illegally. By the time his electronics empire folded, Antar and members of his family had distinguished themselves with a fraud of massive proportions, reaping more than $120 million. A senior official at the Securities and Exchange Commission (SEC) quipped, "This may not be the biggest stock fraud of all time, but for outrageousness it is going to be very hard to beat." The SEC was joined by the FBI, the Postal Inspection Office and the U.S. Attorney in tracking Eddie down. They were able to show a multipronged attack. They claimed that Antar:

1. listed smuggled money from foreign banks as sales;
2. made false entries to Accounts Payable;

3. overstated Crazy Eddie, Inc.'s inventory by breaking into and altering audit records;

4. took credit for merchandise as "returned," while also counting it as inventory;

5. "shared inventory" from one store to boost other stores' audit count;

6. arranged for vendors to ship merchandise and defer the billing, besides claiming discounts and advertising credits; and

7. sold large lots of merchandise to wholesalers, then spread the money to individual stores as retail receipts.

It was a long list and a profitable one for Eddie Antar and the inner circle of his family. The seven action items were designed to make Crazy Eddie's look like it was booming. In fact, it was. It was the single biggest retailer of stereos and televisions in the New York metropolitan area, with a dominant and seemingly impregnable share of the market. That wasn't enough for Eddie. He took the chain public, and then made some real money. Shares that initially sold at $8 each would later peak at $80, thanks to the Antar team's masterful tweaking of company accounts.

Inflating Crazy Eddie's stock price wasn't the first scam that Antar had pulled. In the early days, as Sight and Sound grew into Crazy Eddie's and spawned multiple stores, Eddie was actually underreporting his earnings. Eddie's cousin, Sam Antar, remembered learning how the company did business by watching his father during the early days. "The store managers would drop off cash to the house after they closed at ten o'clock, and my father would make one bundle for deposit into the company account, and several bundles for others in the family," Sam Antar said. "Then he would drive over to their houses and drop off their bundles at two in the morning." For every few dollars to the company, the Antars took a dollar for themselves. The cash was secreted away into bank accounts at Bank Leumi of Israel. Eddie smuggled some of the money out of the country himself, by strapping stacks of large bills across his body. The Antars sneaked away with at least $7 million over several years. Skimming the cash meant tax-free profits and one gargantuan nest egg waiting across the sea.

But entering the stock market was another story. Eddie anticipated the initial public offering (IPO) of shares by quietly easing money from the Bank of Leumi back into the operation. The company really was growing. Shipping in the pilfered funds as sales receipts made the growth look even more impressive. Now this looks sweet: skim the money and beat the tax man, then draw out funds as you need them to boost sales figures. Keeps the ship running smooth and sunny.

But Paul Hayes, a special agent who worked the case with the FBI, pointed out Crazy Eddie's problem. "After building up the books, they set a pattern of double-digit growth, which they had to sustain. When they couldn't sustain it, they started looking for new ways to fake it," Hayes said.

Eddie, his brothers, his cousins, and several family loyalists all owned large chunks of company stock. No matter what actually happened at the stores, they wanted that stock to rise. So the seven-point plan was born. There was the skimmed money waiting overseas, being brought back and disguised as sales. But there were limits to how much cash the family had available and could get back into the country. In the most daring part of the expanded scam, Antar's people broke into auditors' records and boosted the numbers. Inventory numbers could also be fudged. So they took the opportunity to pump up the inventories of selected stores and warehouses. With the stroke of a pen, 13 microcassette players became 1,327.

Better than that, the Antars figured out how to make their inventory do double work. Debit memos were drawn up showing substantial lots of stereos or VCRs as "returned to manufacturer." Crazy Eddie's was given a credit for the wholesale cost due back from the manufacturer. But the machines were kept at the warehouse for counting as inventory. In a variation of the inventory scam, at least one wholesaler agreed to ship Crazy Eddie truckloads of merchandise, deferring the billing for a later date. That way Crazy Eddie's had plenty of VOLUME, plus the return credits listed on the account book. And what if auditors got too close and began asking questions? Executives would throw the records away. A "lost" report was a safe report.

Eddie Antar didn't stop at simple bookkeeping and warehouse games; he "shared inventory" among his nearly 40 stores. After auditors had finished counting a warehouse's holdings and gone for the day, workers tossed the merchandise into trucks. The machines were hauled overnight to an early morning load-in at another store. When the auditors arrived at that store, they found a full stockroom waiting to be counted. Again, this ruse carried a double payoff. The audit looked strong because of the inventory items counted multiple times. And the bookkeeping looked good because only one set of invoices was entered as payable to Eddie's creditors. Also, the game could be repeated for as long as the audit route demanded.

Eddie's trump card was the supplier network. He had considerable leverage with area wholesalers because Crazy Eddie's was the biggest and baddest retail outlet in the region. Agent Paul Hayes remembers Eddie as "an aggressive businessman: he'd put the squeeze on a manufacturer and tell them he wasn't going to carry their product. Now, he was king of what is possibly the biggest consolidated retail market in the nation. Japanese manufacturers were fighting each other to get into this market. . . . So when Eddie made a threat, that was a threat with serious potential impact."

Suppliers gave Crazy Eddie's buyers extraordinary discounts and advertising rebates. If they didn't, the Antars had another method: they made the discount up. For example, Crazy Eddie's might owe George-Electronics $1 million; by claiming $500,000 in discounts or ad credits, the bill was cut in half. Sometimes there was a real discount, sometimes there wasn't. (It wasn't easy, after Eddie's fall, to tell what was a shrewd business deal and what was fraud. "They had legitimate discounts in there," says Hayes, "along with the criminal acts. That's why it was tough to know what was smoke and what was fire.")

Eddie had yet another arrangement with manufacturers. For certain high-demand items, high-end stereo systems for example, a producing company would agree to sell only to Crazy Eddie. Eddie placed an order big enough for what he needed, and then added a little more. The excess he sold to a distributor who had already agreed to send the merchandise outside Crazy Eddie's tri-state area. And then the really good part: by arrangement, the distributor paid for the merchandise in a series of small checks — $100,000 worth of portable stereos would be paid off with ten checks of $10,000 each. Eddie sprinkled this money into his stores as register sales. He knew that *comparable store sales* are used as a bedrock indicator by Wall Street analysts. New stores are compared with old stores, and any store open more than a year is compared with its performance during the previous term. The goal is to outperform the previous year. So the $10,000 injections made Eddie's "comps" look fantastic.

As the doctored numbers circulated enthusiastically in financial circles, CRZY stock doubled its Earnings Per Share during its first year on the stock exchange. The stock split two-for-one in both of its first two fiscal terms as a publicly traded company. As chairman and chief executive, Eddie Antar used his newsletter to trumpet soaring profits, declining overhead costs, and a new 210,000-square-foot corporate headquarters. Plans were underway for a home-shopping arm of the business. Besides the electronics stores, there was now a subsidiary, Crazy Eddie Record and Tape Asylums, in the Antar fold. At its peak, the operation included 43 stores and reported sales of $350 million a year. This was a long way from the Sight and Sound storefront operation where it all began.

It was almost eerie how deliberately the Antar conspirators manipulated investors, and how directly their crimes impacted brokers' assessments. At the end of Crazy Eddie's second public year, a major brokerage firm issued a gushing recommendation to "buy." The recommendation was explicitly "based on 35 percent EPS [earnings per share] growth" and "comparable store sales growth in the low double-digit range (emphasis added)." These double-digit expansions were from the "comps" which Eddie and his gang had cooked up with wholesalers' money and by juggling inventories. CRZY stock, the report predicted, would double and then some during the next year. As if following an Antar script, the brokers declared, "Crazy Eddie is the only retailer in our universe that has not reported a disappointing quarter in the last two years. We do not believe that is an accident. . . . We believe Crazy Eddie is becoming the kind of company that can continually produce above-average comparable store sales growth." The brokers could not have known what herculean efforts were needed to yield just that impression. The report praised Eddie's management skills. "Mr. Antar has created a strong organization beneath him that is close-knit and directed. . . . Despite the boisterous (less charitable commentators would say obnoxious) quality of the commercials, Crazy Eddie management is quite conservative."

Well, yes, in a manner of speaking. They were certainly holding tightly to the money as it flowed through the market. According to federal indictments, the conspiracy inflated the company's value during the first year by about $2 million. By selling off shares of the overvalued stock, the partners pocketed over $28.2 million. The next year they illegally boosted income by $5.5 million and retail sales by

$2.2 million. This time the group cashed in their stock for a cool $42.2 million windfall. In the last year before the boom went bust, Eddie and his partners inflated income by $37.5 million and retail by $18 million. They didn't have that much stock left, though, so despite the big blow-up they only cashed in for about $8.3 million.

Maybe he knew the end was at hand, but with takeovers looming, Eddie kept fighting. He had started his business with one store in Brooklyn almost 20 years before, near the neighborhood where he grew up, populated mainly by Jewish immigrants from Syria. Despite these humble beginnings he would one day be called "the Darth Vader of capitalism" by a prosecuting attorney, referring not just to his professional inveigling but to his personal life as well. Eddie's affair with another woman broke up his marriage and precipitated a lifelong break with his father. Eventually he divorced his wife and married his lover. Rumors hinted that Eddie had been unhappy because he had five daughters and no sons from his first marriage. Neighbors said the rest of the family sided with the ex-wife. Eddie and his brothers continued in business together, but they had no contact outside the company. Allen Antar, a few years younger, should have been able to sympathize — he had also been estranged from the family when he filed for a divorce and married a woman who wasn't Jewish. (Though Allen eventually divorced that woman and remarried his first wife.) Later at trial, the brothers Antar were notably cold to one another. Even Eddie's own lawyer called him a "huckster."

But this Darth Vader had a compassionate side. Eddie was known as a quiet man, and modest. He was seldom photographed and almost never granted interviews. He was said to have waited hours at the bedside of a dying cousin, Mort Gindi, whose brother, also named Eddie, was named as a defendant in the Antars' federal trial. He is remembered by his cousin Sam as "a leader, someone I looked up to since I was a kid. Eddie was strong, he worked out with weights; when the Italian kids wanted to come into our neighborhood and beat up on the Jewish kids, Eddie would stop them. That was when we were kids. Later, it turned out different." Eddie had come a long way. He had realized millions of dollars by selling off company stock at inflated prices. This money was stashed in secret accounts around the world, held under various assumed identities. In fact, Eddie had done so well that he was left vulnerable as leader of the retail empire. When Elias Zinn, a Houston businessman, joined with the Oppenheimer-Palmieri Fund and waged a proxy battle for Crazy Eddie's, the Antars had too little shareholders' power to stave off the bid. They lost. For the first time, Crazy Eddie's was out of Eddie's hands.

The new owners didn't have long to celebrate. They discovered that their ship was sinking fast. Stores were alarmingly understocked, shareholders were suing, suppliers were shutting down credit lines because they were paid either late or not at all. An initial review showed the company's inventory had been overstated by $65 million, a number later raised to over $80 million. In a desperate maneuver, the new management set up a computerized inventory system and established lines of credit. They made peace with the vendors and cut 150 jobs to reduce overhead. But it was too late. Less than a year after the takeover, Crazy Eddie's was dead.

Eddie Antar, on the other hand, was very much alive. But nobody knew where. He had disappeared when it became apparent that the takeover was forcing him out. He had set up dummy companies in Liberia, Gibraltar, and Panama, along with well-supplied bank accounts in Israel and Switzerland. Sensing his days as Crazy Eddie were numbered, he fled the United States, traveling the world with faked passports, calling himself, at different times, Harry Page Shalom and David Cohen. Shalom was a real person, a longtime friend of Eddie's, another in a string of chagrined and erstwhile companions.

It was as David Cohen that Eddie ended his flight from justice and reality. After 28 months on the run, he stalked into a police station in Bern, Switzerland, but not to turn himself in. "David Cohen" was demanding help from the police. He was mad because bank officials refused to let him at the $32 million he had on account there. The bank wouldn't tell Cohen anything, just that he couldn't access those funds. But officials discreetly informed police that the money had been frozen by the U.S. Department of Justice. Affidavits in the investigation had targeted the account as an Antar line. It didn't take long to realize that David Cohen, the irate millionaire in the Bern police station, was Eddie Antar. It was the last public part Crazy Eddie would have for a while. He eventually plead guilty to racketeering and conspiracy charges and was sentenced to eighty-two months in prison with credit for time served. This left him with about three and a half years of jail time. And he was ordered to repay $121 million to bilked investors. Almost $72 million had been recovered from Eddie's personal accounts, but he still stands to incur more debts from pending litigation by the SEC. "I don't ask for mercy," Eddie told the judge at his trial. "I ask for balance."

Eddie's brother, Mitchell, was first convicted and given four and a half years, with $3 million in restitution burdens, but his conviction was overturned because of a prejudicial remark by the judge in the first trial. Mitchell later pled guilty to two counts of securities fraud and the rest of the charges were dropped. Allen Antar was acquitted at the first trial, but he and his father, Sam, still face charges from the SEC.

At last reporting, Eddie had a new job and was doing well. So well, that food service administrators at the Otisville, N.Y., prison made a special petition to the court, asking that he be allowed to keep the job. CRAZY!

*****

As seen in the above case study, fraudulent financial statements can be manipulated in a wide variety of ways. Most manipulation can generally be classified in one or more of the following categories:

Fictitious Revenues

Fictitious or fabricated revenues involve the recording of goods or services sales which never occurred. Fictitious sales most often involve fake or phantom customers, but can also involve legitimate customers. For example, an invoice can be prepared for a legitimate customer although the goods are not delivered or the services not rendered. At the beginning of the next accounting period, the sale is often reversed, concealing the fraud. Another method is to utilize legitimate customers and artificially inflate or alter invoices reflecting higher amounts or quantities than actually sold.

Income and revenue recognition is based primarily upon four criteria: definition, measurability, relevance and reliability. First, the item must be definable as revenue. *FASB Concepts Statement 3* defines revenue as "actual or expected cash inflows (or the equivalent) that have occurred or will eventually occur as a result of the

enterprise's ongoing major or central operations during the period."
Revenue must also be reliably measurable. Item relevance to the
company must be established, and finally, the item must be verifi-
able. Recording revenue which does not meet the above described
criteria is not in accordance with generally accepted accounting principles.

Case 1760 details a typical example of fictitious revenue.
Interested in inflating their financial standing, a publicly-traded company engineered sham transactions for more than seven years. The
company's management utilized several shell companies, supposedly making a number of favorable sales. The sales transactions
were fictitious, as were the supposed customers. As the amounts of
the sales grew, so did the suspicions of internal auditors. The sham
transactions included the payment of funds for assets while the same
funds would be returned to the parent company as receipts on sales.
The management scheme went undetected for so long that the
company's books were inflated by more than $80 million. The crime
did not pay; the perpetrators were discovered and prosecuted in both
civil and criminal courts.

An example of a sample entry from this type of case is detailed below. A fictitious entry is made to record a purchase of fixed
assets. This entry debits fixed assets for the amount of the alleged
purchase and the credit is to cash for the payment:

Date	Description	Ref.	Debit	Credit
12/01/97	Fixed Assets	104	350,000	
	Cash	101		350,000

A fictitious sales entry is then made for the same amount as
the false purchase, debiting accounts receivable and crediting the
sales account. To cover the fictitious sale, the cash outflow that supposedly covered the purchase of assets is returned as payment on the
receivable account:

Date	Description	Ref.	Debit	Credit
12/01/97	Accounts Receivable	120	350,000	
	Sales	400		350,000
12/15/97	Cash	101	350,000	
	Accounts Receivable	120		350,000

The result of the completely fabricated sequence of events is an increase in both company assets and yearly revenue.

Pressures that are placed on owners by bankers, stockholders, and even families and community for companies to succeed often provide the motivation to commit fraud The following two examples are instances in which business managers could not resist the temptation to manipulate the numbers. The facts of Case 2303 catalog a real estate investment company which arranged for the sale of shares that it held in a nonrelated company. The sale occurred on the last day of the year and accounted for 45% of the company's income for that year. A 30% down payment was recorded as received as well as a corresponding receivable. With the intent to show a financially healthier company, the details of the sale were made public in an announcement to the press, but the sale of the stock was completely fabricated. To cover the fraud, off-book loans were made in the amount of the supposed deposit. Other supporting documents were also falsified. The $40 million misstatement was ultimately uncovered and the real estate company owner faced criminal prosecution.

In a similar instance, Case 710, a publicly-traded textile company engaged in a series of false transactions designed to improve its financial image. Receipts from the sale of stock were returned to the company in the form of revenues. The fraudulent management team even went so far as to record a bank loan on the company books as revenue. At the time that the scheme was uncovered, the company books were overstated by some $50,000, a material amount to this particular company.

The pressures to commit fraud often come from within a company. Departmental budget requirements including income and profit goals also promote situations in which financial statement fraud is committed. In Case 1664, the accounting manager of a small company misstated financial records to cover its financial shortcomings. In fact, the statements included a series of entries made by the accounting manager designed to meet budget projections and to cover up losses in the pension fund. Influenced by dismal financial performance in recent months, the accountant also consistently overstated period revenues. To cover his scheme, he debited liability accounts and credited the equity account. The perpetrator finally resigned, leaving a letter of confession. He was later prosecuted in criminal court.

Timing Differences

As we mentioned earlier, financial statement fraud may also involve timing differences; that is, the recording of revenue and/or expenses in improper periods.

MATCHING REVENUES WITH EXPENSES

Remember, according to generally accepted accounting principles, revenue and corresponding expenses should be recorded or matched in the same accounting period. Corresponding revenues and expenses recorded in different accounting periods do not meet GAAP's matching principle. For example, a company may accurately record sales which occurred in the month of December but fail to fully record expenses incurred as costs associated with those sales. Those costs are often recorded in later periods. The effect of this error overstates the net income of the company in the period in which the sales were recorded, and also understates net income when the expenses are reported. The following example depicts a sales transaction in which the cost of sales associated with the revenue is not recorded within the same period. A journal entry is made to record the billing of a project which is not complete. Although a contract has been signed for this project, goods and services for this project have not been delivered and the project is not even scheduled to start until January. In order to boost revenues for the current year, the following sales transaction is recorded fraudulently before year end:

Date	Description	Ref.	Debit	Credit
12/31/97	Accounts Receivable	120	17,000	
	Sales - Project C	401		17,000
	To record sale of product and services - Project C			

Fiscal Year End - 97

In January, the project is started and completed. The entries below show accurate recording of the $15,500 of costs associated with the sale:

Date	Description	Ref.	Debit	Credit
01/31/98	Cost of Sales - Project C	702	13,500	
	Inventory	140		13,500
	To record relief of inventory for Project C			
01/31/98	Labor Costs - Project C	550	2,000	
	Cash	101		2,000
	To record payroll expense for Project C			

If recorded correctly, the entries for the recognition of revenue and the costs associated, for example, with the sale entry would be recorded in the accounting period in which they actually occur, January. The effect on the income statement for the company is shown below.

Income Statements	Incorrectly Stated		Correctly Stated	
	Year YY	Year ZZ	Year YY	Year ZZ
Sales Revenue				
Project B	25,000		25,000	
Project C	17,000		17,000	
Project D		26,500		26,500
Total Sales	42,000	26,500	42,000	26,500
Cost of Sales				
Project B	22,500		22,500	
Project C		15,500	**15,500**	
Project D		21,400		21,400
Total Cost of Sales	22,500	36,900	38,000	21,400
Gross Margin	19,500	(10,400)	4,000	5,100
G&A Expenses	2,500	3,000	2,500	3,000
Net Income	17,000	(13,400)	1,500	2,100

This example depicts exactly how nonadherence to GAAP's matching principle can cause material misstatement in yearly income statements. As the income and expenses were stated in error, year YY yielded a net income of $17,000+ while year ZZ produced a loss, ($13,400). Correctly stated, revenues and expenses are matched and recorded together within the same accounting period showing moderate, yet accurate net incomes of $1,500 and $2,100.

EARLY REVENUE RECOGNITION

Generally, revenue should be recognized in the accounting records when a sale is complete, that is, when title is passed from the seller to the buyer. This transfer of ownership completes the sale and is usually not final until all obligations surrounding the sale are complete. Long-term construction contracts, for example, should use the completed contract or percentage of completion methods. The completed contract method does not record revenue until the project is 100% complete. Construction costs are held in an inventory account until completion of the project. The percentage of completion method recognizes revenues and expenses as measurable progress on a project is made. In the case of recognizing revenues for services, revenue is recognized as the services are rendered and the collection of the revenue is reasonably assured.

Case 861 details how early recognition of revenue not only leads to statement misrepresentation but also can serve as a catalyst to further fraud. A retail drugstore chain's management got ahead of themselves in recording income. In a scheme which was used repeatedly, management would enhance their earnings by recording unearned revenue prematurely, resulting in the impression that the drug stores were much more profitable than they actually were. When the situation came to light and was investigated, several embezzlement schemes, false expense report schemes, and instances of credit card fraud were also uncovered. The fraudsters had their day in criminal court and each was convicted.

Naturally, there are different motivations to commit early recognition and they vary according to each situation. In Case 2639, however, profit was the only reason the fraudsters needed to record income before it was actually received. "It takes money to make money" might be a cliché used to describe the scheme in which the president of a not-for-profit organization was able to illicitly squeeze the maximum amount of private donations by cooking the company books. To enable the organization to receive additional funding which was dependent upon the amounts of already-received contributions, the organization's president recorded promised donations before they were actually received. By the time the scheme was discovered by the organization's internal auditor, the fraud had been perpetrated for more than four years.

RECORDING EXPENSES IN WRONG PERIOD

Often due to pressures to meet budget projections and goals, or due to lack of proper accounting controls, the timely recording of expenses is compromised. As the expensing of certain costs are pushed into periods other than the ones in which they actually occur, they are not properly matched against the income that they help produce. Consider Case 1370 in which supplies were purchased and applied to the current year budget, but were actually used in the following accounting period. A manager at a publicly-traded company completed 11 months of operations remarkably under budget when compared to total year estimates. He therefore decided to get a head start on the next year's expenditures. In order to spend all current year budgeted funds allocated to his department, the manager bought $50,000 in unneeded supplies. The supplies expense transactions were recorded against the current year's budget. Staff auditors noticed the huge leap in expenditures, however, and inquired about the situation. The manager came clean, explaining that he was under pressure to meet budget goals for the following year. Because the manager was not attempting to keep the funds for himself, no legal action was taken.

The correct recording of the above transactions would be to debit supplies inventory for the original purchase and subsequently expense the items out of the account as they are used. The example journal entries below detail the correct method of expensing the supplies over time.

Date	Description	Ref.	Debit	Credit
12/31/YY	Supplies Inventory	109	50,000	
	Accounts Payable	201		50,000
	To record the purchase of supplies			
Record in	Supplies Expense	851	2,000	
Period Used	Supplies Inventory	109		2,000
	To record supplies consumed in the current period			

Similar entries should be made monthly, as the supplies are used, until they are consumed and $50,000 in supplies expense is recorded.

*****

CASE STUDY: THE IMPORTANCE OF TIMING

Several names may have been changed to preserve anonymity

What about a scheme in which nobody gets any money? One that was never intended to enrich its players or to defraud the company they worked for? It happened in Huntsville, Alabama, on-site at a major aluminum products plant with over $300 million in yearly sales. A few shrewd men cooked the company's books without taking a single dime for themselves.

Terry Isbell was an internal auditor making a routine review of accounts payable. He was running a computer search to look at any transactions over $50,000 and found among the hits a bill for replacing two furnace liners. The payments went out toward the last of the year, to an approved vendor, with the proper signatures from Steven Leonyrd, a maintenance engineer, and Doggett Stine, the sector's purchasing manager. However, there was nothing else in the file. Maintenance and repair jobs of this sort were supposed to be done on a time-and-material basis. So there should have been work reports, vouchers, and inspection sheets in the file along with the paid invoices. But there was nothing.

Isbell talked with Steven Leonyrd, who showed him the furnaces, recently lined and working to perfection. So where was the paperwork? "It'll be in the regular work file for the first quarter," Leonyrd replied.

"The bill was for last year, November and December," Isbell pointed out. That was because the work was paid for in "advance payments," according to Leonyrd. There wasn't room in the work schedule to have the machines serviced in November, so the work was billed to that year's nonrecurring maintenance budget. Later, sometime after the first of the year, the work was actually done.

Division management okayed Isbell to make an examination. He found $150,000 in repair invoices without proper documentation. The records for materials and supplies which were paid for in one year and received in the next totalled $250,000. A check of later records and an inspection showed that everything paid for had in fact been received, just some days later than promised.

So it was back to visit Leonyrd, who said the whole thing was simple. "We had this money in the budget, for maintenance and repair, supplies outside the usual scope of things. It was getting late in the year, looked like we were just going to lose those dollars, you know, they'd just revert back to the general fund. So we set up the work orders and made them on last year's budget. Then we got the actual stuff later." Who told Leonyrd to set it up that way? "Nobody. Just made sense, that's all."

Nobody, Isbell suspected, was the purchasing manager who handled Leonyrd's group, Doggett Stine. Stine was known as "a domineering type guy" among the people who worked for him, a kind of storeroom bully. Isbell asked him about the arrangement with Leonyrd. "That's no big deal," Stine insisted. "Just spent the money while it was there. That's what it was put there for, to keep up the plant. That's what we did." It wasn't his idea, said Stine, but it wasn't really Leonyrd's either, just a discussion and an informal decision. The storeroom receiving supervisor agreed it was a grand idea, and made out the documents like he was told to do. Accounting personnel processed the invoices like they were told to do. A part-time bookkeeper said to Isbell she remembered some discussion about arranging to spend the money, but she didn't ask any questions.

Isbell was in a funny position, a little bit like Shakespeare's Malvolio, who spends his time in the play Twelfth Night scolding the other characters for having such a good time. Leonyrd hadn't pocketed anything, and neither had Stine; being a bully was hardly a fraudulent offense. There was about $6,000 in interest lost, supposing the money had stayed in company bank accounts, but that wasn't exactly the point. More seriously, this effortless cash-flow diversion represented a kink in the handling and dispersal of funds. Isbell wasn't thinking rules for their own sake or standing on ceremony—money this easy to come by just meant the company had gotten a break. The next guys might not be so civic-minded and selfless; they might start juggling zeros and signatures instead of dates. If Leonyrd and Stine could crush the controls like an empty soda can, other people could too.

Under Isbell's recommendation, the receiving department started reporting directly to the plant's general accounting division, and its supervisor was assigned elsewhere. Doggett Stine had subsequently retired. Steven Leonyrd was demoted and transferred to another sector. Cynically striped students of human nature will not be disappointed by the apparently fruitless nature of this scheme: Leonyrd was fired a year later. He had approached a contractor to replace the roof on his house, with the bill to be charged against "nonrecurring maintenance" at the plant. But the contractor alerted plant officials to their conniving employee, who was also known to be picking up extra money for "consulting work" with plant-related businesses. Rats, Leonyrd must have thought, foiled again.

*****

Concealed Liabilities

As previously discussed, understating liabilities and expenses is one of the ways financial statements can be manipulated to deceitfully make a company appear more profitable. Understating liabilities has a positive effect on the balance sheet, in that the equity or asset accounts will have to increase by the amount understated in order to keep the books in balance. Understating expenses, on the other hand, has the effect of artificially inflating net income. Overstating net income in turn overstates owners' equity. These omissions state financial statements in a fashion that is more attractive to the user.

Concealed liabilities and expenses can be difficult to detect because there frequently is no audit trail. There are three common methods for concealing liabilities and expenses: Liability/Expense Ommisions, Capitalizing Expenses, and Failure to Disclose Warranty Costs and Liabilities.

LIABILITY/EXPENSE OMISSIONS

The preferred and easiest method of concealing liabilities/expenses is to simply fail to record them. These entries may or may not be recorded at a later time, but a possible future recording does not change the fraudulent nature of the current statements.

Just as they are easy to conceal, omitted liabilities are probably one of the most difficult to uncover. A thorough review of all post-financial-statement-date transactions, such as accounts payable increases and decreases, might aid in the discovery of omitted liabilities in financial statements.

Often, perpetrators of liability and expense omissions believe they can conceal their fraud in future periods. They often plan to compensate for their omitted liabilities with visions of other income sources such as profits from future price hikes. In Case 678, an owner/operator of a publicly traded retail outlet falsified financial statements through concealing company liabilities and inflating inventory counts. The owner hoped to create the false picture of company profitability and entice potential investors. He planned to conceal the fraud by increasing his sales price in future periods when the expense would actually be recorded. However, a tip from someone within the organization caused an investigation by the company's audit committee.

CAPITALIZED EXPENSES

Capital expenditures are costs that provide a benefit to a company over more than one accounting period. Manufacturing equipment is an example of this type of expenditure. Revenue expenditures or *expenses*, on the other hand, directly correspond to the generation of current revenue and only provide benefits for the current accounting period. An example of expenses is labor costs for one week of service. These costs correspond directly with revenues billed in the current accounting period. Capitalizing revenue-based expenses is another way to increase income and assets since they are amortized over of period of years rather than expensed immediately. If expenditures are capitalized as assets and not expensed off during the current period, income will be overstated. As the assets are depreciated, income in subsequent periods will be understated. Generally accepted accounting principles are not always clear about rules for capitalizing costs, thus abuses in this category often occur. The examiner should be diligent in determining the appropriateness of the capitalization. If a company capitalizes the payment for a service because it benefited the company for more than one year, is that an improper capitalization? Or is the company trying to manipulate the income by not reflecting the repair as a current-period expense? Are there really 18 months of supplies available? Is the total dollar amount being considered material? These questions should be asked when considering the capitalization policy of the company under examination.

EXPENSING CAPITAL EXPENDITURES

Just as capitalizing expenses is improper, so is expensing costs which should be capitalized. The organization may want to minimize its net income due to tax considerations. Expensing an item that should be depreciated over a period of time would help accomplish just that — net income is lower and so are taxes. Internal budget constraints also pressure accounting personnel into miscoding capital items to expense accounts.

RETURNS AND ALLOWANCES AND WARRANTIES

Improper returns and allowances liability occur when a company fails to accrue the proper expense and offsetting liabilities for potential product returns or repairs. It is inevitable that a certain percentage of products sold will, for one reason or another, be returned. It is the job of management to try to accurately estimate what that percentage will be over time and make provision for it. In warranty liability fraud, the liability is usually either omitted altogether or substantially understated. Another similar area is the liability resulting from defective products (product liability).

Improper Disclosures

As we detailed earlier, accounting principles require that financial statements and notes include all the information necessary to prevent a reasonably discerning user of the financial statements from being misled. These notes should include narrative disclosure notes, supporting schedules, and any other information required to avoid misleading potential investors, creditors, or any other users of the financial statements.

Management has an obligation to disclose all significant information through a viable medium. If not disclosed in the financial statements, disclosure should appear in the footnotes or management's discussion and analysis. In addition, the disclosed information cannot be misleading. An independent accountant need not disclose ordinary business information, unless that information shows a previous report to have been misleading or incorrect when it was issued. Improper disclosures usually include one of the following inadequacies: Liability Omissions, Significant Events, Management Fraud, Related Party Transactions, and Accounting Changes.

LIABILITY OMISSIONS

Typical omissions include the failure to disclose loan covenants or contingent liabilities. Loan covenants are agreements, in addition to a financing arrangements, which a borrower has promised to keep as long as the financing is in place. The agreements can contain various types of convenants including certain financial ratio limits and restrictions on other major financing arrangements. Contingent liabilities are obligations a firm may be required to honor in certain cases. A pending lawsuit is a representative example of a contingent liability. The company's potential liability, if material, must be discussed.

SIGNIFICANT EVENTS

Examples of significant events might include new products or technology having an impact on sales. Also, obsolescence of merchandise or manufacturing methods should be disclosed. Lawsuits whose outcomes are unknown and any other significant event that, if not disclosed, would mislead the reader when considering the available information should be discussed. In addition, major purchases should be disclosed.

MANAGEMENT FRAUD

Management has an obligation to disclose to the shareholders significant fraud committed by officers, executives, and others in positions of trust. According to the court in *Roeder v. Alpha Industries, Inc., 814 F.2d 22,* (1 Cir. 1987), management does not have the responsibility of disclosing uncharged criminal conduct of its officers and executives. However, if and when officers, executives, or other persons in trusted positions become subjects of a criminal indictment, disclosure is required. In *Roeder*, the officers of the company bribed a defense contractor employee to obtain a subcontract. Only when it was learned that its officers were about to be indicted did the company release that information to the public. The court held that no liability can be imposed if there is no duty to disclose. The mere possession of nonpublic information also does not impose a duty to disclose; there must also be misrepresentation or misleading information as a result of the nonpublic information. See *Backman v. Polaroid Corporation, 910 F. 2d 10* (1st Cir. 1990.)

RELATED-PARTY TRANSACTIONS

Related-party transactions occur when a company official has an undisclosed financial interest in a transaction that causes economic harm to the company. The financial interest which a company official might have may not be readily apparent. For example, common directors of two companies which do business with each other, any corporate general partner and the partnerships with which it does business, and any controlling shareholder of the corporation with which he/she/it does business are all illustrations of related parties. Family relationships can also be considered related parties, such as all lineal descendants and ancestors, without regard to financial interests. Related-party transactions are sometimes referred to as "self-dealing."

The inadequate disclosure of related-party transactions is among the most serious of financial statement frauds. While these transactions are not always non-arm's-length in nature, they often are. Inadequate disclosure of related-party transactions is not limited to any specific industry; it transcends all business types and relationships.

In Case 737, the chairman of the board of trustees of a state employee retirement system failed to disclose that he was also on the board of directors of a savings and loan in which the state retirement system was going to invest over $65 million in debenture bonds. Shortly after the investment, the S&L was seized by federal regulators and the investment was lost. The trustee was convicted in criminal court and had a pending civil action against him.

ACCOUNTING CHANGES

It is important that any major changes to a company's accounting policies and procedures be disclosed in its financial state-

ments. The importance lies in the user's comparison from one period to the next. These changes may cause drastic differences in the
way that statements are presented. Accounting Principles Board
(APB) Opinion No. 20 describes three accounting changes. Changes
in estimates such as depreciation of useful life estimates, bad debt
expense, certain amortization estimates, warranty liability, and earned
revenue estimates must be disclosed. Changes in accounting principle such as depreciation methods, construction reporting, capitalization methods, and changes in certain tax methods are very important to the statement user. Thirdly, changes in the accounting entity
occur and should be reported when the composition of the company
changes from the prior period. Examples of this include mergers
and acquisitions, and selling of company subsidiaries. For these types
of changes, financial statements should be retroactively restated.

Improper Asset Valuation

The cost principle of generally accepted accounting principles,
remember, requires that assets be recorded at their original cost. Some
assets are reported at the lower of cost or market value, but asset
values are not *increased* to reflect current market value. Even so, it
is sometimes necessary to use estimates in accounting with the hope
that it is near the true value. For example, estimates are used in
determining warranty costs, salvage value, and the useful life of a
depreciated asset. Whenever estimates are used, there is an additional opportunity for fraud.

Many schemes are used to inflate the current ratio at the expense of long-term assets. The net effect is seen in the current ratio.
The misclassification of long-term assets as current assets can be of
critical concern to lending institutions that often require the maintenance of certain ratios. This is of particular consequence when the
loan covenants are on unsecured or undersecured lines of credit and
other short-term borrowings. Sometimes these misclassifications are
referred to as "window dressing."

Most improper asset valuations involve the fraudulent overstatement of inventory or receivables. Other improper asset valuations are purchase-versus-pooling accounting methods,
misclassification of fixed and other assets, or improper capitalization of inventory or start-up costs. Improper asset valuations usually
take the form of one of the following classifications: Inventory Valuation, Business Combinations, Accounts Receivable, and Fixed Assets.

INVENTORY VALUATION

Since inventory must be valued at the acquisition cost except when the value is determined to be below current market value, obsolete inventory should be written down to its current value, or written off altogether if it has no value. Failing to write down inventory results in overstated assets and the mismatching of cost of goods sold with revenues. Inventory can also be improperly stated through the manipulation of inventory count, failure to relieve inventory for costs of goods sold, and by other methods. Case 2481 reveals an inventory valuation scheme in which the fraud was committed through tampering of the inventory count. During a routine audit of a publicly traded medical supply company, the audit team found a misstatement of the inventory value that could hardly be classified as routine. The client's inventory was measured in metric volumes, and apparently as the count was taken, the decimal unit was arbitrarily moved by an employee. This resulted in the inventory being grossly overstated. The discovery forced the company to restate its financial statements, resulting in a write-down of the inventory amount by more than $1.5 million.

One of the most popular methods of overstating inventory is through fictitious (phantom) inventory. The case studies summarized below detail two instances in which fictitious inventory fraud was committed. In Case 1696, the president and general manager of a small closely held company shared ownership with three other investors; the president was the only one who actively participated in the management of the business. Over a period of years, he consistently made adjustments to falsely increase inventory and decrease cost of goods sold. When independent auditors discovered the fraud, the president admitted that he did not gain directly from the adjustments. Instead, he had conducted the fraud to create a facade of success for the other owners, his family, and the community.

Most perpetrators of inventory fraud aren't as altruistic. Increasing profit, of course, is the most common reason for tampering with inventory. This was revealed in Case 1666. During a systems control review at a large cannery and product wholesaler in the Southwest, a Certified Fraud Examiner observed a forklift driver constructing a large facade of finished product in a remote location of the warehouse. The inventory was cordoned off and a sign indicated it was earmarked for a national food processor. The cannery was supposedly warehousing the inventory until requested by the customer. When the CFE investigated, he discovered that the inventory held for the food processor was later resold to a national fast-food supplier.

A review of the accounts receivable aging report indicated sales of approximately $1.2 million to this particular customer in prior months. And the aging also showed that cash receipts had been applied against those receivables. An analysis of ending inventory above failed to reveal any improprieties because the relief of inventory had been properly recorded with cost of sales. Copies of all sales documents to this particular customer were then requested. The product was repeatedly sold FOB shipping point and title had passed. But bills of lading indicated that only $200,000 of inventory had been shipped to the original purchaser. There should have been a million dollars of finished product on hand for the food processor. However, there was nothing behind the facade of finished products. An additional comparison of bin numbers on the bill of lading with the sales documents revealed that the same product had been sold twice.

The corporate controller was notified and the plant manager questioned. He explained the "he was doing as he was told." The vice president of marketing and the vice president of operations both knew of the situation but felt there was "no impropriety." The CFO and president of the company felt differently and fired the vice presidents. The company eventually was forced into bankruptcy.

ACCOUNTS RECEIVABLE

Accounts receivable are subject to manipulation in the same manner as sales and inventory, and in many cases, the schemes are conducted together. The two most common schemes involving accounts receivable are fictitious receivables and failure to write down accounts receivable as bad debts (or failure to establish adequate reserves for the future collectability problems).

Fictitious receivables have been discussed in detail earlier. In Case 2647, the manager of a publicly traded company kept two versions of his accounts receivable ledger. One set accurately showed the aging of the accounts. The other set was manipulated to show a more favorable picture, since his compensation was based thereon. Late accounts were redated and debts that were written off were coded to inappropriate accounts. After detection by his company, the manager was demoted.

Accounts receivable should be held at net realizable value; that is, the amount of the receivable less amounts expected not to be collected.

BUSINESS COMBINATIONS

The accounting treatment for business combinations can be extremely complex. In general, the purchase method is used when cash or other assets are distributed as a result of the combination, or if liabilities are incurred as a means of financing the purchase. On the other hand, if only voting common stock is issued to affect the business combination, the pooling-of-interest method is generally favored. The use of both methods in the same transaction is usually prohibited. More than anything, the auditor or fraud examiner should look to the nature of the transaction to see if the primary purpose is to overstate assets or income. The Accounting Principles Board Opinion No. 16, "Business Combinations," provides further information.

FIXED ASSETS

Bogus fixed assets can be created by a variety of methods. They are subject to manipulation through several different schemes. Some of the more common schemes are: Booking Fictitious Assets, Misrepresenting Asset Valuation, and Improperly Capitalizing Inventory and Start-up Costs

Booking of Fictitious Assets

One of the easiest methods of asset misrepresentation is in the recording of fictitious assets. This false creation of assets affects account totals on a company's balance sheet. The corresponding offset account commonly and effectively used is the owners' equity account. Because company assets are often physically found in many different locations, this fraud can sometimes be easily overlooked. One of the most common fictitious asset schemes is to simply create fictitious documents. In other instances, the equipment is leased, not owned, and the fact is not disclosed during the audit of fixed assets. Case 376 reveals instances in which companies created fictitious and overstated assets to cover the truth — their financial ship was sinking. In this situation, a real estate development and mortgage financing company produced fraudulent statements which included fictitious and inflated asset amounts and illegitimate receivables. The company also recorded expenses which actually were for personal, instead of business, use. To cover the fraud, the company raised cash through various illegal securities offerings, guaranteeing over $110 million with real estate projects. They subsequently defaulted. The company declared bankruptcy shortly before the owner passed away.

Case 1664 details additional abuses of fixed asset misrepresentation. The owner of the publicly traded retail outlet wanted his company to appear vibrant and profitable. The only problem was that the company was nowhere close to attaining the owner's lofty goals, so he simply lied. The fraudster misstated financial statements by recording fictitious assets and concealing his company's numerous liabilities. The owner hoped to conceal the fraud long enough to cover his debts by increasing the prices of store items. A tip from someone within the organization caused an investigation by the company's audit committee. The owner was nabbed and prosecuted for significant financial misrepresentation.

Misrepresenting Asset Value

As with other assets, fixed assets should be recorded according to generally accepted accounting principles' cost principle. Estimated values of assets are not to be used in the initial recording. Although assets may appreciate in value, this increase in value should not be recognized on company financial statements. Misrepresentation of asset values frequently goes hand in hand with other schemes. In Case 1749, the partial owner and operator of a $100 million leasing company sold his stock shares of the company and took steps to ensure his financial well-being. First, the owner stipulated that he remain the manager of all company operations, to which the purchasing company agreed. Prior to acquisition, the former owner misrepresented the financial statements of his company by making journal entries to overstate company assets. Then, as an employee of the new company, the former owner perpetrated a cash-skimming scheme by diverting a percentage of company sales to his own personal account and understating sales on the financial statements. The manager's scheme was finally revealed through a tip from one of his employees. He was prosecuted in both civil and criminal courts.

Often, it takes more than one person to pull off a fraud scheme. A powerful figure in a company can pressure his subordinates to perpetrate fraud. In Case 1338, a well-respected, 55-year-old chairman of the board and president of a banking corporation used his considerable influence for his own good. The president powered his employees into committing and concealing several financial statement frauds, misrepresenting over $30 million. The financial statements of the bank included inflated fixed assets and marketable securities, as well as fraudulent purchases of services, supplies, and expenses on travel. Bank deposits were also used for the president's personal benefit. A federal bank examiner detected the fraud and the banker was prosecuted and convicted in civil and criminal proceedings.

Understating Assets

In rare cases, as with some government related or regulated companies, it is advantageous to understate assets. Additional funding is often based on asset amounts. This understatement can be done directly or through accelerated depreciation as in Case 507. The management of the company falsified their financial statements by manipulating the depreciation of the fixed assets. The depreciation reserve was accelerated by the amount of $2.9 million over a six-month period. The purpose of the scheme was to avoid cash contributions to a central government capital asset acquisition account.

Capitalizing Nonasset Cost

Excluded from asset "costs" are interest and finance charges incurred in the purchase. For example, as a company finances a capital equipment purchase, monthly payments include both principal liability reduction and interest payments. On initial purchase, only the original cost of the asset should be capitalized. The subsequent interest payments should be charged against interest expense and not as an increase to the asset. Without reason for intensive review, fraud of this type can go unchecked. In Case 921, a new investor in a closely held corporation sued for rescission of purchase of stock, alleging that the company compiled financial information which misrepresented the financial history of the business. A fraud examination uncovered assets which were overvalued due to capitalization of interest expenses and other finance charges. Also discovered was the fact that one of the owners was understating revenue by $150,000 and embezzling the funds. The parties subsequently settled out of court.

Misclassifying Assets

In order to meet budget requirements, and for various other reasons, assets are sometimes misclassified into general ledger accounts in which they don't belong, as we have seen in previous case examples. The manipulation of entries to accounts in which assets are falsely and incorrectly coded can be beneficial by skewing financial ratios and helping meet borrowing requirements. In another situation, Case 2106 is an example of an employee who purposefully miscoded inventory assets to hide deficiency of his purchasing ability. A purchasing employee at a retail jewelry firm feared being called to the carpet on some bad jewelry purchases. Instead of taking the blame for bad margins on many items, the employee arbitrarily redistributed costs of shipments to individual inventory accounts. The cover-up did not take, as the company's CFO detected the fraud after he initiated changes to control procedures. When the CFO created a separation of duties between the buying function and the costing activities, the dishonest employee was discovered and terminated.

Detection of Fraudulent Financial Satement Schemes

SAS No. 82, Consideration of Fraud in a Financial Statement Audit

While considering today's business environment, with ever-changing technology and the increasing number of business organizations, employees, and federal regulations, the Accounting Standards Board chose to view fraudulent financial reporting as a separate issue. The Board considered it important enough to develop a standard that concentrates solely on material misstatements arising from fraud.

The Treadway Commission

The National Commission on Fraudulent Financial Reporting was formed in 1987 to better define the responsibilities of the auditor in detecting and preventing fraud. The professional auditing organizations — the American Institute of CPAs, the Institute of Internal Auditors and the National Association of Accountants, among others — established the Commission to underwrite a study and make recommendations. The Commission, commonly called the Treadway Commission after its chairman, defined fraudulent financial reporting as follows:

> *"Intentional or reckless conduct, whether [by] act or omission, that results in materially misleading financial statements."*[1]

According to Treadway, the cause of fraudulent financial reporting is the combination of situational pressures on either the company or the manager and the opportunity to commit the fraud without the perception of being detected. These pressures defined by the Treadway Commission are known as "red flags." That is to say, if red flags (situational pressures and opportunity) are present, then the risk of financial reporting fraud increases significantly.

Prior SAS Treatment of Fraud

Previous standards regarding fraudulent misstatement stopped short, only charging auditors to exercise professional skepticism in SAS No. 53. This standard did not define fraud, rather used the terms "errors and irregularities." The primary difference between errors and irregularities is intent. An unintentional misstatement or omission of amounts or disclosures in financial statements is an error. An irregularity, however, is the intentional misstatement or omission. SAS No. 53 stated that auditors were not responsible for finding intentional misstatements concealed by collusion.

SAS No. 54 details an auditor's responsibility regarding discovery of illegal acts. It does call for an auditor to perform audit procedures regarding illegal acts, but not until specific information comes to the auditor's attention indicating that these acts may have a material indirect effect on financial statements.

SAS No. 61 guides auditors when reporting to the audit committee. The new SAS calls for specific communication for fraudulent activity.

A New SAS on Fraud

The new standard, SAS No. 82, supersedes SAS No. 53 and expands the operational guidance given on considering the possibility of fraud in conducting a financial statement audit. It also clarifies an auditor's responsibility for detecting material misstatement of financial statements. The new standard specifically states that an auditor "has a responsibility to plan and perform the audit to obtain reasonable assurance about whether the financial statements are free of material misstatement, whether caused by error or fraud." In addition, the changes provide added guidance on the standard of due professional care in the performance of work, including the need to exercise professional skepticism and the concept of reasonable assurance.

The New SAS consists of the following sections:

*   Description of the characteristics of fraud as well as the difference between Fraudulent Financial Reporting and Misappropriation of Assets
*   Guidance for the consideration, assessment, and response to fraud risk factors
*   Requirements for documentation and communication of fraud considerations to management, the audit committee, and others

Fraudulent Misstatement Defined

SAS No. 82 contains multiple paragraphs describing the characteristics of fraud. The first point made is the fundamental difference between fraudulent financial reporting and the misappropriation of assets. The statement indicates that fraud frequently involves a pressure or incentive to commit fraud and a perceived opportunity to do so. In general, fraudulent reporting occurs through intentional fraudulent omissions or inclusions in the financial statements. Asset misappropriation involves the theft or misuse of company assets. The table below summarizes the distinction between the two.

Characteristic	Fraudulent Financial Reporting	Misappropriation of Assets
Definition	Intentional misstatements or omissions of amounts or disclosures in financial statements to deceive financial statement users.	Theft of an entity's assets.
Perpetrator	Usually perpetrated by management.	Usually perpetrated by employees; may be perpetrated by management.
Who is harmed	Third-party users of the financial statements.	The entity.
Who benefits	The entity: perhaps the perpetrator, though indirectly and usually at some future point in time.	The perpetrator – directly and immediately.
Relevance of internal controls	Ineffective controls may indicate an inappropriate attitude regarding controls of the financial reporting process. Improper attitude may indicate a willingness to commit fraudulent financial reporting (indirect relationship between controls and the risk of fraud).	Ineffective controls provide an opportunity for misappropriation of assets (direct relationship between controls and the risk of fraud).
Likelihood of fraud being material to financial statements	By definition, fraudulent financial reporting is meant to deceive third-party users. Therefore, it is almost always material; otherwise it wouldn't have its desired effect.	May or may not be material to the financial statements.

Assessment of Fraud Risk

In addition, SAS No. 82 gives operational guidance for auditors to meet their responsibilities to material misstatements due to fraud. First, auditors are instructed to consider the presence of fraud risk factors. The statement divides the types of risk into three categories: (1) management's characteristics and influence over the control environment, (2) industry conditions, and (3) operating characteristics and financial stability. Specific examples of each type of risk are detailed in the table below.

Risk Factors Relating to Management's Characteristics and Influence	Risk Factors Relating to Industry Conditions	Risk Factors Relating to Operational Characteristics and Financial Stability
Performance related compensation plans	New accounting or statutory regulations	Cash flow problems while also reporting earnings or growth in earnings
Management's desire to keep stock price high	High degree of market competition with declining margins	Pressure or need to obtain additional capital financing
Need for credit and financing	Declining industry	Assets, liabilities, revenues or expenses bases largely on estimates
Management's desire to reduce tax liability	Industry is rapidly changing, such as technology	Significant related party transactions not in ordinary course of business
Corporate values or ethics not effectively communicated		Significant, unusual, or highly complex transactions
Domination of one person or group of persons in management		Significant bank accounts or subsidiary branch in tax-haven jurisdictions
Lack of control monitoring		Overly complex operational structure or unusual legal entities
Ineffective accounting, information technology, or internal auditing staff		Difficulty in determining individual(s) who control(s) the entity
Non-financial management's excessive involvement in accounting and finance activities		Especially high vulnerability to changes in interest rates
High turnover of management		Unusually high dependence on debt or marginal ability to meet payment requirements
Strained relations between management and employees		Unrealistically aggressive sales or profitability incentive programs
History of fraudulent behavior		Threat of imminent bankruptcy
		Poor, deteriorating financial position when management has personally guaranteed significant debts of entity

The total risk associated with these factors should be formulated and considered. This risk should be assessed separately from other risk assessments, although an assessment may also be performed in conjunction with other audit risks.

Documentation of Fraud Risk

After the risk is assessed, an appropriate audit response should be developed. In the case of relevant levels of risk associated with fraudulent misstatement, changes in typical audit procedures should be adapted. Typical changes include detailed inquiries in the area of possible fraud including revenue recognition, inventory quantities, cash accessibility, or estimates and adjusting entries.

"In planning the audit, the auditor should document in the working papers evidence of the performance of the assessment of the risk of material misstatement due to fraud. Where risk factors are identified as being present, the documentation should include (a) those risk factors identified and (b) the auditor's response to those risk factors, individually or in combination."

Communicating Fraud to Management

SAS No. 82 provides instruction on the communication of fraud to company management. The statement requires that an auditor communicate to an appropriate level of management when there is "evidence that a fraud may exist." This paragraph establishes a threshold of evidence of fraud, regardless of level or relevance of the fraud. The presence of a fraud risk factor does not usually meet this threshold. This obligation to disclose fraud is, in most cases, only to the client's management. In rare occurrences an auditor will be obliged to convey the finding to outside sources. These instances include (1) to comply with certain legal and legislative requirements, (2) when inquired upon by a successor auditor, (3) in response to a subpoena, and (4) to particular government entities for firms who receive funding.

The figure below details the processes discussed in SAS No. 82.

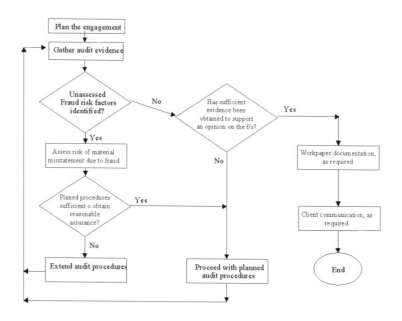

SAS No. 82 Benefit

Overall, SAS No. 82 may provide two major benefits. The first would be to enlighten auditors and fraud examiners as well as company management to the fraudulent statement risk assessment process. Secondly, the procedures and requirements outlined in the statement would, if performed properly, allow examiners and auditors to take an even closer, more explicit look at fraud possibilities while conducting an audit. The result will be specific inquiries into fraudulent misstatement improving an auditor's standard of due professional care as the use of professional skepticism is required.[2]

FINANCIAL STATEMENT ANALYSIS

Comparative financial statements provide information for current and past accounting periods. Accounts expressed in whole dollar amounts yield a limited amount of information. The conversion of these numbers into ratios or percentages allows the reader of the statements to analyze them based on their relationship to each other, as well as to major changes in historical totals. In fraud detection and investigation, the determination of the reasons for relationships and changes in amounts can be important. These determinations are the red flags which point an examiner in the direction of possible fraud. If large enough, a fraudulent misstatement will affect the financial statements in such a way that relationships between the numbers become questionable. Many schemes are detected because the financial statements, when analyzed closely, do not make sense. Financial statement analysis includes the following:

Vertical Analysis	Horizontal Analysis	Ratio Analysis

Percentage Analysis - Horizontal and Vertical

There are traditionally two methods of percentage analysis of financial statements. *Vertical analysis* is a technique for analyzing the relationships between the items on an income statement, balance sheet, or statement of cash flows by expressing components as percentages. This method is often referred to as "common sizing" financial statements. In the vertical analysis of an income statement, net sales is assigned 100%; for a balance sheet, total assets is assigned 100% on the asset side; and total liabilities and equity is expressed as 100%. All other items in each of the sections are expressed as a percentage of these numbers.

Horizontal analysis is a technique for analyzing the percentage change in individual financial statement items from one year to the next. The first period in the analysis is considered the base, and the changes to subsequent periods are computed as a percentage of the base period. Like vertical analysis, this technique will not work for small, immaterial frauds.

The following is an example of financial statements which are analyzed by both horizontal and vertical analysis:

BALANCE SHEET	Vertical Analysis				Horizontal Analysis	
	Year One		Year Two		Change	%Change
Assets						
Current Assets						
Cash	45,000	14%	15,000	4%	(30,000)	-67%
Accts Receivable	150,000	45%	200,000	47%	50,000	33%
Inventory	75,000	23%	150,000	35%	75,000	100%
Fixed Assets (net)	60,000	18%	60,000	14%	-	0%
Total	330,000	100%	425,000	100%	95,000	29%
Acc'ts Payable	95,000	29%	215,000	51%	120,000	126%
Long-term Debt	60,000	18%	60,000	14%	-	0%
Stockholder's Equity					-	
Common Stock	25,000	8%	25,000	6%	-	0%
Paid-in Capital	75,000	23%	75,000	18%	-	0%
Retained Earnings	75,000	23%	50,000	12%	(25,000)	-33%
Total	330,000	100%	425,000	100%	95,000	29%

INCOME STATEMENT	Vertical Analysis				Horizontal Analysis	
	Year One		Year Two		Change	%Change
Net Sales	250,000	100%	450,000	100%	200,000	80%
Cost of Goods Sold	125,000	50%	300,000	67%	175,000	140%
Gross Margin	125,000	50%	150,000	33%	25,000	20%
Operating Expenses						
Selling Expenses	50,000	20%	75,000	17%	25,000	50%
Administrative Expenses	60,000	24%	100,000	22%	40,000	67%
Net Income	15,000	6%	(25,000)	-6%	(40,000)	-267%

Additional Information		
Average Net Receivables	155,000	210,000
Average Inventory	65,000	130,000
Average Assets	330,000	425,000

Vertical Analysis Discussion

Vertical analysis is the expression of the relationship or percentage of component part items to a specific base item. In the above example, vertical analysis of the income statement includes total sales as the base amount, and all other items are then analyzed as a percentage of that total. Vertical analysis emphasizes the relationship of statement items within each accounting period. These relationships can be used with historical averages to determine statement anomalies.

In the above example, we can observe that accounts payable is 29% of total liabilities. Historically we may find that this account averages slightly over 25%. In year two, accounts payable total rose to 51%. Although the change in the account total may be explainable through a correlation with a rise in sales, this significant rise might be a starting point in a fraud examination. Source documents should be examined to determine the rise in this percentage. With this type of examination, fraudulent activity may be detected. The same type of change can be seen as selling expenses decline as a part of sales in year two from 20 to 17%. Again, this change may be explainable with higher volume sales or another bona fide explanation. But close examination may possibly point a fraud examiner to uncover fictitious sales since there was not a corresponding increase in selling expenses.

Horizontal Analysis Discussion

Horizontal statement analysis uses percentage comparison from one accounting period to the next. The percentage change is calculated by dividing the amount of increase or decrease for each item by the base period amount. The resulting percentages are then studied in detail. It is important to consider the amount of change as well as the percentage in horizontal comparisons. A 5% change in an account with a very large dollar amount may actually be much more of a change than a 50% change in an account with much less activity.

In the above example, it is very obvious that the 80% increase in sales has a much greater corresponding increase in cost of goods sold, which rose 140%. These accounts are often used to hide fraudulent expenses, withdrawals or other illegal transactions.

Financial Ratios in Detail

Ratio analysis is a means of measuring the relationship between two different financial statement amounts. The relationship and comparison are the keys to the analysis. This method is used by many professionals including bankers, investors, and business owners, as well as major investment firms. Ratio analysis allows for internal evaluations using financial statement data. Traditionally, financial statement ratios are used in comparisons to an entity's industry average. They can be very useful in detecting red flags for a fraud examination. As the financial ratios present a significant change from one year to the next, or over a period of years, it becomes obvious that there may a problem. As in all other analysis, specific changes are often explained by changes in the business operations. As a change in specific ratios is detected, the appropriate source accounts should be researched and examined in detail to determine if fraud has occurred. For instance, a significant decrease in a company's Current Ratio may point to an increase in current liabilities or a reduction in assets, both of which could be used to cover fraud.

In the analysis of financial statements, each reader of the statements will determine which portions are most important. Like the statement analysis discussed previously, the analysis of ratios is limited by its inability to detect fraud on a smaller, immaterial scale. Some of the types of financial ratio comparisons are shown below.

Current Ratio	Collection Ratio	Debt to Equity
Quick Ratio	Inventory Turnover	Profit Margin
Receivable Turnover	Average Days Inventory in Stock	Asset Turnover

Many of the possible ratios are used in industry-specific situations, but the nine comparisons mentioned above are ratios which may lead to discovery of fraud. The following calculations are based on the example financial statements presented earlier:

RATIO ANALYSIS

Ratio	Calculation		Year 1		Year 2	
Current Ratio	Current Assets		270,000 =	2.84	365,000 =	1.70
	Current Liabilities		95,000		215,000	
Quick Ratio	Cash+Securities+Receivables		195,000 =	2.05	215,000 =	1.00
	Current Liabilities		95,000		215,000	
Receivable Turnover	Net Sales on Account		250,000 =	1.61	450,000 =	2.14
	Average Net Receivables		155,000		210,000	
Collection Ratio	365		365 =	226.30	365 =	170.33
	Receivable Turnover		1.61		2.14	
Inventory Turnover	Cost of Goods Sold		125,000 =	1.92	300,000 =	2.31
	Average Inventory		65,000		130,000	
Average Number of Days Inventory in Stock	365		365 =	189.80	365 =	158.17
	Inventory Turnover		1.92		2.31	
Debt to Equity	Total Liabilities		155,000 =	0.89	275,000 =	1.83
	Total Equity		175,000		150,000	
Profit Margin	Net Income		15,000 =	0.06	(25,000) =	(0.06)
	Net Sales		250,000		450,000	
Asset Turnover	Net Sales		250,000 =	0.76	450,000 =	1.06
	Average Assets		330,000		425,000	

Interpretation of Financial Ratios

CURRENT RATIO

$$\frac{\text{Current Assets}}{\text{Current Liabilities}}$$

The current ratio, current assets to current liabilities, is probably the most-used ratio in financial statement analysis. This comparison measures a company's ability to meet present obligations from its liquid assets. The number of times that current assets exceeds current liabilities has long been a quick measure of financial strength.

In detecting fraud, this ratio can be a prime indicator of manipulation of accounts involved. Embezzlement will cause the ratio to decrease. Liability concealment will cause a more favorable ratio.

In the case example, the drastic change in the current ratio from year one (2.84) to year two (1.70) should cause an examiner to look at these accounts in more detail. For instance, a check tampering scheme will usually result in a decrease in current assets, cash, which will in turn decrease the ratio.

QUICK RATIO

$$\frac{Cash+Securities+Receivables}{Current\ Liabilities}$$

The Quick Ratio, often referred to as the Acid Test ratio, compares assets that can be immediately liquidated. This calculation divides the total of cash, securities, and receivables by current liabilities. This ratio is a measure of a company's ability to meet sudden cash requirements. In turbulent economic times, it is used more prevalently, giving the analyst a worst-case look at the company's working capital situation.

An examiner will analyze this ratio for fraud indicators. In year one of the example, the company balance sheet reflects a Quick Ratio of 2.05. This ratio drops in year two to 1.00. In this situation, a fraud affecting the Quick Ratio might be fictitious accounts receivable which have been added to inflate sales in one year. The ratio calculation will be abnormally high and there will not be an offsetting current liability.

RECEIVABLE TURNOVER

$$\frac{Net\ Sales\ on\ Account}{Average\ Net\ Receivables}$$

Receivable Turnover is defined as net sales divided by average net receivables. It measures the number of times accounts receivable is turned over during the accounting period. In other words, it measures the time between on-account sales and collection of funds. This ratio is one which uses both income statement and balance sheet accounts in its analysis. If the fraud is caused from fictitious sales, this bogus income will never be collected. As a result, the turnover of recievables will decrease, as in the example.

COLLECTION RATIO

$$\frac{365}{\text{Receivable Turnover}}$$

Accounts receivable aging is measured by the collection ratio. It divides 365 days by the Receivable Turnover ratio to arrive at the average number of days to collect receivables. In general, the lower the collection ratio, the faster receivables are collected. A fraud examiner may use this ratio as a first step in detecting fictitious receivables or larceny and skimming schemes. Normally, this ratio will stay fairly consistent from year to year, but changes in billing policies or collection efforts may cause a fluctuation. The example shows an favorable reduction in the collection ratio from 226.3 in year one to 170.33 in year two. This means that the company is collecting its receivables more slowly in year two than in year one.

INVENTORY TURNOVER

$$\frac{\text{Cost of Goods Sold}}{\text{Average Inventory}}$$

The relationship between a company's cost of goods sold and average inventory is shown through the Inventory Turnover Ratio. This ratio measures the number of times inventory is sold during the period. This ratio is a good determinant of purchasing, production, and sales efficiency. In general, a higher Inventory Turnover Ratio is considered more favorable. For example, if cost of goods sold has increased due to theft of inventory (ending inventory has declined, but not through sales), then this ratio will be abnormally high. In the case example, inventory turnover increases in year two, signaling the possibility that an embezzlement is buried in the inventory account. An examiner should look at the changes in the components of the ratio to determine a direction in which to discover possible fraud.

AVERAGE NUMBER OF DAYS INVENTORY IS IN STOCK

$$\frac{365}{\text{Inventory Turnover}}$$

The Average Number of Days Inventory is in Stock Ratio is a restatement of the Inventory Turnover Ratio expressed in days. This rate is important for several reasons. An increase in the number of days inventory stays in stock causes additional expenses, including

storage costs, risk of inventory obsolescence, and market price reductions, as well as interest and other expenses incurred due to tying
up funds in inventory stock. Inconsistency or significant variance in
this ratio is a red flag for fraud investigators. Examiners may use
this ratio to examine inventory accounts for possible larceny schemes.
Purchasing and receiving inventory schemes can affect the ratio. As
well, false debits to cost of goods sold will result in an increase in the
ratio. Significant changes in the Inventory Turnover Ratio are good
indicators of possible fraudulent inventory activity.

DEBT TO EQUITY RATIO

$$\frac{\text{Total Liabilities}}{\text{Total Equity}}$$

The Debt to Equity Ratio is computed by dividing total liabilities by total equity. This ratio is one that is heavily considered
by lending institutions. It provides a clear picture of the comparison
between the long-term and short-term debt of the company, and the
owner's financial injection plus earnings-to-date. This balance of
resources provided by creditors and what is provided by the owners
is crucial when analyzing the financial status of a company. Debt to
Equity requirements are often included as borrowing covenants in
corporate lending agreements. The example displays a year one ratio of 0.89. The increase in the ratio corresponds with the rise in
accounts payable. Sudden changes in this ratio may signal an examiner to look for fraud.

PROFIT MARGIN

$$\frac{\text{Net Income}}{\text{Net Sales}}$$

Profit Margin Ratio is defined by net income divided by net
sales. This ratio is often referred to as the efficiency ratio, in that it
reveals profits earned per dollar of sales. This percentage of net
income to sales relates not only the effects of gross margin changes,
but also charges to sales and administrative expenses. As fraud is
committed, artificially inflated sales will not have a corresponding
increase to cost of goods sold, net income will be overstated, and the
Profit Margin Ratio will be abnormally high. False expense and
fraudulent disbursements will cause an increase in expenses and a
decrease in the Profit Margin Ratio. Over time, this ratio should be
fairly consistent.

Asset Turnover

$$\frac{\text{Net Sales}}{\text{Average Assets}}$$

Net sales divided by Average Operating Assets is the calculation used to determine the Asset Turnover Ratio. This ratio is used to determine the efficiency with which asset resources are utilized. The case example displays a greater use of assets in year two than in year one.

By performing an analysis of the financial statements, the examiner may be directed toward the direct evidence to resolve an allegation of fraud. After performing a financial statement analysis, the examiner can select statistical samples in the target account and eventually examine the source documents. If an irregularity of overstatement is suspected, begin the examination with the financial statements. If, however, an irregularity of understatement is suspected, begin the examination with a review of the source documents. This rule of thumb is of particular effectiveness in the area of omission of liabilities, such as litigation, contingent liabilities, leases, and some product warranties.

Interviews in Financial Statement Fraud Cases

As we have witnessed in so many cases, financial statement fraud does not occur in an isolated environment. People in organizations who have both motive and opportunity are the prime candidates to commit fraudulent misstatements. In the overwhelming majority of situations, two key managers most often participate actively in the fraud: the chief executive officer and the chief financial officer. From there, others become involved largely out of necessity. Those who are not involved and don't need to know aren't told.

To detect or deter financial statement fraud, it is absolutely necessary that both the CEO and CFO be interviewed by a competent and experienced fraud examiner who possesses the ability to solicit honest answers to tough—but vital—questions about whether anyone has cooked the books. Anything less might lead to the same kind of disaster illustrated in the audit of Equity Funding Corporation.

At least 65 insiders were aware and participated in this massive fraud to some extent. At the time, there was no real requirement for auditors to openly ask, "Is there fraud going on in this company?" If they had, would the outcome have been the same? Of course, no one knows. But it certainly wouldn't have hurt to merely inquire, and it might have done some good. As we have repeatedly noted, if the principals are convinced there is a good chance of getting caught, they are less likely to commit financial statement fraud.

INTERVIEWING TECHNIQUES

This book is not about interviewing. But you cannot be, in my opinion, a competent fraud examiner or auditor unless you know the basics. So if you have never had a formal interview course, I highly recommend you add it to your arsenal of antifraud weapons. You will not regret it. Before discussing the basics of interviewing, it would be helpful to explain how the great majority of financial statement cases get started. Although the dialogue below is not verbatim, it could be.

CFO: (To CEO) "Boss, it looks like we will not have a good year financially. We told the shareholders (or bank) that our earnings would be $4 a share, and it looks like we'll be very lucky to make $3."

CEO: "Well, what are we going to do about it? If we miss the earnings projections (or don't get the loan) our gooses will be cooked; we'll both lose our jobs. We must get those earnings up to where they should be."

CFO: "What do you mean?"

CEO: "What I mean is that it is your job to bring in the numbers. You're going to have to find a way to get them up. I'm sure we can probably make up the difference next year, but for now, you get our earnings/assets/equity up however you have to. All financial statements are essentially estimates anyhow. So you figure out how to 'estimate' the numbers more in our favor. I don't know how to do it, and I don't want you to tell me. But get it done."

The CFO is now on the horns of a dilemma: cook the books or lose his job. Which way it will go, of course, is very hard to predict. But if the CFO steps over the edge, chances are he will need to enlist the aid of accounting and clerical personnel to carry out the details, even if these employees do not know what they are actually doing. For example, the CFO may tell the chief accountant to book certain receivables and income, which has the needed effect—pumping up the equity. In some instances, though, that is only apparent to the real insiders.

In order to detect financial statement frauds through interviews, management as well as key support staff must be interviewed. Here are a few essential things you must know to conduct interviews.

A.   There is generally no liability in asking a question to which you have a legitimate interest, no matter how insulting someone might find it. You therefore have the legal right to be fearless in your questions, as long as they are asked privately and under reasonable circumstances. That doesn't extend to accusations—only questions. Example: "Are you still cooking the books?" is an accusation. "Are you cooking the books?" is a question. Know the difference, and frame your questions accordingly.

B.   All interviews should be conducted one person at a time; do not attempt to interview people in groups, because what each says will influence what the others say. Always conduct interviews under private conditions, which permit the respondent to answer candidly.

C.   The secret to being a good interviewer is to be non-threatening in your approach. Think of the kind of person you would confess to, and be that kind of person. That means you should be especially prepared at the beginning: smile, be warm and sociable, and spend time on nonsensitive issues before progressing to tougher questions. It stands to reason that the less threatening you appear, the less reluctant someone will be to answer your questions. Keep your cool, and if you are surprised, disgusted, or judgmental, don't show it—that will inhibit the flow of information.

D.   Warm up the respondent thoroughly before asking sensitive questions. This means that fraud should usually be the last thing discussed in an interview; get all the procedural information and internal control questions out of the way first.

E.   You can almost always ask tough question without offending someone if you do it right. There are two things you can do to make the process easier. First, explain the nature of your interest before asking the question. Example: "As you know, we as auditors are required to actively look for fraud. That means we must ask you some direct questions about the subject. Do you understand?" After obtaining a positive response, proceed with questions, from the easiest to the hardest.

The second thing you can do to make tough questions more palatable is to phrase them hypothetically. For example, if you are interviewing the chief financial officer, you could start—instead of end—with the most direct question, "Have you committed fraud?" The common response of course would be "no," whether that person actually has or not. It would also be common for the respondent to either laugh at the question or to be offended by it.

A better approach is to start with: "Suppose someone in the position of chief financial officer decided to pump up the financials. How would he do it?" You can easily see the first question, although legal and direct, is not as likely to elicit specific information as would the latter.

F.   Before you end an interview with a highly placed executive, ask that person specifically if he or she has committed fraud. Phrase the question something like this: "Mr. Smith, my professional responsibilities require me to ask you one particularly sensitive direct question. Have you committed fraud or illegal acts against the company?"

As stated, the vast majority of respondents will answer "no" without hesitation, whether they have or not. Simply asking this question will give you a much more favorable posture if you are ever attacked professionally for not detecting the fraud. At least you will be able to tell the court or any other authority that you did not shirk your professional responsibilities, that you asked each person you interviewed in connection with the audit or examination, and that you were lied to.

THE INTERVIEW

With the above as a predicate, there is a series of questions you can ask which are designed to elicit the most specific information in a professional manner. These questions also will help the financial statement auditor and examiner in not only uncovering potential problems, but also help complying with requirements under the AICPA's Statement on Auditing Standards No. 82, the Institute of Internal Auditor's Statement on Internal Audit Standards No. 3, and the Association of Certified Fraud Examiners Code of Professional Ethics, Article 1.

The Chief Executive Officer

Generally, the CEO should be interviewed first in any proactive or reactive fraud situation. There are several good reasons for this approach. First of all, the auditor or fraud examiner must have a thorough understanding with management as to what his responsibilities in this area are. Second, it is unwise to conduct sensitive inquiries within any organization without first advising the CEO. If he learns from some other source that you are making discreet fraud-related inquiries without telling him, he is more likely to misunderstand your objectives and take the inquiry as a personal affront. Third, as stated, if there is any significant diddling with the books, the Chief Executive Officer is almost always involved. The fraud-related questions you should ask in connection with a regular audit should include, as a minimum, the following. Note how the questions are for "set up" purposes.

1. Mr. CEO, as you know we are required to assess the risk that material fraud exists in every company, not just yours. This is sort of a sensitive area for everyone, but our professional responsibilities dictate that we address this area. Do you understand? (Wait for an affirmative response before proceeding).

2. Do you have any reason to believe that material fraud is being committed at any level within the organization?

3. Mr. CEO, one trend in fraud is that small frauds are committed by employees with little authority, which means that the largest ones are usually committed with the knowledge of upper management. Do you understand that? (Wait for an affirmative response before proceeding.)

4. Because of that, we are required to at least look at the possibility that all CEOs, including you, might commit significant fraud against customers, investors, or shareholders. Do you understand our situation? (Wait for an affirmative response.)

5. So during this audit (examination) I need to ask direct questions about this subject with you and your staff. As a matter of fact, we will at least discuss the possibility of fraud with every employee we talk with in connection with this audit/examination. Do you have any trouble with that? (Wait for a negative response. If the CEO protests, satisfy his objections. If he cannot be satisfied, assess the risk of whether the CEO is attempting to obstruct the audit or examination.)

6. First, let's look at your CFO position. Can you think of a reason he might have to get back at you and the company by committing fraud?

7. Has the CFO ever asked you to approve any financial transaction you thought might be improper or illegal?

8. Do you know whether the CFO has any outside business interests that might conflict with his duties here?

9. Does the CFO employ any friends or relatives in the company? (Look for possible conflicts or sweetheart deals.)

10. What information do you have about the CFO's lifestyle? (Look for expensive homes, cars, toys, and habits.)

11. What is your general impression of how the CFO gets along with his staff? (Look for abuses of authority, etc. that would motivate employees directly below the CFO to participate in fraud.)

12. How do you think fraud in your company compares with others in the same industry?

13. Of course, Mr. CEO, I must ask you many of the same questions about yourself. Is there any reason that anyone below you might claim you are committing fraud against the company?

14. I must also ask you some personal financial questions. Does that give you any problem? (Wait for negative response.)

15. Please give me a current estimate of your personal assets, liabilities, income, and expenses. (List) What percentage of your net worth is tied directly to this company? (Look for highly leveraged individuals whose company holdings are the significant portion of their net worth.)

16. Are you currently experiencing any personal financial problems? (Look for lawsuits, liens, judgments, or other indicators.)

17. Do you have friends or relatives working for this company? (Look for conflicts of interest.)

18. Do you have friends or relatives working for major suppliers or vendors to your company? (Look for conflicts.)

19. Do you own any portion of a company that does business with this organization? (Look for conflicts.)

20. Hypothetically, if you wanted to artificially pump up your company's profits, what would be the easiest way to do it?

21. As I said, we will be required to ask many questions of your staff. Is there any reason why someone who works for you would say you are at risk to commit significant fraud against the company or its shareholders?

22. Mr. CEO, this is the last question, and it should be obvious why I have to ask it. Have you committed fraud or other illegal acts against the company? (Do not apologize for asking the question; it's your job.)

The CEO's Top Staff

Chief Executive Officers of corporations, large and small, are busy individuals. Because they tend to be "big picture" people by nature, they rely heavily on their staffs—principally their personal assistants—to take care of the details. But personal assistants do not usually get closely tied with the boss without a demonstrated history of loyalty and discretion. In short, if you make the boss's assistant mad, your fraud-related questions are going to be interpreted in the worst possible light, thereby making your job much more difficult.

So the key to interviewing the CEO's top staff is to approach it correctly from the outset. That means laying a great deal of groundwork before you ask sensitive questions. Start with procedural matters or some other nonsensitive topic, and ask the fraud-related questions toward the end of your conversation.

1. Mr. Assistant, part of my job as an auditor (fraud examiner) is to assess the risk that the company's books are not materially correct as a result of fraud by employees or management. I already have talked about these issues to your boss, and he understands the importance of this, and that in the audit I will be talking to everyone about the subject to some extent. Do you have any problem with that? (Wait for negative response.)

2. Do you think fraud is a problem for business in general? (Icebreaker)

3. How do you think this company stacks up with others in terms of honesty of its employees and managers?

4. Have you ever heard rumors in the company that someone is committing fraud, especially someone high up in the organization?

5. Is the company in any kind of financial trouble which would motivate management to misstate the company's profits?

6. Do you think your coworkers are essentially honest?

7. Has anyone you work with ever asked you to do something you felt was not legal or ethical?

8. How would you handle that situation if someone asked you? (Solicit information on fraud reporting program.)

9. If someone in a position of authority in the company wanted to commit fraud, what would be the easiest way to do it?

10. As your auditor, may I ask you to report any instances in the future if someone asks you to do something to the books and records that you feel is not right? (Solicit future cooperation.)

The Chief Financial Officer

In the vast majority of cases the CFO is an integral part of any financial statement fraud, as illustrated previously. As a result, the interview with the CFO should concentrate not only on possible motivations to commit fraud, but the opportunity to do so. Since most CFOs are accountants, they should more readily understand your fraud-related mission. This can be both good and bad; good if the CFO is honest, and bad if he isn't. Among all financial personnel, the CFO is in the best position to know how to cook the books and keep it from being uncovered. If that weren't enough, many CFOs are hired directly from the firms who audit the company. Is there any other person more likely to be at the center of the fraud? Here are some sample questions you can ask the CFO.

1. Mr. CFO, you now know that new audit standards require us to actively assess the risk that material fraud could be affecting the financial statements. We have talked to the CEO, and he is fully aware that we will be inquiring of most everyone we speak with about the possibility of fraud or irregularities. You understand that, don't you? (Wait for affirmative response.)

2. Of the accounts on the company's books, which do you suspect might be the most vulnerable to manipulation, and why?

3. What kind of history does the company have with fraud in general, including defalcations and employee thefts? (Look for signs of a weak corporate culture.)

4. We know that fraud usually exists to some extent—even if it is small—in most companies. How does your company compare to others, do you think?

5. What is your overall impression of the company's ethics and corporate culture?

6. During our assessment of risk of fraud in your company, are there any specific areas you'd like to discuss with us?

7. Is there any reason that someone in the company might say that management had a motive to misstate the financials?

8. Has anyone you work with ever asked you to do something with the books that you thought was questionable, unethical, or illegal?

9. Are you involved in the personal finances of the CEO? If so, is there anything about them that might make you think he is under personal financial pressure?

10. Does the CEO's lifestyle or habits give you any reason to think he may be living above his means?

11. Has anyone in a position of authority ever asked that you withhold information from the auditors, alter documents, or make fictitious entries in the books and records?

12. Is there anything about your own background or finances that would cause someone to suspect that you had the motive for committing fraud?

13. Because of your importance as CFO, I must ask you one final question: Have you yourself committed fraud or illegal acts against this company? (Remember—don't apologize.)

The Accounting Staff

If a financial statement fraud has been ordered by the CFO, either he will do the actual dirty work himself, or he will get his staff to do it. In some cases, the staff will understand the big picture, but in most situations, the employee is told only what he or she needs to know. It is uncommon for a CFO to share with a lower staff person the fact that he is cooking the books.

As a result, the examiner generally must complete his audit work before beginning the interviews of the accounting staff. This will allow specific transactions to be discussed with the people who actually entered them in the company's records. For example, all thorough audits will examine the major journal entries. Frequently, these journal entries will be ordered by the CFO but actually entered by a staff member. There generally would be no record of the CFO requesting the entry, so this fact must be established through interviews.

Interviews of the accounting staff will allow sufficient examination of procedures and controls over assets. After these questions are answered, you can generally pursue the line of inquiry suggested above for the CEO's assistant.

It should be noted that there are similarities and differences in the questions asked of the CEO, the CFO, and their staffs. In the case of the CEO and the CFO, both were specifically asked if they had committed fraud against the company, albeit in a nice way. The staffers were not asked that specific question.

The reasoning is this: significant financial statement fraud, as we have stated, generally originates with one or both of these two executives. Staffers have less motivation to engage in financial statement fraud, and are therefore at less risk to do so. They are also less likely to have the financial authority to enter transactions in the books without higher approval.

So absent of any specific information to the contrary, asking the employees point blank if they have committed fraud is less likely to produce information and more likely to offend them. But with the CFO and the CEO, asking the direct question will add measurably to the detection of fraud. There are few defenses to not asking the question, other than the specter of embarrassing the executives you are auditing. That will, of course, sound pretty weak in a court of law where you are fighting for your professional life.

Prevention of Financial Statement Fraud

Prevention and deterrence of statement fraud consists of those actions taken to discourage the perpetration of fraud and limit the exposure, if fraud does occur. Internal auditing is responsible for helping deter fraud by examining and evaluating the adequacy and the effectiveness of controls, commensurate with the extent of the potential exposure/risk in the various segments of the entity's operations.

The internal audit standard states that the principal mechanism for deterring fraud is control. Primary responsibility for establishing and maintaining control rests with management. Treadway addresses this issue by recommending that internal audit departments or staffs have not only the support of top management, but also the necessary resources available to carry out their mission. The internal auditors' stated responsibility is to aid management in the deterrence of fraud. Specifically, the internal auditor should determine if

- The organizational environment fosters control consciousness
- Realistic organizational goals and objectives are set
- Written corporate policies (for example, code of conduct) exist that describe prohibited activities and the action required whenever violations are discovered
- Appropriate authorization policies for transactions are established and maintained
- Policies, practices, procedures reports and other mechanisms are developed to monitor activities and safeguard assets, particularly in high-risk areas.
- Communication channels provide management with adequate and reliable information

- Recommendations need to be made for the establishment or enhancement of cost-effective controls to help deter fraud.

*****

Case Study: All on the Surface
*Several names may have been changed to preserve anonymity

Michael Weinstein chuckled a lot. He smoked big cigars and laughed at the people who used to think he was just a chubby schmo. *Forbes* and *Business Week* stoked the fire with adoring articles. *Business Week* called Weinstein's Coated Sales, Inc. "the fourth fastest growing company in the country" and predicted greater returns to come. Of Coated Sales's twenty competitors, eleven were either defunct or absorbed. "The survivors," chuckled a writer in *Forbes*, "are more likely to cower than laugh when they see Weinstein." In a few years' time, revenues at Coated had jumped from $10 to $90 million per annum. The stock was peaking at eight times its opening price. "One of my goals," Weinstein stated dramatically, "is to see us be almost alone."

Which didn't take long. Weinstein's auditors walked out on him. The big six firm resigned and announced publicly they had no trust in the management of Coated Sales. Senior management scrambled en masse to get out of the way. Weinstein was suspended. New people started looking at the books. In two months, Coated Sales was filing for bankruptcy. The last laugh fell hollow down the empty hallways.

Michael Weinstein was once the All-American businessman. At nineteen he borrowed $1,000 from his father and bought into a drugstore. At thirty-one he had a chain of stores, which he sold, and reaped several million dollars in take-home pay. Weinstein remembered thinking, "I have a problem." Just when all his contemporaries were reaching their thirty-something years, starting careers, raising their families, he was retiring. What to do with all that time?

His buddy Dick Bober talked him into the coated fabrics business. Weinstein didn't know anything about coated fabrics. But he wasn't a pharmacist either, and that venture had proved fortuitous. Coating fabrics, he learned, was a crucial step in making lots of products, from conveyer belts to bulletproof vests. Things like parachutes, helmet liners, and camouflage suits all use coated fabrics. So there were some bulky government contracts waiting to be served. Uniforms and equipment have to be stainproofed, fungus-proofed, waterproofed, and dyed. According to one estimate, coating adds from ten to fifty percent to the base value of raw material, lending the luster of money to an otherwise workaday industry.

Weinstein threw himself into the business and eventually into the manufacturing process. As a pilot, he hated the life vests stowed on commercial airliners. "They had always bugged me," he said. "They [are] heavy and expensive to make," he told Coated researchers. They designed a prototype using coated nylon which was sixty percent lighter than the standard, and seventy percent cheaper to make. Before his untimely demise, Weinstein could boast that every Western-based airline carried life vests manufactured with materials made by Coated Sales.

The Coated Sales laboratory helped develop a super-proofed denim to protect oil rig workers, firemen, and people handling hazardous materials. Coated sales employees worked on aircraft emergency slides, radiator hoses, telephone earpieces, a sewage filtration fabric, marine dive suits, backpacks and, just for the flair of it, they made some of the sailcloth for the *Stars & Stripes*, the schooner piloted by Dennis Conner to win the America's Cup. Weinstein must have had a charm, wound up and running in his favor. Just two years before the crash, he became the first coated fabrics operator to own a large-scale finishing plant, a $27 million facility without rival in the industry.

At the same time, Weinstein's darling was digging its own grave. Expanding into new markets, developing cutting-edge product lines, herding new companies into the fold — all this takes money. Especially when the CEO and senior management like to live large and let people know about it. There's a constant cash crunch. Larger scale means larger crunch. Inside the workings of Coated Sales, shipments of fabric and equipment were being bought and sold quickly, often at a loss, just to get to the short-term money.

For years, Coated had used Main Hurdman for auditing, with no sign of trouble. But when Main Hurdman was acquired by Peat-Marwick, the new auditors saw a very different picture. One associate called a luggage manufacturer to ask about 750,000 pieces of merchandise purchased from Coated. The luggage company said they never placed an order like that. No idea. When team members spoke about their concerns, Coated sent in their legal counsel to talk with the auditors. Philip Kagan tried to get them to make a deal, to

go ahead and let the financial statement slide; there were some problems, he admitted, but nothing beyond repair. The matter was being
taken care of. No way, said the auditors, and walked out.

In two months' time, the company that flew higher than the
rest had fallen into bankruptcy. Early estimates put shareholder losses
at more than $160 million. Coated's top twenty creditors claimed
they were out at least $17 million. The bankruptcy court appointed
Coopers & Lybrand's insolvency and litigation practice to work with
the debtor in possession. Besides the usual assessments, the group
was to determine what went wrong, and just how wrong, in dollar
amounts, it had gone. CFE Harvey Creem says, "We knew there was
something of concern with a loan and how the money was used. Once
we started poking around, the iceberg got larger." Creem worked
with the debtor's lawyers who determined that the proceeds of a bank
loan had been transferred to a brokerage account, one no longer carried in the ledgers. It was a supposedly dormant account from the
company's first public offering, used for temporary investments until it was zeroed out. During the most recent fiscal year, there had
been some activity on the account. Proceeds from a loan had been
deposited into the brokerage account, transferred out to a cash account, and listed as if it were payments from customers against their
accounts receivable. Coated Sales was due a lot of money, their receivables growing by $20 million a year. But a lot of the payments
on those receivables were being made with Coated's own money,
part of which originated from bank loans. The broad outline of the
fraud was clear. "When you find a single check for, say $2 million,
used to pay off several different accounts, you know something's up.
. . . Usually each customer sends their own check to pay off their
own debt. In this case, a check listed under one name was used to
pay off debts for several different people. Now, a company that not
only pays its own debts, but the debts of other companies, too—
that's not impossible, but it's not likely. . . . The basics of the operation took two or three hours to break," says Creem. "Then it was
tracking the scope of what happened."

Creem describes how he and his colleagues started at the bankruptcy filing date and "went in and analyzed the receivables in depth.
. . . Large chunks of them were totally fallacious; they had nothing
supporting them." The tracking effort was helped along by a number
of lower-level employees: "Some of them didn't really know what
was happening and they were willing to help. Some may have known,

but they were repentant, so they were willing to talk." In about three years of scamming, Weinstein and his management had inflated their sales and profits, resulting in overstated equity by $55 million. They used these phony numbers to get loans from several banks, like a $52 million line of credit from BancBoston, and a $15 million line from First Fidelity in Newark, New Jersey.

The rigged loans solved the cash-flow problem, plus there were very pleasant side effects. Stock in Coated Sales—traded under the ticker symbol RAGS—was headed through the roof. Huge leaps in revenue and a monstrous control of the market had propelled the stock to $12 a share, eight times more than what it opened for. The company's upper echelon, including Ernest Glantz (President) and Weinstein's longtime partner Dick Bober (Vice President), was cashing in in a big way. By himself, Weinstein made more than $10 million in a short-term selling spree. Additionally, one of the myriad lawsuits against him accused Weinstein of departing with $968,000 in company cash.

Creem followed the trail of rigged profits into several intriguing corners. "To float this past the auditors for as long as they did, they found several ways to create the fiction that customers were actually paying the fake receivables. They would create a fake receivable, say $10,000 due from a company. They'd hold it as long as they could, sometimes doctoring the dates on the aging, so it looked more recent than it was." Creem says the next step was "rigging a way to pay the account off: They'd transmit their own cash to a vendor. The vendor presumably was in on the scheme, too, since they had submitted a fake invoice for the $10,000. This vendor keeps one to two percent for their trouble, and sends the rest back to Coated. That money would be reflected as a payment against the phony receivable."

Guys like Bernard Korostoff made the vendor trick work. Korostoff used his Kaye Mills International Corporation to create false invoices for several big Coated orders. Weinstein's team, having used their phony financials to get loans, sent out the money to Korostoff as if they were paying off a debt. Korostoff kept 1.5% for making the transaction possible, turning the rest back to Coated to pay off the falsified receivables. "I never really understood that," says Creem. "These guys are doing this for a measly little percentage. Why would they bother for no more than that? Maybe it was connected in other ways to the business. . . ."

The business, as it was being run, was a labyrinth of finagle and deception. Weinstein was faking how much he owed people in order to pay off receivables, which were also being faked. He was using receivables to get million-dollar loans and plowing chunks of the proceeds back into the system to keep suspicious eyes unaware. The false sales not only brought in loan dollars, they created portfolio dollars by driving RAGS stock higher and higher. To support the scam, Weinstein had three ways to keep his circle of money in motion: he could move loan money from the hidden brokerage account to wherever it was needed, he could use fake vendor invoices to launder funds back into the company, or he and his associates could sell off their own stock in the company and apply some of the proceeds to the delinquent receivables.

Four years of this action and Weinstein had demolished Coated Sales. The company exaggerated its accounts receivable by millions, fictionalizing half or more of their sales at any given point. At the time, it was the largest stock fraud ever in the state of New Jersey. Weinstein and nine other senior managers were charged with planning, executing and profiting from the scheme. Weinstein—called "a tall, plump man with a domineering personality" by *Forbes*—owned more than ten airplanes and several helicopters. He had two Rolls-Royces, one at each of his two residencies, besides five other luxury automobiles scattered here and there. He and the other conspirators had used some of the proceeds to buy themselves smaller companies. For flamboyance, he had no better, and for gall he was unrivaled. After Coated went belly up and federal charges joined the pile of lawsuits against him, Weinstein bought a 13,000-square-foot house in Boca Raton, Florida, valued at $2 million, sitting on a $1 million property. Three different yachts were docked along the Florida coast in case Weinstein needed to get away from all the hassle.

But Weinstein wouldn't slip past this one. He and his inner circle were presented with a 46-page indictment. Bruce Bloom, Coated's Chief Financial Officer, pled guilty and pointed at his cohorts. Coated's lead counsel, Philip Kagan, first declared himself "totally innocent of any wrongdoing," but later decided to plead guilty to the racketeering and conspiracy charges against him. Kagan confessed to helping dupe company auditors, and described trying to entice them into ignoring the facts of their ledgers. He also admitted that he had once accepted $115,000 in legal fees from Coated Sales without reporting the money to the SEC as required. Kagan was sentenced to eighteen months in prison. Jail terms for other low-level players ranged from one year to twenty-four months.

Coated President Ernest Glanz was given a year's sentence, part of a deal he made to cooperate with the government. Richard Bober, Weinstein's longtime friend, drew twenty months in prison and a $3-million fine, besides the $55.9 million civil judgment he shared with Weinstein. Creem remembers that when Bober testified in bankruptcy court, "The judge appeared shocked. He started asking Bober questions himself. I don't believe he had ever heard anything quite like this in his courtroom before."

Michael Weinstein struck a plea bargain which nevertheless carried a pretty stout penalty. He forfeited virtually all of the properties, cars, and boats he had amassed, along with several businesses and numerous bank accounts worth several hundred thousand dollars each. He was given fifty-seven months in federal prison and charged to make restitution for any outstanding stockholder losses.

U.S. Attorney Michael Chertoff saw this as a decisive case, part of what he called "a new genre of corporate board-room prosecutions." Fed up with the mega-scams of the megalomaniacal executive, legal agencies are using the tough Securities Law Enforcement Remedies Act to go after the big players. "Major financial fraud," Chertoff told a press conference after Weinstein's guilty plea, "not only harms banking institutions but also infects the securities market, victimizing the thousands of persons who invest in stock. When dishonesty roams the boardroom, it is the creditors and investors who suffer."

*****

Conclusion

The primary responsibility for a company's financial statements lies with its management and board of directors. Their obligation includes the prevention and detection of material, fraudulent reporting. In general, material misstatements by senior levels of management occur infrequently. These chance circumstances where fraud is committed may involve manipulation of accounting records and supporting evidence in an effort to cover the lack of agreement between accounting records and underlying documentation. It is the rare occurrences, when misstatement is made and concealment is attempted, that result in pervasive effects.

To prevent misstatement it is very important that management maintain effective internal control systems including policies and procedures documentation. The control systems will serve to ensure validity, completeness, accuracy, and security of financial and accounting information and documentation. In addition, corporations should have an independent audit committee whose members are comprised of outside directors. Companies should develop a written charter setting forth the duties and responsibilities of the audit committee. The committee must also have adequate resources and authority to carry out its responsibilities. Given the appropriate resources and authority, the audit committee must also be vigilant and effective in its oversight function.

The purpose of financial statements is to relay the financial health of the organization. Users of the statements rely on the assumption that the statements are prepared in an accurate manner, without misstatement. For this assurance to be conveyed, the user must be reasonably assured that the company's management can be trusted. The perception of their ethical character is very important. This character is part of the way company management as well as employees conduct themselves on a daily basis. Most often, as the integrity of management is held at a high level, employees also feel that they should act in similar fashion. This effect preserves the integrity of professional conduct of a company as a whole and is usually sought after by users of financial statements.

Within each chapter we have included examples of prevention and detection methods for specific fraud schemes. We have also given methods for the financial statement schemes detailed in this fraudulent financial statements chapter. The prevention and detection methods given in this book should be used to enhance your control policies and fraud detection efforts. However, an all-encompassing audit program for financial statements is beyond the scope and purpose of this book.

[1] National Commission on Fraudulent Financial Reporting, 1987, *Report of the National Commission on Fraudulent Financial Reporting* (New York: American Institute of Certified Public Accountants, October).

[2] Jane Mancino, "The Auditor and Fraud", *Journal of Accountancy*, April 1997, pp32-36.

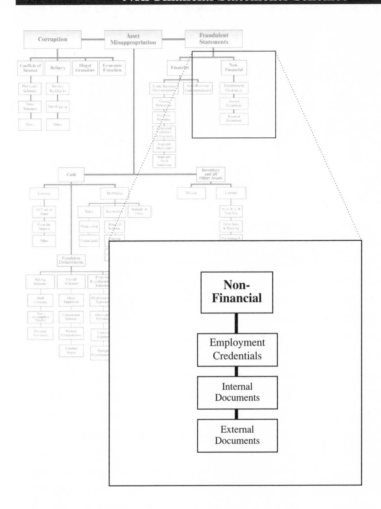

15. NON-FINANCIAL STATEMENTS

*****

Case Study: A Nurse Doctors Her Credentials

*Several names have been changed to preserve anonymity.

David Vasiloff knows the importance of continuing education. Fresh from earning a bachelor's degree in accounting and a master's degree in management science — two fields that require ongoing formal study to stay current — Vasiloff signed on with the government as an entry-level auditor and kept at it, steadily rising in rank and status. "I've worked my way down the road here, no question," said Vasiloff, now based in Washington, D.C.

More than a quarter century of public service has certainly taught him a bit about law, politics, and work ethics as well. And in his present capacity as the central director of the audit division at a large federal agency that commands a multibillion-dollar budget and almost a quarter million employees, Vasiloff continues to learn about the mores of human behavior.

Charged with national audit and review responsibilities for the agency, Vasiloff was once called on to conduct a parity review of its nursing staff's pay system. In the aftermath, he learned a lesson about honesty and class distinctions in America.

The review came about largely in response to pending legislation that mandated special compensation for distinguished nurses. But there was also an allegation that there had been improper manipulation of data used to calculate the improved pay scale, said the government official.

Vasiloff led a three-person team — consisting of himself, a project manager, and an auditor — in an intensive data-gathering effort. Their three-part mission: (1) To determine which nurses were truly entitled to the special pay, (2) to uncover any improprieties by those who stood to benefit, and (3) to make recommendations on how to achieve true parity. "We put together a database of employees who held positions that might be affected by the special pay, listing their assignments and descriptions and cross-referencing their qualifications and designations," said the internal auditor, who had earned his accreditation as a CFE just one year earlier.

The schedule of candidates revealed several discrepancies. Noting that some job descriptions seemingly failed to jibe with the stated requirements or the employee's qualifications, the auditors decided to pull the corresponding personnel files to investigate further, recalled Vasiloff.

One employee record in question belonged to Judith Anne Breed. Requirements for her high-level administrative position clearly stated that the employee must hold an-up-to-date nursing license and certification. Yet no supporting documentation could be found in her file. Owing to years of experience in personnel matters, the glaring absence of such documentation immediately raised red flags in the auditor's mind.

The file did show that she had "moved up the ranks fairly quickly and had transferred from different sites in here to Washington," said Vasiloff. After several promotions with the agency, Breed now pulled down a yearly salary in excess of $90,000.

"This lady was also the wife of a high-ranking official in Washington in one of our departmental elements," added Vasiloff, careful not to reveal too many clues about the husband's identity. "Her husband, who is a physician, occupied a position in the chain of command for the program area that she was involved in. So there was an obvious husband-and-wife connection." Vasiloff said Breed's marriage and successful career accorded her privilege and gave her a well-accepted station both in her community and her workplace.

Her standing did not deter the auditor from further inquiry, however, even though he considered the case a mere side issue to the nurse pay review. "Sometimes you stumble across these irregularities in the course of a routine function. A lot of times it happens this way. It's not something we exactly planned to do."

On her resume and in her detailed government application — "the old form 171" — Breed stated that she earned a Ph.D. from a prominent university. She also certified that she held a current license in nursing. On another form Breed signed, she verified the accuracy of her entire application. (As part of governmental efforts to become more accessible, said Vasiloff in an aside, recent job applicants may simply submit resumes and such for electronic data input in lieu of filling out a formal standardized application.)

One phone call to officials at the university disclosed no record of Breed ever attending the school, let alone earning an advanced degree in graduate studies, whether in the traditional classroom setting or via night school, home-study, or correspondence school, said Vasiloff. They didn't even offer alternative study programs. Obligingly, they also checked listings for students under her other married names. They found none. A few more calls to agents at different state licensing agencies confirmed that Nurse Breed "once had a license but it had expired over two years ago." After receiving verbal confirmations, Vasiloff then requested timely written confirmations to support this case.

Even though proof of her level of education had been requested as part of the hiring process, no proof was ever provided, Vasiloff said. And no follow-up action was taken. "We had a hole there that nobody checked." File notations indicated that human resource employees viewed the documents. "But if they had, they would have seen what we saw." During his short acquaintance with this file, it irked him that the "paper in the file went unsupported by background, experience, and training."

"This fraud went undetected for several years because nursing service officials failed to follow established rules and procedures that require assurance of completeness and accuracy of supporting education and nursing credentials for any nurse being boarded for a position," stated Vasiloff. "It takes an effort to check on training and certification, and people just don't want to spend that kind of time. You have to go behind the application to find out if, in fact, there is something there to support it."

"The perpetrators are betting on average that no one's going to check. And I think in the past that was a pretty good bet. But nowadays there's a better chance that someone's going to check."

Vasiloff cited four important weaknesses in internal controls that contributed greatly to this case and need to be addressed, not only in government but in the private sector as well:

- Lack of separation of duties
- Lack of proper authorization procedures
- Lack of proper required documentation
- Lax attitudes toward rules and policies

In three months the team members had pulled together a thick packet of information on Breed — with all claims thoroughly substantiated —and turned it over to the agency's investigators. "Since this was just a sideline to the nurse pay review, we felt it would be better handled by separate investigators."

When Breed was later approached by the investigators, "she tried to go back and cover some of her tracks. But there was no way to do that. She simply compounded the problem," said Vasiloff. After making a statement that she had recently called to request a more current certification, only then did Breed make the call. It was too late.

The investigators also met with her superiors and raised some serious questions over their screening process for applicants. According to Vasiloff, they should have been reminded, "No matter how nice the person looks or how well equipped they are, there could still be a problem."

"The bottom line is that this individual lied and then was caught," Vasiloff stated. "She apparently did these things to move up the ladder and get where she wanted to go." In her recorded evaluations, Breed's bosses gave her high marks and encouraged her aspirations, as further evidenced by her subsequent pay raises and promotions. "Her job performance was never an issue."

Unknowingly abetting her deceit, the deputy director of nursing once overruled a board of review recommendation not to promote Breed, according to her file, because of the absence of a current nursing license and questions about her education. The audit team drew the conclusion that her husband's position had decidedly eased her upward progression.

Fortunately, "She was in a position that didn't require any nursing duties," said Vasiloff. "This was more of an administrative position, so it had little reliance on those skills anyway."

In his audit findings of the nurse pay review, Vasiloff questioned the wisdom of paying out such high salaries for essentially administrative support workers in the central office. "That level of pay is justified if you're out dealing with direct-patient care. These people weren't. The high salaries weren't even justified for those with legitimate credentials." As a result of the review, salary cuts for administrative personnel were ordered and implemented. "That made a lot of people happy," said Vasiloff sarcastically. On the plus side, the audit team found no basis for the allegation of improper manipulation of data by those who stood to benefit by the new special pay. "Everything they did was appropriate." All other issues were resolved satisfactorily.

As a result of the mounting case against Breed, the nurse resigned her post toward the end of the investigation. "I think it was a shocker when all of a sudden she just departed the department. I don't know how many people actually knew the details surrounding her departure." Her former supporters voiced no objections, however. "When something comes out like this, people can be pretty silent. They know what's going to happen—that person's going to be out the door."

"The results of the investigation were placed in her personnel file and the employee was placed on a list of undesirables for future employment. If she ever tries to get a job here, the investigators want to know."

The U.S. Attorney's office declined to prosecute Judith Anne Breed for her transgressions, which grossed her hundreds of thousands of dollars in undeserved wages. Vasiloff explained, "Around Washington, you've got to have a pretty good amount of money before the attorneys go after a perpetrator. It just wasn't enough money." And comparatively speaking, "The case just wasn't that interesting. There's a lot of other things going on around here that warrant greater attention and energy."

*****

The motives which cause a fraud perpetrator to falsify other types of statements take several forms. The false statements are sometimes self-serving and are often used to hide wrongdoing or to enhance one's standing in the workplace.

Other false statements include:

> Employment Credentials

> Internal Documents

> External Documents

Employment Credentials

When applying for employment, the applicant generally must be qualified to carry out the required duties. Intentionally misstating one's credentials and qualifications is one type of fraud. For example, a position for general counsel in an organization usually requires a law degree from an accredited university and a license from the state bar. If the applicant claims to hold a law degree on an application or resume when in fact he or she does not, the applicant has made a false statement. Not verifying potential employee credentials can cause an organization serious embarrassment as well as potential liability should an incident arise as a result of the employee being underqualified. Case 702 details a case in which a woman more than doubled her salary with the use of false credentials. A Department of Veteran Affairs employee wanted a new, higher paying position, but lacked the qualifications. To obtain the position, she literally reinvented herself. Armed with falsified statements regarding her education and nursing credentials, the employee was able to land a $94,000 per year job, a position which would have been unattainable to her without false documents. The fraud was ultimately discovered through a random employee credentials audit. This case is detailed at the end of this section.

Internal Documents

In today's corporate world, an endless number of internal documents have the potential for fraudulent manipulation and falsification. As discussed in previous chapters, these documents include invoices, time sheets and other payroll documentation, expense forms, company checks, petty cash forms, and inventory records. The list of internal company documents is long.

External Documents

Although abused less frequently, external documents can be falsified to commit occupational fraud. An example would be documentation for cash expenditures in which the company expense is indeed legitimate, but for various reasons the documentation for the expenditure is falsified. A typical example of this is the traveling salesman who physically loses a stack of receipts. When reporting these legitimately incurred company expenses, he falsely recreates a month's worth of expense receipts in order to complete his expense report. Case 2274 is an example of an investment manager who falsified external documentation to cover arbitration losses incurred in a bad investment. A local government investment officer speculated on future issues of GNMA's, hoping to arbitrage capital gains during a period of falling interest rates. He agreed to purchase over $42 million of securities in excess of the organization's projected available cash. The officer's scheme included producing false GNMA serial numbers and amortization schedules. Interest rates began to rise and the office was forced to cover over $900,000 in losses. He wired the money but requested the funds for use in new investments instead of losses.

In conjunction with an outside vendor, the manger in Case 2660 manipulated external invoices to meet documentation requirements for his accounting department. When a facility manager at a cement manufacturing company was denied budget funds on an equipment project, he decided to carry out the project anyway. To do so, the manager persuaded vendors to alter invoice descriptions on the projects and hid all project funds by inflating the expense budget. When a fellow employee tipped off the company, the manager's rebellious scheme came to light and he was terminated.

Prevention and Detection

INFERIOR INFORMATION GATHERING AND REPORTING SYSTEM

The ultimate detection method for false statements is the examination of source documents. The typical auditing approach is termed "Inside-Out," that is, from the source document out to the report or financial statement. However, the analysis of a company's reporting requirements as well as keeping an eye out for possible red flags, may prove to be a more effective manner of detecting fraud in other false statements.

EMPLOYEE REPORTING INADEQUACIES

Employee reporting which is not up to standard control policies is a clear pointer to potential fraudulent activity. The following discussion details potential red flags indicating inadequate employee reporting:

Failure to produce documents in a timely manner may be a type of inaction indicating that there are not source documents to substantiate the summary data. For example, an employee may submit a report for expense reimbursement that does not include supporting receipts and documentation. The employee may ask to provide this documentation at a later time. If the expense is not legitimate or if it did not occur at all, the employee will not be able to produce the substantiation of expense required for reimbursement. The actual reimbursement should not be allowed until proper documentation is received.

If the required reports are consistently late, incomplete, or unsatisfactory, this might be an indication that the source data is either unavailable, nonexistent, or it cannot be retrieved. Source data is derived from source documentation. If the source documentation is false, then summarizing the corresponding data becomes an increasingly more difficult problem.

Frauds are often concealed by altering or "misplacing" the supporting documentation. The tenacity of the fraud examiner to obtain and examine the source documentation may go a long way in proving false statements.

Transactions should be authorized and recorded based on original documentation, not duplicates. Duplicates or photocopied documentation are subject to alteration and manipulation.

In order for supporting documentation to be adequate, it must be sufficient, competent, and relevant. If not, the integrity of the review will be left in question.

PART V - EPILOGUE

16. OCCUPATIONAL FRAUD AND ABUSE: THE BIG PICTURE

Defining Abusive Conduct

The cases we have seen on the preceeding pages were, by and large, on the extreme edge of abusive conduct by employees. In short, this data is merely the tip of the iceberg. How deep and massive that iceberg is varies from one organization to another, depending on a complex set of business and human factors.

The depth of the iceberg is also measured by what is defined as abusive conduct. Obviously, the more rules within the organization, the more employees are likely to run afoul of them. Remember, Hollinger and Clark's study reflected that almost *nine in ten employees* admitted to abusive conduct at some level. Part of that abuse is owing to the diverse nature of individuals. Tom R. Tyler, in his book *Why People Obey the Law* concluded overwhelmingly that individuals obey only laws they believe in. If a rule makes no sense to the employees, they will make their own.[1]

Let me illustrate the point with another personal experience from the FBI. The Federal Bureau of Investigation did a thorough background investigation before they hired me, notwithstanding the Mr. Zac debacle. They investigate each and every agent prospect. So when you are hired, it doesn't mean you're perfect. It just means they have put you through every wringer they can think of, hoping some major imperfection will surface to disqualify you.

Of those who survive that process, a tiny percentage are actually hired and put through training school—like me. From day one, the agents were held to impossibly high standards. To illustrate the mentality at the time, consider what our esteemed instructor told his class of 35 eager, bright-eyed trainees. "The FBI doesn't have any ordinary agents. Every single one of them is above average or better," the instructor bragged. One of the trainees sitting toward the back of the class—a mathematical type of guy—raised his hand. "Excuse me," the trainee questioned, "I don't think it is possible for every FBI agent to be above average. By definition, to be above average, there must be an average, and a below average. So not every agent can be above average—it's statistically impossible." The trainee spoke to the instructor with respect but conviction.

The classroom was silent, and every eye went to the front of the room, where the instructor was carefully formulating his response. "Look, Mister," said the instructor. "If J. Edgar Hoover himself said every agent is above average, that's statistical enough for me." And he meant it.

When we graduated from training class and went into the field, the rookie agents had to come to the real world. In the real world, we all got paid 25% extra for all the overtime we typically incurred. But the record-keeping requirements were so ridiculous that no one—outside the clerks in Washington—paid any attention to the myriad of forms we all had to fill out every month to get paid.

The ridiculous part of the record keeping, as far as the rank-and-file agent was concerned, was that there was no carry-over for overtime accumulated from one period to the next. For example, if you put in 50% overtime in pay period 14, you still got paid 25%. But if you only put in 10% overtime in pay period 15, your overtime would be cut to 10% because you could not use the overtime you burned in period 14. But the kicker was that during the course of the year, all the agents would put in at least 25% overtime, many ran much higher.

As a result, virtually everyone I knew in the field at that time simply claimed 25% each pay period, regardless of the actual time they put in. And we had to certify, under oath, that we had worked that specific amount of overtime—no more, no less. Our agency could not pay us more than 25%, so they didn't "offically" want us to put in more time, because government regulations would have required them to pay compensatory time off. So none of us took seriously the certification that bore our signatures. A sworn false statement under oath to the government—which we regularly signed on our forms—warned us all of the criminal penalties involved. Each and every one of us would sign such a form 26 times a year—just to get our paychecks. I commented on the irony of it all to a salty old FBI Agent one day when both of us were at the sign-in register. "Joe," he said, "welcome to the real world. Here is the way it works: if you've told many lies, you can't get in the FBI. But once you're hired, you have to tell a few just to stay in. And that's all because of these ridiculous regulations."

What is the moral to this story—other than my admitting that during my professional career I have had my own personal experiences with occupational fraud and abuse? There are two morals, in my view. The first is that we cannot eliminate this problem in the workforce without eliminating people. The human race is notoriously subject to periodic fits of bad judgement. Anyone in fraud detection or deterrence who is aiming for perfection from the workforce will not only be disappointed, he will find that such attitudes invariably increase the problem.

That paradox is the second moral to the story: to quote my longtime colleague Dr. Steve Albrecht, "If you set standards too high, you may be inadvertently giving an employee two choices in his mind—to fail or to lie." Your job in establishing antifraud standards, then, is to make them clear and reasonable. More on that later.

Measuring the Level of Occupational Fraud and Abuse

Since the goal of the antifraud professional is to reduce the losses from these offenses, measuring progress in the traditional sense might be difficult. We have clearly established the reasons why—we only know about the frauds that are discovered.

As we discussed in the introduction to this book, 2,608 Certified Fraud Examiners think that the average company loses about 6% of its gross revenues to all forms of fraud and abuse in the workplace. Considering everything we know, it may be the best number we can use for the present. It at least gives organizations a rough measure of their potential exposure. Whether or not that exposure is ever discovered is a different matter. We have seen examples of occupational frauds in this book that have gone undetected for years. Exept for a fluke of circumstance, many of them could still be thriving today. That, of course, is the most troublesome aspect of many occupational frauds: the longer they go, the more expensive they are. People who start committing fraud will generally continue unless there is a compelling reason to quit.

On an organizational basis, one good indicator of the real risks of fraud is what has happened in the past. Surprisingly few organizations—especially the smaller ones—make any effort to gather historical, fraud-related data: how many offenses occur, what are the losses from each, and what patterns emerge, if any? But remember, this data will not tell you the size of the iceberg, only the size of the tip. Most importantly though, gathering historical fraud information will tell you whether the iceberg is growing or melting.

THE HUMAN FACTOR

The diverse case studies in this book have one common element. That is, of course, the human failings that led trusted people to violate that trust. Were these employees, from the mailroom to the boardroom, all simply greedy? Were they all simply liars? Did they always have defective morals which just surfaced when their honesty was tested? Or were they mistreated, underpaid, and only taking what was "rightfully" theirs?

The answer, of course, is that it depends. Crime is a complex tapestry of motive and opportunity. The Sultan of Brunei, reputedly the world's richest man, may have unlimited opportunity to defraud people. But does he have the motive? Contrarily, the miniumum-wage cashier may be very motivated to steal in order to keep his lights turned on. But if he is constantly aware his cash drawer may be counted by surprise, he may not perceive the opportunity to do so. In any antifraud effort, we must always keep in mind that not one factor alone will deter occupational fraud; we must attack the problem on several fronts.

Greed

Michael Douglas uttered the now famous line from the movie, *Wall Street:* "Greed is good." While some may debate whether that is true, there is little debate that greed is certainly a factor in occupational frauds. Indeed, students of this subject are more likely to describe embezzlers and their ilk by that one single word: greedy.

The problem with that definition of a fraud motivator is that it is subjective, and begs for the response, "Greedy? Compared to what?" Most of us consider ourselves greedy to some extent; it is, after all, a very human trait. But there are many greedy people who do not steal, lie, and cheat to get what they want. And how can we measure the amount of greed in any way that will become a predictor of behavior? In sum, there is little we can say about greed as a motive that will help us detect or deter occupational fraud.

Wages In Kind

In nearly all the case studies you reviewed in this book, one common thread prevails: those who chose to commit fraud against their employers felt justified in doing so. A perfect example is the case of Bob Walker, the cashier who began stealing to get even with his employer. Walker had been demoted from a management position to head cashier at his store, a move that included a $300 a month paycut. Feeling morally justified in his theft, Walker went on to process over $10,000 in false refunds, more than 25 times what his demotion cost him in lost wages.

For the purpose of detecting and deterring occupational fraud, it does not matter whether the employee is *actually* justified, but whether he *perceives* he is. Your prevention efforts must begin with education of employees and staff, and attack this misperception on all fronts—the morality, legality, and negative consequences of committing occupational fraud and abuse.

Employers must also understand the concept of "wages in-kind." I can remember a perfect illustration from my days as an anti-fraud consultant in the '80s. A local banker heard me give a speech on fraud prevention, and he later called me. "We have a hell of a time with teller thefts," he confidentially admitted. "I would like to hire you to evaluate the problem and give us some solutions."

I spent several days in the bank, going over the accounting procedures, the history of teller thefts, the personnel policies, and the internal controls. I also interviewed bank supervisors, head tellers, and the rank and file. The interviews were particularly revealing.

When it came time to give my report, the banker requested I meet with his entire board to deliver my conclusions orally and be able to respond to questions. I tried to be as diplomatic as I could, but when the veneer was stripped away, it wasn't a pretty picture. The reason the bank was having problems with teller thefts was because they (1) had inadequate personnel screening procedures, (2) had no anti-fraud training whatsoever, (3) paid inadequate wages to a person entrusted with a drawer full of money, and (4) were perceived by the employees as cheap and condescending. When I finished my presentation to the board, I asked for questions. The silence was deafening. After standing there for what seemed like eternity, my banker colleague meekly thanked me for my suggestions and told me they would call. They didn't.

So employers must be educated in the concept of *wages in-kind*. There are three basics that are absolutely necessary to minimizing (not eliminating) occupational fraud and abuse. First, hire the right people. Second, treat them well. Third, don't subject them to unreasonable expectations.

Unreasonable Expectations

If you have carefully evaluated the case studies in this book, you should have empathy with at least some of the situations which led to an employee deciding to commit fraud. Ernie Philips's situation, for example, reads like the scenario for a Movie-of-the-Week. While trying to support a wife and six adopted children, Philips was forced to undergo several back operations which kept him away from work. He then became addicted to the pills which he was given to alleviate the pain from those operations. His CPA practice was on the verge of folding, and he suffered from depression as well as chronic anxiety. Under such dire circumstances, how many of us might resort to forging checks in order to get by?

In my view, employers sometimes have unreasonable expectations of their employees which may contribute to occupational fraud and abuse. First, employers frequently expect their employees to be honest in all situations. That belies the human condition. According to Patterson and Kim in *The Day America Told the Truth,* a full 91% of people surveyed admitted to lying on a regular basis. Thankfully, most of these lies have nothing to do with fraud. But it must be remembered that while all liars are not fraudsters, all fraudsters are liars. Our approach to deterrence therefore must be not to eliminate lying (since it can't be done), but to keep lies from turning into frauds.

It is easy to see how anyone can confuse the two concepts of lying and fraud. When we lie to our family, our coworkers, our superiors, and our customers, these are typically deceptions motivated by the human desire to tell people what they want to hear: "My, you look nice today!" So keep your eye on the ball: we want to deter fraud specifically; we don't have quite the time to reform humanity, even though that is a lofty goal.

And to deter fraud requires some understanding.

Understanding Fraud Deterrence

Deterrence and prevention are not the same thing, even though we frequently use the terms interchangeably. Prevention, in the sense of crime, involves removing the root causes of the problem. In this case, to prevent fraud, we would have to eliminate the motivation to commit it, such as the societal injustices that lead to crime. We as fraud examiners must leave that task to the social scientists. Instead, we concentrate on *deterrence*, which can be defined as the modification of behavior through the perception of negative sanctions.

Fraud offenders are much easier to deter than run-of-the-mill street criminals. Much violent crime is committed in the heat of the moment, and criminologists agree that those crimes are very difficult to stop in advance. But fraud offenders are very deliberate people, as you have seen in this book. At each stage of the offense, they carefully weigh—consciously or subconsciously—the individual risks and rewards of their behaviors. For that reason, their conduct can be more easily modified.

THE IMPACT OF CONTROLS

Throughout this book, you have witnessed situations that could have been prevented with the most basic control procedure: separating the money from the record-keeping function. Having said that, it is likely that we accountants and auditors ask controls to do too much. After all, many internal controls have nothing to do with fraud. And still others are only indirectly related. My view is that internal controls are only part of the answer to fraud deterrence. However, some others do not share that view. They would argue that if the proper controls are in place, occupational fraud is almost impossible to commit without being detected.

THE PERCEPTION OF DETECTION

As alluded to throughout these pages, the deterrence of occupational fraud and abuse begins in the employee's mind. The perception of detection axiom is as follows:

> *Employees who perceive that they will be caught engaging in occupational fraud and abuse are less likely to commit it.*

The logic is hard to dispute. Exactly how much deterrent effect this concept provides will be dependent on a number of factors, both internal and external. But as you can see, internal controls can have a deterrent effect only when the employee perceives such a control exists and is for the purpose of uncovering fraud. "Hidden" controls have no deterrent effect. Conversely, controls that are not even in place—but are perceived to be—will have the same deterrent value.

How does an entity raise the perception of detection? That, of course, will vary from organization to organization. But the first step is to bring occupational fraud and abuse out of the closet and deal with the issue in an open forum. Companies and agencies must be cautioned that increasing the perception of detection, if not handled correctly, will smack of "Big Brother" and can cause more problems than it solves. There are at least six positive steps organizations can employ to increase the perception of detection.

Employee Education

Unless the vast majority of employees are in favor of reducing occupational fraud and abuse, any proactive fraud deterrence program is destined for failure. It is therefore necessary that the entire workforce be enlisted in this effort. Organizations should provide at least some basic antifraud training at the time workers are hired. In this fashion, the employees become the eyes and ears of the organization, and are more likely to report possible fraudulent activity.

Education of employees should be factual rather than accusatory. Point out that fraud—in any form—is eventually very unhealthy for the organization and the people who work there. Fraud and abuse cost raises, jobs, benefits, morale, profits, and one's integrity.

The fraud-educated workforce is the fraud examiner's best weapon—by far.

Proactive Fraud Policies

When I ask most people how to deter fraud, they typically say something like this: "In order to prevent fraud, we must prosecute more people. That will send a message." There are at least three flaws in this well-meaning argument. First, there is nothing proactive about prosecuting people. As some in Texas would say, it is like closing the barn door after the cows have escaped. Second, whether it really sends much of a message is debatable. This concept is called "general deterrence" by criminologists. As logical as the idea sounds on its face, there is no data—out of scores of studies—that show it actually works.

Without getting into the intricacies of criminological thought, punishment is believed by many experts to be of little value in deterring crime because the possibilities of being punished are too remote in the mind of the potential perpetrator. Think about it for a second. If you were debating whether to commit a crime (of any kind) the first question that comes in to your mind is: "Will I be caught?" not "What is the punishment if I am caught?" If you answer yes to the first question, you are very unlikely to commit the offense. That makes the punishment moot, no matter how severe it is.

The foregoing is not to say that crime should not be punished. Quite the opposite—it is something that must be done in a civilized society. But remember that the primary benefit of any type of punishment is society's retribution for the act, not that punishment will deter others.

A Higher Stance

Proactive fraud policies begin with simply a higher stance by management, auditors, and fraud examiners. That means, as previously stated, bringing fraud out of the closet. At every phase of a routine audit or management review, the subject of fraud and abuse should be brought up in a nonaccusatory manner. People should be asked to share their knowlege and suspicions, if any. They should be asked about possible control and administrative weaknesses that might contribute to fraud. What we are trying to accomplish through this method is to make people subtly aware that if they commit illegal acts, others will be looking over their shoulders.

A higher stance also means making sure that "hidden"controls don't remain that way. Auditors may have a peculiar image to the uninformed. Employees know auditors are there, but they are not quite sure what the auditors actually do. While this attitude can obviously bring benefits if you are trying to conduct your activities in secret, it is counterproductive in proactive fraud deterrence. You must let employees know you are looking.

Increased Use of Analytical Review

If an employee embezzles $100,000 from a Fortune 500 corporation, it will not cause even a blip in the financial statements. And in large audits, the chance of discovering a bogus invoice are remote at best. That is because of the sampling techniques used by auditors—they look at a relatively small number of transactions in total.

But as you can see from the cases in this book, the real risks are in asset misappropriations in small businesses. These of course can be and frequently are very material to the bottom line. And the smaller businesses are those which benefit the most from the increased use of analytical review, most specifically vertical and horizontal analysis. As a reminder, proactive fraud examiners and auditors should be especially mindful of historical trends which reflect the following increases: expenses, cost of sales, receivables with decreasing cash, inventory, sales with decreasing cash, returns and allowances, and sales discounts.

As a part of the anayltical review process it is a good idea to determine the organization's policy on job rotation and enforced vacations. Because many occupational frauds require continuous manual intervention by the perpetrator, a large proportion of these offenses seem to be uncovered when the perpetrator leaves—for vacation, sick time, and job rotation. It stands to reason that the longer a person is in one position, largely unsupervised, the more risks of occupational fraud increase.

Surprise Audits Where Feasible

The story of Bill Gurado best illustrates the concept of the perception of detection in audits. As you recall, Barry Ecker, the auditor, was simply joking when he told Gurado that an audit was imminent. Based on that false information, Gurado confessed that he had been stealing from his branch. The reason? Gurado was convinced his unlawful conduct was about to be discovered.

The threat of surprise audits, especially in businesses which are currency-intensive, may be a powerful deterrent to occupational fraud and abuse. In case after case, all too many fraud perpetrators were aware that audits were coming, so they had time to alter, destroy, and misplace records and other evidence of their offenses. Obviously, surprise audits are more difficult to plan and execute than a normal audit that is announced in advance. But considering the impact of the perception of detection, surprise audits may certainly be worth the trouble.

Adequate Reporting Programs

As many of the cases in this book illustrate, adequate reporting programs are vital to serious efforts to detect and deter occupational fraud and abuse. In situation after situation we encountered, employees were suspicious that illegal activity was taking place, but they had no way to report this information without the fear of being "dragged in" to the investigation.

Reporting programs should emphasize at least six points: (1) fraud, waste, and abuse occur at some level in nearly every organization; (2) this conduct costs jobs, raises, and profits; (3) the organization actively encourages employees to come forward with information; (4) there are no penalties for furnishing good-faith information; (5) there is an exact method for reporting, such as a telephone number or address; and (6) a report of suspicious activity does not have to be reported by the employee to his immediate supervisor.

A hotline is considered by most professionals to be the cornerstone of an employee reporting program. According to some studies, about 5% of hotline calls are actually developed into solid cases. But in many instances, these schemes would not have been discovered by any other method. And as near as we can tell, reports from employees outstrip all other methods of fraud detection combined.

There are three basic kinds of hotlines. The first is a part-time, in-house hotline staffed by an employee with other duties. When the employee is out, a recorder takes the call. These hotlines have the advantage of low cost, but the disadvantages are twofold: (1) some calls might be missed; and (2) some employees are reluctant to report fraud to organizational personnel.

The second type of hotline is a full-time, in-house one. Its advantage is that employees can make calls any time, day or night, and talk to an actual person. These kinds of hotlines are expensive, and they are usually found in only the largest corporations and governmental agencies.

The last type is called a third-party hotline. It is staffed by an outside company, usually 24 hours a day, and is priced to subscribers based upon the number of employees. Third-party hotlines offer three distinct advantages: cost, efficiency, and anonymity.

An example of such a service is EthicsLine, operated by the Association of Certified Fraud Examiners. Trained interviewers and Certified Fraud Examiners staff the telephones 24 hours a day, 365 days a year. Companies subscribe and pay an annual fee, and they post the EthicsLine number within the company on bulletin boards, in company handouts, and in their ethics policies. When a call is received, the caller is debriefed by an interviewer. The caller is not required to provide his identity. After the call is received on the hotline, the information provided is relayed back to the company to take whatever action it sees fit. The annual cost of the service for a small business (fewer than 100 employees) is under $200. Other third-party hotline providers are available, too.

Hotlines, regardless of their type, work to increase the perception of detection. An employee who is aware that his nefarious activities might be reported by a coworker will be less likely to engage in such conduct. One final advantage of a hotline is that it helps comply in part with the federal Corporate Sentencing Guidelines for corporations.

The Corporate Sentencing Guidelines

DEFINITION OF CORPORATE SENTENCING

Guideline legislation is one of the most dramatic changes in criminal law in the history of this country. Not only do the Guidelines seek to make punishments more uniform, they unquestionably and dramatically increase the severity of the punishment — in some cases the fine may be $290 million or more. Additionally, the presence of an effective program to prevent and detect violations of the law is rewarded with a more lenient sentence. That reward may be worth several million dollars at the time of sentencing.

The Guidelines were mandated by Congress in the Comprehensive Crime Control Act of 1984. The Act also established the United States Sentencing Commission (USSC) which began studying sentences for individuals soon after the passage of the Act. It was widely held in Congress that there was a great disparity of penalties for similar crimes committed by individuals.

After three years of study, the USSC announced Sentencing Guidelines for Individuals. In November of 1987, these Guidelines began to be applied in the 94 Federal Courts of the United States.

Shortly after the implementation of the individual guidelines, the USSC began studying sanctions for organizations even though there was no clear direction to do so in either the 1984 Act or the accompanying legislative history. After four years of study and hearings, the USSC submitted to Congress on May 1, 1991, its Proposed Guidelines for Sentencing Organizations. On November 1, 1991, these Guidelines automatically became law. The underlying philosophy of the Guidelines has been characterized as a "carrot and stick" approach to criminal sentencing. That is, if the organization prevents or discloses certain conduct, then the punishment will be reduced.

VICARIOUS OR IMPUTED LIABILITY

Unlike individuals, corporations can legally be held criminally responsible for the criminal acts of their employees if those acts are done in the course and scope of their employment and for the ostensible purpose of benefiting the corporation. See New York Central and Hudson River Railroad v United States 212 U.S. 481(1909); Standard Oil Co. of Texas v United States 307 F.2d 120 (5th Cir. 1962).

The corporation will be held criminally responsible even if those in management had no knowledge or participation in the underlying criminal events and even if there were specific policies or instructions prohibiting the activity undertaken by the employees.

In fact, a corporation can be criminally responsible for the collective knowledge of several of its employees even if no single employee intended to commit an offense. U.S. v Bank of New England, W.A., 921 F. 2d 844, 856 (1st Cir.), cert. denied, 484 U.S. 943 (1987). Thus, the combination of vicarious or imputed corporate criminal liability and the new Sentencing Guidelines for Organizations creates an extraordinary risk for corporations today.

REQUIREMENTS

The following seven minimum steps are required for due diligence:

- Have policies defining standards and procedures to be followed by the organization's agents and employees
- Assign specific high-level personnel who have ultimate responsibility to ensure compliance
- Use due care not to delegate significant discretionary authority to people whom the organization knew or should have known had a propensity to engage in illegal activities
- Communicate standards and procedures to all agents and employees and require participation in training programs
- Take reasonable steps to achieve compliance, e.g., by use of monitoring and auditing systems and by having and publicizing a reporting system where employees can report criminal conduct without fear of retribution (hotline or ombudsman program)
- Consistently enforce standards through appropriate discipline ranging from dismissal to reprimand
- After detection of an offense, the organization must have taken all reasonable steps to appropriately respond to this offense and to prevent further similar offenses — includ-

ing modifying its program and appropriate discipline for
the individuals responsible for the offense and those who
failed to detect it.

The Sentencing Guidelines provide for both criminal and civil
sanctions. Fines up to $290 million can be imposed, plus the corpo-
ration can be placed on probation for up to five years.

The Ethical Connection

Wheelwright defined ethics as:

*that branch of philosophy which is the systematic study
of reflective choice, of the standards of right and wrong
by which a person is to be guided, and of the goods
toward which it may ultimately be directed.*[2]

More generally, moralists believe that ethical behavior is that
which produces the greatest good, and that which conforms to moral
rules and principles. Although ethics is often used interchangeably
with morality and legality, the terms are not precisely the same. Ethics is much more of a personal decision. In theory, ethics is how you
react to temptation when no one is looking.

There are fundamentally two schools of ethical thought. The
first, called the "imperative principle," advocates that there are con-
crete ethical principles that cannot be violated. The second, called
"situational ethics" or the "utilitarian principle," generally advocates
that each situation must be evaluated on its own; in essense, that the
end can justify the means. Probably the majority of people in mod-
ern-day society follow situational ethics. But regardless of one's particular ethical philosophy, the sticky problems exist in defining what
constitutes the "greatest good." It is certainly easy to see how the
CEO of a corporation employing thousands of individuals would rationalize that commiting financial statement fraud will help save jobs,
and therefore his conduct is justified as the "greatest good."

Similarly, an employee can perceive that a major corporation
with lots of money will never miss the amount he so desperately
needs to keep afloat financially. This was demonstrated in the story
of Larry Gunter and Larry Spelber, two employees who saw the opportunity to finance their entire educations by taking six small boxes
of computer chips from their employer's warehouse. In a building
filled to the brim with computer chips, who would miss six boxes?

And it is no surprise that some of the biggest crooks view themselves inwardly as very ethical; to this day, it is doubtful that Charles Keating views himself as more than a victim of circumstance, regardless of the fact that little old ladies across America have lost every dime they owned.

So the reality is that for most, the "greatest good" invariably turns out to be what is the good for the individual making the ethical decision. Coincidence? Probably not. Ancient and modern philosophers usually subscribe to one of three schools of thought about the essence of people: (1) man the good, (2) man the evil, or (3) man the calculator. In the latter situation, people will *always and consistently* seek pleasure and/or avoid pain. This is a lesson most of us learn very young.

Behaviorists tell us that the vast majority of our personalities have been formed by the age of three. A large part of our personality relates to the values we have, which are instilled in us by our parents and mentors. Without being a cynic (which I admit to) it is highly unlikely that ethical policies—no matter how strong they are—will seriously deter those sufficently motivated to engage in occupational fraud and abuse.

There is no ethical policy stronger than the leadership provided by the head of the organization. Modeling of behavior occurs with strong influences such as the boss. Indeed, the Treadway Commission specifically commented on the importance of the "tone at the top." Unfortunately, the formal ethics policies in place right now are thought to exist mostly in large organizations. In the small business—which is much more vulnerable to going broke from asset misappropriations—few of the bosses victimized seem to realize the importance of their own personal example.

When employees hear their leaders telling the customer what he wants to hear, when the small business boss fudges on the myriad taxes he must pay, when the chief executive officer lies to the vendors about when they will be paid, nothing good can possibly result. So setting an example is the *real* ethical connection.

Having said that, formal ethics policies are recommended for all organizations, regardless of their size. They certainly don't do any harm, and just may provide some deterrence. But almost as important is that having an ethics policy makes enforcement of conduct generally easier to legally justify. A sample, from the *Fraud Examiner's Manual,* is in the appendix to this book. Feel free to use the example to develop your own ethics policy. Three things are important regardless of what form your policy finally takes: (1) set out specific conduct which violates the policy, (2) state that dishonest acts will be punished, and (3) provide information on your organization's mechanism for reporting unethical conduct.

Although some professionals will disagree, I think it is a terrible idea to lace your ethics policy with draconian statements such as ". . . all violators will be prosecuted to the maximum extent allowed by law." First, even to many honest people, such a statement smacks of a veiled threat. Second, the victim of fraud does not decide criminal prosecution; this decision is made by the state. As a practical matter, your organization has little control, and it is unlikely that many first-time offenders will get more than a probated sentence.

Finally, your organization's ethical policy, whatever it is, can be only as good as the reinforcement it gets. A company which provides just one training program on ethics, not to mention the subject again, cannot expect results, however marginal. So training must be continuous, and must be positive in tone. Don't preach; keep emphasizing the simple message: fraud, waste, and abuse is eventually bad for the organization and everyone in it.

Concluding Thoughts

Within the pages of this book, many details of occupational fraud and abuse have been revealed. But those searching for a "magic bullet" to detect these offenses are doubtlessly still looking. Indeed, the dream of many in the accounting community is to develop "new" audit techniques which will quickly and easily point the finger of suspicion. To those innocent souls, good luck. Regardless of the ability of computers to automate a great deal of drudgery, there are no new audit techniques, and there haven't been any for the last several centuries.

Another factor makes the detection of occupational fraud and abuse difficult. Fraud is one of the few crimes whose clues are not unique to commission of the offense. For example, clues in a bank robbery case would be the witnesses who saw the robber, the records reflecting the loss, the security cameras and such. By contrast, the indicators of a bank embezzlement can be internal control weaknesses, missing or incomplete documents, and figures that don't add.

The problem, of course, is that none of these latter clues is conclusive evidence of fraud; the red flags could just as easily turn out to be red herrings.

I am confident this book will help you detect and deter fraud. But detection can be almost impossible when committed by someone clever enough and motivated sufficiently to hide his tracks. For those of us who are fraud examiners, that fact is sometimes hard to take. If you are the best fraud examiner in the world, you will detect some cases and resolve them. But you'll never get them all, no matter how hard you try.

In putting forward your best efforts to detect fraud, you'll be tempted to try too hard sometimes. You will weigh in your mind whether you should take an unauthorized look at the suspect's bank account; you'll wrestle with the dilemma of whether to secretly check the fraudster's credit records. Don't do it.

Overreaching an investigation or fraud examination is the quickest way to ruin it. Not only will you be unsuccessful in proving your case, you will subject yourself to possible criminal and civil penalties. If you get to a point in a fraud examination when you don't know what to do, stop. Resolve all doubt in favor of your suspect, or check with counsel on the next step.

In the perfect world, we would probably abandon our efforts to detect fraud and concentrate exclusively on deterrence. As we all know, prevention of any problem—from cancer to crime—is usually cheaper and more effective than the aftermath. In the area of occupational fraud, for reasons we have discussed extensively in this book, deterrence can work better than for most any other type of crime.

Deterrence, as we have explicitly stated, is much more than internal control. And we accountants concentrate primarily on those controls to deter fraud. As history has witnessed, it is an inadequate effort. For a number of years I have advocated the concept of the *Model Organizational Fraud Deterrence Program.* Under the program, we in the audit community would invest the resources to find out what works in organizations who don't have much of a problem with occupational fraud and abuse. What works will be a combination of both accounting and nonaccounting factors. We know some of the factors already, but we need to know more. From new research, we would then develop a complete checklist of the model organization, and use that checklist to audit against. Then the external auditor would attest to the organization's compliance to the model, not whether the auditor has uncovered material fraud. The latter approach, adopted by the accounting community now, is bound to drive up the cost of the audit and the price of litigation.

So the bad news is that we cannot audit ourselves out of the occupational fraud and abuse problem. But the good news is that there are a multitude of new approaches we can try. Some of them are in this book, which is but a beginning. New approaches combine both audit and investigative skills—the precise attributes of tomorrow's corporate cop, the fraud examiner. And since most people don't start their careers to become liars, cheats, and thieves, it is the fraud examiner's job to ensure they do not end up that way.

[1] Tom R. Tyler, *Why People Obey the Law* (New Haven: Yale University Press, 1990)

[2] Association of Certified Fraud Examiners, *Fraud Examiners' Manual, Revised 2nd Edition* (Austin: ACFE, 1996).

PART VI - APPENDIX

CODE OF BUSINESS ETHICS AND CONDUCT

(A SAMPLE)

Introduction

This section reaffirms the importance of high standards of business conduct. Adherence to this Code of Business Ethics and Conduct by all employees is the only sure way we can merit the confidence and support of the public.

Many of us came from a culture that provided answers or direction for almost every situation possible. Managing our business was not so complex, the dilemmas we faced were — for the most part — simple, making our choices relatively easy. We would probably all agree that managing in today's environment is not so simple.

This code has been prepared as a working guide and not as a technical legal document. Thus, emphasis is on brevity and readability rather than providing an all-inclusive answer to specific questions. For example, the term "employee" is used in its broadest sense and refers to every officer and employee of the company and its subsidiaries. The word "law" refers to laws, regulations, orders, etc.

In observance of this code, as in other business conduct, there is no substitute for common sense. Each employee should apply this code with common sense and the attitude of seeking full compliance with the letter and spirit of the rules presented.

It is incumbent upon you, as an employee of the company, to perform satisfactorily and to follow our policies and comply with our rules as they are issued or modified from time to time.

These policies and rules are necessary to effectively manage the business and meet the ever-changing needs of the marketplace. Good performance and compliance with business rules lead to success. Both are crucial since our ability to provide you with career opportunities depends totally upon our success in the marketplace.

Nonetheless, changes in our economy, our markets, and our technology are inevitable. Indeed, career opportunities will vary between the individual companies. For these reasons, we cannot contract or even imply that your employment will continue for any particular period of time. While you might terminate your employment at any time, with or without cause, we reserve that same right. This relationship might not be modified, except in writing signed by an appropriate representative of the company.

This Code of Business Ethics and Conduct is a general guide to acceptable and appropriate behavior at the company and you are expected to comply with its contents; however, it does not contain all of the detailed information you will need during the course of your employment. Nothing contained in this code or in other communications create or imply an employment contract or term of employment. We are committed to reviewing our policies continually. Thus, this code might be modified or revised from time to time.

You should familiarize yourself with this code so that you might readily distinguish any proposal or act that would constitute a violation. Each employee is responsible for his actions. Violations can result in disciplinary action, including dismissal and criminal prosecution. There will be no reprisal against an employee, because the employee in good faith reported a violation or suspected violation.

The absence of a specific guideline practice or instruction covering a particular situation does not relieve an employee from exercising the highest ethical standards applicable to the circumstances.

If any employee has doubts regarding a questionable situation that might arise, that employee should immediately consult his supervisor or higher level.

COMPETITION AND ANTITRUST

Fair Competition

The company supports competition based on quality, service, and price. We will conduct our affairs honestly, directly, and fairly. To comply with the antitrust laws and our policy of fair competition, employees:

- ❏ Must never discuss with competitors any matter directly involved in competition between ourselves and the competitor (e.g. sales price, marketing strategies, market shares and sales policies).

❏ Must never agree with a competitor to restrict competition by fixing prices, allocating markets or other means.

❏ Must not arbitrarily refuse to deal with or purchase goods and services form others simply because they are competitors in other respects.

❏ Must not require others to buy from us before we will buy from them.

❏ Must not require customers to take from us a service they don't want just so they can get one they do want

❏ Must never engage in industrial espionage or commercial bribery.

❏ Must be accurate and truthful in all dealings with customers and be careful to accurately represent the quality, features, and availability of company products and services.

Compliance with Laws and Regulatory Orders

The applicable laws and regulatory orders of every jurisdiction in which the company operates must be followed. Each employee is charged with the responsibility of acquiring sufficient knowledge of the laws and orders relating to his duties in order to recognize potential dangers and to know when to seek legal advice.

In particular, when dealing with public officials, employees must adhere to the highest ethical standards of business conduct. When we seek the resolution of regulatory or political issues affecting the company's interests we must do so solely on the basis of the merits and pursuant to proper procedures in dealing with such officials. Employees might not offer, provide, or solicit, directly or indirectly, any special treatment or favor in return for anything of economic value or the promise or expectation of future value or gain. In addition, there shall be no entertaining of employees of the U.S. Government.

Foreign Corrupt Practices Act

No employee will engage in activity which might involve the employee or the company in a violation of the Foreign Corrupt Practices Act of 1977. The Foreign Corrupt Practices Act requires that the company's books and records accurately and fairly reflect all transactions and that we maintain a system of internal controls; transactions conform to management's authorizations; and the accounting records are accurate. No employee will falsely report transactions or fail to report the existence of false transactions in the accounting records. Employees certifying the correctness of records, including vouchers or bills, should have reasonable knowledge that the information is correct and proper.

Under the Act it is also a federal crime for any U.S. business enterprise to offer a gift, payment, or bribe, or anything else of value, whether directly or indirectly, to any foreign official, foreign political party or party official, or candidate for foreign political office for the purpose of influencing an official act or decision, or seeking influence with a foreign government in order to obtain, retain, or direct business to the company or to any person. Even if the payment is legal in the host country, it is forbidden by the Act and violates U.S. law.

Conflicts of Interest

There are several situations that could give rise to a conflict of interest. The most common are accepting gifts from suppliers, employment by another company, ownership of a significant part of another company or business, close or family relationships with outside suppliers, and communications with competitors. A potential conflict of interest exists for employees who make decisions in their jobs that would allow them to give preference or favor to a customer in exchange for anything of personal benefits to themselves or their friends and families.

Such situations could interfere with an employee's ability to make judgments solely in the company's best interest.

GIFTS AND ENTERTAINMENT

Definition of Gifts

"Gifts" are items and services of value which are given to any outside parties, but do not include items described under 1), 2), 3), and 4) below.

1) Normal business entertainment items such as meals and beverages are not to be considered "gifts."
2) Items of minimal value, given in connection with sales campaigns and promotions or employee services, safety, or retirement awards are not to be considered "gifts" for purposes of this code.

3) Contributions or donations to recognized charitable and non-profit organizations are not considered gifts.
4) Items or services with a total value under $100 per year are excluded.

Definition of Supplier

"Supplier" includes not only vendors providing services and material to the company, but also consultants, financial institutions, advisors, and any person or institution which does business with the company.

Gifts

No employee or member of his immediate family shall solicit or accept from an actual or prospective customer or supplier any compensation, advance loans (expect from established financial institutions on the same basis as other customers), gifts, entertainment or other favors which are of more than token value or which the employee would not normally be in a position to reciprocate under normal expense account procedures.

Under no circumstances should a gift or entertainment be accepted which would influence the employee's judgment. In particular, employees must avoid any interest in or benefit from any supplier that could reasonable cause them to favor that supplier over others. It is a violation of the code for any employee to solicit or encourage a supplier to give any item or service to the employee regardless of its value, no matter how small. Our suppliers will retain their confidence in the objectivity and integrity of our company only if each employee strictly observes this guideline.

Reporting Gifts

An employee who receives, or whose family member receives, an unsolicited gift prohibited by these guidelines should report it to his supervisor and either return it to the person making the gift or, in the case of perishable gift, give it to nonprofit charitable organization.

Discounts

An employee might accept discounts on a personal purchase of the supplier's or customer's products only if such discounts do not affect the company's purchase price and are generally offered to others having a similar business relationship with the supplier or customer.

Business Meetings

Entertainment and services offered by a supplier or customer might be accepted by an employee when they are associated with a business meeting and the supplier or customer provides them to others as a normal part of its business. Examples of such entertainment and services are transportation to and from the supplier's or customer's place of business, hospitality suites, golf outings, lodging at the supplier's or customer's place of business, and business lunches and dinners for business visitors to the supplier's or customer's location. The services should generally be of the type normally used by the company's employees and allowable under the applicable company's expense account.

OUTSIDE EMPLOYMENT

Employees must not be employed outside the company (1) in any business that competes with or provides services to the company or its subsidiaries, and/or (2) in a manner which would affect their objectivity in carrying out their company responsibilities, and/or (3) where the outside employment would conflict with scheduled hours, including overtime, or the performance of the company assignments. Employees must not use company time, materials, information or other assets in connection with outside employment.

RELATIONSHIPS WITH SUPPLIERS AND CUSTOMERS

Business transactions must be entered into solely for the best interests of the company. No employee can, directly or indirectly, benefit from his position as an employee or from any sale, purchase or other activity of the company. Employees should avoid situations involving a conflict or the appearance of conflict between duty to the company and self-interest.

No employee who deals with individuals or organizations doing or seeking to do business with the company, or who makes recommendations with respect to such dealings, should:

1) serve as an officer, director, employee or consultant; or
2) own a substantial interest in any competitor of the company, or any organization doing or seeking to do business with the company. Substantial interest means an economic interest that might influence or reasonably be thought to influence judgment or action, but shall not include an investment representing less than 1% of a class of outstand-

ing securities of a publicly held corporation. The Conflict of Interest Questionnaire included with this book must be completed by every employee.

In addition, no employee who deals with individuals or organizations doing or seeking to do business with the company, or who makes recommendations with respect to such dealings, might:

1) have any other direct or indirect personal interest in any business transactions with the company (other than customary employee purchases of company products and services as consumers and transactions where the interest arises solely by reason of the employee relationship or that of a holder of securities);

2) provide telecommunications or information service or equipment, either directly or as a resaler in a manner which would place the objectivity or integrity of the company in question.

Our policy is that employees will no do business on behalf of the company with a close personal friend or relative; however, recognizing that these transactions do occur, they must be reported on the Conflict of Interest Questionnaire.

This policy is applicable equally to the members of the immediate family of each employee, which normally includes your spouse, children and their spouses, and the father, mother, sisters and brothers of yourself and your household.

EMPLOYMENT OF RELATIVES

Relatives of employees will not be employed on a permanent or temporary basis by the company where the relative directly reports to the employee or the employee exercises any direct influence with respect to the relative's hiring, placement, promotions, evaluations, or pay.

CONFIDENTIAL INFORMATION AND PRIVACY OF COMMUNICATIONS

Confidential Information

Confidential information includes all information, whether technical, business, financial or otherwise concerning the company, which the company treats as confidential or secret and/or which is not available or is not made available publicly. It also includes any private information of or relating to customer records, fellow employees, other persons or other companies, and national security information obtained by virtue of the employee's position.

Company policy and various laws protect the integrity of the company's confidential information which must not be divulged except in strict accordance with established company policies and procedures. The obligation not to divulge confidential company information is in effect even though material might not be specifically identified as confidential and the obligation exists during and continues after employment with the company.

A few examples of prohibited conduct are: (a) selling or otherwise using, divulging, or transmitting confidential company information; (b) using confidential company information to knowingly convert a company business opportunity for personal use; (c) using confidential company information to acquire real estate which the employee knows is of interest to the company; (d) using, divulging, or transmitting confidential company information in the course of outside employment or other relationship or any succeeding employment or other relationship at any time; (e) trading in the company stocks, or the stocks of any company, based on information which has not been disclosed to the public or divulging such information to others so that they might trade in such stock. Insider trading is prohibited by company policy and federal and state law.

Employees shall not seek out, accept, or use any confidential company information of or from a competitor of the company. In particular, should we hire an employee who previously worked for a competitor, we must neither accept not solicit confidential information concerning that competitor from our employee.

Classified National Security Information

Only employees with proper government clearance and a need to know have access to classified national security information. Government regulations, outlined in company instructions, for safeguarding must be followed. Disclosing such information, without authorization, even after leaving employment, is a violation of law and this code.

Adverse information about employees having government clearance must be reported to the Security or Law Departments' representatives having responsibility for clearances.

Company Assets

CASH AND BANK ACCOUNTS

All cash and bank account transactions must be handled so as to avoid any question or suspicion of impropriety. All cash transactions must be recorded in the company's books of account.

All accounts of company funds, except authorized imprest funds, shall be established and maintained in the name of the company or one of its subsidiaries and might be opened or closed only on the authority of the company's Board of Directors. Imprest funds must be maintained in the name of the custodian and the custodian is wholly responsible for these funds. All cash received shall be promptly recorded and deposited in a company or subsidiary bank account. No funds shall be maintained in the form of cash, except authorized petty cash, and no company shall maintain an anonymous (numbered) account at any bank. Payments into numbered bank accounts by the company might leave that company open to suspicion of participation in a possibly improper transaction. Therefore, no disbursements of any nature might be made into numbered bank accounts or other accounts not clearly identified to the company as to their ownership.

No payments can be made in cash (currency) other than regular, approved cash payrolls and normal disbursements from petty cash supported by signed receipts or other appropriate documentation. Further, corporate checks shall not be written to "cash," "bearer," or similar designations.

COMPANY ASSETS AND TRANSACTIONS

Compliance with prescribed accounting procedures is required at all times. Employees having control over company assets and transactions are expected to handle them with the strictest integrity and ensure that all transactions are executed in accordance with management's authorization. All transactions shall be accurately and fairly recorded in reasonable detail in the company's accounting records.

Employees are personally accountable for company funds over which they have control. Employees who spend company funds should ensure the company receives good value in return and must maintain accurate records of such expenditures. Employees who approve or certify the correctness of a bill or voucher should know that the purchase and amount are proper and correct. Obtaining or creating "false" invoices or other misleading documentation or the invention or use of fictitious sales, purchases, services, loans entities, or other financial arrangements is prohibited.

Employees must pay for personal telephone calls and use, except to the extent that specifically defined benefit programs or allowances provide otherwise.

EXPENSE REIMBURSEMENT

Expenses actually incurred by an employee in performing company business must be documented on expense reports in accordance with company procedures. In preparing expense reports, employees should review these procedures for the documentation which must be submitted in order to be reimbursed for business expenses.

COMPANY CREDIT CARDS

Company credit cards are provided to employees for convenience in conducting company business. No personal expenses can be charged on company credit cards except as specifically authorized by company procedures. Any charged personal expenses must be paid promptly by the employee. Company credit cards should not be used to avoid preparing documentation for direct payment to vendors. Where allowed by local law, charges on company credit cards for which a properly approved expense report has not been received at the time of an employee's termination of employment might be deducted from the employee's last paycheck. The company will pursue repayment by the employee of any amounts it has to pay on the employee's behalf.

SOFTWARE AND COMPUTERS

Computerized information and computer software appear intangible, but they are valuable assets of the company and must be protected from misuse, theft, fraud, loss, and unauthorized use or disposal, just as any other company property.

Use of mainframe computers must be customer service or job related. Employees can not access company records of any kind for their personal use. Misappropriation of computer space, time, or software includes, but is not limited to using a computer to create or run unauthorized jobs, operating a computer in an unauthorized mode, or intentionally causing any kind of operational failure.

Personal computers can be used for company-sanctioned education programs as well as personal use incidental to company business use with the permission of your supervisor. However, personal use cannot be allowed for personal financial gain.

It is also understood that personal computers will occasionally be used at home with the permission of your supervisor.

Political Contributions

Federal law and many state laws prohibit contributions by corporations to political parties or candidates. The term "political contributions" includes, in addition to direct cash contributions, the donation of property or services, and the purchases of tickets to fund-raising events. Employees can make direct contributions of their own money, but such contributions are not reimbursable. In addition, employees can make contributions to a company-sponsored Political Action Committee.

Where corporate political contributions are legal in connection with state, local, or foreign elections, such contribution shall be made only from funds allocated for that purpose, and with the written approval of the president of the company making the contribution. The amounts of contributions made shall be subject to inter-company allocation.

It is improper for an employee to use his position within the company to solicit political contributions from another employee for the purpose of supporting a political candidate or influencing legislation. It is also improper for an employee to make a political contribution in the name of the company.

Employee Conduct

CONDUCT ON COMPANY BUSINESS

Dishonest or illegal activities on company premises or while on company business will not be condoned and can result in disciplinary action, including dismissal and criminal prosecution. The following illustrates activities that are against company policy, and which will not be tolerated on company premises, in company vehicles, or while engaged in company business:

1) Consumption and storage of alcoholic beverages, except where legally licensed or authorized by an officer of the company.

2) The use of controlled substances, such as drugs or alcohol. The unlawful manufacture, distribution, dispensation, possession, transfer, sale, purchase, or use of a controlled substance.

3) Driving vehicles or operating company equipment while under the influence of alcohol or controlled substances.
4) Illegal betting or gambling.
5) Carrying weapons of any sort on company premises, in company vehicles, or while on company business. Even employees with permits or licenses can not carry weapons on company property or while on company businesses.

The company reserves the right to inspect any property that might be used by employees for the storage of their personal effects. This includes desks, lockers, and vehicles owned by the company. It is a violation of company policy to store any contraband, illegal drugs, toxic materials or weapons on company property.

REPORTING VIOLATIONS

All employees are responsible for compliance with these rules, standards, and principles. In the area of ethics, legality, and propriety, each employee has an obligation to the company which transcends normal reporting relationships. Employees should be alert to possible violations of the code anywhere in the company and are encouraged to report such violations promptly. Reports should be made to the employee's supervisor, the appropriate security, audit, or legal department personnel, or elsewhere as the circumstances dictate. Employees will also be expected to cooperate in an investigation of violations. In addition, any employee who is convicted of a felony, whether related to these rules or not, should also report that fact.

All cases of questionable activity involving the code or other potentially improper actions will be reviewed for appropriate action, discipline, or corrective steps. Whenever possible, the company will keep confidential the identity of employees about or against whom allegations of violations are brought, unless or until it has been determined that a violation has occurred. Similarly, whenever possible, the company will keep confidential the identity of anyone reporting a possible violation. Reprisal against any employee who has, in good faith, reported a violation or suspected violation is strictly prohibited.

All employees are required to notify the company within five (5) days of any conviction of any criminal statute violation occurring on the job. In addition, any employee who is convicted of a felony, whether related to these rules or not, should report that fact.

DISCIPLINE

Violation of this code can result in serious consequences for the company, its image, credibility and confidence of its customers, and can include substantial fines and restrictions on future operations as well as the possibility of fines and prison sentences for individual employees. Therefore, it is necessary that the company ensure that there will be no violations. Employees should recognize that it is in their best interest, as well as the company's, to follow this code carefully.

The amount of any money involved in a violation might be immaterial in assessing the seriousness of a violations since, in some cases, heavy penalties might be assessed against the company for a violation involving a relatively small amount of money, or no money.

Disciplinary action should be coordinated with the appropriate Human Resources representatives. The overall seriousness of the matter will be considered in setting the disciplinary action to be taken against an individual employee. Such action, which might be reviewed with the appropriate Human Resources organization, might include:

Reprimand
Probation
Suspension
Reduction in salary
Demotion
Combination of the above
Dismissal

In addition, individual cases might involve:

Reimbursement of losses or damages
Referral for criminal prosecution or civil action
Combination of the above

Disciplinary action might also be taken against supervisors or executives who condone, permit, or have knowledge of illegal or unethical conduct by those reporting to them and do not take corrective action. Disciplinary action might also be taken against employees who make false statements in connection with investigations of violations of this code.

The disciplinary action appropriate to a given matter will be determined by the company in its sole discretion. The listing of possible actions is informative only and does not bind the company to follow any particular disciplinary steps, process or procedure.

The company's rules and regulations regarding proper employee conduct will not be waived in any respect. Violation is cause for disciplinary action including dismissal. All employees will be held to the standards of conduct described in this booklet.

The company never has and never will authorize any employee to commit an act which violates this code or the direct a subordinate to do so. With that understood, it is not possible to justify commission of such an act by saying it was directed by someone in higher management.

Compliance Letter and Conflict of Interest Questionnaire

Annually, all officers of the company will represent in writing that there are no violations of this code known to the officer, after the exercise of reasonable diligence, or if such violations have been committed, to disclose such violations in a format to be specified.

Annually, each employee will review the Code of Business Ethics and Conduct, sign the code's Acknowledgment form and complete and sign the Conflict of Interest Questionnaire. If the employee's circumstances change at any time, a new Conflict of Interest Questionnaire or letter of explanation must be completed.

The Code of Business Ethics and Conduct Acknowledgment form should be signed and given to your supervisor for inclusion in your personnel file.

BIBLIOGRAPHY

Albrecht, W. Steve, Keith R. Howe, and Marshall B. Romney. Deterring Fraud: The Internal Auditor's Perspective. Altamonte Springs: The Institute of Internal Auditors Research Foundation, 1984.

Albrecht, W. Steve, Gerald W. Wernz, and Timothy L. Williams. Fraud: Bringing Light to the Dark Side of Business. Burr Ridge, IL: Irwin Professional Publishing, 1995.

Albrecht, W. Steve, Marshal B. Romney, David J. Cherrington, I. Reed Payne, and Allan J. Roe. How to Detect and Prevent Business Fraud. Englewood Cliffs: Prentice-Hall, Inc., 1982.

American Institute of Certified Public Accountants, Inc. Accounting Standards, Original Pronouncements November 1972 - May 1996.
— "The Auditor's Responsibility to Detect and Report Errors and Irregularities," SAS No. 53. New York, NY, 1900.
— "Illegal Acts by Clients," SAS No. 54. New York, NY, 1990
— "Auditing Accounting Estimates," SAS No. 57. New York, NY, 1990.
— "Communication with Audit Committees," SAS No. 61. New York, NY, 1990.
— "Special Reports," SAS No. 62
— "Compliance Auditing Applicable to Governmental Entities and Other Recipients of Governmental Financial Assistance," SAS No. 63.
— "Consideration of Fraud in a Financial Statement Audit," SAS No. 82, 1996

Androphy, Joel M. White Collar Crime. New York: McGraw-Hill, Inc., 1992.

Associated Press. "Software Executive Pleads Guilty to Stock Fraud." USA Today. January 31, 1997.

Association of Certified Fraud Examiners, The. Fraud Examiners' Manual, Revised 2nd Edition. ACFE, 1996.

Beckett, Paul. "SEC, Publisher of On-Line Newsletter Settle Fraud Case Involving the Internet." The Wall Street Journal, February 26, 1997.

Bintliff, Russell L. White Collar Crime Detection and Prevention. Englewood Cliffs, New Jersey: Prentice Hall, 1993.

Binstein, Michael and Charles Bowden. Trust Me: Charles Keating and the Missing Millions. New York: Random House, 1993.

Black, Henry Campbell. Black's Law Dictionary, Fifth Edition. St. Paul, Minnesota: West Publishing Co., 1979.

Bliven, Bruce. "The Tempest Over Teapot." American Heritage. September-October, 1995.

Bologna, Jack. Corporate Fraud: The Basics of Prevention and Detection. Boston: Butterworth-Heinemann, 1984.

Bologna, Jack and Robert J. Lindquist. Fraud Auditing and Forensic Accounting. New York: John Wiley & Sons, 1987.

Bologna, Jack. Handbook on Corporate Fraud. Boston: Butterworth-Heinemann, 1993.

Caplan, Gerald M. ABSCAM Ethics: Moral Issues & Deception in Law Enforcement. Cambridge, Massachusetts: Ballinger, 1983.

Clarke, Michael. Business Crime: Its Nature and Control. New York: St. Martin's Press, 1990.

Clarkson, Kenneth W., Roger LeRoy Miller, and Gaylord A. Jentz. West's Business Law: Text & Cases, Third Edition. St. Paul: West Publishing Company, 1986.

Clinard, Marshall B., and Peter C. Yeager. Corporate Crime. New York: Macmillan Publishing Co., Inc., 1980.

Cressey, Donald R. Other People's Money. Montclair: Patterson Smith, 1973.

Davis, Robert C., Arthur J. Lurigio, and Wesley G. Skogan, ed. Victims of Crime, Second Edition. Thousand Oaks: Sage Publications, 1997.

Dirks, Raymond L. and Leonard Gross. The Great Wall Street Scandal, New York: McGraw-Hill Book Company, 1974

Drake, John D. The Effective Interviewer: A Guide for Managers, New York: AMACOM, 1989.

Ermann, M. David and Richard J. Lundman. Corporate Deviance. New York: Holt, Rhinehart and Winston, 1982.

Financial Accounting Standards Board. Original Pronouncements, Accounting Standards as of June 1, 1990. "Statement of Financial Accounting Standards No. 2; Accounting for Research and Development Costs." Vol. 1, Norwalk, CT, 1990
— "Statement of Financial Accounting Standards No. 68; Research and Development Arrangements." Norwalk, CT, 1990.

Financial Accounting Standards Board. Original Pronouncements, Accounting Standards as of June 1, 1990, Vol. 2. "Accounting Research Bulletin No. 45 Long-Term Construction-Type Contracts. ARB No. 45, Norwalk, CT, 1990.
— "Reporting the Results of Operations-Reporting the Effects of Disposal of a Segment of a Business, and Extraordinary, Unusual and Infrequently Occurring Events and Transactions." APB No. 30, Norwalk, CT, 1990.
— "Statement of Financial Accounting Concepts No. 2; Qualitative Characteristics of Accounting Information." CON No. 2, Norwalk, CT, 1990.
— "Statement of Financial Accounting Concepts No. 5; Recognition and Measurement in Financial Statements of Business Enterprises." CON No. 5, Norwalk, CT, 1990.

Flesher, Dale L., Paul J. Miranti and Gary John Previts. "The First Century of the CPA." Journal of Accountancy, October 1996.

Fridson, Martin S. Financial Statement Analysis. New York: John Wiley & Sons, Inc., 1991.

Gardner, Dale R. "Teapot Dome: Civil Legal Cases that Closed the Scandal." Journal of the West. October 1989.

Geis, Gilbert. On White-Collar Crime. Lexington, Mass: Lexington Books, 1982.

Geis, Gilbert and Robert F. Meier. White-Collar Crime: Offenses in Business, Politics, and the Professions. Revised Edition. New York: The Free Press, A Division of Macmillan Publishing Co., Inc., 1977.

Georgiades, George. Audit Procedures. New York: Harcourt Brace Professional Publishing, 1995.

Hall, Jerome. Theft, Law and Society. 2nd Edition. 1960.

Hayes, Read. Retail Security and Loss Prevention. Stoneham, MA: Butterworth-Heinemann, 1991.

Inbau, Fred E., John E. Reid, and Joseph P. Buckley. Criminal Interrogation and Confessions. Baltimore: Wilkins, 1986.

Inkeles, Alex. National Character: A Psycho-Social Perspective. New Brunswick: Transaction Publishers, 1997.

Institute of Internal Auditors. Standards for the Professional Practices of Internal Auditing. Altamonte Springs, 1978.

Hubbard, Thomas D. and Johnny R. Johnson. Auditing, 4th Edition. Houston: Dame Publications, Inc., 1991.

Kant, Immanuel. Lectures on Ethics. New York: Harper & Row, 1963.

Mancino, Jane. "The Auditor and Fraud." Journal of Accountancy. April 1997.

Marcella, Albert J., William J. Sampias and James K. Kincaid. The Hunt for Fraud: Prevention and Detection Techniques. Altamonte Springs: Institute of Internal Auditors, 1994.

Marshall, David H. and Wayne W. McManus. Accounting: What the Numbers Mean, Third Edition. Chicago: Irwin, 1996.

Mee Jr., Charles L. The Ohio Gang: The World of Warren G. Harding. New York: M. Evans and Company, 1981.

Mill, Hohn Stuart. Utilitarianism. Indianapolis: The Bobbs-Merrill Company, Inc., 1957.

Miller, Norman C. The Great Salad Oil Swindle. Baltimore: Penguin Books, 1965.

Nash, Jay Robert. Hustlers & Con Men: An Anecdotal History of the Confidence Man and His Games. New York: Lippincott, 1976.

National Commission on Fraudulent Financial Reporting, 1987. Report of the National Commission on Fraudulent Financial Reporting. New York: American Institute of Certified Public Accountants, October.

Noonan, John T. Jr. Bribes. New York: Macmillan Publishing Company, 1984.

O'Brian, Keith. Cut Your Losses! Bellingham: International Self-Press Ltd., 1996.

Patterson, James and Peter Kim. The Day America Told the Truth. New York: Prentice Hall Publishing, 1991.

Ramos, Michael J. Consideration of Fraud in a Financial Statement Audit: The Auditor's Responsibilities Under New SAS No. 82. New York: The American Institute of Certified Public Accountants, Inc., 1997.

Robertson, Jack C. Auditing, Sixth Edition. Homewood: BPI Irwin, 1990.

Robertson, Jack C. Auditing, Seventh Edition. Boston: BPI Irwin, 1991.

Robertson, Jack C. Fraud Examination for Managers and Auditors. Austin: The Association of Certified Fraud Examiners, 1996.

Sarnoff, Susan K. Paying For Crime. Westport: Praeger, 1996.

Seidler, Lee J., Fredrick Andrews, and Marc J. Epstein. The Equity Funding Papers: the Anatomy of a Fraud. New York: John Wiley & Sons, 1997.

Sharp, Kathleen. In Good Faith. New York: St. Martin's Press, 1995.

Siegel, Larry J. Criminology, 3rd Edition. New York: West Publishing Company, 1989.

Siegel, Larry J. Criminology, 4th Edition. New York: West Publishing Company, 1993.

Snyder, Neil H., O. Whitfield, William J. Kehoe, James T. McIntyre, Jr., and Karen E. Blair. Reducing Employee Theft: A Guide to Financial and Organizational Controls. New York: Quorum Books, 1991.

Thornhill, William T. Forensic Accounting: How to Investigate Financial Fraud. Burr Ridge, IL: Irwin Professional Publishing, 1995.

Tyler, Tom R. Why People Obey the Law. New Haven: Yale University Press, 1990.

Vaughan, Diane. Controlling Unlawful Organizational Behavior. Chicago: The University of Chicago Press, 1983.

Wells, Joseph T., CFE, CPA. Fraud Examination: Investigative and Audit Procedures. New York: Quorum Books, 1992.

Wells, Joseph T., CFE, CPA., Tedd A. Avey, BComm, CA, G. Jack Bologna, JD, CFE, BBA, and Robert J. Lindquist, CFE, FCA. The Accountant's Handbook of Fraud and Commercial Crime. Toronto: Canadian Institute of Chartered Accountants, 1992.

Wells, Joseph T., CFE, CPA. "Accountancy and White-Collar Crime." The Annals of the American Academy of Political and Social Science. January 1993.

Wells, Joseph T., CFE, CPA. "The Billion Dollar Paper Clip." Internal Auditor. October 1994.

Wells, Joseph T., CFE, CPA. "Collaring Crime at Work," Certified Accountant. August 1996.

Wells, Joseph T., CFE, CPA. "Fraud Assessment Questioning." Internal Auditor. August 1992.

Wells, Joseph T., CFE, CPA. "Getting a Handle on a Hostile Interview." Security Management. July 1992.

Wells, Joseph T., CFE, CPA. "Six Common Myths About Fraud." Journal of Accountancy. February 1990.

Welsch, Glenn A., D. Paul Newman, and Charles T. Zlatkovich. <u>Intermediate Accounting, Seventh Edition</u>. Homewood: Irwin, 1986.

Wojcik, Lawrence A. "Sensational Cases and the Mundane—Lessons to be Learned." <u>The First Annual Conference on Fraud</u>. The American Institute of Certified Public Accountants, 1996.
— "Judas Escariot." <u>Encyclopedia Brittanica</u>, 1990 edition.

— "Arrest Ordered in Alleged Embezzlement from Revisionist Group." <u>San Diego Daily</u>, November 22, 1996.

— "Auto Dealer Rick Hendrick to Plead Not Guilty." <u>Reuter's News Service</u>, December 5, 1996.

ABOUT THE AUTHOR

Joseph T. Wells, white-collar criminologist, is founder and Chairman of the Association of Certified Fraud Examiners, a 20,000-member professional organization headquartered in Austin, Texas.

Mr. Wells graduated with honors from the University of Oklahoma with a bachelor's Degree in Business Administration, and spent two years on the audit staff of Coopers and Lybrand. In 1972, he was appointed a Special Agent of the FBI, specializing in the investigation of white-collar crime. Over the next 10 years, he assisted in nearly 200 criminal convictions, including that of former U.S. Attorney General John Mitchell for his involvement in the Watergate case.

In 1981, Mr. Wells left the FBI to form Wells & Associates, a consulting group of criminologists dealing with fraud detection and deterrence. In 1988, he became Chairman of the Association of Certified Fraud Examiners.

In addition to administrative duties as Chairman, Mr. Wells writes, researches, and lectures to business and professional groups on white-collar crime issues. He was a Faculty Member of the Federal Financial Institution Examinations Council, a Visiting Scholar at the University of Nebraska , and is a Visiting Lecturer for the University of Texas.

Mr. Wells is the author of scores of articles and training programs on fraud. He has authored four other books: *The Fraud Examiners Manual, First and Second Editions; Fraud Examination: A Guide to Investigative and Audit Procedures; and The Accountant's Handbook of Fraud and Commercial Crime.*

He is the recipient of an Outstanding Contributor Award for his writing. He is featured frequently in the national media, including *The Wall Street Journal, Forbes Magazine, The New York Times, ABC News 20/20, Nightline,* and *60 Minutes.*

Mr. Wells is a member of the Association of Certified Fraud Examiners, the American Institute of Certified Public Accountants, the Institute of Internal Auditors, the National Criminal Justice Association, and the American Society of Industrial Security. He has served on the Practice Advisory Council of the American Accounting Association and the Ethics Committee of the Texas Society of CPAs. He has also served on the Board of Directors for CrimeStoppers.